D0765749

The Impact of 9/11 and the New Legal Landscape

Also by Matthew J. Morgan

A Democracy Is Born

The American Military after 9/11: Society, State, and Empire
The Impact of 9/11 on Politics and War
The Impact of 9/11 on Business and Economics
The Impact of 9/11 on the Media, Arts, and Entertainment
The Impact of 9/11 on Psychology and Education
The Impact of 9/11 on Religion and Philosophy

The Impact of 9/11 and the New Legal Landscape

The Day That Changed Everything?

Edited by
Matthew J. Morgan

with a Foreword by
Senator Bob Graham

palgrave
macmillan

THE IMPACT OF 9/11 AND THE NEW LEGAL LANDSCAPE
Copyright © Matthew J. Morgan, 2009.

First published in 2009 by
PALGRAVE MACMILLAN®
in the United States—a division of St. Martin's Press LLC,
175 Fifth Avenue, New York, NY 10010.

Where this book is distributed in the UK, Europe and the rest of the world, this is by Palgrave Macmillan, a division of Macmillan Publishers Limited, registered in England, company number 785998, of Houndmills, Basingstoke, Hampshire RG21 6XS.

Palgrave Macmillan is the global academic imprint of the above companies and has companies and representatives throughout the world.

Palgrave® and Macmillan® are registered trademarks in the United States, the United Kingdom, Europe and other countries.

ISBN: 978–0–230–60838–2

Library of Congress Cataloging-in-Publication Data

The impact of 9/11 and the new legal landscape : the day that changed everything? / edited by Matthew J. Morgan ; with a Foreword by Bob Graham.
        p. cm.
Includes bibliographical references and index.
ISBN-13: 978–0–230–60838–2 (alk. paper)
ISBN-10: 0–230–60838–8 (alk. paper)
  1. War on Terrorism, 2001—Law and legislation—United States. 2. Due process of law—United States. 3. Terrorism—Government policy—United States. 4. Civil rights—United States. 5. Internal security—United States. 6. September 11 Terrorist Attacks, 2001. 7. War and emergency powers—United States. I. Morgan, Matthew J.

KF9430.I47 2009
345.73′02—dc22   2008055139

A catalogue record of the book is available from the British Library.

Design by Newgen Imaging Systems (P) Ltd., Chennai, India.

First edition: September 2009

10 9 8 7 6 5 4 3 2 1

Printed in the United States of America.

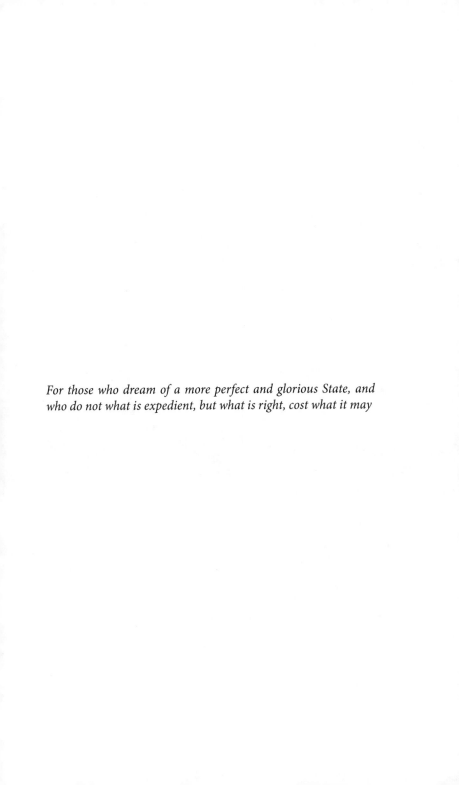

For those who dream of a more perfect and glorious State, and who do not what is expedient, but what is right, cost what it may

Contents

Foreword

Bob Graham

Now is a timely period to reflect upon the horrible tragedy of September 11, to understand the impact of those terrible events, and to prevent them in the future. The series of which this volume is a part, *The Day That Changed Everything?*, is an important project. Painful as it is to revisit memories of such a terrible time, it is a necessary process to prevent future catastrophes.

I believe such reflective processes have led to a growing realization that our leaders did not do everything that they could have done and should have done to protect Americans from a terrorist attack. The 9/11 Commission, for example, has reported that they endorse the recommendations of the Joint Congressional Inquiry into the 9/11 terrorist attacks, which I cochaired with my friend and colleague and fellow Floridian, Porter Goss. We found that failures of intelligence collection and analysis, compounded by a lack of information sharing within the intelligence community and between the intelligence community and the law enforcement community, cost us the chance to detect and disrupt the plot of the 19 hijackers. In short, September 11 could have—indeed, should have—been prevented.

In order to prevent future terrorist attacks on our homeland, we must enhance our domestic intelligence-gathering capabilities. We need to have a full and open debate in this country about the balance between domestic security and personal liberties and how we go about identifying and tracking terrorist suspects who live among us. This book is a major step in that direction.

Whether it is our domestic civil liberties or whether it is our responsibility to be an advocate for human rights, we must not forget the centrality of concern for human rights in our national values and history. Jimmy Carter articulately expressed something that seems to have been lost in our current dialogue on human rights: "Human rights were not the product of the United States of America; the United States of America was the product of human rights." Staying true to these values while protecting our security will be imperative as we move into a dangerous new century. Challenging old assumptions and advancing the dialogue are a necessary part of this process, and I am encouraged to see those so well achieved in *The Impact of 9/11 and the New Legal Landscape.*

Acknowledgments

September 11, 2001, was an event that for most Americans will be remembered for a lifetime as a pivotal moment in history. Like the Kennedy assassination a generation before on November 22, 1963, Americans share a collective memory and trauma of the event, often asking each other and reminiscing about what one was doing during that fateful moment. Now, with several years passed since 9/11, this series reflects on that event by bringing together from a broad spectrum of disciplines the leading thinkers of our time.

In undertaking such an ambitious project as this, appreciation must go to a wide range of people. First and foremost are the distinguished and skillful writers who have contributed to the series. Their willingness to share their talents and follow through with their commitment to this effort made all the difference. I cannot thank them enough for the sacrifices they have made to contribute their work to this series.

As I thank the many authors from such diverse backgrounds, perspectives, and even countries, I should caution readers that opinions expressed in this series reflect the views of each contributing author of each chapter and should not be contrived to represent views of the contributing authors generally or even my own views. The series has self-consciously attempted to include a "big tent" of different perspectives, some highly critical of policy decisions, others supportive of government actions in difficult times, some dubious of the significance of 9/11, others finding it a disruptive event that "changed everything." I have tried to reserve my own views to allow this series to collect these perspectives.

I would like to thank several people who have made special contributions to this process. First, two friends have proven themselves adept at finding my errors and improving my work, which is an invaluable skill for an author to find in a trusted colleague. These two distinguished professionals—Jennifer Walton of JPI Capital and Linda Nguyen of Deloitte Consulting—have taken time out of their busy schedules to review these manuscripts, and I am eternally grateful to them. Second, many of our authors are extremely busy top leaders at the pinnacles of their careers.

In these cases, their professional assistants and staff have been incredibly helpful in managing correspondence and facilitating the timely completion of these contributions. Among these helpful professionals are Flip Brophy of Sterling Lord Literistic, Minna Cowper-Coles, Chip Burpee, Sarah Neely, Toni Getze, Nancy Bonomo, Elizabeth Ong Baoxuan, Brooke Sweet, and Janet Conary. I also owe gratitude to institutions with colleagues very supportive of my writing during my time with them: Bentley College of Waltham, Massachusetts, and McKinsey & Company.

Finally, I owe a debt of gratitude to several members of the publishing community to bring this massive effort to fruition. First, Hilary Claggett of Potomac Books, my editor at Greenwood/Praeger for my first book (*A Democracy Is Born*, 2007), envisioned an interdisciplinary series reflecting on the national tragedy that was 9/11. This concept was initially to be set out in four volumes, but due to the enthusiastic response from the scholarly and writing communities the series expanded to six—allowing for a full treatment of each major area we have undertaken. Next, Toby Wahl of Westview Press, and former political science editor at Palgrave Macmillan, supported me with my publication of *The American Military after 9/11: Society, State, and Empire* at Palgrave (2008) and provided energy and commitment in the initial stages of the development of *The Day That Changed Everything?* After his departure, Farideh Koohi-Kamali, editorial director at Palgrave, assumed Toby's responsibilities and provided excellent advice and support, taking the series through its last stages in the summer of 2008. Those dedicated professionals who completed the production process, including Allison McElgunn of Palgrave Macmillan and the team at Newgen Imaging Systems led by Maran Elancheran, deserve my gratitude as well as that of our contributing author team. Finally, Editorial Assistants Asa Johnson and Robyn Curtis deserve heartfelt appreciation for their efforts to bring the book to publication in its final form, exceeding all expectations. In my experience as an author, I have never before demanded nor received the support that Asa and Robyn mustered for this massive series. Working with both of them was an absolute pleasure and they reflect great credit upon Palgrave Macmillan.

MATTHEW J. MORGAN
White Plains, New York

About the Contributors

Foreword. Senator Bob Graham served as the governor of Florida from 1979 to 1986 and served in the U.S. Senate from 1987 to 2005, including as the chair of the Select Committee on Intelligence from 2001 to 2003. He is the author of *Intelligence Matters: The CIA, the FBI, Saudi Arabia, and the Failure of America's War on Terror* (2004).

Mashood A. Baderin is Professor of Law at the School of Oriental and African Studies, University of London.

Christopher P. Banks is Associate Professor of Political Science at Kent State University and author of several books.

John C. Blakeman is Associate Professor of Political Science at the University of Wisconsin-Stevens Point.

Kelly R. Damphousse is Presidential Professor of Sociology and Associate Dean in the College of Arts and Sciences at the University of Oklahoma. He is the Associate Director of the American Terrorism Study.

Alan M. Dershowitz has been called "the nation's most peripatetic civil liberties lawyer," one of its "most distinguished defenders of individual rights," and "the best-known criminal lawyer in the world." He is the Felix Frankfurter Professor of Law at Harvard Law School and the author of 20 works of fiction and nonfiction, including 6 bestsellers, selling more than a million copies worldwide. His writing has been praised by Truman Capote, Saul Bellow, and Elie Wiesel. His recent work includes *The Case for Peace: How the Arab-Israeli Conflict Can Be Resolved*, *Rights from Wrongs: A Secular Theory of the Origins of Rights*, *The Case for Israel*, *America Declares Independence*, *Why Terrorism Works*, *Chutzpah* (a #1 bestseller), *Reversal of Fortune* (which was made into an Academy Award–winning film), and many others.

Joanne D. Eisen, a Senior Fellow at the Independence Institute, has written ten cutting-edge articles for numerous scholarly and popular periodicals and is a contributor to the award-winning academic encyclopedia, *Guns in American Society: An Encyclopedia of History, Politics, Culture, and the Law*.

Amber Ferris is a doctoral candidate in the School of Communication Studies at Kent State University.

Rene Flores is a graduate student in political science at the University of Texas, El Paso.

Paul Gallant, a Senior Fellow at the Independence Institute, has written cutting-edge articles for numerous scholarly and popular periodicals and is a contributor to the award-winning academic encyclopedia, *Guns in American Society: An Encyclopedia of History, Politics, Culture, and the Law.*

Paul Haridakis is an attorney and Associate Professor of Communication Studies at Kent State University.

Aziz Z. Huq teaches at the University of Chicago School of Law.

Moushumi M. Khan is a civil rights attorney and the founding President of the Muslim Bar Association of New York.

Peter N. Kirstein is Professor of History at St. Xavier University and author of *Anglo over Bracero: A History of the Mexican Worker in the United States from Roosevelt to Nixon.* He is Vice President, American Association of University Professors—Illinois.

David B. Kopel is one of the leading scholarly writers on gun control. He is Research Director of the Independence Institute and coauthor of the only college and graduate textbook on the subject, *Gun Control and Gun Rights.* He is also the author of dozens of published articles on the subject, in journals of law, criminology, sociology, medicine, and media.

Joanne K. Lekea is a visiting lecturer at the Hellenic Air Force Academy and a postdoctoral researcher and a visiting lecturer at the University of Athens.

Brent G. McCune is Assistant Director at the Institute for Policy and Economic Development and the principal prelaw advisor for the Law School Preparation Institute (LSPI). He teaches in the LSPI and the Master of Public Administration and Intelligence Community Center of Academic Excellence programs.

Tara McKelvey is a senior editor at *The American Prospect*, a frequent contributor to *The New York Times Book Review* and a former research fellow at NYU School of Law's Center on Law and Security. A 2009 Templeton-Cambridge Fellow, she is the author of *Monstering: Inside America's Policy on Secret Interrogations and Torture in the Terror War.*

Anne Joseph O'Connell is Assistant Professor of Law at University of California-Berkeley.

Leanne Piggott is Deputy Director of the Centre for International Security Studies at the University of Sydney.

Christopher A. Shields is a Visiting Assistant Professor and ATS Project Manager for the Terrorism Research Center at the University of Arkansas.

Brent L. Smith is Distinguished Professor and chair of the Department of Sociology and Criminal Justice and Director of the Terrorism Research Center in Fulbright College at the University of Arkansas. He is the author of *Pipe Bombs and Pipe Dreams.*

Dennis L. Soden is Dean of the University College and Executive Director of the Institute for Policy and Economic Development at the University of Texas at El Paso. He is author of over 100 articles and technical reports and author or coauthor of 9 books ranging from *The Environmental Presidency, Global Environmental Policy and Administration,* and *Digame: Politics and Policy in the Texas Border.*

William G. Weaver is Associate Professor of Political Science at the University of Texas, El Paso, and author of *Presidential Secrecy and the Law* and *New Perspectives on American Law.*

Dewi Williams is Lecturer in Law, Staffordshire Law School.

Kim M. Williams is Associate Professor of Public Policy at the John F. Kennedy School of Government at Harvard University. Her first book was *Mark One or More: Civil Rights in Multiracial America* (2006), and she is currently at work on her second book, *Transition: The Politics of Racial and Ethnic Change in Urban America.*

Introduction

Matthew J. Morgan

This book is the third volume of the six-volume series *The Day That Changed Everything?* With some time having passed now since the attacks of September 11, 2001, it is possible to reflect upon the attacks and assess their impact. The series brings together from a broad spectrum of disciplines the leading thinkers of our time to reflect on one of the most significant events of our time. This volume is devoted to the new legal landscape that has emerged after 9/11.

Some observers have been highly critical of these developments, while others have found the legal changes needful in response to a newly revealed threat. It is the way in which authorities have constructed the threat that has fostered the new, post–9/11 legal environment.

The declaration of War on Terror is a major development that has allowed the current threat environment to have significant legal consequences. The attacks, the first on the continental United States since the War of 1812, led to the "state of war" narrative,[1] and the domestic and international use of military force since September 11, 2001 has further justified this construction. Nonetheless, the term has been controversial.[2] American leaders have often adopted a call to war to struggle against social ills, and the war on drugs has also included limited international military activity and enhanced domestic security policies, but there is mixed similarity of the War on Terror to more traditional wars. Gore Vidal argued, however, that U.S. case law requires war be declared against "a sovereign nation, not a bunch of radicals."[3] The ambiguity and permanence of the War on Terror are reminiscent of the war on poverty, but the political stakes, the use of military force, and the effects on civil society are reminiscent of historical examples of American armed conflict.

Problems do emerge from the declaration of a War on Terror. The unclear enemy leads to an indefinite stalemate. Declaring war on an idea leads to little chance for resolution, but in the case of terror the threat to the survival of society produces restrictions on civil liberties that wars on poverty or even crime or drugs do not. Chief Justice Rehnquist documented, with approval, the necessity of suspending American civil liberties during wartime, but his argument implied that civil liberties would be suspended temporarily because war is a temporary matter.[4] The prospective continued threat of non-state terrorism distinguishes today's situation from previous conflicts.

Harold Lasswell developed a garrison state theory in the opening years of the cold war.[5] He envisioned an international system where hostile states would eventually evolve into opposing armed camps, with domestic life transformed by military preparedness. As Jay Stanley observed about the Lasswell garrison thesis, "The central hypothesis here is that the presence of continued crises radically alters the structure of societies."[6] While the garrison state failed to evolve during the cold war, the debate in the post–9/11 world has once again made Lasswell's hypothesis relevant. A permanent, rather than temporary, heightened threat leads to permanent, rather than temporary, reduction in freedoms.

Another issue that makes the current concept of homeland security problematic is the mingling of the two categories "acts of war" and "disasters."[7] In a war, it is possible for the government to engage its role of defense to protect its citizens from harm. In a disaster, the best that can be accomplished is rapid emergency response. The latter situation is thus more threatening to the local populace. Hannah Arendt considered this mingling in terms of nuclear weapons: "…the history of warfare in our century could almost be told as the story of the growing incapacity of the army to fulfill [the basic function of defense], until today the strategy of deterrence has openly changed the role of the military from that of a protector into that of a belated and essentially futile avenger."[8] This analysis realized the implications of the aerial bombing of World War II and the nuclear threat of the cold war. They could not have foreseen the destructive asymmetric power of terrorists with means of mass destruction (whether these be airplanes filled with fuel, homemade bombs as used in the Oklahoma City bombing, or more conventional weapons of mass destruction of a radiological, chemical, or biological variety obtained on a black market). Lasswell seems prophetic in his statement, "In some periods of modern warfare, casualties among civilians may outnumber casualties of the armed forces."[9]

The threat has thus assumed a combination of urgency and permanence that exceeds past circumstances. Legal systems and institutions have responded to the new threat levels. Critics have argued that these developments have not been positive. Two centuries ago, Alexander Hamilton expressed the domestic dangers of heightened threats:

> The violent destruction of life and property incident to war, the continual effort and alarm attendant on a state of continual danger, will compel

nations the most attached to liberty to resort for repose and security to institutions which have a tendency to destroy their civil and political rights. To be more safe, they at length become willing to run the risk of being less free.[10]

This volume explores the legal consequences of 9/11 in three parts. The first contains a series of chapters exploring the impact on American civil liberties of the terrorist attacks and the government's response to them. Part II is devoted to legal changes to structures and systems, and Part III considers new standards in international law. Alan M. Dershowitz, the prominent attorney at Harvard Law School, begins with an overview chapter on fundamental changes in our legal system with his articulation of the "preventative state," a new paradigm after 9/11. Professor Dershowitz both recognizes the challenges to civil liberties brought about by the trade-off for greater security and argues that this trade-off must be assessed democratically and thoughtfully. He also points to the systematic evolution of the law that has been taking place and must take place. In so doing, he sets the stage well for the following parts of the book.

In Part I on civil liberties, Dewi Williams begins by questioning the logic by which the post–9/11 legal system would curtail liberties to achieve improved security. In chapter 3, Paul Haridakis and Amber Ferris of Kent State University consider the first amendment by exploring how post–9/11 "speech zones" have been used to control public discourse. Peter N. Kirstein, a well-known lecturer on post–9/11 academic freedom from St. Xavier University, explores this dimension of freedom of speech in chapter 4, which focuses on challenges to academic freedom. Moving to the second amendment, in chapter 5 David B. Kopel, Paul Gallant, and Joanne D. Eisen of the Independence Institute consider the right to bear arms after 9/11. Next in chapter 6, Christopher P. Banks of Kent State University provides an assessment of privacy rights that he argues are diminishing in light of new government powers granted in the Patriot Act. Moushumi M. Khan, the founding president of the Muslim Bar Association of New York, and Kim M. Williams of Harvard University's Kennedy School of Government explore consequences to freedom of movement in chapter 7, which focuses on entry and exit registration. Finally, John C. Blakeman of the University of Wisconsin at Stevens Point considers victims' civil rights in his discussion on civil litigation against terrorists and terrorist states in chapter 8.

Kelly Damphousse of the University of Oklahoma and Christopher Shields and Brent L. Smith of the University of Arkansas begin Part II with a chapter on how 9/11 changed the investigation and prosecution of terrorism. Moving into constitutional law and legal systems of governance,

Aziz Z. Huq of the University Chicago School of Law considers the role of the commander-in-chief after 9/11 in chapter 10. Two chapters on oversight follow. First Anne Joseph O'Connell of the University of California at Berkeley considers intelligence oversight in chapter 11, and then in chapter 12 William G. Weaver of the University of Texas El Paso and Rene Flores argue that institutionalized accountability has failed in the post–9/11 world. In chapter 13 Weaver's colleagues at UT El Paso—Brent G. McCune and Dennis L. Soden—consider U.S. border security policies after 9/11.

Part III considers post–9/11 international law. In chapter 14 Joanna K. Lekea of the Hellenic Air Force Academy/National and Kapodistrian University of Athens considers broadly the impact on humanitarian law and human rights due to counterterrorist operations. In chapter 15 Tara McKelvey, a prominent journalist and author, writes on interrogation techniques and procedures following 9/11, focusing in particular on the notorious "torture memo." Leanne Piggott of the University of Sydney follows with chapter 16, which focuses on the Bush Doctrine and the legal use of force post–9/11. Lastly, Mashood A. Baderin of the University of London discusses collective security law in light of Islamic law in chapter 17.

The contributing authors of this volume—and the entire series—deliberately have divergent perspectives on 9/11 and its aftermath. Some have interpreted legal developments after the 9/11 attacks as a serious setback for democratic governance and individual rights; others view the response as a necessity in difficult times. This series attempts to bring together leading minds from a variety of perspectives. Without any particular "ax to grind," I believe the approach to reflect on the impact of the attacks is best to explore the question of whether September 11, 2001, was the day that changed everything.

Notes

1. Melvin J. Dubnick, "Postscripts for a 'State of War': Public Administration and Civil Liberties after September 11," *Public Administration Review* 62 (September/October 2002): 86–91.
2. Michael Howard, "What's in a Name? How to Fight Terrorism," *Foreign Affairs* 81 (January/February 2002): 8–13.
3. Gore Vidal, *Perpetual War for Perpetual Peace: How We Got to Be So Hated* (New York: Thunder's Mouth Press/Nation Books, 2002).
4. William H. Rehnquist, *All the Laws but One: Civil Liberties in Wartime* (New York: Vintage Books, 1998).
5. Harold D. Lasswell, "The Garrison State," *The American Journal of Sociology* 46 (January 1941): 455–468.

6. Jay Stanley, "Harold Lasswell and the Idea of the Garrison State," *Society* 33, no. 6 (September/October 1996): 46–52.
7. Michael Barkun, "Defending against the Apocalypse: The Limits of Homeland Security," in *Critical Concepts in Political Science: Terrorism*, ed. David Rapoport (London: Routledge, 2005).
8. Hannah Arendt, *On Revolution* (New York: Viking Press, 1963), 5.
9. Lasswell, "The Garrison State."
10. Alexander Hamilton, "Federalist Paper No. 8: The Consequences of Hostilities between the States," *The Federalist Papers* (available on-line at http://www.foundingfathers.info/federalistpapers/fed08.htm, accessed on May 1, 2009.)

I

The Preventative State: Uncharted Waters after 9/11

*Alan M. Dershowitz**

The attack on the United States perpetrated by a small group of Islamic extremists on September 11, 2001, has brought about fundamental changes in our legal and political cultures. Among the most controversial of these changes is the dramatic shift from what I call the "reactive state" to what I call the "preventive state."

From the beginning of recorded history, governments have reacted to harms by punishing the harm-doers after the harm has been done. The goals of such punishment are multiple: to isolate the offender and thus preclude him from inflicting future harms during his period of isolation (or if isolation takes the form of execution, to preclude him from ever repeating his crime); to deter the offender from recidivating if and when he is free from isolation; to deter others from committing crimes; to channel the understandable feelings of revenge that would otherwise lead to private vengeance; and to demonstrate society's abhorrence of the crime. These and other mechanisms all presuppose the willingness and the ability of

* **Alan M. Dershowitz** has been called "the nation's most peripatetic civil liberties lawyer," one of its "most distinguished defenders of individual rights," and "the best-known criminal lawyer in the world." He is the Felix Frankfurter Professor of Law at Harvard Law School and the author of 20 works of fiction and nonfiction, including 6 bestsellers, selling more than a million copies worldwide. His writing has been praised by Truman Capote, Saul Bellow, and Elie Wiesel. His recent work includes *The Case for Peace: How the Arab-Israeli Conflict Can Be Resolved*, *Rights from Wrongs: A Secular Theory of the Origins of Rights*, *The Case for Israel*, *America Declares Independence*, *Why Terrorism Works*, *Chutzpah* (a #1 bestseller), *Reversal of Fortune* (which was made into an Academy Award–winning film), and many others.

the society to absorb the harmful conduct and to respond only after it has occurred. They also presuppose the capacity of the potential harm-doer to be deterred by the threat of punishment.

The events of 9/11 challenged these presuppositions. The event itself was so cataclysmic—more than 3,000 civilian deaths—and the possibility of even greater cataclysms in the future so frightening that our nation does not seem prepared to wait for the second shoe to drop. Citizens demand that our government take preventive action designed to anticipate and stop any comparable acts *before* they occur.

Moreover, those who inflicted it, the harms of 9/11, do not seem amenable to traditional forms of deterrence. They welcome death and martyrdom and anticipate great rewards in a future world. It is difficult to deter a suicide terrorist.

This combination of factors has led us away from exclusive reliance on reactive mechanisms and toward greater reliance on preventive mechanisms. This shift from the reactive state to the preventive state has enormous implications for civil liberties, human rights, criminal justice, national security, foreign policy, and personal morality—implications that are not being sufficiently considered. It is a shift that carries enormous implications for how society controls dangerous human behavior, ranging from targeted killing of terrorists to preemptive attacks against nuclear and other weapons of mass destruction, to preventive warfare, to proactive crime prevention techniques (stings, informers, wiretaps), to psychiatric or chemical methods of preventing sexual predation, to racial, ethnic, or other forms of profiling, to the inoculation or quarantine for infectious diseases (whether transmitted "naturally" or by means of "weaponization"), to prior restraints on dangerous or offensive speech, to the use of torture (or other extraordinary measures) as a means of gathering intelligence deemed necessary to prevent imminent acts of terrorism.

Although the seeds of this change were planted long ago and have blossomed gradually over the years, it was the terrorist attack against the United States on September 11, 2001 that expedited and, in the minds of many, legitimated this important development. Following that attack, the former Attorney General John Ashcroft described the "number one priority" of the Justice Department as "prevention." The prevention of future crimes, especially terrorism, is now regarded as even "more important than prosecution" for past crimes, according to the current Justice Department. In his confirmation hearings of January 5, 2005 former Attorney General Alberto Gonzales reiterated that the administration's "top priority is to prevent terror attacks." Attorney General Michael Mukasey has made similar statements. The tactics that have been employed as part of this preventive approach include tighter border controls, profiling, preventive detention, the gathering of preventive intelligence through rough interrogation and more expansive surveillance, targeting of potential terrorists for assassination, preemptive attacks on terrorist bases, and full-scale preventive war. We are doing all this and more without a firm basis in law, jurisprudence, or morality, though there certainly are historical precedents—many quite questionable—for preventive actions.

The Checkered History of Prevention

From the beginning of recorded history, prophets have attempted to foresee harmful occurrences, such as flood, famine, pestilence, earthquake, volcanic eruption, tsunami, and war. Attempting to predict crime—to determine who is likely to become a criminal—has also captured the imagination of mankind for centuries. From the Bible's "stubborn and rebellious son," identifiable by his gluttony and drunkenness; to nineteenth-century criminologist Cesare Lombroso's "born criminal and criminaloid," identifiable by the shape of his cranium; to Sheldon and Eleanor Glueck's three-year-old delinquent, identifiable by a composite score derived from familial relationships—"experts" have claimed the ability to spot the mark of the potential criminal before he or she has committed serious crimes. Though the results have not generally met with scientific approval, it is still widely believed—by many policeman, judges, psychiatrists, lawyers, and members of the general public—that there are ways of distinguishing real criminals from the rest of us, even before they commit serious crimes.

In the 1920s and 1930s eugenicists—not only in Nazi Germany, but in the United States, Great Britain, and other Western nations—believed that they could prevent criminal behavior in specific, and the weakening of particular races or of humankind in general, through sterilization and other eugenic measures. Even before the Holocaust, the German government forcibly sterilized 400,000 men and women—nearly 1 percent of Germans of childbearing age—believing that "[i]t is better to sterilize too many rather than too few." The legislation authorizing sterilization was called the "Law for the Prevention of Genetically Diseased Offspring." Although this "science" became widely discredited following the Holocaust, as recently as the 1970s, it was suggested that the presence of the XYY karyotype in a man might be associated with—and consequently predictive of—certain kinds of violent crime. The mapping of the human genome has stimulated contemporary genetic research about the predictability of violence and other harms. Racial, ethnic, religious, and other "profiling" is now thought by some to hold some promise in the effort to identify potential criminals, especially terrorists.

Historically, the widespread use of early intervention to preempt serious threats to the state and its rulers has been associated with tyrannical regimes. Hitler and Stalin excelled at killing their enemies before they could rise up against them. But preventive approaches have been championed by progressive forces as well.

Over the past several decades, especially in Europe, the so-called precautionary principle has become "a staple of regulatory policy." It postulates that one should "[a]void steps that will create a risk of harm. Until safety is established, be cautious; do not require unambiguous evidence. In a catchphrase: Better safe than sorry."[1]

The New York Times Magazine listed the precautionary principle as among the most "important ideas" of 2001.[2] This principle, which originated in Germany and grew out of efforts to prevent environmental and other "natural" disasters, has now moved beyond these concerns that have traditionally been raised by the Left. According to Professor Cass Sunstein, the precautionary principle has now

> entered into debates about how to handle terrorism, about "preemptive war," and about the relationship between liberty and security. In defending the 2003 war in Iraq, President George W. Bush invoked a kind of Precautionary Principle, arguing that action was justified in the face of uncertainty. "If we wait for threats to fully materialize, we will have waited too long." He also said, "I believe it is essential that when we see a threat, we deal with those threats before they become imminent."[3]

Professor Sunstein points to an interesting paradox in the different attitudes in Europe and the United States:

> [T]he United States appears comparatively unconcerned about the risks associated with global warming and genetic modification of foods; in those contexts, Europeans favor precautions, whereas Americans seem to require something akin to proof of danger. To be sure, the matter is quite different in the context of threats to national security. For the war in Iraq, the United States (and England) followed a kind of Precautionary Principle, whereas other nations (most notably France and Germany) wanted clearer proof of danger.[4]

This observation can be generalized beyond Europe and the United States and beyond the contemporary scene: all people in all eras have favored *some* preventive or precautionary measures, while opposing others. The differences over which preventive measures are favored and which opposed will depend on many social, political, religious, and cultural factors. As I argue throughout this essay, it is meaningless to declare support for, or opposition to, prevention or precaution as a general principle, because so much properly depends on the values at stake—on the *content* of the costs and benefits and on the *substance* of what is being regulated.

One can, of course, sympathize with efforts to predict and prevent at least some harms before they occur, rather than to wait until the victim lies dead. Indeed, Lewis Carroll put in the Queen's mouth an argument for preventive confinement of predicted criminals that Alice found difficult to refute. The Queen says:

> "[T]here's the King's Messenger. He's in prison now, being punished; and the trial doesn't even begin till next Wednesday; and of course the crime comes last of all."
>
> "Suppose he never commits the crime?" said Alice.
>
> "That would be all the better, wouldn't it?" the Queen said...
>
> Alice felt there was no denying *that*. "Of course that would be all the better," she said: "But it wouldn't be all the better his being punished."
>
> "You're wrong..." said the Queen. "Were *you* ever punished?"
>
> "Only for faults," said Alice.
>
> "And you were all the better for it, I know!" the Queen said triumphantly.
>
> "Yes, but then I *had* done the things I was punished for," said Alice: "that makes all the difference."
>
> "But if you *hadn't* done them," the Queen said, "that would have been even better still; better, and better, and better!" Her voice went higher with each "better," till it got quite to a squeak...
>
> Alice [thought], "There's a mistake here somewhere—"[5]

There are numerous mistakes and perils to liberty implicit in this kind of thinking, and they are not being sufficiently debated today.

Our Traditions

Part of the reason for our neglect of the issues surrounding prevention is the mistaken assumption that any form of preventative detention would be alien to our traditions. Lord Justice Denning, one of the most prominent common-law jurists of the twentieth century, purported to summarize the irreconcilability of preventive punishment with democratic principles: "It would be contrary to all principle for a man to be punished, not for what he has already done, but for what he may hereafter do." It may be contrary to all *principle*, but as we shall see it is certainly not contrary to all *practice*.

The shift from *responding* to past events to *preventing* future harms is part of one of the most significant, but unnoticed, trends in the world today.

It challenges our traditional reliance on a model of human behavior that presupposes a rational person capable of being deterred by the threat of punishment. The classic theory of deterrence presupposes a calculating evildoer who can evaluate the cost/benefits of proposed actions and will act—and forbear from acting—on the basis of these calculations. It also presupposes society's ability (and willingness) to withstand the blows we seek to deter and to use the visible punishment of those blows as threats capable of deterring future harms. These assumptions are being widely questioned as the threat of weapons of mass destruction in the hands of suicide terrorists becomes more realistic, and our ability to deter such harms by classic rational cost-benefit threats and promises becomes less realistic.

Among the most frightening sources of danger today are religious zealots whose actions are motivated as much by "otherworldly" costs and benefits as by the sorts of punishments and rewards that we are capable of threatening or offering. The paradigm is the suicide terrorist, such as the ones who attacked us on September 11. We have no morally acceptable way of deterring those willing to die for their cause, who are promised rewards in the world to come. (There are, of course, immoral ways of deterring suicide killers, by threatening their loved ones, as the Nazis did. But a civilized nation may not punish the innocent to deter the guilty.) Recall the serene looks on the faces of the suicide terrorists as they were videotaped in the final hours of their lives passing through airport security. It is not that they are incapable of making "rational" cost-benefit calculations, by their own lights. But these calculations involve benefits that we cannot confer (eternity in Paradise) and costs (death) that to them are outweighed by the expected benefits. They are, in some respects, like "insane" criminals who believe that God or the devil told them to do it. Because they are not deterrable, the argument for taking preventive measures against them becomes more compelling. Blackstone made this point in the context of "madmen": "as they are not answerable for their actions, they should not be permitted the liberty of acting…."[6] Nations whose leaders genuinely—as opposed to tactically—believe that their mission has been ordained by God (such as some in today's Iran) may also be more difficult to deter than those who base their calculations on earthly costs and benefits (such as today's North Korea or Cuba).

The *New York Times*, in its lead editorial on September 10, 2002—a year after the 9/11 attacks and six months before the invasion of Iraq—recognized the distinction between the theory of deterrence and the theory of prevention (or "preemption" or "first strike") in the context of the War on Terror:

> The suddenness and ferocity of last September's terror attacks tore the United States free from the foreign-policy moorings that had served the

nation well for more than five decades, including the central notion that American military power could by its very existence restrain the aggressive impulses of the nation's enemies. In its place, the Bush administration has substituted a more belligerent first-strike strategy that envisions Washington's attacking potential foes before they hit us. That may be appropriate in dealing with terror groups, but on the eve of the anniversary of Sept. 11 there is still an important place in American policy for the doctrine of deterrence.[7]

Deterrence, in the context of international relations, boils down to "a brutally simple idea": if America or its allies are attacked, we will retaliate massively. "Deterrence is diplomatic parlance for a brutally simple idea: that an attack on the United States or one of its close allies will lead to a devastating military retaliation against the country responsible. It emerged as the centerpiece of American foreign policy in the early years of the cold war."[8] According to the *Times*, this approach has the advantage of inducing "responsible behavior by enemies as a matter of their own self-interest.... Aggression becomes unattractive if the price is devastation at home and possible removal from power."[9]

The *Times* then argued that while preemption may be appropriate against terrorists, it was a far more questionable strategy in dealing with Iraq:

> In the wake of Sept. 11, President George W. Bush has made a convincing case that international terrorist organizations, which have no permanent home territory and little to lose, cannot reliably be checked by the threat of retaliation and must be stopped before they strike. Whether Saddam Hussein falls into that category is a question that the country will be debating in the days ahead.[10]

The debate predicted by the *Times* did occur, but only in the relatively narrow context of the Iraq war. In this essay, I broaden it beyond any specific war, and even beyond the issue of war itself, to the wide range of harms that may not be subject to (or may not be *thought* to be subject to) the strategy of deterrence.

The Limitations of Deterrence

The classic theory of deterrence contemplates the state absorbing the first harm, apprehending its perpetrator, and then punishing him publicly and proportionally, so as to show potential future harm-doers that it does not pay to commit the harm. In the classic situation the harm may be a single murder or robbery that, tragic as it may be to its victim and his family, the society is able to absorb. In the current situation the harm may be a terrorist attack with thousands of victims, or even an attack with weapons of mass destruction capable of killing tens of thousands. National leaders capable of preventing such mass attacks will be tempted to take preemptive action, as some strategists apparently were during the early days of the cold war: "During the Truman administration, some strategists suggested attacking the Soviet Union while it was still militarily weak to prevent the rise of a nuclear-armed Communist superpower. Wiser heads prevailed, and for the next 40 years America's reliance on a strategy of deterrence preserved an uneasy but durable peace."[11]

With the benefit of hindsight that decision was clearly correct, but if the Soviet Union had, in fact, subsequently used its nuclear arsenal against us our failure to take preventive action, when we more safely could have, would have been criticized, just as England's failure to prevent the German arms buildup in the years prior to World War II has been criticized. One of the great difficulties of evaluating the comparative advantages and disadvantages of deterrence versus preemption is that once we have taken preemptive action, it is almost never possible to know whether deterrence would have worked as well or better. Moreover, at the time the decision has to be made—whether to wait and see if deterrence will work or whether to act preemptively now—the available information will likely be probabilistic and uncertain. It is also difficult to know with precision the nature and degree of the harm that may have been prevented. For example, if a preemptive attack on the German war machine had succeeded in preventing World War II, we would never know the enormity of the evil it prevented. All history would remember is an unprovoked aggression by England.

The conundrum, writ large, may involve war and peace. Writ small it may involve the decision whether to preventively incarcerate an individual who is thought to pose a high degree of likelihood that he will kill, rape, assault, or engage in an act of terrorism. At an intermediate level, it may involve the decision to quarantine dozens, or hundreds, of people, some of whom may be carrying a transmittable virus such as SARS. At yet another level it may raise the question of whether to impose prior restraint on a magazine, newspaper, television network, or Internet provider that is planning to publish information that may pose an imminent danger to the safety of our troops, our spies, or potential victims of aggression. Since the introduction of the Internet—which, unlike responsible media outlets, has no "publisher" who can be held accountable after the fact—there has been more consideration of before-the-fact censorship.

The Uncertainty of Preventive Decisions

At every level preventive decisions must be based on uncertain predictions, which will rarely be anywhere close to 100 percent accurate. We must be prepared to accept some false positives (predictions of harms that would not have occurred) in order to prevent some true positives (predictions of harm that would have occurred had we not intervened) from causing irreparable damage. The policy decisions that must be made involve the acceptable ratios of inevitable errors in differing contexts.

Over the millennia we have constructed a carefully balanced jurisprudence or moral philosophy of after-the-fact reaction to harms, especially crimes. We have even come to accept a widely agreed-upon calculus: "better 10 guilty go free than even one innocent be wrongly convicted." Should a similar calculus govern preventative decisions? If so, how should it be articulated? Is it better for 10 possibly preventable terrorist attacks to occur than for one possibly innocent suspect to be preventively detained? Should the answer depend on the nature of the predicted harm? The conditions and duration of detention? The past record of the detainee? The substantive criteria employed in the preventive decision? The ratio of true positives to false positives and false negatives? These are the sorts of questions we will have to confront as we shift toward more preventative approaches—whether it be terrorism, crime in general, the spread of contagious diseases, or preventive warfare.

Decisions to act preemptively generally require a complex and dynamic assessment of multiple factors. These factors include at least the following:

(1) The nature of the harm feared,
(2) The likelihood that it will occur in the absence of preemption,
(3) The possibility that the contemplated preemption will fail,
(4) The costs of a successful preemption,
(5) The costs of a failed preemption,
(6) The nature and quality of the information on which these decisions are based,
(7) The ratio of successful preemptions to unsuccessful ones,
(8) The legality, morality, and potential political consequences of the preemptive steps,
(9) The revocability or irrevocability of the harms caused by the feared event,
(10) The revocability or irrevocability of the harms caused by contemplated preemption, and
(11) Many other factors, including the inevitability of unanticipated outcomes (the law of unintended consequences).

A Jurisprudence for Prevention

In light of the complexity, dynamism, and uncertainty of these and other factors that must go into rationally making any preemptive decision, it would be difficult to construct a general formula with which specific decisions could be quantified, evaluated, and tested. At the simple level any such formula would begin by asking whether the seriousness of the contemplated harm, discounted by the unlikelihood that it would occur in the absence of preemption, would be greater than the likelihood of the harms caused by successful preemption, discounted by the likelihood (and costs) of failed preemption. This simple formula can be made more complex by the inclusion of other factors, such as the appropriate burdens of action and inaction, the legal and moral status of the intervention, and the likelihood of long-term, unintended consequences. Any formula will necessarily mask subtlety, nuance, and indeterminacy. But a formula that even comes close to approximating reality will help clarify the relationship among the factors that—either explicitly or implicitly—should be considered by any rational decision-maker responsible for taking preemptive actions.

There have been several legal contexts in which judges have tried to construct gross formulae for analyzing decisions with predictive implications. In the First Amendment context, Judge Learned Hand formulated a "clear and present danger" exception to protected free speech in the following terms:

> In each case [the judge] must ask whether the gravity of the "evil," discounted by its improbability, justifies such invasion of free speech as if necessary to avoid the danger....We can never forecast with certainty; all prophecy is a guess, but the reliability of a guess decreases with the length of the future which it seeks to penetrate. In application of such a standard courts may strike a wrong balance; they may tolerate "incitements" which they should forbid; they may repress utterances they should allow; but that is a responsibility that they cannot avoid.

That formulation was used by the Supreme Court to sustain the conviction of the leaders of the American Communist Party in 1951, despite the miniscule likelihood that this weak and unpopular party could actually succeed in overthrowing our government "by force or violence." The "clear and present danger" test was made more speech-friendly by the Supreme Court in its 1969 *Brandenburg* decision, which required that the danger be both likely *and* imminent. This is the current view of the First Amendment.

In the context of issuing an injunction, the courts also write about balancing future harms and likely outcomes. Justice Stephen Breyer summarized "the heart of the test" as "whether the harm caused plaintiff without the injunction, in light of the plaintiff's likelihood of eventual success on the merits, outweighs the harm the injunction will cause defendants."[12]

Applying Jurisprudence to Real Problems

These rather simple formulas do not even begin to capture the subtleties and difficulties of balancing the claims of prevention again those of freedom. Consider the following preemptive decisions, all of which potentially involve life-and-death choices.

The most far-reaching may be whether a democratic nation, committed to humane values, should go to war before it is attacked in order to prevent an anticipated attack or provide it a military advantage in what it regards as an inevitable, or highly likely, war. We can call this the "preemptive" or "preventive" war decision. Related to that exercise in anticipatory self-defense is the decision to engage in military action to prevent genocide or ethnic cleansing of others within a given country. This can be called the "humanitarian intervention" decision.

Another may be whether to vaccinate all, most, or some people against a contagious germ that can be, or has been, weaponized, under circumstances where a small, but not insignificant number of those vaccinated may die or become seriously ill from the infection. The decision becomes especially difficult when it is only possible, but not probable, that an attack using the weaponized germ will occur. We will call this the "preventive inoculation" decision.

Yet another may involve the decision to try to identify and confine (or otherwise incapacitate) potentially dangerous individuals (rapists, killers, terrorists, child molesters), or groups (Japanese-Americans, Arab-Americans, those who fit certain "profiles" or others). We will call this the preventive detention decision (or "Minority Report" approach, based on the motion picture about a futuristic law enforcement system that relies on predicting and preventing crime).

A particularly difficult decision may be whether a government should try to prevent certain kinds of speech (or other expression) that is thought to incite, provoke, facilitate, or otherwise cause (or contribute significantly to) serious harms, ranging from genocide to rape to the killing of spies to an overthrow of a government. The causative mechanisms may vary: in some situations the mechanism is informational (revealing the names of spies, the location of a planned military attack, the instructions for making a nuclear weapon, the names and locations of ethnic enemies, as in Rwanda); in other situations it may be emotional (incitements, degrading the intended victims, issuing religious decrees); while in still others it may contain a combination of elements. We will call this the "censorship" or "prior restraint" decision.

The question is whether decisions as diverse as the aforementioned share enough common elements so that there is some benefit in trying to construct a common decision-making formula. Such a formula may, with appropriate variations, help clarify the balancing judgments that must be made before preemptive or preventive action is deemed warranted. Even in the absence of a single formula, comparative discussion of these different but related predictive decisions may contribute to clarification of the policies at stake in each type of decision.

The Difficulty of Prediction

Human beings make both predictive and retrospective decisions every day. Routine predictive decisions include marriage proposals, weather reports, college admission decisions, stock purchases, vacation plans, bets on sporting events, and voting choices. Routine retrospective decisions include trial verdicts, historical reconstructions, and punishing children for misbehavior that they deny. Many decisions are, of course, a mixture of retrospective and prospective elements. These include sentencing, issuing protective orders against feared abusers, and denying bail to criminal defendants.

In theory we should be no worse at predicting at least some types of future events than we are at reconstructing some past ones, because the accuracy of our predictions (at least our short-term, visible ones, such as weather, stocks, sports, and college performance) are easily tested by simply observing future events as they unfold, whereas past reconstructions (such as whether a particular crime, tort, or historical event actually occurred) are often not retrievable or observable.

Yet in practice we seem better (or we believe we are better) at reconstructing the past than in predicting the future, perhaps because we fail to learn from our predictive mistakes. It has been argued that prediction is more difficult than reconstruction, because predictive decisions are inherently probabilistic (e.g., how likely is it that it will rain tomorrow), whereas retrospective decisions are either right or wrong (Booth either assassinated Lincoln or he did not). But this is really a matter of how the issue is put. Predictive decisions are also either right or wrong: it will either rain tomorrow or it will not. And the question of whether a past act did or did not occur can also be stated in probabilistic terms: jurors are asked to decide "beyond a reasonable doubt" or by "a preponderance of the evidence" whether a disputed past event occurred. In both instances, the target event either did or will occur or it did not or will not occur, but in the absence of full information, we cannot be sure and must state our level of certainty in probabilistic terms—for example, it seems highly likely (or 90 percent likely) that x occurred; it seems highly likely (or 90 percent likely) that x will occur. Our ability to predict the future as well as to reconstruct the past has almost certainly improved with developments in science (predictive computer modeling, DNA etc.), but we are still far from any level of accuracy that eliminates the problems of false positive and false negatives and thus the moral challenge of assigning proper weights to these inevitable errors.

In real life, as distinguished from controlled experiments, most important decisions involve both predictive and retrospective judgments, often in combination. Consider the sentencing decision a judge must make with regard to a convicted defendant. Although the jury has already decided (beyond a reasonable doubt) that the defendant almost certainly committed the specified crime with which he was charged, the judge will generally also consider other uncharged past crimes (his record), as well as the likelihood that he will recidivate. Or consider the decision to hire a lawyer. When a potential client interviews me, he wants to know my past record (which is more complex than simply the ratio of wins to losses, because the difficulty of the cases is relevant). But he also wants to assess my current status—have I gotten too busy or too old for a long, complex case?—as well as my likely future performance when his case comes before the court. Similarly with regard to a potential pinch hitter at a crucial stage of a baseball game the manager looks at past performance—batting average on base percentage, success against a particular pitcher—and then makes a prospective judgment; how will he do in this specific situation?

Or consider the much more serious—even monumental—decision to go to war against Saddam Hussein. The primary considerations were future-looking: what is the likelihood that he would use weapons of mass destruction against the United States, his own people, or one of our allies? What is the likelihood he would sell or otherwise transfer such weapons to terrorist groups? Those future-looking probabilistic judgments had to be based on past- and present-looking assessments: What is the probability that he currently has weapons of mass destruction? Did he have them in the past, and, if so, what did he do with them? Did he use them in the past against his own people and against Iran? Similarly a decision to target a "ticking bomb" terrorist for arrest, assassination, or other form or incapacitation will inevitably be based on a combination of past- and future-looking probabilistic judgments: what is the likelihood that he has engaged in terrorist activities in the recent past? Has anything changed to make it less likely that he will persist in these activities? Is there current, reliable intelligence about his plans or activities for the future? How many people will he likely kill if he is not incapacitated? How many people (and of what status—other terrorists, supporters of terrorists, innocent bystanders) will likely be killed or injured in the effort to incapacitate him? Will killing him cause others to resort to more terrorism? Or might it deter others?

Asking the broad question of whether preemption is good or bad is as meaningless as asking whether deterrence is good or bad. Preemption is a mechanism of social control that is sometimes good and sometimes bad, depending on many factors. Just as deterrence can be used for bad purposes or in bad ways (in the 1930s, in parts of the South, any black person who acted "inappropriately" toward a white woman could be lynched), so too preemption can be used for good purposes and in good ways (planting informers within the Ku Klux Klan to learn about and prevent anticipated lynchings). There is, however, something understandingly unsettling about giving the government broad powers to intervene in the lives of its citizens before a harm has occurred in an effort to prevent anticipated harm, rather than responding once it has occurred.

Requiring a past harm, as a precondition to the exercise of certain governmental powers, serves as an important check on the abuse of such powers. But this check—as most checks—comes with a price tag. The failure to act preemptively may cost a society dearly, sometimes even catastrophically. For example, when the UN Charter was originally drafted in the wake of World War II, it demanded that an actual "armed attack occur" before a nation could respond militarily. Now, in the face of potential weapons of mass destruction in the hands of terrorists or rogue nations, that charter is being interpreted to permit preemptive self-defense "beyond an actual attack to an imminently threatened one." But acting preemptively also comes with a price tag, often measured in lost liberties and other even more subtle and ineffable values. That is perhaps why deterrence, rather than preemption, is the norm—the default position—in most democracies for the exercise of most extraordinary governmental powers, such as waging war, confining dangerous people, requiring citizens to submit to medical procedures and restraining speech. But more and more, this presumption against preemptive actions is being overcome by the dangers of inaction—of not acting preemptively. The stakes have increased both for taking and not taking preemptive steps, as we live in a world of both increasing physical dangers and increasing dangers to our liberty. Hence the need for thoughtful consideration of the values at stake whenever an important preemptive action is contemplated.

The Politics of Prevention

Since the debate throughout the world has become politicized, it has too often focused on the yes-no questions of whether preemption is a good policy, rather than on the more nuanced issues discussed earlier. Even for those adamantly opposed to all preemption—or even to all preemption of a particular sort, such as preemptive war—the reality is that preemptive actions of different types and degrees are becoming routine throughout the world. And these actions are being taken without the level of careful, rational consideration that carries with it the prospect that this important, if controversial, mechanism of social control can be cabined in a way that maximizes its utility, while minimizing its potential for misuse and abuse. Precise quantification of many of the factors that are relevant to predictive decisions probably exceeds our current capacity. Some may indeed go beyond our inherent ability to quantify. A profound observation, made centuries ago, and included in the Jewish prayer service, cautions that there are certain things—such as helping the poor and doing acts of loving kindness—that cannot be measured or quantified. Despite this caution, it may still be true that thinking about the costs and benefits of an important mechanism of social control in a roughly quantified manner can be a helpful heuristic.

The elusiveness of any quest for a precise formula capable of quantifying the elements that should govern preemptive decisions must not discourage efforts at constructing a meaningful jurisprudence of preemption. After all, we still lack a precise formula for evaluating retrospective decisions. We have been struggling with efforts to quantify punitive decisions since biblical times when Abraham argued with God about how many false positives would be acceptable in an effort to punish the sinners of Sodom:

> Will you really sweep away the innocent along with the guilty?
> Perhaps there are fifty innocent within the city,
> will you really sweep it away? . . .
> Heaven forbid for you!
> The judge of all the earth—will he not do what is just?
> YHWH said:
> If I find in Sodom fifty innocent within the city,
> I will bear with the whole place for their sake.
> Avraham spoke up, and said: . . .
> Perhaps there will be found there only forty!
> He said:
> I will not do it, for the sake of the forty.
> But he said: . . .
> Perhaps there will be found there only thirty!

He said:
I will not do it, if I find there thirty.
But he said:...
Perhaps there will be found there only twenty!
He said:
I will not bring ruin, for the sake of the twenty.
But he said:
Pray let my Lord not be upset that I speak further just this one time:
Perhaps there will be found there only ten!
He said:
I will not bring ruin, for the sake of the ten.
YHWH went, as soon as he had finished speaking to Avraham, and
Avraham returned to his place.

In other words, 50 false positives—innocents punished along with the guilty—would be too many. So would 40, 30, 20, even 10! But Abraham seems to concede that less than ten would not be unjust, since he stops his argument and returns to his place, after God agrees that he "will not bring ruin, for the sake of the ten." Even this powerful story does not contain sufficient data on which to base a formula, since we do not know how many false negatives (sinners who deserve punishment) are being spared "for the sake" of the ten—or how many future crimes that could have been prevented would now occur. Despite incompleteness of the data, this biblical account—perhaps the first recorded effort to quantify important moral judgments—almost certainly served as the basis for the formula later articulated by Maimonides, Blackstone, and others that it is better for 10 guilty defendants (some have put the number at 100, others at 1,000) to go free (to become false negatives) than for 1 innocent to be wrongly condemned (to become a false positive). That primitive formula is about the best we have come up with in the thousands of years we have been seeking to balance the rights of innocent defendants against the power of the state to punish guilty defendants for their past crimes.

We apply—or at least claim to apply—the identical formula to suspected murderers, pickpockets, corporate criminals, and drunken drivers. (There are some historical exceptions, such as treason, which our Constitution made especially difficult to prosecute; and rape, which historically was difficult to prosecute because of sexist distrust of alleged victims—a phenomenon that has been undergoing significant change during the past several decades.) A rational, calibrated system might well vary the number depending on the values at stake. The U.S. Constitution contains no specific reference to the maxim that it is better for ten guilty to go free than for one innocent to be convicted, but the Supreme Court has repeatedly invoked it as part of the requirement of proof beyond a reasonable doubt. Although the maxim was first articulated in the context of the death penalty, which was the routine punishment for all serious felonies, over time it came to be applied to imprisonment as well. Many Americans (and many jurors) probably do not prefer to see ten murderers go free in order to prevent the false imprisonment of even one wrongly accused defendant. Nonetheless, the maxim has become enshrined among the principles that distinguish nations governed by the rule of law from nations governed by the passion of persons. The maxim emerged, of course, from a criminal justice system that dealt with crime as a retail, rather than a wholesale, phenomenon. The guilty murderer who might go free as a result of its application was not likely to engage in future mass murders. The cost of applying the maxim could be measured in individual deaths, terrible as any preventable murder might be. Now, with the advent of terrorists using weapons of mass destruction, the calculus may have to change. It, in my view, remains true that it is better for ten guilty criminals (even murderers) to go free (and perhaps recidivate on a retail basis) than for even one innocent person to be wrongfully convicted. But it does not necessarily follow from this salutary principle that it is also better for ten potential mass terrorists to go free (and perhaps recidivate on a *wholesale* basis) than for even one innocent suspect to be detained for a limited period of time, sufficient to determine that he is not a potential terrorist.

These are the sorts of issues that must now be faced squarely as we shift from a primarily deterrent focus to a significantly preemptive approach, especially in the war against terrorism.

Conclusion

As we face these complex and difficult issues, we must always remember that we are a nation under law. Whatever balance we decide to strike between liberty and security must be struck openly and with democratic input. In the end, our policy choices will reflect the diversity of our society. They will not and should not reflect a single ideology. The result will be a compromise, but that is as it should be in a society as diverse and heterogeneous as our own. There is rarely one right answer to complex issues of the sort we face following 9/11. There are often wrong answers. The challenge of democracy is to strike the delicate balance between those who would give up all liberty in quest of total security and those who would surrender all security in quest of total liberty. Both of these extreme positions are wrong. Where the right balance should be struck must eventually be decided by democratic processes subject to the checks and balances of our Constitution.

Notes

1. Cass R. Sunstein, "Precautions & Nature," *Daedalus* 137, no. 2 (Spring 2008): 49–58.
2. Michael Pollan, "The Year in Ideas: A to Z: Precautionary Principle," *New York Times Magazine*, December 9, 2001.
3. Sunstein, "Precautions & Nature."
4. Ibid.
5. Lewis Carroll, *Alice's Adventures in Wonderland* (New York: Sterling, 2005 [1865]).
6. William Blackstone, *Commentaries on the Laws of England* (San Francisco: Bancroft-Whitney Company, 1916), 2185.
7. "In Defense of Deterrence," *New York Times*, September 10, 2002.
8. Ibid.
9. Ibid.
10. Ibid.
11. Ibid.
12. United Steelworkers of America, *AFL-CIO v. Textron, Inc.*, 836 F.2d 6, 252 (1st. Cir. 1987), citing *Vargas-Figueroa v. Saldana*, 826 F.2d 160, 162 (1st. Cir. 1987).

Part I

The Impact on
American Civil Liberties

2

The Logic of
Suspending Civil Liberties

*Dewi Williams**

> Those who would give up essential Liberty, to purchase a little tempo-
> rary Safety, deserve neither Liberty nor Safety.
>
> *Benjamin Franklin*

This is a nation which has been tested in adversity, which has survived
physical destruction and catastrophic loss of life. I do not underestimate
the ability of fanatical groups of terrorists to kill and destroy, but they do
not threaten the life of the nation.... [T]errorist violence, serious as it is,
does not threaten our institutions of government or our existence as a civil
community.... [T]he real threat to the life of the nation, in the sense of a
people living in accordance with its traditional laws and political values,
comes not from terrorism but from laws such as these.[1]

With these words, the U.K. government's response to the events
of September 11, 2001 was declared unlawful by one of Britain's
most eminent judicial figures, Lord Hoffmann. The government's contention was simple—that the detention, without charge or trial, of a small
number of foreign suspects was a necessary and proportionate response
to the threat posed by a nihilistic organization, with which these individuals were intimately associated. The Law Lords, Britain's most senior
judicial authorities, however, held otherwise.

Contemporary discourse surrounding antiterrorism legislation post–
September 11 almost universally acknowledges notions of sacrifice, which

---

* **Dewi Williams** is Lecturer in Law, Staffordshire Law School.

resonates with the Hobbesian dilemma; how does the state defend a liberal democratic society from imminent threats without compromising the individual freedoms and rights, which are the hallmarks of such societies?

Increasingly even those passionate human rights advocates and civil libertarians have accepted, to a varying extent, the notion of offering a "proportionate" sacrifice of individual liberty in light of the threat posed.[2]

This chapter seeks to challenge this perceived mantra in favor of recognizing and acknowledging the fact that the threat of terrorism and terrorists generally does not differ so considerably from regular crime and that in our highly legislated societies, domestic criminal law and criminal procedures offer a favorable route to bringing suspects to justice—as opposed to the draconian antiterrorism laws, which often serve only the cause and ultimate goals of the very organizations that the state seeks to "defeat."

The governments of the United States and United Kingdom regularly seek to reiterate the threat posed by nihilistic Islamic fundamentalists, those who pose a "clear and present danger" to our way of life.[3] In the United States the post–September 11 discourse is dominated by the neoconservative notion of the War on Terror in which the opposing belligerents form a subcategory of combatants who evade the protections and privileges of domestic civil law, in addition to those of international humanitarian law. The U. K. government sought to follow a similar, though not identical, approach in that it also identified the threat faced as being grave and yet somehow different from previous politically motivated violence. That is, the level and form of violence employed by al Qaeda-inspired terrorist is perceived as being on a previously unimagined scale. In response to this "new" threat the former British Prime Minister Tony Blair famously declared that "the rules of the game are changing."[4]

Witnesses to the events of the attacks of September 11, Bali, Madrid and London bombings would undoubtedly agree. This author, while not in the slightest way belittling the suffering of the victims of such atrocities, must query whether the legal response of the state was actually even necessary, let alone proportionate. This essay concerns itself with two fundamental questions posed by contemporary, post–September 11 discourse concerning the nature of liberty, security, and the law's response.

Terrorism and Crime, Spot the Difference?

First what, if anything, makes terrorism different from other threats posed to the social order, in particular criminal offences committed by major organized criminal networks? And, second, does the state actually require specific legal rules with which to combat terrorism?

The first question must, therefore, address the perceived wisdom which dictates that terrorism, in particular al Qaeda-inspired terrorism, differs from other crime. This author would question what precisely is it that creates such a distinction between terrorism and other criminal activity?

As Freeman observed, "In evaluating restrictions of human rights for the sake of security we must evaluate the threat from which we are said to need protection."[5] What therefore is the exact threat posed, and to whom is that threat addressed? This fundamental question is often responded to with glib references to "our way of life," "our freedoms," and "us." Wiser authorities have sought to explain and examine the nature and scale of the threat posed, and this author will avoid contributing further to this particular debate.[6] One would, however, observe that determining the actual threat posed cannot be an exact science, given the polemical rhetoric employed by governments and certain elements of the media. Freeman acknowledged that "demonization is a barrier to understanding, and understanding is necessary to just and effective solutions of political problems."[7]

An oft-cited metaphor to describe the "menace" of Islamic fundamentalist violence is the notion of a pervasive cancer of secret networks, which evade standard police detection. Tesón interestingly noted that "democratic societies can be besieged as much by fundamentalist Islamic terrorists as by, say, the mafia or drug lords (think about Colombia)."[8]

One therefore would repeat, what, if anything, distinguishes a terrorist organization that engages in nondiscriminatory violence from an organized criminal network such as the Camorra or Cosa Nostra—which often appear to behave in a similar fashion? The crux of Tesón's argument appears to be that the distinction between terrorism and crime can be simplified and that one must examine the victim group targeted. He argues that terrorists attack society not just the people. This distinction, in one's opinion, is deliberately simplistic, if not wholly inappropriate in this context. What, therefore, is society if not the people within it?

A criminal act can damage society as gravely as any act of terrorism; judges in criminal courts regularly describe those convicted of serious crimes as a "menace to society" in order to justify imposing lengthy prison sentences. To maintain this fiction demonstrates, once again, a failure to comprehend the nature of terrorism.

Proponents of this distinction, between terrorism and crime, often highlight the global nature of contemporary terrorist violence. They often cite the need to break complex computer-based networks and the need for unprecedented levels of international police collaboration and cooperation.[9] Similarly though we are now familiar with international police cooperation involving, for example, the viewing, purchasing, and production of child pornography through operations such as Operation

Ore, which involved considerable cooperation between the U.S. and U.K. police. Collaboration in the fields of financial crime, money laundering, narcotics, and people trafficking is now a common feature of all but the most routine police work in major Western cities.

In seeking to distinguish terrorism as its own separate and unique phenomenon, and more problematically taking it as read that terrorist suspects differ from criminal suspects, the possibility of making such an individual subject to varying standards emerges. A disturbing feature of the so-called War on Terror are the persistent allegations that terrorist suspects are subjected to torture and inhuman and degrading treatment,[10] in the name of interrogation and intelligence gathering. Furthermore as Ibrahim noted, "every dictator in the world is using what the U.S. has done under the Patriot Act and other derivative measures to justify their violations of human rights, as well as declaring a licence to continue to abuse human rights at present and in the future."[11]

The former British Ambassador to Uzbekistan Craig Murray highlighted these very serious concerns in his insightful autobiography.[12] Murray cautioned that intelligence obtained through torture in Uzbekistan was used in counterterrorism operations within the United Kingdom. This information was often little more than a flight of fantasy; as Dershowitz cautioned, suspects will sign or agree to anything, however ridiculous, in order for the interrogators to stop.[13] However, in the case of *Ajouaou & Others v. Secretary of State for the Home Department*,[14] the Court of Appeal accepted that such evidence was admissible, provided that the evidence had not been obtained through the actions or cooperation of a U.K. official. Furthermore such evidence could form the basis of initial police enquiries in the United Kingdom. Britain's then Attorney General Lord Goldsmith repeated the government's assertions that such intelligence was necessary in the light of the threat posed by the suspects, which reminds one of the Jacobin motto, "C'est affreux mais nécessaire."[15]

Such an approach should, of course, be abhorrent to the values of a liberal democracy; an approach that runs contrary to the spirit, if not also the letter, of several binding international instruments.[16] This position is also repugnant to the very ideals that such a War on Terror is alleged to champion. The "outsourcing" of torture via the semantic nicety of "extraordinary rendition" was neatly encapsulated by Lord Steyn,[17] who described the process as "sending suspects by flights of the CIA to certain foreign countries…the purpose of such rendition [being] coercive questioning of suspects." Worryingly as Gearty noted, "much of this activity is predicated on a definition of terrorism so vague that it permits action against persons whose only offence is that of radical political activity."[18] Such behavior is clearly paradoxical to the virtues that our governments claim to uphold and protect.

The alternative, therefore, appears obvious, which is to regard terrorism as a crime and to accord those suspected of having committed terrorism-related offences as criminal suspects. Gearty suggested that "…the laws on terrorism should be restricted to the core of serious criminal acts to which they ought exclusively to refer: murder, manslaughter, causing explosions and the like—not general, destabilising behaviour as is often the case today."[19] He continues and advocates that "the civil libertarian should argue unashamedly for the replacement of the language of terrorism with the language of the criminal law, for a return to policing rather than military metaphors to describe this branch of serious crime," so as to "…show that all the threats posed by terrorism can be catered to by the criminal process."

Regarding terrorist suspects as being beyond the pale of ordinary criminal law appears only to elevate them to the standing of supercriminal from which they gain the publicity and exposure they so desire, while simultaneously creating a climate of fear, suspicion, mistrust, and often near-panic and hysteria within the population the state claims it protects.[20] As Lord Hoffmann acknowledged, "[T]hat is the true measure of what terrorism may achieve. It is for Parliament to decide whether to give terrorist such a victory."[21]

In adopting specific antiterrorism provisions, the state may already have facilitated that victory.

Special Laws for Special Cases?

The premise of Joseph Conrad's novel, *The Secret Agent*, is an attempt by a foreign diplomat, Vladimir, to provoke the U.K. government into introducing punitive, if not repressive, antiterrorism legislation. Vladimir claims that "England lags. This country is absurd with its sentimental regard for individual liberty."[22] He encourages Verloc, the secret agent of the title, to instigate a terrorist incident within the United Kingdom. Ultimately the attempted bombing of the Greenwich Meridian fails to provoke the desired reaction and Vladimir is uncovered. Conrad's policeman, Chief Inspector Heat, unravels the details of the plot through classic detective work, forensic examination, and standard criminal investigative procedures. The Government Minister, the "distinguished personage," maintains that Britain does not require such draconian measures, despite Vladimir's efforts. The implication of the novel is that we in Britain pride ourselves on cool, considered response and not hot-blooded "continental" reaction—qualities that Conrad, evidently, admired.

This position now appears as antiquated as the novel itself. Specific antiterrorism legislation emerges throughout Europe during the 1970s and

1980s, in reaction to the proliferation of radical left-wing groups such as the Red Army Faction (Baader-Meinhof Gang), Red Brigades, and nationalist paramilitary organizations such as the Irish Republican Army (IRA) and Euskadi Ta Askatasuna (ETA).[23] These provisions variously provided for internment, detention without trial, special trials, and a general erosion of suspects' rights. Although almost all these measures were initially envisaged as being temporary or provisional, they were, however, maintained in force long after the groups renounced violence.[24] Gearty described, "...the terrorism laws prior to September 11, 2001...were sharply focused and usually applied with the kind of restraint that could only flow from a culture whose commitment to freedom and democracy did not feel challenged by the sporadic acts of relatively weak—albeit it is true occasionally very violent—subversives."[25] While this author would generally agree with this proposition, there were of course examples of terrible abuses conducted by the state. In particular the revelations of the *Ireland v. United Kingdom*[26] and *McCann v. United Kingdom*[27] cases make for disturbing reading. As Freeman identified, "In Northern Ireland, heavy handed laws that were meant to be temporary soon became permanent and those were notoriously ineffective and often damaging...these coercive measures were counterproductive, created new sources of grievance and failed to prevent the recurrence of terrorist atrocities."[28]

One defining distinction between previous antiterrorism legislation and the variety now employed post–September 11 is the apparently permanent nature of the threat faced and consequently of the legislation itself. The War on Terror appears to be an almost Orwellian concept of a never-ending, self-perpetuating, conflict against a "foreign" enemy, which requires a variety of sacrifices to be made by the citizenry of the state. As Luban acknowledged, though,

> [A]t this point, the plea of emergency no longer makes sense: calling long-term conditions (like the standing danger of terrorism)...an "emergency" is a confusion. Emergencies are temporary departures from normal conditions. September 11 was an emergency, daily life under long-term risk is not. Any abrogation of rights due to long-term "emergency" conditions should be regarded as permanent, not temporary.[29]

In introducing legislation such as the Patriot Act and, in the United Kingdom, several Terrorism Acts the governments of both the United States and United Kingdom appear to have learnt little from the experiences gleaned from the past 30 or more years. To justify such draconian measures as detention without charge for up to 42 days[30] and making suspects subject to virtual house arrest via the mechanism of control orders,[31] the state reiterates the threat posed and reminds the skeptic of the old IRA threat, "...remember we only have to be lucky once. You will have to be lucky always."[32] Furthermore, the state frequently seeks to alleviate the concerns of civil libertarians by subjecting the provisions to judicial scrutiny, though this is by no means guaranteed.[33] This places the judiciary in a rather novel position, as Gearty notes, "...the authoritarian tendency (of the state) has made such advances recently that the judges have found themselves in the front line of the defence of freedom."[34]

While the pronouncements of Lord Hoffmann and Justice Stevens in the case of *Hamdi v. Rumsfeld*[35] are a welcome check against the excess of the executive and compliant legislature, reliance on the judiciary as the last bastion against tyranny is fraught with uncertainty. In both the United States and United Kingdom, during periods of declared "emergency," the supreme courts of both nations have held that government legislation which provided for the detention of foreign nationals was justified and lawful.[36] While one would concede that such decisions now appear an extreme example from a "less enlightened age," it must, nevertheless, be borne in mind that such decisions still resonate and that judgments, such as those cited, often represent and indeed reflect the prevailing current of public opinion.

In seeking to justify the adoption of specific antiterrorism provisions the state appears to be handing a propaganda victory to al Qaeda-inspired terrorists, by exaggerating the threat to near-biblical proportions. Why, therefore, do states such as the United States and United Kingdom, which both espouse, and allegedly embody, the values and virtues of liberal democracies, introduce such measures? Starmer acknowledged, "[I]t may seem odd at first blush that while serious offences such as murder and rape are routinely tried in our courts, such insuperable problems exist when it comes to the prosecution of those suspected of terrorism that they must be detained, controlled or deported instead."[37]

Starmer appears to charge the state security apparatus with responsibility for encouraging and maintaining such a position. He appreciates that such agencies were not envisaged, nor do they function, as law enforcement agencies. Consequently as Mr. Justice Newman held, "[T]he Security Service (MI5) material...is not recorded and prepared for the purposes of being presented and used as evidence in an adversarial hearing."[38] Gearty goes further and claims that "[T]he intelligence services have never understood the need for a criminal process: their ideal world would be one in which official suspicion led straight to incarceration. That is why they so fervently oppose the idea that any of the 'evidence' they build up should be exposed to the rigours of a criminal trial."[39]

Thus it appears that the state has sought to dispense with one of the most fundamental concepts of a democratic society, the presumption of innocence and the right to a fair trial, all in the name of expedient security. As Starmer[40] notes, by dispensing with the notion of a criminal trial and the inherent features of due process in favor of preventative measures with no trial and no concept of due process, suspects can be detained indefinitely on the basis of mere suspicion and on the justification of "preventative detention."[41]

Aharon Barak recognized that "sometimes, a democracy must fight with one hand tied behind its back. Nonetheless, it has the upper hand. Preserving the rule of law and recognition of individual liberties constitute an important components of its understanding of security."[42]

And fight we must, not only against those who threaten our lives but also against the indifference, apathy, and ignorance[43] that allows an adroitly pernicious state to erode our traditional and hard-fought freedoms; as the authors of the *9/11 Commission Report* argued, "...if our liberties are curtailed, we lose the values that we are struggling to defend."[44]

The events of September 11, catastrophic as they were, did not change everything. Those events, however, might change everything if we permit, or are sufficiently reticent to allow, our elected officials to strip all of us of our rights and liberties in the name of safety. In which case, as Benjamin Franklin cautioned, we deserve neither.

Notes

1. Judgment of Lord Hoffmann in the joined cases of *A(FC) and Others v. Secretary of State for the Home Department and X(FC) and Others v. Secretary of State or the Home Department* [2004] U.K.HL 56 at 96 and 97, available at www.bailii.org.
2. Michael Ignatieff, e.g., claimed that the War on Terror requires a "new ethics of emergency" that may require the suspension of many cherished human rights. Ignatieff argues that emergency powers and radical counterterror measures are lesser evils, "forced on unwilling liberal democracies by the exigencies of their own survival." See Michael Ignatieff, *The Lesser Evil: Political Ethics in an Age of Terror* (Princeton: Princeton University Press, 2004), 136–143. This led Jonathan Raban to ascribe to Ignatieff the title of "in house philosopher" of the "terror warriors"; see Jonathan Raban, "The Truth about Terrorism," *New York Review of Books* LII, no. 1 (January 2005): 22–26, cited in R. A. Wilson, ed., *Human Rights in the "War on Terror"* (Cambridge, MA: Cambridge University Press, 2007), 19. Ignatieff is, however, not alone. Jeremy Waldron also believed that in light of the events of September 11 "some adjustment in our scheme of civil liberties is inevitable." See J. Waldron, "Security and Liberty: The Image of Balance," *The Journal of Political Philosophy* 11, no. 2 (2003): 191. Most significant perhaps is the fact that neither Ignatieff nor Waldron could be described as illiberal reactionary right-wing commentators.

3. In particular see the findings of the 9/11 Commission report, which commentated upon the extremist ideology of al Qaeda and described the problem: "It is not a position with which Americans can bargain or negotiate. With it there is no common ground—not even respect for life—on which to begin a dialogue. It can only be destroyed or utterly isolated." *The 9/11 Commission Report: Final Report of the National Commission on Terrorist Attacks upon the United States* (New York: W.W. Norton & Co, 2004), 362. While this may be a further example of the bellicose rhetoric employed by the U.S. authorities, it is telling that the report's findings have widely resonated within American society.

4. Prime Ministerial Press Conference on August 5, 2005.

5. Michael. Freeman, "Order, Rights and Threats: Terrorism and Global Justice," in *Human Rights in the "War on Terror,"* ed. R. A. Wilson, 49.

6. See, e.g., Rohan Gunaratna, *Inside Al Qaeda* (Berkley: Penguin, 2000); Jason Burke, *Al-Qaeda: The True Story of Radical Islam* (London: I B Taurus & Co, 2003).

7. Freeman, "Order, Rights and Threats," 52.

8. Fernando R Tesón, "Liberal Security," in *Human Rights in the "War on Terror,"* ed. Richard A. Wilson, 59.

9. Though as Wilson noted, a "classic" terrorist organization such as the IRA possessed, "…several hundred terrorists [which] were organised after 1978 into secret cells that could strike at the heart of the British political and economic institutions pretty much indefinitely. The IRA was embedded within a deterritorialized and global terror network that included Marxist guerrillas in South America, ETA in Spain and foreign Governments such as Libya." R. A. Wilson, "Human Rights in the 'War on Terror,'" in *Human Rights in the "War on Terror,"* ed. R. A. Wilson, 31–32. This revelation makes a mockery of Blair's assertion that Britain faced a new global threat in al Qaeda.

10. See, e.g., U.S. Torture Memo—August 1, 2002. Memorandum on "Standards of Conduct for Interrogators [Under 18 U.S.C §§ 2340–2340A].

11. Opening remarks by Professor Saad Eddin Ibrahim at the "Human Rights Defenders on the Frontlines of Freedom," Conference, November 11–12, 2003, cited in N Hicks, "The Impact of Counter Terror on the Promotion and Protection of Human Rights: A Global Perspective," in *Human Rights in the "War on Terror,"* ed. R. A. Wilson, 219. Similar remarks were made to Irene Khan, director of Amnesty International by the then Russian President Vladimir Putin—which she later related to this author in July 2006.

12. Craig Murray, *Murder in Samarkand* (Edinburgh: Mainstream, 2007).

13. Alan Dershowitz, *Why Terrorism Works* (New Haven, CT: Yale University Press, 2002).

14. [2004] EWCA (Civ.) 1123, available at www.bailii.org.

15. From the anonymous print, "It is dreadful but necessary" ("Cest affreux mais nécessaire"), from the Journal *d'Autre Monde*, 1794. Perhaps most concerning was the position of the United Kingdom's independent reviewer of anti-terrorism legislation, the noted QC Lord Carlyle who publicly stated that "we should have confidence in this intelligence"—a position he maintained when questioned further by this author.

16. For example, the UN Convention against Torture and Other Cruel, Inhuman or Degrading Treatment or Punishment (adopted on December 10, 1984, entered into force on June 26, 1987) 1465 UNTS 85 (CAT), International Convention on Civil and Political Rights (adopted on December 16, 1966, entered into force on March 23, 1976) 999 UNTS 171 (ICCPR), and the Convention for the Protection of Human Rights and Fundamental Freedoms (European Convention on Human Rights, as amended) (ECHR) art. 3. This was acknowledged in a later House of Lords decision, *A(FC) and Others v. Secretary of State for the Home Department* [2005] U.K.HL 71, which rejected the approach adopted by the Court of Appeal. In particular see the judgments of Lord Bingham of Cornhill, Lord Nicholls of Birkenhead, and Lord Hope of Craighead, available at www.bailii.org.

17. Lord Steyn, "Our Government and the International Rule of Law since 9/11," *European Human Rights Law Review* 1 (2007): 1–7, at page 4.

18. Conor Gearty, "Rethinking Civil Liberties in a Counter-Terrorism World," *European Human Rights Law Review* 1 (2007): 111–119, at page 115.

19. Ibid., 117–119.

20. See, e.g., the BBC Documentary produced by Adam Curtis, "The Power of Nightmares: The Rise of the Politics of Fear," which aired on BBC 2 in the Autumn of 2004.

21. Lord Hoffmann, note 1 supra, 97.

22. Joseph Conrad, *The Secret Agent* (London: Penguin Group, 2007 [1907]), 23.

23. For example, see the Prevention of Terrorism Acts (Northern Ireland) 1974–1989.Though in the United Kingdom specific provisions dated back to the 1920s; see the Civil Authorities (Special Powers) Act 1922.

24. As the French would say, "tout ce qui est temporaire ont par habitude de devenir permanent." (All that is temporary has a habit of becoming permanent.)

25. Gearty, "Rethinking Civil Liberties in a Counter-Terrorism World," 115.

26. European Human Rights Reports 2 (1978): 25.

27. European Human Rights Reports 21 (1996): 97.

28. Wilson, "Human Rights in the 'War on Terror,'" 32.

29. David Jay Luban, "Eight Fallacies about Liberty and Security," in *Human Rights in the "War on Terror,"* ed. R. A. Wilson, 249.

30. See the Counter-Terrorism Bill 2008, which is currently being debated in the House of Lords, available at www.publications.parliament.uk/pa/cm200708/cmbills/063/08063.i-v.html.

31. For a withering criticism of the British governement's legislative response to the events of September 11, see Kier Starmer, "Setting the Record Straight: Human Rights in an Era of International Terrorism," *European Human Rights Law Review* 1 (2007): 123–132.

32. Peter Taylor, *Brits: The War against the IRA* (London: Bloomsbury Publishing, 2001), 265. Gearty puts the post–September 11 threat into some perspective by offering that "…in fact such bouts of violence are few and far between–hardly ever occurring in North America and practically absent from a Western European society that has endured far more frequent bouts

of subversive political violence in the past"—violence, which was more often than not officially regarded as criminal, and the perpetrators regarded as criminal offenders, not terrorists; Gearty, "Rethinking Civil Liberties in a Counter-Terrorism World," 111.

33. Sadat Sayeed notes that Section 1005 of the Detainee Treatment Act 2005, the "Graham—Levin" Amendment, sought to remove the right of a habeas corpus petition to those detained at Guantanamo Bay; see Sadat Sayeed, "Guantanamo Bay–Five Years On," *Journal of Immigration Asylum and Nationality Law* 21, no. 2 (2007): 109–128, at page 110.

34. Gearty, "Rethinking Civil Liberties in a Counter-Terrorism World," 115.

35. Justice Stevens declared that "...for a nation to remain true to the ideals symbolized by its flag, it must not wield the tools of tyranny even to resist an assault by the forces of tyranny." *Hamdi v. Rumsfeld* (124 S. Ct. 2711, 2735 (2004)).

36. See, e.g., the House of Lords decision in *Liversage v. Anderson* [1942] AC 206, which upheld Regulation 18B of the Defence Regulations—which provided that the home secretary could order a person detained if the home secretary, "has reasonable cause to believe [the] person to be of hostile origin or association." Similarly in the United States the Supreme Court upheld the legitimacy of interment during World War II; see *Korematsu v. United States*, 323 U.S. 214. Richard Goldstone describes the decision as the "low watermark" of the Supreme Court's jurisprudence; see Richard Goldstone, "The Tension between Combating Terrorism and Protecting Civil Liberties," in *Human Rights in the "War on Terror,"* ed. R. A. Wilson, 160.

37. Starmer, "Setting the Record Straight," 128.

38. Newman J in *MK v. Secretary of State for the Home Department* (SIAC Appeal No. SC/29/2004, September 5, 2006 at para. 6).

39. Conor Gearty, "Short Cuts," *London Review of Books*, March 17, 2005. Cited in Starmer, "Setting the Record Straight," 131.

40. Starmer, "Setting the Record Straight," 131.

41. Significantly as Starmer, "Setting the Record Straight," 132, notes of the 17 detainees held at HMP Belmarsh without charge, no charges were ever brought; most tellingly though is the fact that no files were even passed to the Crown Prosecution Service.

42. President of the Israeli Supreme Court, Aharon Barak in A Barak, "A Judge on Judging: The Role of a Supreme Court in a Democracy," *Harvard Law Review* 116, no. 1 (2002): 19–162 at page 148.

43. Luban, "Eight Fallacies about Liberty and Security," 243, quotes the comedian Mel Brooks, "...tragedy is when I break a fingernail, and comedy is when you fall down a manhole and die." It would appear that for the majority of people living in the United States and United Kingdom infringements of rights and inhuman treatment occurring to other people are not their concern, provided of course it does not happen to them!

44. *9/11 Commission Report*, 395.

3

The Use of "Speech Zones" to Control Public Discourse in Twenty-First-Century America

Paul Haridakis and Amber Ferris*

The health of democracy in the United States, which is grounded in civic debate and participation, requires that we remain vigilant in monitoring restrictions on public discourse. One reason for close scrutiny today is that heightened controls on expression in the twenty-first century are not always highly visible. They often are reflected in mere restrictions on the time, place, or manner of public discussion. Recent courts' interpretation of First Amendment rights increasingly has supported strict controls on the time, place, or manner of protest and other forms of political dissent.

The purpose here is not to trace the history of the regulation of speech in public places or to review in depth the myriad restrictions on public discourse in the United States over the years. There has been a wealth of literature on these important topics.[1] This essay focuses on one specific mechanism to control public discourse in twenty-first-century America: the creation of specifically defined speech zones that designate *where* public expressive activities can occur. This manifestation of governmental constraints on the time, place, and manner of public discourse warrants

* **Paul Haridakis** is an attorney and Associate Professor of Communication Studies at Kent State University.

Amber Ferris is a doctoral candidate in the School of Communication Studies at Kent State University.

close attention, because the use and level of acceptance of speech zones to control discourse provide a gauge of the current level of societal commitment to free speech.

First, we summarize briefly the development of judicial thinking pertaining to controls on expression in government-owned public forums in the United States, including the tradition of time, place, and manner restrictions. Next, we provide examples of the creation of speech zones outside of which expressive activity is not tolerated, and recent cases in which courts addressed their constitutionality. Finally, we consider some potential ramifications of "zoning" public discourse in post–9/11 America.

The Regulation of Speech in Public Areas

In the late nineteenth century, the U.S. Supreme Court held that a city could control speech on public property it owned.[2] However, in 1939, the Court altered the view that the government could exercise total control of expression in public areas. In *Hague v. CIO*,[3] the Court ruled that the U.S. Constitution mandated that public areas such as streets, parks, and the like had to be open for "assembly, communicating thoughts between citizens, and discussing public questions."[4] Although a city had discretion to regulate use of public areas for communication activities, it could not prohibit expression in public places at its whim.

Over the years, courts have struggled to find a consistent approach to clarifying precisely when a public forum was an open forum for free speech purposes and when public expressive activities could be regulated constitutionally. Generally, *Hague* stood for the proposition that public property was presumptively open for public discourse. However, there was a countervailing recognition that governmental entities had a right to preserve the intended purpose for which those places exist (e.g., recreation, transportation) that might not be compatible with speakers' access in all instances.[5]

Consistent with *Hague*, the U.S. Supreme Court invalidated laws that prohibited entire forms of expression such as the distribution of leaflets and handbills.[6] The Court declared that democratic principles mandated that streets be open for the public to "impart information through speech or the distribution of literature."[7] The Court did recognize that cities could legitimately control the time, place, and manner of distribution without infringing on speaker rights. Such controls, though, had to be content-neutral. Accordingly, controls were invalidated that gave public officials too much discretion to restrain a speaker based on message content, and/or were vague in describing what was appropriate speech.[8]

Courts did uphold content-neutral time restrictions such as the authority to prevent "confusion by overlapping parades or processions,"[9] place restrictions, such as authority to control protest outside of courthouses (in order to avoid disruption of trials)[10] and schools (to control disruption of classes),[11] as well as manner restrictions, such as controls on the use of amplified speakers on sound trucks.[12]

In short, in cases where courts felt the public forum was compatible with public discourse, the rights of speakers were protected, subject to content-neutral and reasonable time, place, and manner restrictions. When courts felt that speakers' activities were not compatible with the nature of the public forum, the courts often upheld restrictions and even outright bans on expression.[13] As the Court noted in *Adderley v. Florida*, the First Amendment does not guarantee speakers the right of expression "whenever and however and wherever they please."[14]

Therefore, one major development in public forum jurisprudence was the articulation of three distinct categories of public fora,[15] as well as criteria for assessing the constitutionality of the regulation of expression in each of them. The three classifications of public forums are: traditional public forums, designated forums, and nonpublic forums.[16]

Traditional public forums are those locales in which public discourse historically has taken place. As Justice Owen Roberts put it in the *Hague* opinion he authored, such forums "have immemorially been held in trust for the use of the public and, time out of mind, have been used for purposes of assembly, communicating thoughts between citizens, and discussing public questions."[17] Classic examples are streets, parks, and sidewalks.[18]

Designated public forums, on the other hand, are places that would not have a tradition of openness or be available for public discourse but for the fact that the government has permitted them to be used for that purpose. The government can designate such a forum as open for just certain types of expression or for only certain classifications of speakers, such as student groups.[19] Therefore, in determining whether a forum has been designated for discourse, the courts have to make a factual determination as to the class of speakers for whom it has been open and for what types of expressive activities.[20] If the forum has been opened to certain classifications of speakers (e.g., students) or expression (e.g., employee family announcements), it can be maintained as a nonpublic forum for other speakers (e.g., nonstudents) or expression (e.g., picketing) for which it has not been designated as public.[21]

A nonpublic forum is public property that does not have a tradition of use for public discourse and has not been opened by the government for expressive activity. Here the government has considerable reign to restrict the use of the property and/or refuse speakers access to it.

Degree of Scrutiny Applied in Judicial Review

The type of public forum involved is an important factor in judicial assessment of the propriety of time, place, and manner restrictions.[22] Restrictions on expressive activities in a nonpublic forum simply must be "reasonable" in light of the intended purpose for which the forum exists.[23] In the case of traditional and designated forums, the standard of review is much stricter. First, the restrictions must be content-neutral. Second, they must be narrowly tailored to serve a substantial government interest. Third, if restricted, the speakers must have reasonable alternative communication channels available to reach their intended audience.[24]

Generally, content neutrality mandates that the government refrain from regulating speech because of opposition with the message.[25] However, courts have ruled at times that restrictions were content-neutral even though they were applied to or had a greater impact on certain groups.[26] In *Ward v. Rock against Racism*, the Court noted that "the requirement of narrow tailoring is satisfied 'so long as the...regulation promotes a substantial government interest that would be achieved less effectively absent the regulation.'"[27] The requirement that reasonable time, place, and manner restrictions leave speakers with sufficient alternative means of communication often depends on factors such as the speaker's access to the intended audience, as well as the cost and level of accessibility of using alternative channels of communication.[28]

In sum, the history of the regulation of public discourse in the United States provides specific guidance for considering the propriety of the current practice of limiting public expressive activities to specific speech "zones" or locales. First, governmental entities and officials can regulate but cannot prohibit speech in public forums. Second, in the case of traditional and designated public forums, regulation of public discourse must be content-neutral, narrowly tailored to serve significant government interests, and leave the speakers with reasonable alternatives for getting the message to their intended audience.

The Growing Practice of the Use of Speech Zones

As noted earlier, courts historically have upheld reasonable narrow constraints that limited expression in specific locales such as areas immediately surrounding post offices[29] and polling places.[30] However, the establishment of specified speech zones is qualitatively different. Speech zones are not often used to quarter off narrowly defined areas within which speech can be limited. Rather, they are generally used to quarter off small, designated areas in which speech can occur, and exclude large public areas outside of these zones from public discourse and dissent.

Here we focus on three specific contexts in which speech zones (by various names)[31] have been used in recent years to confine expression to narrowly defined areas: college campuses, political conventions, and post–9/11 public political events.

University Free Speech Zones

Numerous universities and colleges in recent years have established designated speech zones to control the situs of public discourse on campuses.[32] Pursuant to these policies, campuses define specific locales within which protest, demonstrations, and other expressive activities may occur. Such expressive activities on university property outside these designated locales generally are prohibited.

One concern with such policies is that the wealth of authority suggests that many public areas on campuses are, at a minimum, designated public forums.[33] As the U.S. Supreme Court suggested several years ago portions of a public university campus, "at least for its students, possesses many of the characteristics of a public forum."[34] Thus, declaring all but small designated areas of a college campus as off-limits for expressive activities would seem to exclude some areas that have the characteristics of public forums.

Particular zones or locales for student expression occasionally have been established over the years.[35] For example, at the end of the 1960s, students at Southwest Texas State University challenged a policy that limited expressive activities to a "student expression area." In *Bayless v. Martine*,[36] the Fifth Circuit Court of Appeals ruled that the regulation was a valid time, place, and manner restriction primarily because the court did not interpret the policy as banning expressive activity outside of the "expression area." In fact, the university had sought to provide students with alternative options to assemble. In concurrence, though, Judge Thornberry noted that if the student expression zone had been strictly enforced "it would restrict student assemblies to so small an area and so brief a time" that it would have been unreasonable.[37]

This latter attribute is reflected in some of the recent campus policies limiting where speakers (individuals, groups) can express themselves.[38] Several of these policies have been challenged by affected speakers and garnered opposition by concerned interest groups.[39] When faced with challenges to such regulations, courts have applied public forum and time, place, and manner rationales to determine whether regulations were constitutional. Below are a few examples.

In *Pro-Life Cougars v. University of Houston*,[40] a federal district court invalidated a restriction that was used to limit a pro-life student group that wanted to display photos of aborted fetuses to an area of campus that had been designated for "potentially disruptive" activities. The judge ruled that public university areas were "public fora designated for student speech,"[41] and that the policy gave the administration too much discretion to control what speech activity could occur at the university.[42] Similarly, in *Burbridge v. Sampson*[43] and *Khademi v. South Orange County Community College*,[44] courts ruled that regulations requiring college approval before distributing information, limitations placed on groups of 20 or more, and restriction of the use of amplified sound to particular "preferred areas" of campus (as opposed to other locales that had been traditionally used for expression) also gave administrators too much discretion to control speech on campus.

The U.S. District Court for the Northern District of Texas ruled in 2004 that Texas Tech's designation of a 20-foot-diameter gazebo as a speech zone was unconstitutional.[45] Judge Sam R. Cummings ruled that student expression should be permitted on "park areas, sidewalks, streets, or other similar common areas" because "these areas are public forums, at least for the University's students, irrespective of whether the University has so designated them or not."[46]

At West Virginia University, administrators designated two specific areas of campus for assemblies and other expressive activities.[47] The university cited "limitations of space on the downtown campus" as justification for creating these two speech zones.[48] After pressure from free speech advocates and the student body West Virginia abolished the speech zones in November 2002, providing that "assemblies of persons may occur on any grounds on the campus outside of buildings."[49]

Courts have been more receptive to curtailments of nonstudent expression. In 2004, the Maryland District Court ruled that the University of Maryland-College Park could restrict speech of people who were not associated with the university, unless the groups were sponsored by a university-affiliated group.[50] Concluding that the campus was a limited public forum, the judge explained that the purpose of the university was education, "not to provide an open meeting place for the unstructured expression of public points of view that are not sponsored or requested by any member of the University community."[51] Therefore, the university did not have to provide unfettered access to the public.

Zoning Political Discourse at Recent National Political Conventions

Speakers who wish to affect political dialogue often choose locales for public expression strategically to confront an intended audience and maximize the effect of the message. It is no accident, for example, that abortion clinics have been targets of antiabortion protests,[52] antiwar protesters have targeted recruitment centers[53] or naval parades,[54] and Nazi marchers have chosen towns with a significant Jewish community in which to conduct marches.[55]

One can hardly envision a more symbolic place for political expression in the United States than the conventions at which candidates for the president of the United States are nominated. One of the more controversial expressive activities during a convention occurred when Gregory Lee Johnson burned an American flag in front of the Dallas City Hall during the Republican National Convention in 1984.[56] The U.S. Supreme Court ruled that the First Amendment protected such symbolic speech.

In light of the protection of such controversial behavior exercised at prior political conventions, a fairly clear example of an emerging trend at controlling public discourse can be seen in the handling of protesters at the most recent Democratic and Republican National Conventions. At the 2000 Democratic National Convention in Los Angeles government officials attempted to restrict protesters to designated areas. The police department established a security zone surrounding the Staples Center that housed the Convention. All "expressive activity" within the security zone was foreclosed. A demonstration zone for expressive activity was established, but it was over 200 yards away from the Staples Center.

Various groups wanting to speak, protest, or demonstrate sought an injunction against enforcement of the security zone. Determining that the security zone encompassed traditional public forums (e.g., streets and sidewalks), the district court ruled that the restriction was not narrowly tailored (noting that the size of the security zone was greater than necessary to satisfy the government's concern for safety) and failed to provide the demonstrators with ample alternate channels of communication.[57]

Attempts to regulate speech during the 2000 Republican National Convention in Philadelphia involved concerns about both the place and manner in which public discourse was restricted. The city of Philadelphia gave the Republican National Committee (RNC) exclusive use of the major public forums near the convention site. The agreement gave the RNC the discretion to review other groups' applications for permits to assemble and, in essence, to determine who could engage in expressive activities (e.g., demonstrate, assemble) and where they would be permitted to do so. The American Civil Liberties Union (ACLU) challenged the agreement.[58] However, the propriety of the agreement was never litigated. The dispute was resolved when the issue was settled and various groups were permitted to demonstrate.

By 2004, however, a different view of the balance between security needs and expressive activities in public forums resulted in the imposition of strict controls on demonstrations and other expressive activities during the Democratic and Republican National Conventions. Municipal officials surrounded the DNC Convention site in Boston (the Fleet Center) with a security zone. The city also established a "designated demonstration zone." A coalition of activists who wanted to parade and/or demonstrate near the Fleet Center challenged the restriction that they limit their activities to the demonstration zone. Despite District Court Judge Woodlock's reservation of the atmosphere created by the demonstration zone,[59] he ruled that restricting protesters at the Convention to the demonstration zone did not violate their freedom of speech. He stated that the restriction was content-neutral and narrowly tailored (based on the City's argument that public safety necessitated keeping the streets and sidewalks clear).

On appeal, the Third Circuit Court of Appeals affirmed this ruling, indicating that limiting the protesters to the designated speech zone was a reasonable time, place, and manner restriction. In *Bl(a)ck Tea Society v. City of Boston*,[60] the appellate court accepted the district court's conclusion that the restriction was content-neutral and narrowly tailored. The court also ruled that the restriction left the plaintiffs with sufficient alternative channels to get their message to their intended audience. Specifically, the court determined that the demonstration zone was "within sight and sound of the delegates,"[61] and suggested the protesters also could "reach the delegates through television, radio, the press, the internet, and other outlets."[62]

At the 2004 Republican National Convention in New York, police used pens and orange netting to corral protesters.[63] By the time the Convention was over, perhaps more than 1,700 people had been arrested for not remaining in the confined areas provided. Demonstrations on the Great Lawn in Central Park also were restricted. In *National Council of Arab Americans v. City of New York*,[64] a federal court ruled that the restrictions on demonstrations in the park were reasonable.

Zoning Political Discourse near the President, Public Officials, and at Public Events

The trend of limiting political discourse to specific locales has occurred in settings other than college campuses and political conventions. Events involving the president come readily to mind.

Particularly after 9/11, when President Bush made public appearances, the Secret Service and/or local law enforcement personnel often enforced speech zones. There has been some criticism of this practice.[65] The locales designated for expressive activity often have been quite remote from the President and the media covering his visits.[66] They also are often placed behind fences, buses, and other types of physical barriers.[67]

In *Acorn v. City of Philadelphia*,[68] the ACLU filed a lawsuit on behalf of three organizations seeking an order to enjoin the Secret Service from enforcing such restrictions on expression, alleging that it violated the First Amendment. The district court judge determined that the plaintiff's claims of likely future harm were too amorphous to support an injunction and that if such harm arose in the future, it should be dealt with "in the jurisdiction where such disputes arise, and where the specific factual context can readily be developed."[69] Accordingly, the district court judge dismissed the case for lack of subject-matter jurisdiction.[70]

Although the judge in the *Acorn* case may have felt that claims were too speculative to support an injunction on the government's use of speech zones, the consequences for protesters who refuse to abide by the geographic restrictions imposed are very real. Arrests, for example, have become relatively commonplace.[71] In one fairly well-publicized instance, protester Brett Bursey was arrested at the Columbia Metropolitan Airport in South Carolina for carrying an antiwar sign outside of the designated zone located on the edge of a highway.[72] Bursey was convicted pursuant to a 1971 federal statute making it unlawful to "enter or remain in any posted, cordoned off, or otherwise restricted area of…grounds where the President…is or will be temporarily visiting, in violation of the regulations governing ingress or egress thereto."[73] Although it is likely that few would argue with the logic of the statute, the cordoned-off area designated by the Secret Service was extensive. Bursey was approximately half a mile from the president.[74]

Some attempts to create designated speech zones to control political protest that may occur near the president or other public officials have not withstood judicial scrutiny. For example, in *Lederman v. United States*,[75] the D.C. Circuit Court of Appeals ruled that a ban on "demonstration activity" outside the U.S. Capitol building was unconstitutional.[76] The events leading to the case began when Lederman allegedly refused to stop passing out leaflets in a "no demonstration zone" after police informed him that such activity was not permitted there.[77] Assessing the restriction under time, place, and manner principles, the Circuit Court of Appeals noted that the areas around the Capitol were "traditionally" public forums and that "their intended use is consistent with public expression."[78] Accordingly, the court ruled that the total ban on all expressive activities was not narrowly tailored because alternatives less egregious than banning all speech around the Capitol could have been used to serve the government's interests such as safety and orderly traffic flow.[79]

However, the *Lederman* case stands in stark contrast to cases in which courts have permitted public expressive activities, particularly since the September 11, 2001 terrorist attacks on the World Trade Center and Pentagon, to be confined to stationary areas. For example, shortly after the *Lederman* decision, a federal district court denied a motion for a preliminary injunction filed by a coalition of organizations challenging New York City's refusal to permit a demonstration protesting the Iraq war that was to include a march in front of the United Nations.[80] Finding that the city had banned other post–9/11 demonstrations in front of the United Nations, the judge felt that (1) the city's decision was content-neutral,[81] (2) the city's security concerns posed by terrorism were significant,[82] (3) the city's consent to permit the demonstrators to hold a stationary rally at nearby locations was narrowly tailored,[83] and (4) that a stationary rally was a reasonable alternative because it provided the plaintiff with "ample opportunity to express its views in close proximity to the United Nations."[84] Once the rally did take place, police exercised crowd control by setting up barricades and metal pens into which demonstrators were herded.[85]

The Ramifications of Speech Zones in Post–9/11 America

According to the Supreme Court, the type of public forum dictates the extent to which speech and debate can be controlled and the level of scrutiny the courts apply to test the constitutionality of restrictions on the time, place, or manner of expression. The highest level of scrutiny is applied to assess restrictions on speech in locales that traditionally have been open or designated for free expression.[86]

In each of the aforementioned contexts in which speech was constrained to designated speech zones, such analysis was triggered and applied. Courts upheld the sequestering of demonstrators in "free speech zones" at the 2004 Democratic National Convention far from the convention site. Similar remote speech zones recently have been upheld in other post–9/11 situations in which speakers wanted to hold protests, demonstrations, and marches. Thus far, courts have been less receptive to the designation of small free speech zones on college campuses.

In each of these contexts, the courts assessed the content-neutrality of the regulations, how narrowly tailored they were, and whether there were adequate alternative means of communication. This approach is designed to balance speakers' First Amendment rights with significant government interests such as maintaining order and public safety. However, the fact that courts increasingly have used the analysis to uphold the constitutionality of stationary speech zones has led some commentators to question whether this approach, as currently being applied by the courts, adequately guards against dilution of free speech rights, particularly public demonstrations and dissent.[87]

Over the years there have been a number of restrictions upheld as constitutional that restricted speech in specific narrowly defined places such as outside a courthouse, jails, polling areas, and the like.[88] These constraints usually restricted speech in small narrowly defined areas that were not compatible with public use for free expression. College campus free speech zones and the free speech zones created at the recent national political conventions and other public events are qualitatively different. Specific narrowly prescribed areas are not designated as off-limits for public discourse. Rather, narrowly prescribed areas are designated as acceptable places for expression, and large areas—regardless of whether they have been traditional public forums in the past—are deemed off-limits for public discourse.

In light of this change in the treatment and control of the public forum, one of the more important First Amendment questions in the early twenty-first century is whether the courts and public are becoming more amendable to use of such constraints. Thus the use and acceptance of speech zones to control public discourse provides a visible gauge of where we, as a society, currently draw boundaries on freedom of speech in public places in post–9/11 America.

Those boundaries change from time to time in the United States. There have been periods in U.S. history of greater protection and/or expansion of free speech rights and other periods of acceptance of greater restrictions and/or diminishment of such rights.[89] Crises can precipitate the latter. It has been suggested that during crises, "the balance between liberty and security is more like a pendulum that gets pushed off-center by significant events (such as those of September 11) than a spiral. Over time, after Americans have recovered from the understandable human reaction to catastrophe and after the threat recedes, the pendulum returns to center."[90] The point is that eras of greater controls on speech (often precipitated by times of crises) are followed by later eras of relaxed controls and greater protection of free speech and other individual liberties (often precipitated by the lessening of the crisis and emergence of a time of relative tranquility).

In light of such recognition, how do we put the current era of the protection of expression in historical perspective? Why in an era that has not produced the type or volume of student activism present in the 1960s have colleges felt compelled to create and enforce speech zones? Why were there more arrests of members of the public at the 2004 Republican National Convention than at previous conventions? Could a protester get away with burning an American flag at a national political convention today?[91] These are questions that we must ask ourselves as we consider the acceptable balance between free expression and control of it in the United States today.

It is easy to point to events such as the War on Terror and the tragic events of September 11, 2001 as the crisis that has led to constraints on civil rights, such as the closing of deportation hearings to the public, the prospect of closed military trials, USA Patriot Act restrictions, controls of access to information,[92] and, perhaps, speech zones.[93] For example, prior to 9/11, speech zones established for the 2000 Democratic National Convention were deemed to be an unreasonable restriction on speech. Four years later similarly restrictive speech zones at the 2004 Convention were deemed reasonable time, place, and manner restrictions. In the late 1980s the Supreme Court indicated that it was unreasonable to prevent dissenters from congregating within 500 feet from a foreign embassy.[94] In 2003, preventing protesters from using the public street near the UN building was deemed reasonable.

In his concurring opinion issued in the *Bl(a)ck Tea Party* case, Appellate Court Judge Lipez hinted that we may be in an era stressing security. Noting that the 2004 Democratic National Convention was the first post–9/11 national political convention held, Judge Lipez acknowledged that

> the events of 9/11 and the constant reminders in the popular media of security alerts color perceptions of the risks around us, including the perceptions of judges.... I am not suggesting that this new reality makes the First Amendment rights of the demonstrators any less important or the vigilance that the courts must have for those rights any less imperative. But I am suggesting that the always difficult balancing between those First Amendment rights and the demands of security has become even more difficult.[95]

Similarly, when affirming the district court decision in *United for Peace and Justice v. City of New York*, the Second Circuit Court of Appeals stressed that judges "are ever mindful of our role in the preservation of our system of ordered liberty, especially in times of war."[96] Speech zones seem to be a current mechanism being used to balance these interests in the new century.

In the *Bl(a)ck Tea Party* case, the court claimed that there was no inherent First Amendment guarantee to direct face-to-face access to persons who are the intended recipients of a message,[97] and suggested that protesters who were limited to expressing their message from the free speech zone corrals could seek access through mediated channels such as the Internet.

But, is that right? Electronic channels may provide more security, more orderly streets, and less human clutter. But the point of public discourse is to interact directly with one's intended audience. Supreme Court Justice

William Douglas stated more than half a century ago, the purpose "of free speech...is to invite dispute. It may indeed best serve its high purpose when it induces a condition of unrest, creates dissatisfaction with conditions as they are, or even stirs people to anger."[98]

Speech zones thwart that purpose. They often force dissenters into controlled locales in which their message is at best placed outside the public eye,[99] and at worst, where "its very effectiveness can be minimized and perhaps eliminated."[100] Eloquently put by the Supreme Court as far back as 1939, a speaker should not "have the exercise of his liberty of expression in appropriate places abridged on the plea that it may be exercised in some other place."[101]

Speech zones contradict this long-standing précis. The criteria that time, place, and manner restrictions be narrowly tailored would seem to suggest that the extremity of zoning speech should be a last resort. Too often, however, speech zones are a first resort, carefully preestablished regardless of whether they are truly necessary. Coupling them with cages, pens, and other physical confinement of speakers creates an ominous aura of overbreadth.

In addition, because speech zones often sequester speakers from their intended audience and the media, the functional value of alternative media channels is questionable. The court's suggestion in *Bl(a)ck Tea Party* that the Internet was an alternative for those who wanted to demonstrate at the 2004 Democratic National Convention is a pretty sweeping generalization, and research challenges that proposition. It has been suggested, for example, that when choosing Internet content, people selectively expose themselves to messages that serve their needs and desires.[102] Such findings should give us pause when suggesting that newer media can supplement the physical public forum. The Internet certainly may be beneficial for reaching an audience of like-minded people who agree with the message content and/or its advocates. But it strains logic to suggest that those who are not willing recipients of a message would go to the Internet for information they do not want. The public forum may be the only functional channel for reaching such a reticent audience. Thus, circumventing it cuts off a powerful channel for registering dissent.

Conclusion

In short, to judge the reasonableness of time, place, and manner restrictions, the courts do have specific criteria to apply (e.g., whether the restrictions are content-neutral, narrowly tailored, and provide alternative means for speakers to reach their intended audience). But the atmosphere in which the restrictions are imposed and reviewed often seems to be as or more important than the criteria used to assess their reasonableness. During times of crisis, such as post–9/11 America, government officials, including judges, are not always at their best in defending constitutional ideals. As former Fifth Circuit Appellate Court Justice Learned Hand once cautioned, we may sometimes "rest our hopes too much upon constitutions, upon laws and upon courts…Liberty lies in the hearts of men and women; when it dies there, no constitution, no law, no court can save it."[103]

Notes

1. See, e.g., Ronnie J. Fischer, "'What's in a Name?': An Attempt to Resolve the 'Analytic Ambiguity' of the Designated and Limited Public Fora," *Dickinson Law Review* 107 (2003): 639–674; Calvin Massey, "Public Fora, Neutral Governments, and the Prism of Property," *Hastings Law Journal* 50 (1999): 309–353; Kevin Francis O'Neill, "Disentangling the Law of Public Protest," *Loyola Law Review* 45 (1999): 411–526.
2. *Davis v. Massachusetts*, 167 U.S. 43 (1897).
3. *Hague v. Committee for Industrial Organization*, 307 U.S. 496 (1939).
4. Ibid., 515.
5. See, e.g., *Adderley v. Florida*, 385 U.S. 39 (1966); *Grayned v. Rockford*, 408 U.S. 104 (1972).
6. *Schneider v. State*, 308 U.S. 147 (1939).
7. Ibid., 160.
8. See, e.g., *Shuttlesworth v. Birmingham*, 394 U.S. 147 (1969); *Kunz v. New York*, 340 U.S. 290 (1951).
9. *Cox v. New Hampshire*, 312 U.S. 569, 576 (1941).
10. *Cox v. Louisiana*, 379 U.S. 559 (1965).
11. *Grayned v. Rockford*, 408 U.S. 104 (1972).
12. *Kovacs v. Cooper*, 336 U.S. 77 (1949).
13. For a discussion of the evolution of this jurisprudence, see Thomas L. Tedford and Dale A. Herbeck, *Freedom of Speech in the United States*, 4th ed. (State College, PA: Strata Publishing, 2001), 261–271.
14. *Adderley*, 385 U.S. at 48. See also, *Greer v. Spock*, 424 U.S. 828, 836 (1976).
15. *Perry Education Association v. Perry Local Educators' Association*, 460 U.S. 37 (1983).
16. Ibid., 44–46.
17. *Hague*, 307 U.S. at 515.
18. See, e.g., *Frisby v. Schultz*, 487 U.S. 474, 479–481 (1988); *Cornelius v. NAACP Legal Defense & Education Fund, Inc.*, 473 U.S. 788, 802 (1985).
19. See, e.g., *Widmar v. Vincent*, 454 U.S. 263 (1981).
20. See, e.g., *Cornelius*, 473 U.S. at 802. For a discussion of this issue and a review of relevant cases, See O'Neill, "Disentangling the Law of Public Protest," 426.

21. See Massey, "Public Fora, Neutral Governments, and the Prism of Property," 321–327.

22. *Good News Club v. Milford Central School*, 533 U.S. 98 (2001).

23. *Perry Education Association*, 460 U.S. at 49; See also, *International Society for Krishna Consciousness, Inc. v. Lee*, 505 U.S. 672, 688–689 (1992) (O'Connor, J., concurring).

24. *Ward v. Rock against Racism*, 491 U.S. 781, 802 (1989).

25. Ibid., 791.

26. See *United States v. Fee*, 787 F. Supp. 963 (D. Colo. 1992) (upholding convictions of environmentalists for entering a portion of a national forest that had been closed in response to prior actions of environmentalists); see also, *Frisby v. Schultz*, 487 U.S. 474 (1988) and *Madsen v. Women's Health Center*, 512 U.S. 753 (1994) (upholding bans on protesting outside residences and/or abortion clinics which, in essence, were applied only to antiabortion protesters).

27. *Ward*, 491 U.S. at 799 (quoting *United States v. Albertini*, 472 U.S. 675, 689 (1985)).

28. See O'Neill, "Disentangling the Law of Public Protest," 441–447 for a discussion.

29. *United States v. Kokinda*, 497 U.S. 720 (1990).

30. *Burson v. Freeman*, 504 U.S. 191 (1992).

31. Although we are using the term "speech zone" here, other names for such mandated stationary areas for discourse include "free speech zones," "protest zones," "demonstration zones," "security zones," and the like.

32. See Thomas J. Davis, "Assessing Constitutional Challenges to University Free Speech Zones under Public Forum Doctrine," *Indiana Law Journal* 79 (2004): 267–297 for a review of several examples of such policies. See also, Carol L. Zeiner, "Zoned Out! Examining Campus Speech Zones," *Louisiana Law Review* 66 (2005): 1–61.

33. See Davis, "Assessing Constitutional Challenges to University Free Speech Zones under Public Forum Doctrine," 271–272; see also Michael Schwartz, "The Place of Dissent in Inquiry, Learning and Reflection," *Peace & Change* 21, no. 2 (1996): 169–181.

34. *Widmar v. Vincent*, 454 U.S. 263, 268 (1981).

35. United States President's Commission on Campus Unrest, *The Report of the President's Commission on Campus Unrest* (Washington, DC: U.S. Govt. Print. Off., 1970).

36. *Bayless v. Martine*, 430 F.2d 873 (1970).

37. Ibid., 881 (Thornberry, J., concurring).

38. See Davis, "Assessing Constitutional Challenges to University Free Speech Zones under Public Forum Doctrine."

39. Ibid., 267–268.

40. *Pro-Life Cougars v. University of Houston,* 259 F. Supp. 2d 575 (S.D. Tex. 2003).

41. Ibid., 582.

42. Ibid., 584.

43. *Burbridge v. Sampson*, 74 F. Supp. 2d 940 (C.D. Cal. 1999).

44. *Khademi v. South Orange County Community College*, 194 F. Supp. 2d 1011 (C.D. Cal. 2002).
45. *Roberts v. Haragan*, 346 F. Supp. 2d 853 (N.D. Tex. 2004).
46. Ibid., 861.
47. The case and university policy is cited and discussed in Davis, "Assessing Constitutional Challenges to University Free Speech Zones under Public Forum Doctrine," 294–295.
48. Ibid., 295 (note 247).
49. Quoted in FIRE, "Victory at West Virginia University: The End of a Censorship Zone," *FIRE Press Release* (December 5, 2002), http://www.the-fire.org/index.php/article/55.html (accessed July 31, 2008).
50. *ACLU Student Chapter-University of Maryland, College Park v. C.D. Mote, Jr.*, 321 F. Supp. 2d 670 (2004).
51. Ibid., 680.
52. For example, *Hill v. Colorado*, 530 U.S. 703 (2000).
53. *Gooding v. Wilson*, 405 U.S. 518 (1972).
54. *Bay Area Peace Navy v. United States*, 914 F.2d 1224 (9th Cir. 1990).
55. *Collin v. Smith*, 578 F.2d 1197 (7th Cir. 1978).
56. *Texas v. Johnson*, 491 U.S. 397 (1989).
57. *Service Employee International Union Local 660 v. City of Los Angeles*, 114 F. Supp. 2d 966 (C.D. Cal. 2000).
58. For a thorough discussion of this issue, see Jonathan Janiszewski, "Silence Enforced through Speech: Philadelphia and the 2000 Republican National Convention," *Temple Political & Civil Rights Law Review* 12 (2002): 121–140.
59. Coalition to Protest the Democratic National Convention v. City of Boston, 327 F. Supp. 2d 61, 67 (D. Mass. 2004).
60. *Bl(a)ck Tea Society v. City of Boston*, 378 F.3d 8 (1st Cir. 2004).
61. Ibid., 14.
62. Ibid.
63. See Timothy Zick, "Speech and Spatial Tactics," *Texas Law Review* 84 (2006): 581–651, 597–598; James J. Knicely and John W. Whitehead, "The Caging of Free Speech in America," *Temple Political & Civil Rights Law Review* 14 (2005): 455–493, 466–467.
64. *National Council of Arab Americans v. City of New York*, 331 F. Supp. 2d 258 (S.D. NY, 2004). Cited and discussed in James C. Kozlowski, "Protesters in Public Parks," *Parks & Recreation*, November 2004, 51–55.
65. See, e.g., Mary M. Cheh, "In the Aftermath of September 11: Defending Civil Liberties in the Nation's Capital: The Treatment of Demonstrators: Demonstrations, Security Zones, and First Amendment Protection of Special Places," *University of the District of Columbia Law Review* 8 (2004): 53–76, 58; Michael J. Hampson, "Protesting the President: Free Speech Zones and the First Amendment," *Rutgers Law Review* 58 (2005): 245–274, 256–259.
66. See Cheh, "In the Aftermath of September 11,"58; see also, Hampson, "Protesting the President," 257 (noting an example in South Carolina in which a free speech zone was more than half a mile from the president).

67. See Hampson, "Protesting the President," 256–260 for a discussion. See also James Bovard, " 'Free Speech Zone': The Administration Quarantines Dissent," *The American Conservative*, December 15, 2003, available at http://www.amconmag.com/12_15_03/feature.html (accessed July 31, 2008) (noting that when the president visited the Pittsburgh area in 2002, the Secret Service established a "designated free speech zone" a third of a mile away from the president on a baseball field surrounded by chain-link fence).

68. *Acorn v. City of Philadelphia,* 2004 U.S. Dist. LEXIS 8446 (E.D. PA 2004).

69. Ibid., 8.

70. Ibid.

71. See Cheh, "In the Aftermath of September 11" for a discussion of the use of preemptive arrests as a police tactic.

72. For a discussion of the facts, see *United States v. Bursey,* 416 F.3d 301 (4th Cir. 2005), in which the Fourth Circuit Court of Appeals affirmed Bursey's conviction.

73. 18 U.S.C.S. 1752(a)(1)(ii) (cited in *United States v. Bursey,* 416 F.3d at 306).

74. See Bovard, " 'Free Speech Zone.' "

75. *Lederman v. United States*, 291 F.3d 36 (DC Cir. 2002).

76. Ibid., 39.

77. Ibid., 39–40.

78. Ibid., 41.

79. Ibid., 45–46.

80. *United for Peace & Justice v. City of New York*, 243 F. Supp. 2d 19 (S.D. NY 2003).

81. Ibid., 24.

82. Ibid., 25.

83. Ibid., 29.

84. Ibid.

85. For a description of the rally and a discussion of police tactics, See Nick Suplina, "Crowd Control: The Troubling Mix of First Amendment Law, Political Demonstrations, and Terrorism," *The George Washington Law Review* 73 (2005): 395–428, 416–417.

86. See, e.g., *Perry Education Association v. Perry Local Educators' Association*, supra note 15; *Ward v. Rock against Racism*, supra note 24.

87. See Suplina, "Crowd Control," 398, 409–412, and 427 (where Suplina suggested that "time, place, manner jurisprudence is susceptible to manipulation by the state, particularly through proffered terrorism-prevention state interests"); see also, Cheh, "In the Aftermath of September 11," 53 (suggesting that the time, place, and manner analysis "has become too flabby and unstable to reliably counter the government's sophisticated dilution and weakening of public demonstrations and the consequent enervation of dissent").

88. See, e.g., *Cox v. Louisiana*, 379 U.S. 559 (1965); *Adderley v. Florida*, 385 U.S. 39 (1966); *Burson v. Freeman*, 504 U.S. 191 (1992).

89. Margaret A. Blanchard, " 'Why Can't We Ever Learn?' Cycles of Stability, Stress and Freedom of Expression in United States History," *Communication Law & Policy* 7 (2002): 347–378. Professor Blanchard referred to this ebb and

flow as corresponding eras of greater restrictions on speech followed by eras of reactions to those restrictions. See also, Michael Kent Curtis, "Teaching Free Speech from an Incomplete Fossil Record," *Akron Law Review* 34 (2000): 231–260, 240. Law professor Michael Kent Curtis referred to these fluctuations as revolutions and counterrevolutions.

90. Paul Rosenzweig, "Civil Liberty and the Response to Terrorism," *Duquesne Law Review* 42 (2004): 663–723, 671.

91. See *Texas v. Johnson*, 491 U.S. 397 (1989) (in which the U.S. Supreme Court held that burning of an American flag outside the Dallas City Hall during 1984 Republican National Convention was protected by the First Amendment).

92. See, e.g., Paul Haridakis, "Citizen Access and Government Secrecy," *Saint Louis University Public Law Review* 25, no. 3 (2006): 3–32.

93. See Zick, "Speech and Spatial Tactics," 589. Zick referred to the displacement of political protest as a "noticeable and disturbing recent trend."

94. *Boos v. Barry*, 485 U.S. 312 (1988).

95. *Bl(a)ck Tea Society v. City of Boston*, 378 F.3d 8, 19 (1st Cir. 2004).

96. *United for Peace and Justice v. City of New York*, 323 F.3d 175, 177–178 (2nd Cir. 2003).

97. *Bl(a)ck Tea Society v. City of Boston*, 378 F.3d 8, 14 (1st Cir. 2004).

98. *Terminiello v. Chicago*, 337 U.S. 1, 4 (1949).

99. See Zick, "Speech and Spatial Tactics," 591. Zick asserted that speech zones around the president during his campaigns and presidency not only separated protesters from the president, "they also separated protesters from the media."

100. Don Mitchell, "The Liberalization of Free Speech: Or, How Protest in Public Space is Silenced," *Stanford Agora* 4 (2004): 1–45, 42.

101. *Schneider v. State*, 308 U.S. 147, 163 (1939).

102. Silvia Knobloch-Westerwick, Francesca Dillman Carpentier, Andree Blumhoff, and Nico Nickel, "Selective Exposure Effects for Positive and Negative News: Testing the Robustness of the Informational Utility Model," *Journalism and Mass Communication Quarterly* 82 (2005): 181–185.

103. Quoted in Susan Dente Ross, "An Apologia to Radical Dissent and a Supreme Court Test to Protect It," *Communication Law & Policy* 7 (2002): 401–430, 403.

4

Challenges to Academic Freedom since 9/11

*Peter N. Kirstein**

During war, American democracy is imperiled less by external threats than by demands for internal conformity that restrict free speech. Despite the mythic belief that America's wars extend democracy and preserve civil liberties, they frequently are accompanied by rampant nationalism that dehumanizes the enemy and demands reverential patriotism. "War is the health of the state" was the sardonic observation of essayist and progressive intellectual Randolph Bourne during World War I when ruling elites maximized their power by seeking total allegiance to the state.[1] Columbia University President Nicholas Murray Butler abolished academic freedom on his campus in 1917 during the Great War when he issued at commencement a "warning to any among us...who are not with whole heart and mind and strength committed to fight with us to make the whole world safe for democracy."[2]

Edward Bemis may have been the first professor dismissed for extramural activities while teaching at the University of Chicago. He tried to mediate an end to the epic Pullman Strike in 1894. Scott Nearing, an economist at the University of Pennsylvania, became the first progressive professor fired for opposing child labor in the coal mines in 1915.[3] Supporting antiwar and internationalist activism have replaced antiestablishment economic advocacy as the most likely to unleash challenges to academic freedom.

* **Peter N. Kirstein** is Professor of History at St. Xavier University and author of *Anglo over Bracero: A History of the Mexican Worker in the United States from Roosevelt to Nixon.* He is Vice President, American Association of University Professors—Illinois.

During the height of cold-war McCarthyism from 1952 to 1954, nationalistic show trials and suppression of dissent were notorious when hundreds of academics were fired for resisting congressional inquiries into alleged Communist Party affiliation. First Amendment and Fifth Amendment efforts to avoid self-incrimination were disallowed by this crusade for militant anticommunism. Thirty-seven presidents from leading universities issued a statement disparaging the "fitness" of any professor unwilling to report or silence alleged communists or opponents of the cold war. Also, hundreds of secondary-school teachers were purged after a "local loyalty probe" or following testimony before the House Un-American Activities Committee.[4]

Academic freedom is defined by the landmark American Association of University Professors "1940 Statement of Principles on Academic Freedom and Tenure." Academic freedom gives professors the right to pursue research and publish its results; academicians have "freedom in the classroom" to determine their pedagogy. Instructors have the right to "speak and write as citizens... [and] should be free from institutional censorship or discipline."[5] Professors should strive for accuracy, respect the opinions of others, and not claim to speak for their institution.[6] "A faculty member's expression of opinion as a citizen cannot constitute grounds for dismissal unless it clearly demonstrates the faculty member's unfitness to serve. Extramural utterances rarely bear upon the faculty member's fitness for continuing service.... In a democratic society freedom of speech is an indispensable right of the citizen."[7]

In *Keyishian v. Board of Regents*, academic freedom was dramatically elevated by the Supreme Court to a quasi-constitutional right. Justice William J. Brennan, Jr., delivered the majority opinion:

> Our Nation is deeply committed to safeguarding academic freedom which is of transcendent value to all of us and not merely to the teachers concerned. That freedom is therefore a special concern of the First Amendment, which does not tolerate laws that cast a pall of orthodoxy over the classroom.... The Nation's future depends upon leaders trained through wide exposure to that robust exchange of ideas which discovers truth.[8]

While not as sweeping as *Keyishian*, Justice Lewis F. Powell, Jr., in *Regents of the University of California v. Bakke* reaffirmed that "[a]cademic freedom, though not a specifically enumerated constitutional right, long has been viewed as a special concern of the First Amendment." A university must "make its own judgments as to education...."[9] Nevertheless since World War I, academic freedom has periodically been vulnerable to war's conformist regimen of ideological obedience.

The threat to academic freedom is multidimensional. Overt government repression, "departmental colleagues, university administrators, students, trustees, media pundits, organized campaigns by groups unrelated to the university and local politicians" attempt to police and regulate academic speech, teaching, and research.[10] After September 11, 2001, a pronounced campaign against academic freedom emerged. The attacks on the Pentagon and World Trade Center, followed by the "Global War on Terror," now called "Overseas Contingency Operations" by the Barack Obama administration, exacerbated the culture wars and unleashed organized campaigns against critical thinking. At risk were academicians who denounced the Iraq war, questioned the innocence of America prior to the 9/11 attacks, and rejected U.S. support of Israel's continued brutal occupation of Palestine and Syria's Golan Heights.

Following the American Airlines Flight 77 attack on the Pentagon, Richard Berthold, professor of classical history at the University of New Mexico, told his class on September 11, 2001, "Anybody who blows up the Pentagon gets my vote." Although this was an opinion confined to the classroom and later retracted, Berthold was reprimanded and prohibited from teaching future sections of Western Civilization.[11] He was ultimately cashiered into early retirement.[12]

Nicholas De Genova, an assistant professor of Anthropology and Latino Studies at Columbia University, denounced American imperialism at an Iraq war teach-in on March 27, 2003, and advocated America's military defeat: "I personally would like to see a million Mogadishus (in Iraq).... The only true heroes are those who find ways that help defeat the U.S. military." One hundred and four Republican members of the House of Representatives demanded that Columbia University President Lee C. Bollinger fire the professor. Alumni threatened to terminate financial support, and death threats against De Genova necessitated police protection on campus.[13] Bollinger appropriately refused to suspend or fire the non-tenured professor but denounced De Genova's antiwar remarks. On Columbia's website, the university president castigated the professor's teach-in comments as "outrageous," "appall[ing]," and "especially disturbing."[14] Pandering to American militarism, Bollinger apologized to military personnel and their families.

In a subsequent appearance before the National Press Club, Bollinger again excoriated the professor's teach-in comments as "shocking," "horrific," and "especially sickening."[15] University presidents should refrain from condemning extramural utterances by the professoriate. Such reprobation threatens critical thinking on a campus and should be limited to claiming that an academician's statement represents only the opinion of the individual and not the university. Professors rarely claim to speak for a university, however, and should not be coerced into making redundant, self-effacing disclaimers.

Norman G. Finkelstein was an assistant professor of political science at DePaul University. He is a transformative, daring scholar who published *The Holocaust Industry* and *Beyond Chutzpah: On the Misuse of Anti-Semitism and the Abuse of History*.[16] Finkelstein claimed that elements of the Jewish community exploit the sufferings of the Holocaust to advance Israel's geostrategic interests and gratuitously exaggerate the prevalence of anti-Semitism in order to deflect criticism from the 42-year occupation of Palestinian land with its expanding settlement population. The son of Holocaust survivors, Finkelstein's parents survived the Warsaw Ghetto and Nazi death camps during World War II.[17]

In *Beyond Chutzpah*, Finklestein relentlessly assails Alan M. Dershowitz's *The Case for Israel*.[18] He claims the work is inaccurate, that Dershowitz disingenuously cites primary sources that were not consulted but instead lifted from other authors' footnotes, and that the entire work is essentially derivative from the discredited scholarship of Joan Peters. *The Case for Israel* is dismissed as mere propaganda to justify Israel's colonization of Palestine.[19] Dershowitz, Frankfurter Professor of Law at the Harvard Law School, attempted to prevent the University of California Press from publishing *Beyond Chutzpah* with a direct appeal to Governor Arnold Schwarzenegger and threatened defamation litigation if charges of plagiarism and nonauthorship of *The Case for Israel* were not redacted from the published text.[20] The governor's office responded by informing Dershowitz that, "[y]ou have asked for the Governor's assistance in preventing the publication of this book...[but] he is not inclined to otherwise exert influence in this case because of the clear, academic freedom issue it presents."[21]

For almost two years Dershowitz tried to derail Finkelstein's application for tenure and promotion through a sustained media blitz. Dershowitz used the *Wall Street Journal*, *FrontPageMag.com*, *The Jerusalem Post*, *InsiderHigherEd.com*, *The New Republic* online, his website, and numerous media outlets to derail the DePaul professor. Dershowitz referred to Finkelstein as an "anti-Semite," his publications as "trash," and called him a "neo-Nazi supporter, a Holocaust trivializer, and a liar...and...like a little worm."[22] Political Science Professor Patrick Callahan requested that Dershowitz share with the Political Science Department Personnel Committee more than 50 pages of allegations concerning Finkelstein's academic misconduct. Callahan opposed granting tenure to Finkelstein and warned the Personnel Committee that if they did not consider the Dershowitz dossier, he would distribute it to the entire department.[23] Dershowitz eagerly complied and sent these *j'accuse* materials to the

Department of Political Science and even the DePaul University College of Law faculty.

The twelve-member Liberal Arts and Sciences' Faculty Governance Council decided on November 17, 2007, to send a letter to the president of Harvard University, the Harvard Law School dean, and DePaul University President Reverend Dennis H. Holtschneider. The Faculty Governance Council wanted their support in ending Dershowitz's intrusion into the proceedings of the university's personnel review process.[24]

The Political Science Department's Personnel Committee unanimously rejected by 4–0 all charges of academic misconduct and dishonesty claimed by Alan Dershowitz, Daniel Jonah Goldhagen, and Peter Novick. The Department of Political Science recommended by a 9–3 majority the granting of tenure and promotion to associate professor. The five-person College of Liberal Arts and Sciences' Personnel Committee voted unanimously for Finkelstein's tenure and promotion.[25] The dean of the college, Chuck Suchar, rejected the departmental and college-level recommendations for promotion and tenure in a memorandum on March 22, 2007, which was first published in its entirety on my web log on April 5, 2007.[26]

Suchar's main argument in opposing Finkelstein receiving tenure was the tone and supposed lack of civility in his writings and interactions with colleagues. The dean's outrageous claim that the professor lacked collegiality toward departmental colleagues was based upon a rumor from the "General Consul's [sic] office," that Finkelstein "was considering filing a law suit" against those opposing his tenure.[27] He avers that "the tone and substance... [are] inconsistent with DePaul's Vincentian values." Suchar provided a single example from a huge body of published work to claim grave rhetorical misconduct: "My reading of Dr. Finkelstein's work, especially *The Holocaust Industry*, where in one chapter alone Goldhagen, [Benny] Morris, [Elie] Wiesel, [Jerzy] Kosinski and many others are collectively attacked as 'hoaxters and *huxters*,' typifies his apparent penchant of reducing an argument and oppositional views to the inevitable personal and reputation damaging attack, demeaning those with whom he disagrees" (emphasis added).[28] Dershowitz's compilation of alleged Finkelstein transgressions also contained this accusation: "Among the dozen or so Jewish writers whose careers Finkelstein has tried to destroy with the same accusations— 'fraud,' '*huxter*,' 'shake-down artist,' 'plagiarist'—he has only ever written a full book about one other: Daniel Goldhagen" (emphasis added).[29]

Suchar also misspelled "huckster" as "huxter." It is arguable the DePaul University dean used Dershowitz's misspelling of "huckster" and other egregious charges in compiling his anti-tenure memorandum.

The Finkelstein case became a cause célèbre that galvanized groups across the political spectrum. *The Guardian*, *Haaretz*, and *The Jerusalem*

Post provided spacious coverage of the academic freedom controversy.[30] The Middle East Studies Association, the Illinois Conference of the American Association of University Professors (AAUP), and the DePaul Academic Freedom Committee wrote letters and conducted public fora in support of Finklestein.[31] Opponents included neoconservatives and ardent supporters of an Israel can-do-no-wrong policy.[32] On May 11, 2007, DePaul's University Board on Promotion and Tenure (UBPT) voted 4–3 against granting tenure to Norman Finklestein. On June 8, 2007, Holtschneider announced that Finkelstein had been denied tenure and on September 5, 2007, a settlement was reached between the parties.[33] Mehrene E. Larudee, assistant professor of International Studies and an intrepid supporter of Finkelstein, was the only other probationary faculty member in 2007 who was denied tenure in the College of Liberal Arts and Sciences. Unlike Finkelstein, Suchar recommended her for tenure and promotion, but Larudee was still denied tenure by Holtschneider upon receiving a non-recommendation by the UBPT.[34]

Sami Al-Arian, a Kuwaiti-born Palestinian, was fired from the University of South Florida by President Judy Lynn Genshaft on February 26, 2003, a mere six days after a fifty-count indictment was handed down by a federal grand jury. It contained charges of terrorism and using the university as a front for materially supporting Palestinian Islamic Jihad, an alleged terrorist organization according to the Department of State.[35]

At various stages, culminating in Al-Arian's dismissal, the University of South Florida used extremely questionable arguments and tactics to terminate the continuous tenure of a professor who had resided in the United States since 1975. Al-Arian's public utterances were described as "disruptive."[36] Genshaft also accused Al-Arian of having "repeatedly abused his position."[37]

On December 6, 2005, Al-Arian was found not guilty on eight of seventeen counts "including conspiracy to maim or murder." The jurors could not reach a verdict on nine other counts, but a majority was apparently in favor of acquittal on each count.[38] He languished in jail pending a decision by the Tampa office of the U.S. attorney whether to retry the case on the deadlocked counts. Al-Arian has argued that his suspension, firing, and indictment resulted from his support of Palestinian resistance and his fierce denunciation of the occupation policies of the State of Israel.[39]

University of South Florida Presidents Betty Castor and Genshaft abused their power in first suspending and then firing Al-Arian. While Genshaft was implementing a 12–1 vote in favor of dismissal by her board of trustees, she could have resigned in protest. While Genshaft was purportedly concerned about "disruptions," administrators should give priority in defending a professor's academic freedom and right of free speech at a public university. Al-Arian's indictment was used as a pretext to terminate his employment. This reckless abandonment of due process that buttresses academic freedom is symptomatic when aggressive nationalism silences legitimate dissent of American and, in this case, even another state actor's foreign policy.

In February 2006, Al-Arian pled guilty as part of a plea bargain to one count of the indictment in return for deportation after his sentence expired in April 2007. On June 26, 2008, the Justice Department, which could not win a conviction at trial, indicted Al-Arian for criminal contempt for not testifying before a federal grand jury.[40] The federal government continues to incarcerate Al-Arian as he approaches seven years as a prisoner of conscience.

Ideologically inspired interest groups that engaged the post–9/11 world in cold-war Manichaean terms of good (United States) versus evil ("Islamofascism") have attempted to cleanse ideologically progressive internationalists from the academy. In September 2002, Daniel Pipes, director of the Middle East Forum, launched his "Campus Watch" website to blacklist and marginalize progressive Middle Eastern scholars who were described as fifth columnists, supporters of "radical Islam," and apologists for terrorism. Middle East specialists who did not support Israel in its conflict with the stateless Palestinians were smeared with charges of ideologically distorted scholarship and displaying bias toward pro-Israel students. Pipes's censorious campaign triggered a robust challenge when hundreds of nonspecialists demanded that their names be included alongside the Campus Watch blacklist. Pipes then published a companion list with a McCarthyism-invoking title, "Solidarity with the Apologists."[41]

In 2004, the David Project Center for Jewish Leadership produced an incendiary film, "Columbia Unbecoming," that attacked Columbia University's Middle East Asian Languages and Cultures Department as anti-Semitic and discriminatory against ideologically oppositional students. Although Columbia's Barnard College anthropology Professor Nadia Abu El-Haj was granted tenure in the fall of 2007, her seminal monograph, *Facts on the Ground: Archaeological Practice and Territorial Self-Fashioning in Israeli Society*, generated websites, blogs, and online petitions that demanded her dismissal.[42] Her book instigated a propaganda campaign between Israel Firsters, who charged the book was fatally flawed and even anti-Semitic, and revisionists—who supported her critique of Israeli archeologists who politicized and extrapolated a dubious biblical claim to the territory of the current State of Israel.[43]

Like the Phoenix, a New McCarthyism has arisen as highly partisan ideological-pressure groups bully and intimidate academicians. Examples of this quest for intellectual rigidity include NoIndoctrination. org, the American Council of Trustees and Alumni, founded by Lynne Cheney, David Horowitz's Freedom Center, Horowitz's Students for

Academic Freedom, media pundit Laura Ingraham and Roger Kimball, editor and publisher of *The New Criterion*. Horowitz's online magazine, *FrontPageMag.com*, engages in a relentless stream of vituperative attacks against activist academics.[44] His most daring book, *The Professors: The 101 Most Dangerous Academics in America*, attempts to identify the most radical and "un-American" scholars and is quite similar to the 1950 McCarthy-era Red Channels blacklist.[45] His most recent work, *One Party Classroom*, continues his allegation that professors have transformed traditional pedagogy into crusading Marxist and victim-emphasizing propaganda. Horowitz berates and mocks socially conscious instructors who offer courses in Peace Studies, Women Studies, and race and ethnic discrimination.[46]

Ward Churchill, a tenured professor of ethnic studies at the University of Colorado, wrote an essay that deplored American foreign relations and claimed that the September 11, 2001 attacks were not a bolt out of the blue but part of an asymmetrical response to American imperialism and capitalism. Churchill described the 2,751 casualties from the attack on the World Trade Center towers in Lower Manhattan as "little Eichmanns" and "as a cadre of faceless bureaucrats and technical experts…making America's genocidal world order hum with maximal efficiency."[47] Years later in February 2005, the statement was resurrected to muzzle Churchill and prevent his appearance on a dissent and critical-thinking panel at Hamilton College in New York State. The event was canceled as a progressive administration, committed to academic freedom, was frightened and startled with public threats of violence and financial pressure from alumni and other donors.

Bill Owens, Republican governor of Colorado, called for Churchill's firing on February 2, 2005. The University of Colorado investigated Churchill's 9/11 statement and initially refused to impose sanctions when it concluded the obvious: the 9/11 essay was protected speech under the First Amendment. However, in an insidious manner, Churchill was then conveniently charged with academic misconduct ranging from plagiarism, ghostwriting, and deceptive misuse of sources. Churchill alleged the U.S. army and others disseminated small pox by distributing infected blankets to Native Americans in 1837. The Standing Committee on Research Misconduct, despite the absence of Native American scholars, recommended the termination of his continuous tenure. Interim-Chancellor Phil DiStefano urged Churchill's dismissal on June 26, 2006.[48] Another university panel, the Privilege and Tenure Committee, recommended after a due process appeal, a one-year suspension and reduction in rank from professor to assistant professor.[49] Churchill was relieved of his teaching duties and placed on paid leave during the 2006–2007 academic year.

Instructors are being capriciously and arbitrarily suspended or reassigned to other duties for an assortment of reasons. AAUP policies on such sanctions are precise. The suspension of a professor must be restricted to cases in which "immediate harm to the faculty member or others is threatened." The ninth "1970 Interpretive Comment" of the "1940 Statement of Principles on Academic Freedom and Tenure," the "1958 Statement on Procedural Standards in Faculty Dismissal Proceedings," and the revised 1999 "Recommended Institutional Regulations on Academic Freedom and Tenure" clearly articulate this policy.

Hank Brown, then president of the University of Colorado and a supporter of the American Council of Trustees and Alumni, recommended Ward Churchill's termination in a letter to the Board of Regents. Democratic Colorado Governor August William "Bill" Ritter, Jr., also joined the chorus for dismissal.[50] The Board of Regents, by a vote of 8–1, fired the tenured Churchill with a laconic public statement on July 25, 2007.[51] Churchill won a wrongful-termination law suit against the university on April 2, 2009, when the six-person jury decided he was fired for the "little Eichmann" remarks, which was protected speech, and not for alleged scholarly misconduct. Despite Churchill's winning a $1 damage award from a Denver jury, Denver District Court Judge Larry Naves on July 7, 2009, denied the professor reinstatement to his tenured position and any "front pay" damages.[52]

Even though the University of Colorado is a public university, governors should exercise appropriate restraint in personnel matters involving rank and tenure. In the landmark Supreme Court case *Sweezy v. New Hampshire*, Justice Felix Frankfurter admonished governments to avoid eviscerating the intellectual vitality of a university: "For society's good—if understanding be an essential need of a society...political power must abstain from intrusion into this activity of freedom, pursued in the interest of wise government and the people's well-being, except for reasons that are exigent and obviously compelling."[53]

Chief Justice Earl Warren also wrote in *Sweezy* that government "should be extremely reticent to tread" and conduct an "invasion...of liberties in the areas of academic freedom and political expression."[54]

I was suspended and reprimanded for an antiwar email response to Robert Kurpiel, an Air Force Academy cadet, who had requested assistance from dozens of professors to publicize and recruit students for an on-campus conference. My suspension reflected, in post–9/11 America, an aroused, nationalistic fervor that construed my statement as unpatriotic, un-American, and insulting to the military. I condemned war, with its inevitable toll of civilian casualties, by referring to the "aggressive baby killing tactics of collateral damage." I described "top guns [who] rain death and destruction upon nonwhite peoples throughout the world." I objurgated both "cowards who bomb countries without A.A.A., without possibility of retaliation" and "imperialists who are turning the whole damn world against us." Although using different rhetoric than comparing civilian casualties to Nazi leaders, my email response complemented Ward Churchill's accusation of a lack of American innocence prior to the 9/11 attacks: "September 11 can be blamed in part for what you and your cohorts have done to the Palestinians, the V.C., the Serbs, a retreating army at Basra."[55] I initially apologized two days later and frequently thereafter for some unwarranted personal references to Kurpiel.

External pressure on Saint Xavier University to sanction me was astonishing as tens of thousands of emails, letters, phone calls, blogs, and websites demanded retribution. Kurpiel and the enraged cadet wing disseminated my email to friends and family, which unleashed a frenzied international response to the incident. Both the cadet and Air Force Captain Jim Borders, who organized the forthcoming campus symposium, apologized for causing the escalating distribution of my email and attempted unsuccessfully to contain the growing controversy. Tolerating controversial and provocative speech, the Air Force Academy, unlike former Saint Xavier University President Richard A. Yanikoski, did not seek punishment.

Former Deputy Undersecretary of Defense Jed Babbin described me in *The Weekly Standard* as "a hate-the-military type" and as "barely literate." He questioned whether I was "fit to teach at any college" and implied my tenure should be terminated.[56] The military press varied from neutral reportage to advocacy journalism.[57] Kimball wrote a piece for *The American Legion Magazine* with a McCarthyite title, "Academia v. America." He claimed universities are "havens for displaced radicals" and named professors including myself that he construed as disloyal and anti-American. After my suspension, he complained that I would "soon be back molding young minds."[58]

My academic freedom was vigorously defended by disparate groups including elite conservative organizations such as the Foundation for Individual Rights in Education (FIRE) and the National Association of Scholars.[59] Even Yanikoski informed me the incident was over during an office appointment on Monday, November 4, 2002, following a weekend of mutual, contrite email exchanges with the cadet. I was praised for my academic service and as I was departing told to inform him of any further attempts to damage my career! Seven days later Yanikoski suspended me on Veterans Day, November 11, 2002.[60]

In post–9/11 America, the suppression of academic freedom has extended offshore to prevent the entry of "undesirable" foreign scholars.[61] Section 411 of the Uniting and Strengthening America by Providing Appropriate Tools Required to Intercept and Obstruct Terrorism Act of 2001 (Patriot Act) empowers the government to exclude those who "endorse or espouse terrorist activity or persuade others to endorse or espouse terrorist activity or support a terrorist organization."[62] The American Civil Liberties Union and AAUP have litigated against the Patriot Act, which they claim is an antidemocratic weapon to "exclude and stigmatize prominent critics of U.S. foreign policy—individuals who may have never supported terrorism and in at least some cases have vocally opposed it."[63] The Department of Homeland Security and the Department of State determine when speech by foreign scholars is permissible on a college campus or at an academic conference. In *Sweezy*, Frankfurter warned against unjustifiable state censorship of the academy: "In the political realm, as in the academic, thought and action are presumptively immune from inquisition by political authority."[64]

Yet an alarming number of progressive academicians are subjected to a xenophobic ideological litmus test not seen since the deportation statutes emanating during the Great War and the cold war with the Alien Immigration Act (1917), Alien Registration Act (Smith Act) (1940), the Cold War Internal Security Act of 1950, and the 1952 Immigration and Nationality Act (McCarran-Walter Act).[65]

Tariq Ramadan, a Muslim scholar born in Egypt, was offered in 2004 a tenured position in Islamic Studies as Luce Professor of Religion, Conflict, and Peace-Building at the University of Notre Dame. Ramadan had enrolled his children in school, rented a house in South Bend, Indiana, and even shipped his furniture before he was notified that his visa had been revoked because he endorsed "terrorism" and was subject to the "ideological exclusion" provision of the Patriot Act.[66] The government later recanted those arbitrary charges when faced with a lawsuit, but concocted a different allegation that his donations, totaling $940 to charitable organizations, actually supported Hamas in Israeli-occupied Palestine. Hamas is designated as a "terrorist" organization by the Department of State despite its victory in the January 2006 Palestinian Authority general legislative elections. Ramadan asserted he was the victim of political persecution when denied his prestigious appointment at Notre Dame: "I am increasingly convinced that the [George W.] Bush administration has barred me for a much simpler reason: It doesn't care for my political views. In recent years, I have publicly criticized U.S. policy in the Middle East, the war in Iraq, the use of torture, secret C.I.A. prisons and other government actions that undermine fundamental civil liberties."[67]

Waskar T. Ari received his Ph.D. from Georgetown University and was offered a position in the Department of History at the University of Nebraska at Lincoln. Ari is from Bolivia and ethnically a member of the Aymara indigenous community. During a brief visit to Bolivia following the successful doctoral defense of his dissertation, Ari learned in June 2005, as he was preparing to return to the United States, that his visa was no longer valid.[68] The apparent reason for his exclusion was growing political tension between the United States and Bolivia.[69] Evo Morales, the charismatic, indigenous president of Bolivia, is Aymaran and seeks greater control over the nation's raw-material resources through the nationalization of natural gas and other energy assets. Morales's relationship with the United States is spirited and he is closely allied with Hugo Chávez, the president of Venezuela. The Department of Homeland Security, upon the petition of the University of Nebraska at Lincoln, finally granted him a visa two years later that enabled Ari to accept his appointment as assistant professor of history and ethnic studies.[70]

Karim Meziane, a physicist at the University of New Brunswick in Canada, is another scholar denied entry despite any evidence of being a security threat. He was barred from attending a conference on "Multi-Spacecraft Observations on Field Aligned Beams" in 2004 at the invitation of the University of New Hampshire. An Algerian native who lived in the United States for many years, he was questioned for six hours at the Canadian border about his religion, the American invasion of Iraq, and the Israeli-Palestinian conflict. The Department of Homeland Security, which frequently fails to proffer a reason for exclusion, in this instance bizarrely asserted that Meziane had a criminal background. Even though Canadian authorities stated there was no record of criminality, there has been no reversal of the government's exclusionary action.[71]

Fifty-five Cuban scholars were prohibited from attending the Latin American Studies Association annual meeting in Puerto Rico when they were denied visas in March 2006.[72] A Greek Marxist economist John (Yoannis) Milios was intercepted from entering the United States on June 8, 2006 by the Department of State and the Department of Homeland Security. Milios is from the National Technical University in Athens and was invited to attend a "How Class Works" conference at the State University of New York at Stony Brook.[73] Milios stated that the interrogation focused "on my political beliefs and affiliations, which I finds [sic] totally repellent, an extravagant theatre of the absurd, and a clear clue of the extremist right-wing policy of the present-day U.S. administration."[74] In the spring of 2008, Milios was finally granted a visa and spoke at the June AAUP annual meeting in Washington, DC.[75]

The Customs and Border Protection on October 25, 2006 also denied entry to Adam Habib of South Africa when he arrived at New York's John F. Kennedy Airport to attend several meetings. A political scientist and a Muslim, he earned his Ph.D. from the City University of New York and was deputy vice-chancellor of research, innovation, and advancement at the University of Johannesburg in South Africa. He was also prohibited from attending the 2007 American Sociological Association annual meeting in New York.[76] It is indisputable that scholars from various nations, who are neither dissidents nor opponents of their regimes, are being denied entry for ideological reasons or bilateral diplomatic disputes wholly unrelated to a foreign scholar's legitimate credentials.

Academic freedom not only is essential for teachers and researchers but also for the educational mission of tens of millions of students at American colleges and universities. David Horowitz's Students for Academic Freedom is construed by many as a misnomer due to its frequent attempts to stifle progressive pedagogy in the classroom through a series of ad hominem, unsubstantiated charges of professor discrimination against noncompliant conservative students. To its credit, the organization has thrust the frequently ignored topic of student academic freedom into the national conversation on student rights.[77] FIRE has more persuasively supported student rights to organize conservative and faith-based clubs and in a bipartisan manner has aggressively challenged campus speech codes. Although AAUP does not adequately address the academic freedom of students, along with several other organizations, it did release the "Joint Statement on Rights and Freedoms of Students."[78]

The "Joint Statement" affirms the rights of students to be evaluated only on academic performance, to challenge the views and ideas of their instructors through "reasoned exception," and to publish student newspapers "free of censorship and advance approval of copy."[79] While right-wing charges of progressive professor discrimination against dissenting students are usually anecdotal exercises in disinformation, the suppression of student newspapers, by university and college administrations, is a growing and gathering threat to academic freedom.

The University of South Carolina's alternative newspaper, *The Trojan Horse*, was stolen and vandalized for weighing in on the Israel-Palestinian struggle. Editors of the *College Voice*, College of Staten Island, were threatened and their office was damaged due to antiwar advocacy. A student reporter for Amherst's *The Daily Collegian* was denounced by the university president and left for Puerto Rico while under death threats. He had written a derogatory story about Army Ranger Pat Tillman, former National Football League player who was killed in April 2004 by "friendly fire" in Afghanistan.[80] Student newspaper editors have been rebuked and censored by administrators who demand student editors serve as public-relations surrogates for the University of Scranton, Baylor University, Long Island University, Brigham Young University, Governors State University, and Lewis University.[81]

Laurence Tribe, Carl M. Loeb University Professor at the Harvard Law School, wrote, "Free speech is an empty freedom if not possessed by a free mind."[82] Academic freedom, which is the sine qua non for an independent and dynamic system of higher education, cannot endure if there is a closing of the American mind. All too frequently, a call to arms abroad against the latest threat to American hegemony has a domestic battleground as well. From World War I to the nationalistic excesses following the September 11 attacks, public and private entities have tried to purge free speech from the academy without which the pursuit of truth would be futile. American and foreign progressive scholars seeking admission into the United States and their students are at risk as the national-security elites and their acolytes pursue their imperial agendas with little regard for their toxic impact on higher education in the United States.

Notes

1. Howard Zinn, *A People's History of the United States* (New York: HarperCollins, 2001), 297.
2. Robert Post, "The Structure of Academic Freedom," in *Academic Freedom after September 11*, ed. Beshara Doumani (Brooklyn: Zone Books, 2006), 61. Somewhat ironically Butler shared the Nobel Peace Prize with Jane Addams in 1931.
3. Bertell Ollman, "The Ideal of Academic Freedom as the Ideology of Academic Repression, American Style," 1, "Freedoms at Risk Conference," New York University, February 23, 2008.
4. Ellen Schrecker, *The Age of McCarthyism: A Brief History with Documents*, 2nd ed. (New York: Bedford Books, 2002), 37–38.
5. "1940 Statement of Principles of Academic Freedom and Tenure," *A.A.U.P. Policy Documents and Reports, "Redbook,"* 10th ed. (Baltimore: Johns Hopkins University Press, 2006), 3.
6. Ibid., 4.
7. "Committee A Statement on Extramural Utterances," *A.A.U.P. Policy Documents and Reports, "Redbook,"* 9th ed. (Baltimore: Johns Hopkins University Press, 2001), 32.
8. *Keyishian v. Board of Regents*, 385 U.S. 589 (1967); Thomas L. Tedford and Dale A. Herbeck, eds., *Freedom of Speech in the United States*, 6th ed. (State College, PA: Strata Publishing, 2009), 312–313.
9. *Regents of the University of California v. Bakke*, 438 U.S. 265 (1978).
10. Project of the Taskforce on Middle East Anthropology, "Academic Freedom and Professional Responsibility after 9/11: A Handbook for Scholars and Teachers," 2006, 4–5.
11. "Professor Reprimanded for Joke," *Houston Chronicle*, December 10, 2001. Online edition.
12. Richard M. Berthold, "My Five Minutes of Infamy," History News Network, November 25, 2002, http://hnn.us/articles/1121.html.
13. Peter N. Kirstein, "Academic Freedom and the New McCarthyism," *Situation Analysis* 3 (Spring 2004): 24–25.
14. Remarks appeared on April 3, 2003, http://www.columbia.edu/cu/news/03/04/statement_genova.html; Peter N. Kirstein, "Campus to Courts: The Silencing

of the Left in Wartime," 13–14, Historians against the War Conference, University of Texas, February 18, 2006.

15. Ibid.; http://www.npr.org/programs/npc/2003/030402.lbollinger.html; http://www.columbia.edu/cu/news/03/04/press_club.html.

16. Norman G. Finkelstein, *The Holocaust Industry: Reflections on the Exploitation of Human Suffering*, 2nd ed. (New York: Verso Press, 2003); Norman G. Finkelstein, *Beyond Chutzpah: On the Misuse of Anti-Semitism and the Abuse of History* (Berkeley: University of California Press, 2005).

17. Patricia Cohen, "Outspoken Political Scientist Denied Tenure at DePaul," *New York Times*, June 11, 2007.

18. Alan Dershowitz, *The Case for Israel* (Hoboken, NJ: John Wiley & Sons, 2003).

19. Joan Peters, *From Time Immemorial* (New York: Harper and Row, 1984). Peters claimed erroneously an absence of a Palestinian presence in the areas from which Israel was created in 1948.

20. Alan Dershowitz, "Tsuris over Chutzpah," *The Nation*, August 29/September 5, 2005, 2.

21. Jon Weiner, "Weiner Replies," *The Nation*, August 29/September 5, 2005, 2, 30.

22. Jeffrey Felshman, "Whose Holocaust Is It Anyway?: Why Alan Dershowitz Wants DePaul Professor Norman Finkelstein Fired," *Chicago Reader*, August 26, 2005.

23. DePaul Political Science Department, "Personnel Committee," November 1, 2006, http://english.sxu.edu/sites/kirstein/?p=696.

24. Michal Lando, "Dershowitz, Finkelstein and a Bitter Tenure Battle," *Jerusalem Post*, April 19, 2007, http://www.jpost.com/servlet/Satellite?apage=2&cid=1176152838045&pagename=JPost%2FJPArticle%2FShowFull; Christopher Brown, "Academic Repression Update/A Question of Scholarship," *The Advocate* (CUNY Graduate Center), May 4, 2007.

25. Callahan, a former department chair, Michael L. Mezey, the previous dean of the College of Liberal Arts and Sciences, and Jim Block submitted a minority report opposing tenure for Finkelstein.

26. Peter N. Kirstein blog: http://english.sxu.edu/sites/kirstein/?p=680.

27. Ibid. The right to litigate and sue is an American right that should not be cited as a lack of collegiality to deny an academician tenure and promotion to associate professor.

28. Ibid., http://english.sxu.edu/sites/kirstein/?p=680; DePaul University is a Roman Catholic institution founded under the charism of the Vincentians, a priestly religious order. In *The Holocaust Industry*, the second chapter, pp. 39–78, is titled with correctly spelled words: "Hoaxers, Hucksters, and History." This is in reference to Zionists who used the Holocaust to exaggerate Israel's vulnerability and to extract excessive reparations from successor governments or financial institutions allegedly complicit with Germany during World War II.

29. Ibid., http://english.sxu.edu/sites/kirstein/?p=691.

30. http://www.guardian.co.uk/world/2007/jun/12/usa.highereducation; http://www.jpost.com/servlet/Satellite?pagename=JPost%2FJPArticle%2FShowFull&cid=1176152838045; http://www.haaretz.com/hasen/spages/901583.html.

31. Zachary Lochman to The Rev. Dennis H. Holtschneider, C.M., Ed.D., April 10, 2007; Leo Welch to The Rev. Dennis H. Holtschneider, C.M., Ed.D., June 22, 2007.

32. For opposition to the granting of tenure see Steven Plaut, "The Finkelstein Affair," *FrontPageMag.com*, April 23, 2007, http://frontpagemag.com/Articles/Read.aspx?GUID=9B47A2C9-CA6B-43DE-9D09-970B2EE29405. The phrase "Israel-can-do-no-wrong policy" from Roger Cohen, "The Fierce Urgency of Peace," *New York Times*, March 26, 2009.

33. http://sherman.depaul.edu/media/webapp/mrNews2.asp?NID=1655.

34. Sierra Millman, "DePaul Professor Who Supported Finkelstein Also Was Denied Tenure," *The Chronicle of Higher Education*, June 12, 2007.

35. Scott Smallwood, "U. of South Florida Fires Professor Accused of Terrorism," *The Chronicle of Higher Education*, March 7, 2003.

36. Foundation for Individual Rights in Education, http://www.thefire.org/index.php/article/49.html.

37. *Tampa Tribune* Online, *TBO*, http://news.tbo.com/news/MGAV3LY9OCD.html.

38. Peter Whoriskey, "Ex-Professor Won His Court Case but Not His Freedom," *Washington Post*, December 14, 2005, A02.

39. British Broadcasting Corporation, December 6, 2005, http://news.bbc.co.uk/1/hi/world/americas/4505248.stm.

40. Josh Gerstein, "Al-Arian Indicted for Refusal to Testify in Charities Cases," *New York Sun*, June 27, 2008.

41. Colin Wright, "Editorial Introduction"; "Campus Watch: Surveying a Non-Apologetic Solidarity," *Situation Analysis* 3 (Spring 2004): 1–20. Both lists were eventually removed from Pipes's Campus Watch website.

42. Jane Kramer, "The Petition: Israel, Palestine, and a Tenure Battle at Barnard," *New Yorker*, April 14, 2008, 50–59.

43. "Israel Firster" term encountered on Tikun Olam blog, http://www.richard-silverstein.com/tikun_olam/.

44. Steven Plaut, "The Eviction of Norman Finkelstein," FrontPageMag, May 29, 2008. Finkelstein's denial of tenure is endorsed, and he is slandered as a "crackpot" for supporting "Holocaust denial." http://frontpagemag.com/Articles/Read.aspx?GUID=94D46D9E-C1E5-4CE9-99BF-7C1EF803CADA.

45. David Horowitz, *The Professors: The 101 Most Dangerous Academics in America* (Washington, DC: Regnery Publishing, 2006). Quotation is from inside cover. I was included among the 101 professors. See also David Horowitz, *Indoctrination U* (New York: Encounter Books, 2007).

46. David Horowitz, *One-Party Classroom: How Radical Professors at America's Top Colleges Indoctrinate Students and Undermine Our Democracy* (New York: Crown Forum, 2009).

47. Ward Churchill, *On the Justice of Roosting Chickens: Reflections on the Consequences of U.S. Imperial Arrogance and Criminality* (Oakland, CA: AK Press, 2003), 19; Anthony DePalma, "For the First Time, New York Links a Death to 9/11 Dust," *New York Times*, May 24, 2007.

48. Hank Brown to Patricia "Pat" Hayes, May 25, 2007.

49. Jennifer Brown, "CU Plans to Fire Churchill," *Denver Post*, August 14, 2006; "Ward Churchill Defends His Academic Record & Vows to Fight to Keep His Job at University of Colorado," *Democracy Now with Amy Goodman!* September 27, 2006, http://www.democracynow.org/article.pl?sid=06/09/27/146255.

50. Press Release: "National Project in Defense of Dissent and Critical Thinking in Academia," June 13, 2007. www.defendcriticalthinking.org.

51. The dissenting vote was cast by Cindy Carlisle who represented the second congressional district. She argued that regents should not impose sanctions beyond those recommended by the Privilege and Tenure committee.

52. DeeDee Correll, "Colorado Professor Wins Wrongful Termination Suit," *Los Angeles Times*, April 3, 2009; DeeDee Correll, "Judge Upholds Ouster of Professor in 'little Eichmann' Scandal," *Los Angeles Times*, July 8, 2009.

53. *Sweezy v. New Hampshire*, 354 U.S. 234 (1957).

54. Ibid.

55. Peter N. Kirstein to Robert Kurpiel, October 31, 2002.

56. Jed Babbin, "When Professors Attack They Make Fools of Themselves," *The Weekly Standard*, December 2, 2002; Peter N. Kirstein, "Kirstein Strikes Back," *The Weekly Standard*, January 20, 2003, 5.

57. "The Professor and the Cadet," *Navy Times*, November 25, 2002; "Pacifist Professor Feels Blowback from Comments," *AIR FORCE Magazine*, December 20, 2002, 20.

58. Roger Kimball, "Academia vs. America," *The American Legion Magazine*, April 2003, 34–38; Peter N. Kirstein, "New McCarthyism," *The American Legion Magazine*, June 2003, 4–6.

59. Alan Charles Kors to Richard Yanikoski, November 20, 2002, http://www.thefire.org/index.php/article/5129.html; Stephen Balch, "Don't Sink Any Deeper into Free-Speech Morass," *The Wall Street Journal*, November 25, 2002. FIRE's intervention may have deterred dismissal when they informed the administration by letter and publicly on Milt Rosenberg's WGN radio program in Chicago, "Extension 720," that legal options would be explored if additional sanctions were imposed.

60. *The Wall Street Journal*, November 12, November 19, 2002; "The Historian Who Denounced the Military for 'Baby-Killing' Tactics," History News Network, November 8, 2002, http://hnn.us/articles/1095.html; Kirstein, "Academic Freedom," 29.

61. Wendi Maloney, "University Sues Government over Scholar's Exclusion," *Academe*, May–June 2007, 11. The United States is unfortunately one of many nations that constrains the transnational exchange of ideas among scholars. Norman Finkelstein was arrested by Shin Bet security personnel in Israel on May 23, 2008 and deported the following day with a ten-year entrance ban. He was traveling to the occupied territories when apprehended at Ben Gurion Airport. Iran detained Iranian-Americans Haleh Esfandiari and Dariush Zahedi for several months.

62. *A.A.U.P., Ramadan, et al. v. Secretaries of State and Homeland Security*; *A.C.L.U., A.A.U.P. et al. v. Departments of State, Homeland Security, and*

Justice, and Central Intelligence Agency, A.A.U.P. Report of the Office of Staff Counsel, November 2006–June 2007, 1–3.

63. Ibid., 3.
64. *Sweezy v. New Hampshire*; John J. Simon, "*Sweezy v. New Hampshire*: The Radicalism of Principle," *Monthly Review,* April 2000, 35–37.
65. John Chalberg, *Emma Goldman* (New York: HarperCollins, 1991), 144; Paul Boyer, *Promises to Keep: The United States since World War II* (Lexington, MA: D.C. Heath, 1995), 88, 114.
66. "Scholars Excluded from the United States," *Academe,* September–October 2007, 15.
67. Tariq Ramadan, "Why I Am Banned in the U.S.A.," *Washington Post,* October 1, 2006.
68. Barbara Weinstein, "The A.H.A. and Academic Freedom in the Age of Homeland Security," *Perspectives,* January 2007, 3.
69. Jason DeParle, "Should We Globalize Labor Too?" *The New York Times Magazine,* June 10, 2007, 83.
70. Burton Bollag, "Bolivian Scholar Receives Visa," *The Chronicle of Higher Education,* August 3, 2007.
71. Scott Jaschik, "Kafka at the Border," *InsideHigherEd.com,* March 13, 2007, http://www.insidehighered.com/news/2007/03/13/canada.
72. "Scholars Kept Out: Foreign Academics Barred by the United States," *The Chronicle of Higher Education,* June 15, 2007, A41.
73. Jonathan Knight, AAUP Director of Program on Academic Freedom and Tenure, to Condoleezza Rice and Michael Chertoff, June 20, 2006.
74. John Milios to Outline on Political Economy Listserve, June 11, 2006, http://archives.econ.utah.edu/archives/marxism/2006w24/msg00002.htm; "Scholars in Peril," *Academe,* May–June 2008, 4.
75. Gwendolyn Bradley, "Excluded Scholar Granted Visa," *Academe,* July–August 2008, 7.
76. Craig Timberg, "Prominent S. African Denied Entry into U.S.," *Washington Post,* October 26, 2006.
77. http://www.studentsforacademicfreedom.org.
78. "Joint Statement on Rights and Freedoms of Students," *Redbook,* 10th ed. (Baltimore, MD: Johns Hopkins University Press, 2006), 273–279.
79. Ibid., 274, 276.
80. John K. Wilson, *Patriotic Correctness: Academic Freedom and Its Enemies* (Boulder, CO: Paradigm Press, 2008), 179–180.
81. Ibid., 183, 186–190; "Quick Takes," *InsideHigherEd.com,* February 26, 2008, http://www.insidehighered.com/news/2008/02/26/qt; Sophia Tareen, "Newspaper Editors Quit over Alleged Censorship at Catholic College," Associated Press, February 27, 2008.
82. Laurence H. Tribe and Michael C. Dorf, *On Reading the Constitution* (Cambridge, MA: Harvard University Press, 1991), 78.

5

Gun Control and the Right to Arms after 9/11

David B. Kopel, Paul Gallant, and Joanne D. Eisen*

How did September 11 affect the gun control debate in the United States? The gun control lobby attempted to use terrorism fears to promote some of their long-standing action items—such as restrictions on gun shows, and bans on .50 caliber firearms. The gun control efforts were generally unsuccessful. The pro-gun lobby gained some marginal benefit from an increase in the number of gun owners, and from greater support for "right to carry" legislation.

Pro-control and pro-gun legislators united on one issue: authorizing gun possession by airline pilots, after appropriate training. Despite overwhelming bipartisan support in both houses of Congress armed pilots legislation was opposed by airline executives, who feared tort liability problems. After the armed pilots law was enacted (and later expanded to include cargo pilots) the Bush administration used administrative prerogatives to strangle the armed pilots program, making certification and training as inconvenient as possible. Regarding the armed pilots issue, the Bush administration put corporate interests ahead of national security.

** **David B. Kopel** is one of the leading scholarly writers on gun control. He is Research Director of the Independence Institute and coauthor of the only college and graduate textbook on the subject, *Gun Control and Gun Rights*. He is also the author of dozens of published articles on the subject, in journals of law, criminology, sociology, medicine, and media.

Paul Gallant and **Joanne D. Eisen** are Senior Fellows at the Independence Institute and have written articles for numerous scholarly and popular periodicals. They each have contributed to the award-winning academic encyclopedia, *Guns in American Society: An Encyclopedia of History, Politics, Culture, and the Law*.

The Antigun Agenda

Before September 11

Not long before the September 11 attacks, Josh Sugarmann of the Violence Policy Center reiterated his organization's long-term goal of banning all handguns.[1] He acknowledged, however, that such a ban would be highly unlikely anytime soon. He also restated one of his long-standing complaints about the Brady Campaign, America's largest gun control group, and about much of the rest of the gun control movement: "Buffeted by the winds of opinion polls, the guiding principle became not what would work most effectively, but what would sell to the general public most easily."[2] As Sugarmann pointed out, because of public resistance to broad bans on guns, the gun control lobby has tended to concentrate on promoting bans of narrower classes of firearms. In the decade before September 11, the main targets of such bans were as follows:

- "Saturday-Night Specials" (a pejorative term for small handguns)
- .50 caliber firearms (a caliber for long-distance rifles).
- "Assault weapons" (an amorphous collection of rifles, shotguns, and handguns, generally defined by cosmetic features that give the gun a military appearance).[3]
- All new handguns other than "smart-guns"—that is, guns with internal computers that prevent the gun from being fired by anyone except the authorized user. The state of New Jersey has such a ban, which takes effect upon the market introduction of functional smart guns. (Such guns exist in laboratories, but have thus far proven too unreliable to market.)[4]

Gun control advocates had also pressed for a variety of non-prohibitory laws, all of which aimed for ever-greater layers of bureaucratic control on gun owners and gun sales. In the United Kingdom, decades of ever-increasing bureaucratization of gun ownership (higher and higher fees, more and more paperwork, months of time spent in application processes) gradually diminished the number of gun owners, as ever more people gave up sport shooting. As the number of gun owners dwindled, the imposition of even more severe bureaucratization became politically possible. Today, only about 5 percent of British homes contain a legal firearm.[5] American gun control advocates have often expressed admiration for the British system; as an example of Fabian tactics being used successfully to eliminate a culture of lawful firearms ownership, the British model is a good one.[6] Canadian gun laws, while less drastic than British ones, have often served as a model for Americans hoping to move incrementally to a British-style system. In the United States, some of the major pre–9/11 proposals to advance the United States in a British direction included the following:

- Gun-owner licensing, ideally under a system by which the licensing agency would have discretion to deny licenses based on the belief that the applicant does not "need" a gun.[7]
- National registration of all firearms—which as demonstrated by the United Kingdom and Canada—can be used to impose significant financial and time burdens on registrants, and can later be used as a database for confiscating newly illegalized guns.[8]
- Reducing the number of licensed firearms sellers (businesses with a Federal Firearms License). For example, there is not a single gun store in the city of Chicago.
- Adding more categories of persons to existing federal and state laws banning certain classes of persons (e.g., persons dishonorably discharged from the military, aliens without a green card) from possessing firearms.
- Bringing private sales of firearms (e.g., between friends in a hunting club) under the same paperwork and regulatory system as sales by persons who are in the business of selling firearms (that is, Federal Firearms Licensees (FFLs)).[9]

The high watermark of the gun control movement came in 1993–1994, when Congress passed the broadest federal gun ban ever (the "assault weapon" ban), enacted a slew of new bureaucratic controls, and the Clinton administration used its own executive powers to ban still more guns, and impose many more gun controls. But the 1994 mid-term elections led to a Republican landslide. In the Grand Old Party's (GOP) greatest congressional victory in half a century, not a single incumbent Democrat endorsed by the National Rifle Association (NRA) was defeated. In December 1994, President Clinton said that "[t]he NRA is the reason the Republicans control the House."[10] According to President Clinton, the NRA also cost Al Gore the 2000 election.[11] Indeed, Gore had narrowly lost his home state of Tennessee, Clinton's home state of Arkansas, traditionally Democrat West Virginia, Missouri, and Florida—all of them pro-gun states where the NRA and the National Shooting Sports Foundation (the lobby for gun manufacturers and gun stores) had conducted major advertising and grassroots campaigns.

Thus, the conventional political wisdom on September 10, 2001 was that, whatever the merits of gun control, it was dangerous politically—except in a few urban enclaves. The gun control lobby moved quickly to try to make September 11 the day that changed everything.[12]

After September 11

The gun control movement's public relations campaigns have always featured villains who are the most frightening type of character in the contemporary culture. In the late 1980s and early 1990s, during the height of the "war on drugs," the villain was an armed drug dealer. In the 1960s, he was a militant black or a white racist. After the Oklahoma City bombings, he was a member of the "militia movement" (even though the only connection that Timothy McVeigh and Terry Nichols had with the movement was attending two meetings of the Michigan Militia and being thrown out because of their talk about violence).[13] In the late 1990s, and especially after Columbine, the gun control movement's favorite villain was a school shooter.

Quickly after September 11, the gun control movement pivoted to bring the terrorist with a gun front and center. The terrorist imagery has remained prominent in gun control advocacy; a wide-ranging presentation of gun control terrorism imagery can be found in the book *One Nation under Guns: An Essay on an American Epidemic*, by Arnold Grossman, head of Colorado's affiliate of the Brady Campaign. He wrote: "What is always held in the hands of the terrorist? A gun. Why? Because it sends a message of power over the powerless, intended to instill fear, to force capitulation, to demean our nation and its people...."[14]

Grossman's particular policy prescriptions amounted to the same as the late 1990s agenda of the Brady Campaign, except that counterterrorism arguments were prominent. Some critics of the conduct of the War on Terror have claimed that supporters of constrictions on civil liberty have deliberately created a false climate of public fear in order to tighten restrictions on freedom. Certainly some of the fears raised by Grossman and other gun control advocates were unrealistic.

Consider, for example, Grossman's warning that .50 caliber machine guns could be bought at gun shows without a background check. According to Grossman, a terrorist could collect "a devastating armory of those weapons and wage a mini-war against police on duty, civilians at a sporting event, or workers coming out of an office building."[15]

Actually, it is impossible to buy any machine gun at a gun show. Pursuant to the National Firearms Act of 1934, the purchase of a machine gun requires a lengthy process involving a background check and letter of authorization from local law enforcement (known as Form 4), fingerprinting, registration of the owner and the gun with the Bureau of Alcohol, Tobacco, Firearms and Explosives (BATFE), and a $200 tax. Moreover, the only .50 caliber machine guns an ordinary citizen can buy are World War II antiques. They are rare, and would likely cost a collector over $20,000. The claim that they are on sale "at most gun shows" was ludicrous.

Although the "fifty caliber machine gun" does not exist, in a practical sense, on the civilian market, there are ordinary rifles and handguns in the .50 caliber size. Gun control advocates moved quickly to use September 11 to bolster their campaign to ban .50 caliber guns. A few weeks after the attacks, U.S. Rep. Rod Blagojevich (D-Ill.) labeled the guns "the terrorist weapon of choice." (The rhetoric tracked previous gun control claims that "assault weapons" were the "weapon of choice" of drug dealers or other villains.) Blagojevich declared: "In response to these terrorist tragedies we have to get them off the market."[16] California Senator Dianne Feinstein claimed that .50 caliber rifle owners were "terrorists, doomsday cultists, and criminals."[17] The campaign against .50 caliber guns was bolstered by an influential segment on the TV show *60 Minutes*.[18] In the late summer of 2004, the California legislature did narrowly enact a .50 caliber ban; given the slender margin, the terrorism issue might have made the difference. But none of the efforts to enact .50 caliber bans in other states, or federally, succeeded.

Gun shows had long been a target of the gun control lobbies. The phrase "gun show loophole" was successfully used to create the impression that gun shows existed in some sort of legal Brigadoon, exempt from ordinary laws about gun sales. Actually, the laws controlling sales at gun shows were exactly the same as for gun sales anywhere else; the gun control lobbies who complained about a "loophole" were really advocating special restrictions that would apply only at gun shows.[19]

Arguing for federal restrictions on gun shows, gun control lobbyists pointed the case of Ali Boumelhem, who had obtained firearms at gun shows. On September 10, 2001, he had been convicted in federal district court in Detroit of unlawfully possessing weapons and attempting to ship them to Hezbollah.[20] However, close examination of the facts of the case did not support the argument for special laws against gun shows.

Even before Boumelhem went shopping for Hezbollah, he was a convicted felon, so it was illegal for him to acquire or possess firearms or ammunition. Yet like most convicted felons, he knew someone who could make purchases legally. Boumelhem brought his brother to gun shows to make "straw purchases." More laws against gun shows would not stop straw purchases, since the straw purchaser (the surrogate for the real buyer) is chosen because he has a clean record; and if there were no gun shows he could buy the guns at a gun store. (Straw purchases have been illegal under federal law since 1986; the criminalization of straw purchase was part of an NRA-backed bill that reformed various practices of the Bureau of Alcohol, Tobacco and Firearms.)

Moreover, Boumelhem also managed to acquire grenades and rocket launchers—none of which can be bought at gun shows or gun stores—so he apparently had some source unrelated to gun shows from which he obtained very powerful weapons.

Before September 11, the FBI had kept a list of names on a "Violent Gang and Terrorist Organization File" (VGTOF). After September 11, the Transportation Security Administration compiled a "No-Fly" list of persons who would not be allowed to board airplanes in the United States. The No-Fly list was notorious for its overbreadth; Senator Ted Kennedy (D.-Mass.) was placed on the list.

From 2005 onward, proposals were made to add persons in the VGTOF, or the No-Fly list, to the group of "prohibited persons" who are forbidden by federal law to possess a gun. Critics argued that a person should not lose a civil right simply because she is placed on a list without due process. The FBI did not support the proposals. According to the *Rocky Mountain News*, "FBI spokesman Carl Schlaff said there's no cause to deny someone a gun just because he or she is on the watch list. Some people are on the list simply because the FBI wants to interview them about someone else who may have a connection to terrorism. 'You're innocent until proven guilty,' he said."[21] The proposals did not get even a committee vote in the Republican-controlled Congress of 2005–2006, nor in the Democratic-controlled Congress of 2007–2008.[22]

The terrorist with a gun attacking victims in America was not an imaginary figure. It is true that the September 11 hijackers did not use guns, and that the United States has not been attacked by foreign terrorist groups such as Hezbollah, Hamas, the Palestine Liberation Organization, or others that are known for carrying out attacks using firearms. However, there have been cases of what might be termed "auto-jihad"—attacks by self-directed individuals using firearms.

For example, on July 4, 2002, Egyptian legal immigrant Hesham Mohamed Hadayet used a handgun to murder two Israelis near the El Al ticket counter at the Los Angeles airport. Acquaintances said that he had frequently expressed hatred for the United States and Israel.

And in October 2002, the Washington, DC, metropolitan area was terrorized by attacks perpetrated by John Allen Muhammad (who had joined the Nation of Islam) and Lee Boyd Malvo. One of them drove a Chevrolet, while the other hid in the trunk, using a small opening to shoot people from 50 to 100 yards away. They murdered 10 people with a stolen Bushmaster XM-15 rifle. Previously they had murdered six other people in six states. Gun control advocates used the shootings to argue for restrictions on self-loading firearms such as the Bushmaster, but opponents pointed out that almost every rifle can shoot accurately up to 100 yards.

Despite ardent efforts, the gun control movement was not successful in using September 11 to advance its agenda. The .50 caliber ban in California was one of the gun control movement's very few significant victories between 2001 and 2008. In general, September 11 did not lead to an improvement in the political situation for gun control advocates.

To the contrary, conventional political wisdom was that the "pro-gun" side did very well in the 2002 congressional elections, in which terrorism was a major issue. In 2004, John Kerry's 95 percent antigun voting record (by NRA metrics) was thought to have cost him the presidential election (most noticeably in the swing state of Ohio, which he lost by 60,000 votes). In 2005, Sarah Brady admitted "we've hit rock bottom."[23] The 2006 elections were good news for Democrats, but not for the gun control movement, as Democratic election leaders such as Sen. Charles Schumer (D-NY) and Rep. Rahm Emanuel (D-Ill.)—both of whom were personally strong supporters of gun control—successfully recruited pro-gun Democrats to win races in swing districts.

Had the 2000 election turned out differently, September 11 might have worked well for the gun control movement. Based on Al Gore's record as vice president, he would have been a staunch and energetic advocate for gun control, and could have used the bully pulpit to set a national gun control agenda. President Gore's version of the Patriot Act likely would have included sweeping gun controls.

But it might not have passed. After the Oklahoma City bombing, President Clinton had pushed an "antiterrorism" law that included many new restrictions on the Bill of Rights, including the Second Amendment. He was defeated in the House of Representatives by a lobbying coalition led by the American Civil Liberties Union, and including the National Rifle Association and Gun Owners of America. Eventually, President Clinton was able to pass much of his restrictive agenda piecemeal, often as attachments to other bills, but none of the gun provisions ever passed.[24]

President Bush was politically shrewd in keeping gun control out of the Patriot Act, and out of his general counterterrorist program—for he thereby kept the NRA on the sidelines, and did not have to face resistance from one of the most powerful lobbies in the United States.

The Pro-Gun Agenda

September 11, 2001, was, of course, preceded by January 1, 2000. There were many warnings about a Y2K computer crash: mainframe computers, built decades before, had only two digits for the year, and so when the year changed from "99" to "00," the computer would think that the year was 1900, and technological infrastructure would collapse, for days, weeks, or longer. Many people did take extra precautions—ranging from procuring extra batteries for flashlights, to stockpiling survival rations, to purchasing reserve supplies of ammunition. January 1, 2000 turned out to cause nothing more than minor problems in a few areas, but the Y2K publicity of 1999 had put civic preparedness into the national zeitgeist.

September 11 was neither foreseen nor minor. Everything was disrupted, from public transportation, to communications, to emergency care, to police protection of civilians. But there was no need for firearms in the disaster area, or in the periphery. While New York City's police were deployed at ground zero, crime in the unprotected outer boroughs fell.[25] Apparently even New York's criminals shared in the mood of national solidarity.

Nobody on September 12 had a clear idea whether more attacks were on the way. Was September 11, like Pearl Harbor, a devastating initial attack that would be followed by many more? Would the overseas tactics used by al Qaeda and its allies—such as attacks on shopping malls, restaurants, schools, busses, churches, and synagogues—be duplicated in the United States?

Many Americans decided to buy their first gun. Retail gun sales in the United States must be authorized by the National Instant Check System (NICS), by which a licensed firearms dealer sends a query to law enforcement officials who check the buyer against databases of prohibited persons. Changes in the number of NICS record inquiries are thus an excellent proxy for changes in the number of firearm sales. According to NICS data, firearms sales in the United States increased in September 2001 and skyrocketed in October. In November, sales were higher than any month before September 2001.[26] Anecdotally, journalists reported from many locations that local gun shops described an increase in firearm and ammunition sales.[27]

As one NRA critic acknowledged, "the 9/11 al-Qaeda terrorist attacks had spurred a wave of gun buying nationwide. Soccer moms became 'security moms' (joined by their husbands and dads). Owning firearms became much more acceptable among the suburban middle class."[28] A poll in *U.S. News & World Report* announced that "45 percent more Americans value Second Amendment rights to pack heat than before the attacks."[29]

Many of the gun buyers were first-timers. The acquisition of a new firearm was accompanied by a desire to become informed about safe firearm practices. ABC reported: "Amy Doherty never wanted a gun in her home and certainly never thought she and her husband would find themselves on a firing range. Like many Americans, they also never thought they would spend their evenings in gun classes."[30] Many citizens had similar experiences.[31]

The gun control lobby, while warning about how effective guns would be in terrorist hands, tried to argue that guns should not be owned by persons at risk of being attacked by a terrorist. Josh Sugarmann, of the Violence Policy Center, cautioned: "A handgun purchased for self-defense is more likely to be used against yourself, your friends or your family than to kill a criminal or to stop a terrorist."[32]

However, the warnings did not work. It is one thing to say, "We need gun control to prevent other people (drug dealers, radical blacks, Klansmen, or other villains *du jour*) from having guns." It is quite another to tell ordinary

Americans, in effect, "You are too hot-tempered and incompetent to own a gun. You will more likely kill yourself in an accident or your wife in a domestic dispute than you will kill a criminal." Insulting the audience has rarely been a route to public relations success.

The wave of new gun purchases ended after November 2001, and gun sales settled back to historically normal levels.[33]

It was on September 11, 2003, that the Missouri legislature overrode a governor's veto, and made Missouri one of the now 40 states that allow citizens to obtain a concealed handgun carry permit under objective, reasonably attainable standards—similar to a driver's license. The importance of ordinary armed citizens being able to resist a terrorist attack had become an important part of the right-to-carry debate.

In 2005, Congress passed, and the president signed, the Protection of Lawful Commerce in Arms Act (PLCAA). The Act prohibited lawsuits against gun manufacturers or gun stores for gun sales that were conducted in compliance with all federal, state, and local gun controls. Beginning in 1998, the Brady Center (the legal arm of the Brady Campaign) had orchestrated several dozen lawsuits—mostly by big-city mayors—claiming that gun manufacturers should be held financially responsible for gun criminals. Shortly before the Senate passed the Protection law, the bill was endorsed by the U.S. Department of Defense, which said it "strongly supports" passage to "help safeguard our national security by limiting unnecessary lawsuits against an industry that plays a critical role in meeting the procurement needs of our men and women in uniform." Indeed, almost every handgun ever used by the U.S. military was first invented for civilians, and only later sold to the military. The PLCAA was going to pass anyway, but support from the Department of Defense during a time when U.S. forces were at war in Afghanistan, Iraq, and other terrorist centers perhaps provided some extra impetus.

At the margins, September 11 did move American culture in a pro-gun direction, but the movement was small compared to the change wrought by Hurricane Katrina. The August 2005 hurricane devastated southern Mississippi and Louisiana, and turned New Orleans into a brutal Hobbesian hellhole. The disaster response of the federal, Louisiana, and New Orleans governments was shockingly inept. For a while, civil government collapsed, gangs of murders and looters roamed wild, and desperate citizens shared their guns with neighbors to protect their families from the predators who came when night fell. A few days after the storm, the New Orleans police, assisted by federal and out-of-state officers, began breaking into homes to confiscate guns from law-abiding citizens.[34]

One reason that Katrina had so much more impact, in terms of making America more supportive of gun ownership, than did September 11, was that natural disasters are not uncommon occurrences. Tornadoes hit the Midwest every year, as do hurricanes on the Gulf and South Atlantic Coasts, and sometimes the Pacific Coast. Snowstorms can sometimes paralyze government for several days in many parts of the northern two-thirds of the United States. In contrast, organized terrorist attacks such as September 11, as well as auto-jihadi attacks within U.S. territory, are rare.

Thus, public response to September 11 probably played a role in aiding the pro-gun agenda, but the effect was relatively minor, and did no more than give a boost to a movement that was already politically ascendant. Culture matters enormously, and the public reactions to September 11 and to Katrina were part of a much larger pro-gun movement in American culture that started well before September 11, and which is still taking place. However, it is difficult to point to any particular pro-gun law enacted after September 11 and say "But for September 11, this would not have been enacted."

Thus, the Second Amendment fared very differently after September 11 than did the Fourth and Fifth Amendments, or the right of habeas corpus. One reason for the different results is that the constitutional guarantee of habeas corpus, unlike the Second Amendment, does not have a national advocacy group with over 3 million members who are avidly dedicated to preserving the right. Habeas corpus is a critically important right, but hardly anyone exercises the right even once in her lifetime, and only a few ardent felony prisoners exercise the petition for a writ of habeas corpus frequently. In contrast, there are tens of millions of gun owners in the United States, all whom exercise their Second Amendment right daily by, at least, knowing that they own a gun, and many of whom exercise the right frequently by engaging in the shooting sports, or in carrying a licensed handgun for lawful protection. Thus, the natural membership base of a Second Amendment lobby is far larger than the natural membership base of a habeas corpus lobby.

The Consensus Agenda

There was one firearms issue for which September 11 really did change everything. Within weeks, the idea of armed pilots went from being unthinkable to being an overwhelming bipartisan consensus. Polls after 9/11 indicated 68–75 percent public support for arming airline pilots.[35] Forty-nine percent said they would switch their business to an airline that armed pilots.[36]

With such palpable popular support, and with a cadre of pilots—at least half of whom already were experienced with firearms because of their prior service in the military—it was not surprising that there would be bipartisan support in Congress.[37]

In the Homeland Security Act of 2002, pro-gun and antigun legislators came together to craft an armed pilots program that combined the most attractive features from both sides: acknowledgment of the life-

saving value of handguns in the right hands, along with reasonable training requirements. The armed pilots law was sponsored by California
Democratic Senator Barbara Boxer (a long-standing gun control advocate)
and Kentucky Republican Mitch McConnell (who boasted a nearly 100
percent pro-NRA voting record).

That same bipartisan support was seen when Senators Barbara Boxer and
Jim Bunning (R-Ky.) cosponsored a 2003 law that closed a loophole, thereby
permitting commercial cargo pilots to carry firearms as well. Although freight
carriers opposed the bill, Senator Boxer won by pointing out that a hijacked
cargo plane can damage a ground target, such as a nuclear power plant, just as
severely as can a passenger plane. Proponents also noted that security of cargo
planes was very poor. Cockpit doors were not reinforced, and it was easy for
unauthorized persons to sneak onto the tarmac and get on a plane.

Opponents of the armed pilots program argued that it was unnecessary because federal sky marshals could protect aircraft from hijackers. A
U.S. Federal Sky Marshal program was created in 1968, and was originally
intended to prevent hijackings to Cuba.[38] However, with about 25,000
commercial airline flights per day, even the minimal Flight Coverage Index
of 3 percent was rarely approached.[39] Needing about 35,000 air marshals
to attain full coverage, Transportation Secretary Norman Mineta speedily
hired 6,000 new marshals. The Cato Institute noted the poor quality of the
newly hired marshals.[40] The Sky Marshal Program, as implemented, had
a fatal flaw that impaired its already limited effectiveness: the bureaucrats
running the program insisted on a dress code and transparent identification system that permitted easy recognition of sky marshals by civilians
and would-be terrorists alike.[41]

Airlines hated the armed pilots idea. Apparently the airline executives
preferred to take their chances of another 9/11 rather than risk that an
armed pilot might use his gun illegally, and the airline might be sued.
While the Bush administration adopted the corporate view and opposed
the armed pilots law, President Bush did not veto the homeland security
bills that contained the armed pilot provisions. Instead, the Bush administration used its new Transportation Security Administration to adminis-
tratively obstruct the arming of pilots.

According to Captain David Mackett, president of the Airline Pilots
Security Alliance:

> TSA began using its self-styled psychiatric screens to deliberately elimi-
> nate, and insult highly qualified pilots. Their message was clear when they
> eliminated former federal, state and local law enforcement agents, as well
> as a large pool of military pilots who were cleared to carry nuclear weap-
> ons and carry pistols; pilots who were still serving our country in the U.S.
> Armed Forces were also eliminated.[42]

Ninety percent of volunteers withdrew from the program as a result.[43] Oregon Rep. Peter DeFazio, who represents a very left-wing district including Eugene, home of the University of Oregon, is a fervent gun control advocate; he introduced nine gun control bills within three days after a school shooting in his district. Yet DeFazio, the ranking Democrat on the Aviation Subcommittee, denounced the TSA's psychological intrusions: "We waste time and resources screening people who are not a threat."[44]

The TSA insisted on conducting the pilot training program itself, in a course that cost $12,000, even though well-established firearms training academies conduct similar courses for less than a thousand dollars, and some academies had offered to train the pilots for free. The Bush administration, however, remained impervious to year after year of bipartisan criticism from Congress and from pilots.[45]

Eighty-five percent of pilots had expressed interest in being armed.[46] Yet by 2008, only about 15 percent of flights were protected by a single armed pilot. About 3 percent are protected by two armed pilots, and about 2 percent are protected by air marshals. The air marshals program's paltry coverage costs over half a billion dollars a year. Even with the TSA's grotesquely inflated training costs, protection of 97 percent of flights could be achieved for $11 million a year.[47]

Mackett explained that the solution would be "applying the same procedures to pilots as are applied to every other Federal officer." He expressed no hope that TSA would fix the problem of its own volition: "It would take corrective legislation to make our skies safe, as the TSA has not been amenable to implementing the required changes."[48]

Conclusion

September 11 changed a great deal with regard to American civil liberties, and other constitutional values. But it did not change much with regard to the Second Amendment. The gun control movement was unable to exploit September 11 to advance the gun control agenda. For the gun rights movement, September 11 did no more than somewhat amplify trends that were already running in favor of gun rights. The only gun issue for which September 11 made a decisive difference was the armed pilots program, one of the very rare examples of pro-gun and antigun congresspersons uniting to craft a widely supported federal gun law. However, the practical effect of the armed pilots law has been drastically reduced by executive branch subversion.

Notes

1. Josh Sugarmann, *Every Handgun Is Aimed at You* (New York: The New Press, 2001).

2. Ibid., xii.

3. The "assault weapon" laws applied to guns that looked like automatic machine guns, but did not function like them. Real automatics had been very strictly controlled ever since the National Firearms Act of 1934. 18 U.S. Code § 922(v)&(w) (enacted 1994, expired by its own terms in 2004). In 1986 the sale of new automatics to the public was outlawed; 18 U.S. Code § 922(o); The Firearm Owners' Protection Act (FOPA), Pub. L. No. 99-308, 100 Stat. 449 (May 19, 1986).

4. For discussion of the various technologies of "smart guns," see Cynthia Leonardatos, David B. Kopel, and Paul Blackman, "Smart Guns/Foolish Legislators," *Connecticut Law Review* 34, (2001): 157–219.

5. Martin Killias, "Gun Ownership and Violent Crime: The Swiss Experience in International Perspective," *Security Journal* 1, 169, 171 (1990): 169, 171.

6. Joseph Olson and David B. Kopel, "All the Way Down the Slippery Slope: Gun Prohibition in England, and Some Lessons for America," *Hamline Law Review* 22 (1999): 399.

7. Erik Eckholm, "A Little Gun Control, a Lot of Guns," *New York Times*, August 15, 1993, sec. 4, p. 1 (interviewing Sarah Brady and quoting her objective of "needs-based licensing").

8. Gary Mauser, "Misfire: Firearm Registration in Canada," Public Policy Sources, No. 48, Fraser Institute Occasional Paper, The Fraser Institute, Vancouver, B.C., 2001. Among the leading U.S. advocates of gun registration is U.S. Rep. Bobby Rush (D-Chicago), a former Black Panther. "Congressman Rush Introduces Gun Legislation Named after Blair Holt, Julian High School Hero," *States News Service* (Chicago), June 11, 2007. According to Rush's press release, his bill "will implement a nationwide program of licensing all individuals who possess firearms and require all guns to be registered in a national gun registry."

9. Sugarmann, *Every Handgun Is Aimed at You*, 184. Secondary sales can be defined as all firearm sales transfer do not involve a Federal Firearms Licensee—e.g., a gift between family members, or a sale between criminals. The latter are already illegal, under federal law banning gun possession by, and gun transfer to, persons with a felony conviction; 18 U.S. Code § 922(d)&(g).

10. Stephen Koff, "Weapons Ban under the Gun: Republicans and Democrats Quietly Allowing Law to Expire," *The Plain Dealer*, September 9, 2004.

11. Bill Clinton, *My Life* (New York: Vintage Books, 2004), 928; Bill Clinton interview, The Charlie Rose Show, transcript, June 23, 2004 ("The NRA and Ralph Nader stand right behind the Supreme Court in their ability to claim that they put George Bush in the White House").

12. The Brady Campaign to Prevent Gun Violence, "Closing the Terror Gap: Denying Firearms to Terrorists," http://www.bradycampaign.org/xshare/ pdf/terror-gap.pdf (updated September 21, 2007); Violence Policy Center, "Firearms Training for Jihad in America" (2001).

13. David B. Kopel and Joseph Olson, "Preventing a Reign of Terror: Civil Liberties Implications of Terrorism Legislation" *Oklahoma City Law Review* 21 (1996): 247.

14. Arnold Grossman, *One Nation under Guns: An Essay on an American Epidemic* (Golden, CO: Fulcrum Publishing, 2006), 70–71.

15. Grossman, *One Nation under Guns*, 42.

16. Tom McCann, "Sniper Rifle Ban Urged Again: Blagojevich Says They're Terrorists' 'Weapon of Choice,'" *Chicago Tribune*, October 22, 2001. For more on the alleged link between .50 caliber firearms and terrorists, see Tom Diaz, "Voting from the Rooftops: How the Gun Industry Armed Osama bin Laden, Other Foreign and Domestic Terrorists, and Common Criminals with 50 Caliber Sniper Rifles," Violence Policy Center (VPC) (October 2001), http://www.vpc.org/studies/roofexec.htm. Although the VPC claimed that .50 caliber rifles were bought by al Qaeda, Ronnie Barrett, the inventor of the modern .50 caliber rifle (and the owner of Barrett Firearms, which makes the guns), states that all his guns that ended up in Afghanistan were sold to U.S. government officials; Dave Kopel and Timothy Wheeler, "Guns and (Character) Assassination," *National Review Online* (December 21, 2001), http://davekopel.org/NRO/2001/Guns-and-Character-Assassination.htm.

17. Senator Feinstein's "assault weapon" law, which was enacted in 1994 and sunset in 2004, had specifically listed the .50 caliber Barrett Model 90 Bolt Action Rifle as among the legitimate "recreational firearms" that were not to be considered "assault weapons"; 18 U.S. Code § 922(v), Appendix B.

18. "Big Rifle a Terrorist Tool?" CBS News (January 9, 2005), http://www. cbsnews.com/stories/2005/01/06/60minutes/main665257.shtml.

19. David B. Kopel and Alan Korwin, "Should Gun Shows Be Outlawed?" Independence Institute, Issue Paper no. 1-2002, January 23, 2002.

20. Grossman, *One Nation under Guns*, 77.

21. Ann Imse, "Gun Shoppers on Terrorism Watch List: Law Won't Let State Learn Outcome of Attempts," *Rocky Mountain News*, March 9, 2005.

22. Government Accountability Office, *Gun Control and Terrorism: FBI Could Better Manage Firearm-Related Background Check Involving Terrorist Watch List Records*, GAO-05-127, January 2005) (proposing various technical improvements in FBI procedures, but not proposing merging the No Fly list into the prohibited persons list). David B. Kopel, "The New McCarthyism: Restricting Constitutional Rights Based on Mere Suspicion," Independence Institute Issue Backgrounder, no. 2005-B, June 2005.

23. Grossman, *One Nation under Guns*, 48.

24. Kopel and Olson, "Preventing a Reign of Terror."

25. Roberto Santiago, "Crime Rate Plunges after Terror Attack," *New York Daily News*, September 20, 2001; "Crime Rate in New York Fell Sharply after Attack," *Wall Street Journal*, September 19, 2001; Kevin Flynn, "Crime Down 18% as Murders Fall in a City Stunned by Wholesale Death," *The New York Times*, September 25, 2001. Crime rates in New York City had already been in a 15-year decline, but the September 11 effect was separable from the broader trend.

26. The lone exception here is the month of November 1999, a month in which gun sales seem to have benefited from the combined imminence of Y2K and of Christmas. In some states, the check is conducted by state law enforcement, but aggregate sales data are transmitted to NICS. For data, see "Total NICS Checks November 30, 1998–March 31, 2006," http://www.nafr,org/NICS/current/checks.pdf.

27. "Gun Frenzy Raises Concerns," *The Journal News* (Rockland County, New York), October 11, 2001 (reprint of *Washington Post* editorial noting: "The

terrorist attacks of Sept. 11 have sparked dramatic increases in gun and ammunition purchases around the country, particularly by women, older citizens and first-time gun-buyers."); Al Baker, "Steep Rise in Gun Sales Reflects Post-Attack Fears," *New York Times*, December 16, 2001 ("there has been a steady stream of serious-minded first-time buyers"); Aline McKenzie, "Texans Rush to Arm Selves after Sept. 11 Attacks," *The Dallas Morning News*, November 8, 2001 (According to Ken Goldberg, owner of DFW Gun Range and Firing Center in the Love Field area, "People are frightened, people are uncertain. These are uncertain times. The unimagined has been imagined.... We've got people who would never have considered owning a gun coming in here"); "Americans Shaken by Terrorist Attacks in New York and Washington Seek Comfort in Handguns," *Associated Press*, September 14, 2001.

28. Richard Feldman, *Ricochet: Confessions of a Gun Lobbyist* (Hoboken, NJ: John Wiley & Sons, 2008). Feldman had been an NRA lobbyist, and had later headed his own gun industry lobby, the American Shooting Sports Council (ASSC). Feldman was pushed out of the ASSC in 1998 as the result of his collaboration with the Clinton administration and with California gun control advocates in supporting some of their agenda—moves that Feldman considered to be legitimate tactical compromises. His book strongly criticizes the NRA, and he has served as an advisor to gun control advocates.

29. Paul Bedard, Suzi Parker, and Christopher H. Schmitt, "Washington Whispers," *U.S. News & World Report* (November 5, 2001): 7.

30. John Cochran and Steve Walsh, "Americans Arm Themselves," *ABCnews. com*, October 1, 2001, http://web.archive.org/web/20020305190323/http://www.federalobserver.com/archive.php?aid=526.

31. Travis Baker, "Residents Enrolling in Personal Safety Courses," *The Cincinnati Post*, Cincinnati.com, September 26, 2001, http://www.cincypost.com/2001/sep/26/armed092601.html ("Terrorist attacks against the United States have increased interest in personal safety instruction and gun ownership, according to some Washington state firearms dealers. The Kitsap Rifle and Revolver Club will run an extra personal safety course in October, because of a three-fold increase in inquiries about firearms training, Marcus Carter of the club says").

32. "Americans Shaken by Terrorist Attacks in New York and Washington Seek Comfort in Handguns," *Associated Press*, September 14, 2001.

33. This is the last yearly total provided by "Total NICS Checks: November 30, 1998–March 31, 2006," http://www.nafr.org/NICS/current/checks.pdf.

34. Gordon Hutchinson and Todd Masson, *The Great New Orleans Gun Grab* (Boutte, LA: Louisiana Publishing, 2007).

35. Fabrizio, McLaughlin and Associates, September 17–20, 2001 (800 adults, conducted between September 17 and September 20, 2001, 73% supported "training and arming all U.S. pilots with specially manufactured handguns that are designed not to penetrate an airliner's outer skin or fuselage"); George Gallup Jr., *The Gallup Poll: Public Opinion, 2001* (Lanham, MD: Rowman & Littlefield, 2002) at 245 (CNN/USA Today/Gallup poll conducted on October 21–29, 2001, 68% in favor of arming airline pilots); Newsweek Poll, conducted by Princeton Survey Research Associates, September 27–28, 2001

(1,000 adults, conducted on September 27–28, 2001, 68% in favor of "arming pilots on flights"); *Pollingreport.com*, Transportation, Air Travel, http://www.pollingreport.com/transport.htm (Fox News/Opinion Dynamics Poll of 900 registered voters, conducted on June 4–5, 2002, 68% approval).

36. John H. Fund, "Cocked Pit: Armed Pilots Would Mean Polite Skies," *Jewish World Review*, October 30, 2001. In addition, Fund noted that, in a survey conducted for the Allied Pilots Association, in which 800 registered voters were interviewed on October 9–10, 2001, 75% of Americans were in favor of arming pilots.

37. Homeland Security Act of 2002, H.R. 5005, 107th Congress, Public Law 107-296, at Title XIV—Arming Pilots against Terrorism, November 25, 2002, http://www.dhs.gov/xlibrary/assets/hr_5005_enr.pdf; Federal flight deck officer program.

38. The current Federal Air Marshal program stems from Public Law 99-83, the International Security and Development Cooperation Act, enacted on August 8, 1985. See FAA News, USA Federal Air Marshal Program, Federal Aviation Administration, September 2001, http://www.unitedstatesaction.com/air-marshals.htm.

39. Alexandra Marks, "Air Marshals Stretched Thin," *Christian Science Monitor* 98 (December 28, 2005): 1.

40. Gene Healy and Robert A. Levy, "Restoring the Right to Bear Arms," in *Cato Handbook for Congress: Policy Recommendations for the 108th Congress*, ed. Edward H. Crane and David Boaz (Washington, DC: Cato Institute, 2003), 185.

41. "Plane Clothes : Lack of Anonymity at the Federal Air Marshal Service Compromises Aviation and National Security," Investigative Report by the Committee on the Judiciary, 109th Congress, 2nd Sess., May 25, 2006; "Air Marshals across Country Warn Passengers Aren't Safe: Marshals Say Managers Causing Total System Failure," *TheDenverChannel.Com* (July 20, 2006), http://www.thedenverchannel.com/news/9552850/detail.html.

42. David Mackett, "Deliberate Apathy—Arming America's Pilots against Terrorism," *Biz&Aviationpub.com* (2004), http://www.bizandaviationpub.com/2004_articles/April/Deliberate%20Apathy.htm.

43. Ibid.

44. Kevin Mooney, "More Armed Pilots Needed, Aviation Experts Say," *CNSNews.com*, March 28, 2007.

45. "Air Marshal Association Challenges Agency Rules and Practice," PRWeb (June 7, 2005), http://politics.press-library.com/releases/2005-06-07/FEDERAL-AIR-MARSHAL-ASSOCIATION/Air-Marshal-Association-Challenges-Agency-Rules-Practice.htm.

46. Annie Jacobsen, "Annie Get Your Gun," *WomensWallStreet.com* (February 18, 2007), http://www.womenwallstreet.com/columns/ArticlePrint.aspx?aid=1178 (citing pilot organization polls).

47. Ibid.

48. David Mackett, telephone conversation with Joanne D. Eisen, March 28, 2008.

6

National Security Letters and Diminishing Privacy Rights

*Christopher P. Banks**

Imagine you are a small-town librarian on the executive board of a nonprofit consortium of about twenty-five public libraries in Iowa. One day two agents from the Federal Bureau of Investigation (FBI) come to see you at work. After you greet them, they hand you a two-page letter, over official letterhead, stating that "Under the authority of Executive Order 12333, dated December 4, 1981, and pursuant to Title 18, United States Code (U.S.C.) Section 279," you must provide to the FBI "subscriber information, billing information, and access logs of any person or entity related to" a specific Internet protocol address for a forty-five-minute period on June 3, 2008. You quickly realize that you are being asked, under authority of law, to disclose the private information of a patron using a library computer in your consortium. As you read on, you see that the letter says that a "Special Agent in Charge" has signed it and certifies that the "information sought is relevant to an authorized investigation to protect against international terrorism or clandestine intelligence activities." The letter, somewhat ominously, "advises" you that you cannot tell anyone that the FBI is seeking the information.[1]

What would you do next? One option may be to refuse the demand while citing the privacy and free speech concerns of the library patron, and yourself (as a representative of the library consortium). But if you do not cooperate, it is possible to become an unwitting accomplice to a terrorist plot and at least be indirectly responsible for causing the deaths of

* **Christopher P. Banks** is Associate Professor of Political Science at Kent State University and author of several books.

innocents if the government does not get the information in time to stop it. Another option might be to delay compliance by seeking the advice of a colleague, a boss, or an attorney about what to do. But the letter declares, in unequivocal terms, that you cannot tell anyone about the FBI's request: the "gag order" accompanying the letter suggests that if word leaks out, you may wind up in jail. There are few, it seems, good options about how to manage the request to disclose personal information sent over the Internet by a customer using a public library's computer.

It may be only a small comfort to know in mulling your choices that thousands of others in the United States face similar predicaments in light of the new legal landscape that emerged after September 11. The hypothetical registers a new and controversial post–9/11 reality: in only a short six-week span after al Qaeda's attack, Congress enacted the USA Patriot Act, a provocative antiterrorism measure that aggressively seeks out enemies of the state before they strike. As a result, the federal government has unprecedented power to utilize national security letters (NSLs) as a tool in the preliminary stages of terrorist- or counterintelligence investigations.[2] Under the Patriot Act, NSLs are issued by the federal agencies without first making a showing in court that the investigation's target engaged in wrongdoing that ordinarily justifies the inquiry's need. Between 2003 and 2006, an average of nearly 50,000 NSLs per year was distributed to companies, schools, and libraries supplying Internet access.[3] Nearly 60 percent of the 2006 NSL requests were served on U.S. citizens.[4] One year after 9/11, a study reported that federal officials, armed with NSLs, made nearly 550 visits to libraries to obtain the kind of information that was at issue in the hypothetical.[5]

Furthermore, not only is the aforementioned scenario very real, it is similar to only a handful of court challenges opposing attempts to obtain customer Internet data. Most times, NSL recipients secretly, and without any public dissent, comply with the government's information-gathering requests. In one case brought before a court in 2004, a federal district judge observed that no one had judicially opposed an NSL request in a span of almost two decades.[6] Accordingly, this chapter surveys the growing practice of using national security letters as a new post–9/11 antiterrorism reality. It first traces the origin and rationale of using national security letters in terrorism investigations before September 11. Next, it explains how the law governing the use of NSLs changed after the terrorist attacks on the World Trade Center and Pentagon. Thereafter, it explains how the changes have led to more abuse by executive agencies in charge of preventing terrorism, and it details the responses to NSLs by federal courts and the U.S. Congress in their attempts to provide meaningful oversight and accountability to executive officials. The last section offers some conclusions about the likelihood and feasibility of reforming the NSL process in the future.

Pre–September 11 Use of National Security Letters

NSLs are direct written requests, akin to administrative subpoenas,[7] used by the FBI in counterintelligence investigations involving threats to national security. Their original purpose was to obtain customer records from third-party communication and financial providers without court order, often referred to as "transactional" information (not involving the disclosure of the content of information). Usually this includes securing documents relating to telephone bills (listing the numbers dialed to a phone) and bank account transactions (reflecting money transfers to specific lenders). Before 9/11 this meant NSLs did not directly involve criminal prosecutions. Instead, they gathered information by spying on foreign intelligence officers in an effort to identify, prevent, and disrupt terrorist activities. As a result, a legal "wall" was erected between counterintelligence agents and criminal law investigators, and laws such as the Foreign Intelligence Surveillance Act (1978) (FISA) tried to keep information taken in one type of investigation separate from the other.[8] Since the late 1970s, Congress has given executive agencies the power to issue NSLs through several laws.

Legislation such as the Right to Financial Privacy Act (1978) (RFPA) generally protects customer privacy in financial transactions. But, in a 1986 amendment, Congress created the first NSL law by granting the FBI and other counterintelligence agencies the power to compel production of customer banking records in legitimately established foreign intelligence cases. Before then, under the RFPA agencies could only ask for voluntary compliance.[9] Likewise, the Electronic Communication Privacy Act (1986) (ECPA) safeguards the privacy of electronic and wire communications stored by third parties, such as telephone companies or corporate networks; but it allows NSLs to be used for compelling access to customer subscriber data and tolling billing records. Notably, each law required a certification from a high-ranking FBI official that there was "specific and articulable facts giving reason to believe" that the target of the counterintelligence investigation was a foreign power or their agent.[10]

Two developments in the mid-1990s led to changes in the law, which increased the scope and application of NSLs. To ease agency discovery of where targets held financial accounts in counterintelligence investigations, in 1996 Congress modified the Fair Credit Reporting Act (1970) to give the FBI the flexibility to use credit reports to identify financial institutions. While the modification let the FBI obtain the same kind of facts that it could ordinarily compel through a subpoena in a criminal prosecution, an NSL's validity depended upon an agency certification that there were specific facts that the target was a foreign power or agent, and that the information pertained to a foreign counterintelligence investigation.[11] Also, in the wake of the 1994 arrest and conviction of Aldrich Ames, a CIA agent spying for the Russians, Congress altered the National Security Act (1947) to make it easier to get credit and banking information from federal employees suspected of leaking classified information. As with the earlier NSL statutes, the new provision had restrictions that narrowed the scope of NSL requests to specific circumstances.[12]

Other laws, such as FISA, gave federal officials general wiretap, and pen register and trace/trap authority in foreign counterintelligence cases.[13] FISA complemented NSL laws and together they controlled much of how the government secured transactional information in national security cases.[14] For supporters and critics alike, the 9/11 tragedy exposed the problems of striking a balance between individual freedom and public safety while trying to prevent terrorism acts in a legal system defined by a wall that stood between foreign intelligence and criminal law agencies. By most accounts, the wall disrupted the free flow of information between them; so after 9/11 the federal government devised new legislation to break it down in order to prevent, and not just respond to, terrorism.[15] Although the pre–9/11 legal standards were created as safeguards to limit the executive branch's unfettered control over information gathering, federal officials complained that they put too many obstacles in the way of stopping terrorists from inflicting mass casualties and untold property damage. The law governing NSLs, and its official certification process, was thought to be too unwieldy and slow in fighting terrorists in a 9/11 era that was increasingly dominated by sleeper cells, cell phones, and the Internet.[16]

The Post–9/11 Legal Landscape

The growing influence of the Internet, as well as the unpredictability and magnitude of the 9/11 attacks, are manifested by Congress's decision to enact USA Patriot Act Section 505, the law governing national security letters.[17] By allowing the federal government to seek information from entities providing Internet service to the public, the new law had three effects. By compulsion, and in secret and without court order, it expanded the quantity of information sought; it enlarged the type of information desired; and it amplified the number of agency officials empowered to ask for information in terrorism investigations.[18] Section 505's impact was put into motion by revising the Right to Financial Privacy Act, the Electronic Communication Privacy Act and the Fair Credit Reporting Act, and by lowering the legal standards in those statutes and others that affect NSL creation, issuance, and enforceability.[19] Each change created a distinct type of NSL that enabled the government to obtain private information from financial institutions, telecommunication providers, and consumer credit bureaus.

In contrast to the old certification process requiring senior FBI officials from verifying that there is specific proof that the target was a foreign power or agent, Section 505 permits FBI Special Agents in charge in field offices to certify that the information sought is merely *relevant* to a foreign intelligence investigation. Establishing relevance is easier than proving specific facts, and delegating signatory authority for issuing NSLs to an expanded base of agents in 56 field offices greatly accelerated how NSLs were prepared, reviewed, and issued.[20] Apart from Section 505, the Fair Credit Reporting Act was revised by licensing *any* government agency involved in a terrorism investigation to compel a credit agency to furnish a customer's credit report upon a written certification of *necessity*.[21] Also, two other changes significantly facilitated NSL usage. In 2003, the U.S. attorney general issued new guidelines that let the FBI distribute NSLs in preliminary national security investigations (as opposed to the old standard of only being allowed in "full investigations"). And, in 2004, the Right to Financial Privacy Act was revised to allow the FBI to apply NSLs to a greater range of financial institutions, including: banks, credit unions, thrift institutions, securities brokers, investment banks, currency exchanges, insurance companies, credit card companies, precious metals dealers, travel agencies, pawnbrokers, vehicle sellers (cars, boats, airplanes), real estate agents, telegraph companies, the U.S. Postal Service, and casinos.[22]

Once issued post–Patriot Act NSLs, which often include multiple requests for information from different customers, could secure histories of telephone calls and email records (calls made, billing records, email addresses, screen names, plus subscriber and payment information), financial information (account, safe deposit, and transaction information), and consumer credit information (including full credit reports in international terrorism cases) from telephone companies, financial institutions, Internet providers and consumer credit agencies, all without judicial oversight. In addition, it placed a gag order on those served with NSLs, thus preventing recipients from telling anyone that they were asked to disclose the records.

After 9/11, the FBI took full advantage of its enhanced authority. In 2000, the FBI issued about 8,500 NSL requests; whereas, in 2003 it issued 39,346; in 2004, 56,507; in 2005, 47,221; and, in 2006, 49,425, for a total of 192,499 NSL requests in a four-year period.[23] The increase in executive powers pertaining to NSLs in terrorism investigations, when coupled with minimal legislative or court oversight, has been troubling to civil libertarians. As a result, both the U.S. Congress and federal courts have responded with new laws and litigation attempting to limit NSLs.

Political and Judicial Oversight of NSLs

From World War I to the Vietnam eras, executive agencies consistently abused the rule of law in the course of watching, investigating, and preventing individuals and groups suspected of subversive activities. In response to anarchist and criminal violence, the infamous "Palmer Raids," so-named after Attorney General A. Mitchell Palmer after his house was bombed in 1919, were responsible for aggressively and randomly amassing files, arresting, and deporting thousands of people under the pretext of protecting national security. An identical, and highly secretive, approach to curbing dissidents was at the core of J. Edgar Hoover's efforts to combat the Communist threat when he was director of the FBI in the 1950s. From 1936 to 1976, Hoover's FBI also conducted a covert counterintelligence operation, code-named COINTELPRO, aimed at domestic antiwar and civil rights groups. Over roughly the same period, the National Security Agency, the Central Intelligence Agency, and the U.S. Army each conducted one or more surveillance operations that often broke the law while claiming it was necessary to do so in the interest of national security.[24]

During each episode of abuse Congress and the federal courts responded by enacting reform legislation or creating new precedents limiting agency powers. Yet ongoing threats to the social order, such as 9/11, often work to undo reform because public fear intensifies and citizens demand that government take immediate action to protect national security. This dynamic explains the urgent lobbying efforts by the Bush administration to have Congress enact antiterrorism laws such as the USA Patriot Act and national security letters. But it also underscores the determined efforts by civil libertarians to constrain executive power once the crisis passes. Thus it is not surprising that the political debate whether to reauthorize the most controversial parts of the USA Patriot Act climaxed after President George W. Bush's 2004 reelection. It culminated with the passage of two laws that increased judicial and political oversight over NSL application and executive agencies. The USA Patriot Act Improvement and Reauthorization Act of 2005, and the USA Patriot Act Additional Reauthorizing Amendments Act of 2006 (Reauthorization statutes), were intended to correct the flaws in the original Patriot Act's Section 505 that caused two federal courts to nullify part of the post–9/11 NSL statutory regime.[25]

The court decisions are significant because in times of war the judiciary usually upholds legislation safeguarding public safety even though it diminishes personal liberty. Still, in *Doe v. Ashcroft* (2004) (*Doe* I),[26] Section 505, and its amendment to Section 2709 of the Electronic Communication Privacy Act, was struck down by a New York federal district court judge after an NSL was issued to an ISP provider that was asked to deliver

Internet records of a customer. The ISP provider was also gagged in order to stop the information request's disclosure. District Judge Victor Marreo held that the NSL law violated the Fourth Amendment's ban on unreasonable searches because it was coercive and lacked judicial oversight. Also, the gag order ran afoul of the First Amendment's ban on prior restraints, or censorship. Shortly thereafter in *Doe v. Gonzalez* (2005) (*Doe* II),[27] a case involving an NSL demand to turn over patron records from a library consortium, a Connecticut federal district court judge issued an injunction preventing the FBI from enforcing an NSL gag order because it violated the First Amendment's free speech clause on similar grounds.

In response and while both *Doe* cases were on appeal,[28] Congress passed the Reauthorization statutes. Both laws add several new procedures and controls designed to curb agency power, including giving NSL recipients the right to challenge both the underlying request and any accompanying gag order in federal court. Also, NSL recipients were given the explicit right to consult an attorney, presumably as part of initiating such challenges. At the same time, however, the government was given the right to enforce and penalize through a contempt decree NSL recipients who failed to comply with demands to produce records. Furthermore, gag orders are still allowed, but they are valid only if the agency certifies through a high-ranking official (generally a department head or deputy) that disclosure might: (1) endanger the physical safety of individuals or national security; or (2) interfere with diplomatic relations; or (3) interfere with a criminal, counterterrorism, or counterintelligence investigation. In certain instances, unless agencies display bad faith, an agency gag order decision cannot be reversed by a court because it is legally deemed conclusive. If there is disclosure, recipients must identify who was told (except for attorneys). Regarding political oversight, the Reauthorization statutes require that agencies report to relevant congressional intelligence, judiciary, and banking committees about NSL usage. Also, it empowers the Department of Justice's inspector general to conduct NSL audits on a regular basis. Unless they deliver "electronic communication services" to patrons (e.g., email), libraries are generally not subject to NSLs.[29]

Whether the Reauthorization statutes will survive additional court challenges remains an open question in light of subsequent *Doe* litigation and continuing political oversight. In *Doe v. Gonzalez* (2007)[30] (*Doe* III), the same New York district court that invalidated the USA Patriot Act's Section 505 ruled that the revised certification and gag order procedures under the Reauthorization statutes were unconstitutional violations of the First Amendment free speech and separation of powers' principles. As in *Doe* I, Judge Marreo reasoned that they manipulated the content of speech and imposed government censorship. But he also added that Congress gave too much discretion to FBI officials which, in turn, created a licensing system that allowed them to pick and choose what speech should be heard. The legislative decision to change the law affecting basic constitutional principles, furthermore, upset the balance of power between Congress and the courts because courts, and not Congress, are entrusted with the authority to make constitutional judgments.[31] Also, two reports filed by the DOJ's inspector general (IG) (in accordance with the Reauthorization statutes) relating to how the FBI and other agencies have utilized NSLs clouds the issue further.[32] The IG reports illustrate that agencies routinely employ NSLs to capture a wide array of private information and increasingly the government is misapplying the law to use them, often against U.S. citizens.

The 2007 report covered NSL agency operations from 2003 to 2005. It found that 74 percent of NSLs involved counterterrorism investigations, whereas the balance of NSL usage pertained to counterintelligence operations.[33] The 2008 report analyzed NSL activity for 2006. For that year, NSLs were aimed at gaining telephone or email information, the same pattern found in earlier years.[34] Still, a wide scope of financial information, amassed from banks, credit card companies, finance companies and consumer credit agencies, often were targets for disclosure.[35] Nearly 60 percent of the 2006 NSL requests involved investigations of U.S. persons, a finding mirroring the sharp increase that was reported from 2003 (39 percent) to 2005 (53 percent).[36] Not surprisingly, the rate of NSLs directed at non-U.S. persons, who presumably represent a more significant international terrorist threat, fell from 2003 (10,232) to 2004 (8, 494) after leveling off to about the same rate in 2005 (8,536) and 2006 (8,605).[37]

Although it was conceded that NSLs were an important law enforcement tool in foreign intelligence cases, the IG's 2007 report documents multiple intelligence violations by the FBI in using NSLs between 2003 and 2005. In part, the FBI was struggling to manage the way it collected NSL statistics and that caused the agency to fail to record or underreport its misuse of NSLs. In addition, among other things NSLs were not issued under proper legal authority; in numerous instances the FBI sought information that it was not legally entitled to get; in over 700 instances the agency issued "exigent letters," or expedited information requests that are supposed to be distributed on an emergency basis before an NSL is used, in violation of its own guidelines and policy; and, the FBI's Counterterrorism Division approved over 300 NSLs without proper authorization.[38] Similarly, in its follow-up 2008 report, at least 84 possible NSL intelligence violations were recorded for 2006.[39] In sum, the IG reports illustrate that the widespread usage of NSLs after September 11 has caused multiple logistical, legal, and political difficulties that have renewed calls for further reform.

Conclusion

The problems with NSLs are registered by additional litigation and congressional hearings debating their legal and political feasibility. As manifested by the *Doe* cases and the determined efforts by civil libertarians to reform NSLs through the courts, the constitutionality of NSLs in the post–9/11 legal era remains unclear.[40] Two bills from the House of Representatives (HR 3189) and Senate (S. 2088) introduced in 2007 are mindful of the *Doe* rulings and offer the prospect of reform. The proposals, in new legislation styled "The National Security Letters Reform Act of 2007," indicate that Congress may limit NSLs by returning to pre–9/11 specificity legal requirements for NSL issuance, tightening the circumstances under which gag orders are placed, and guarantying judicial review of NSL requests. Other ideas expressed in the proposals include requiring the destruction of information that is obtained illegally, creating a right to file a civil lawsuit if there is abuse of NSLs, and devising new agency procedures to record and track the distribution of NSLs.[41] Regardless of whether NSLs will be reformed in the future, NSLs are not likely to disappear in the post–9/11 legal regime as a controversial political issue because the FBI and other agencies highly value their use in fighting terrorists and perceived enemies of the state in a rapidly changing global theater dominated by the Internet, satellite, and wireless communications.

Notes

1. A reproduction of the "national security letter" that is the basis of the hypothetical is found at American Civil Liberties Union, "Safe and Free, National Security Letters, Librarians' NSL Challenge," at http://www.aclu.org/safefree/nationalsecurityletters/25680res20060526.html (accessed April 30, 2009).
2. Christopher P. Banks, "Protecting (or Destroying) Freedom through Law: The USA Patriot Act's Constitutional Implications," in *American National Security and Civil Liberties in an Age of Terrorism*, ed. David B. Cohen and John W. Wells (New York: Palgrave MacMillan, 2004), 29. See also USA Patriot Act, Pub. L. No. 107-56, 115 Stat. 272 (2001).
3. U.S. Department of Justice, Office of the Inspector General, *Review of the FBI's Use of National Security Letters: Assessment of Corrective Actions and Examination of NSL Usage in 2006* (Washington, DC: U.S. Department of Justice, 2008), 9; Laura K. Donohue, *The Cost of Counterterrorism: Power, Politics, and Liberty* (New York: Cambridge University Press, 2008), 237.
4. U.S. Department of Justice, Office of the Inspector General, *Review of the FBI's Use of National Security Letters*, 111, 112.
5. Donahue, *The Cost of Counterterrorism*, 237.

6. Ibid., 239, citing *Doe v. Ashcroft*, 334 F. Supp. 2d 471 (SDNY, 2004), 502.
7. Courts generally rule that subpoenas issued by governmental agencies are constitutional if they are reasonable in scope and application. The information sought must be substantially connected to the agency's regulatory interest and be deemed an appropriate subject of inquiry. They are subject to judicial review, before or after their issuance, under the Fourth Amendment's probable cause standard, which makes them different from national security letters. Donahue, *The Cost of Counterterrorism*, 236. See also David M. O'Brien, *Constitutional Law and Politics: Civil Rights and Liberties (Volume Two)*, 7th ed. (New York: W.W. Norton & Company, 2008), 939–942.
8. Michael J. Woods, "Counterintelligence and Access to Transactional Records: A Practical History of USA Patriot Act Section 215," *National Security Law and Policy* 1 (2005): 37, 39–41. FISA was in part a response to domestic terrorism, and with it Congress created a special "secret" court whose purpose is to review and approve government wiretap applications in foreign intelligence investigations. Banks, "Protecting (or Destroying) Freedom through Law," 34–35.
9. Woods, "Counterintelligence and Access to Transactional Records," 43. See *Right to Financial Privacy Act of 1978*, 12 U.S.C. Sections 3401–3422 (2000).
10. Charles Doyle, *National Security Letters in Foreign Intelligence Investigations: Legal Background and Recent Amendments (Updated March 28, 2008)* (Washington, DC: Congressional Research Service, 2008), 2–3; Woods, "Counterintelligence and Access to Transactional Records," 46–47. See *Electronic Communication Privacy Act of 1986*, 18 U.S.C. Section 2709 (2000).
11. Woods, "Counterintelligence and Access to Transactional Records," 49. See *Fair Credit Reporting Act of 1970*, 15 U.S.C. Section 1681 (2000).
12. Doyle, *National Security Letters in Foreign Intelligence Investigations*, 3–4. See *National Security Act of 1947*, 50 U.S.C. Section 402 (2000).
13. Pen registers capture outgoing numbers in telephone calls via a wiretap, and trap and traces record incoming call numbers. Woods, "Counterintelligence and Access to Transactional Records," 47, note 64. *See Foreign Intelligence Surveillance Act of 1978*, 50 U.S.C. Sections 1801–1811 (2000).
14. Woods, "Counterintelligence and Access to Transactional Records," 52.
15. Banks, "Protecting (or Destroying) Freedom through Law," 50–55.
16. Woods, "Counterintelligence and Access to Transactional Records," 5.
17. *USA Patriot Act*, Section 505.
18. Donahue, *The Cost of Counterterrorism*, 236–237.
19. Doyle, *National Security Letters in Foreign Intelligence Investigations*, 4–5.
20. Woods, "Counterintelligence and Access to Transactional Records," 5; Donahue, *The Cost of Counterterrorism*, 241.
21. Doyle, *National Security Letters in Foreign Intelligence Investigations*, 5–6 (discussing Section 358(g) of USA Patriot Act, amending the Fair Credit Reporting Act).
22. Doyle, *National Security Letters in Foreign Intelligence Investigations*, 6, note 30; Donahue, *The Cost of Counterterrorism*, 241. See *Intelligence*

Authorization Act for Fiscal Year 2004, P.L. 108–177, Section 374, 117 Stat. 2628 (2004).

23. U.S. Department of Justice, Office of the Inspector General, *Review of the FBI's Use of National Security Letters*, 9. See also Donahue, *The Cost of Counterterrorism*, 236.

24. Donahue, *The Cost of Counterterrorism*, 223, lists the following as examples: the NSA's Operation SHAMROCK and Project MINARET; the CIA's Operation CHAOS; and the Army's Operation CONUS. See also David Coleand James X. Dempsey, *Terrorism and the Constitution: Sacrificing Civil Liberties in the Name of National Security* (New York: The New Press, 2002).

25. Brian T. Yeh and Charles Doyle, *USA Patriot Improvement and Reauthorization Act of 2005: A Legal Analysis (Updated December 21, 2006)* (Washington, DC: Congressional Research Service, 2006). See also *USA Patriot Act Improvement and Reauthorization Act of 2005*, P.L. 109–177, 120 Stat. 192 (2006) and *USA Patriot Act Additional Reauthorizing Amendments Act of 2006*, P.L. 109–178, 120 Stat. 278 (2006).

26. *Doe v. Ashcroft*, 334 F. Supp.2d 471 (SDNY 2004).

27. *Doe v. Gonzalez*, 334 F. Supp.2d 66 (D. Conn. 2005).

28. The U.S. Court of Appeals for the Second Circuit, in *Doe v. Gonzales*, 449 F.3d 415 (2d Cir. 2006), vacated the part of the New York district court's *Doe* opinion (*Doe* I, 334 F. Supp. 2d 471) relating to the Fourth Amendment because of the changes Congress made in the 2005 Reauthorization Act (allowing for judicial challenge to NSLs); but the First Amendment gag order issue remained alive, and the appeals court sent the case back to the New York district court to decide whether the Reauthorization Act fixed the problems with the gag order. Also, after a procedural ruling by Supreme Court Justice Ruth Bader Ginsburg (sitting as a Circuit Justice) relating to the validity of the district court's injunction (*Doe v. Gonzalez*, 127 U.S. 1 [2005]), in *Doe v. Gonzales*, 449 F.3d 415 (2d Cir. 2006) the Second Circuit mooted the Connecticut district court's ruling (*Doe* II, 334 F. Supp. 2d 66) because the Reauthorization Act's changes allowed for disclosure of the NSL's requests; so the government dropped its appeal of the injunction that stopped its efforts to compel non-disclosure.

29. Doyle, *National Security Letters in Foreign Intelligence Investigations*, 9–14; Yeh and Doyle, *USA Patriot Improvement and Reauthorization Act of 2005*, 10–16.

30. *Doe v. Gonzalez*, 500 F. Supp.2d 379 (SDNY 2007).

31. *Doe v. Gonzalez*, 500 F. Supp.2d 379 (SDNY 2007). The government has filed an appeal that is pending in the Second Circuit.

32. U.S. Department of Justice, Office of the Inspector General. *A Review of the Federal Bureau of Investigation's Use of National Security Letters (March 2007)* (Washington, DC: Department of Justice, 2007); U.S. Department of Justice, Office of the Inspector General, *A Review of the FBI's Use of National Security Letters: Assessment of Corrective Actions and Examination of NSL Usage in 2006 (March 2008)* (Washington, DC: Department of Justice, 2007).

33. U.S. Department of Justice, Office of the Inspector General, *A Review of the Federal Bureau of Investigation's Use of National Security Letters (March 2007)*, 120. "Counterterrorism" investigations apply to efforts stopping terrorist threats to the homeland, whereas "counterintelligence" operations are designed to stop infiltration of government's intelligence programs by those who seek to discover or undermine them. See Mark M. Lowenthal, *Intelligence: From Secrets to Policy*, 2nd ed. (Washington, DC: CQ Press, 2003), 113.

34. U.S. Department of Justice, Office of the Inspector General, *A Review of the FBI's Use of National Security Letters: Assessment of Corrective Actions and Examination of NSL Usage in 2006 (March 2008)* 107; U.S. Department of Justice, Office of the Inspector General, *A Review of the Federal Bureau of Investigation's Use of National Security Letters (March 2007)*, 120.

35. U.S. Department of Justice, Office of the Inspector General, *A Review of the FBI's Use of National Security Letters: Assessment of Corrective Actions and Examination of NSL Usage in 2006 (March 2008)*, 107.

36. U.S. Department of Justice, Office of the Inspector General, *A Review of the FBI's Use of National Security Letters: Assessment of Corrective Actions and Examination of NSL Usage in 2006 (March 2008)*, 111 and 112; see also, U.S. Department of Justice, Office of the Inspector General, *A Review of the Federal Bureau of Investigation's Use of National Security Letters (March 2007)*.

37. U.S. Department of Justice, Office of the Inspector General, *A Review of the FBI's Use of National Security Letters: Assessment of Corrective Actions and Examination of NSL Usage in 2006 (March 2008)*, 111 and 112.

38. U.S. Department of Justice, Office of the Inspector General, *A Review of the Federal Bureau of Investigation's Use of National Security Letters (March 2007)*, 121–124.

39. U.S. Department of Justice, Office of the Inspector General. *A Review of the FBI's Use of National Security Letters: Assessment of Corrective Actions and Examination of NSL Usage in 2006 (March 2008)*, 11.

40. See House Subcommittee on the Constitution, Civil Rights, and Civil Liberties, "Testimony of Jameel Jaffer, Director of the National Security Project of the American Civil Liberties Union Foundation before the House Subcommittee on the Constitution, Civil Rights, and Civil Liberties (April 15, 2008)," in *Oversight Hearing on H.R. 3189, the National Security Letters Reform Act of 2007*, 110 Cong., 2nd sess., 2008 (accessed June 2, 2008) (outlining the litigation efforts by the American Civil Liberties Union to reform NSLs).

41. A summary of each bill is found at the online Library of Congress search engine under "Bills, Resolutions," at http://thomas.loc.gov (accessed June 2, 2008). See also Carrie Johnson, "Lawmakers Want FBI Access to Data Curbed," *Washington Post*, April 15, 2008, A04.

7

National Security Entry and Exit Registration

*Moushumi M. Khan and Kim M. Williams**

> In this new war, our enemy's platoons infiltrate our borders, quietly
> blending in with visiting tourists, students and workers. They move
> unnoticed through our cities, neighborhoods and public spaces.... Their
> tactics rely on evading recognition at the border and escaping detection
> within the United States.
>
> *Attorney General John Ashcroft announcing NSEERS on June 6, 2002*

The attacks of September 11, 2001 led to a change in the public's percep-
tion and experience of border security and immigration policy. Whether
in the form of actual legislation modifying existing immigration policies,
delays in citizenship processing, or increased scrutiny of those entering or
exiting the United States, many people—citizens and noncitizens, native
and foreign born—are affected in varying degrees by changes in our immigration regulations. Immigration enforcement is now treated by the government as an integral part of national security policy. The challenge is to
balance national security concerns with the need for an open society that
also protects economic and political interests. This chapter advances recommendations about how to strike a more appropriate balance and argues that
abolishing "Special Registration" is an important step in this direction.

---

* **Moushumi M. Khan** is a civil rights attorney and the founding President of the Muslim
Bar Association of New York.

Kim M. Williams is Associate Professor of Public Policy at the John F. Kennedy School
of Government at Harvard University. Her first book was *Mark One or More: Civil Rights
in Multiracial America* (2006), and she is currently at work on her second book, *Transition:
The Politics of Racial and Ethnic Change in Urban America.*

Changes to Immigration Procedures after 9/11

The National Security Entry/Exit Registration System (NSEERS) or "Special Registration" was one of the major overhauls to the U.S. immigration system after 9/11 ostensibly instituted to improve our national security. The Department of Justice, through Attorney General John Ashcroft, issued a notice on August 12, 2002 calling for the registration of certain male nonimmigrant aliens from designated countries.[1] This notice required these men to appear before and answer questions from the Department of Homeland Security (DHS). While the domestic components of NSEERS were suspended in December 2003, it is long overdue for the entire program to be abolished.

Special Registration was initiated by the Department of Justice and continued by the DHS in compliance with Congress's requirement of a comprehensive entry-exit program for all visitors to the United States. Among other things, this involved the registration of certain non-U.S. citizens or immigrants entering or living in the United States as outlined in the USA Patriot Act. The USA Patriot Act required the Immigration and Naturalization Service (INS) to track within three years all of the estimated 35 million foreign visitors to the United States. Some requirements, such as that by 2004 all official travel documents used to enter the United States contain biometric identifiers (like fingerprints) in addition to photo identification, still have not been strictly enforced. U.S. law has previously required aliens who reside in the country for more than 30 days to be registered and fingerprinted, but this requirement had been suspended for decades for most visiting foreign nationals. As things currently stand, however, the law allows the attorney general to require any number of nationals from any country to follow special registration procedures when he or she determines that it is in the national security or law enforcement interests of the country.

Legal Authority for NSEERS

The NSEERS program reinstated these earlier rules with the addition of exit controls and was presented as the first step toward implementing an entry/exit program that would cover all visitors to the United States. The primary rationale was that the attacks of 9/11 demonstrated the need to more closely monitor certain nonimmigrant aliens. The legal authority for this program came from section 265 (b) of the Immigration and Nationality Act, as amended, 8 U.S.C. 1305 (b); and under section 263 (a) of the Immigration and Nationality Act, 8 U.S.C. 1303 (a). It required that certain male citizens and nationals of 25 different countries who reside temporarily in the

United States to register in person with immigration authorities. Special Registration applies only to nonimmigrants in the United States or to holders of temporary visas, such as those held by all of the 9/11 hijackers. It does not apply to U.S. citizens, naturalized citizens, lawful permanent residents ("green card" holders), those with certain diplomatic passports, refugees, asylum seekers, or asylees. Ironically, those who entered the United States without being inspected by immigration authorities, that is, those who entered without proper documents or using false documents ("entry without inspection") were not required to register. Thus the argument that NSEERS would be a useful tool to capture terrorists or protect the homeland by verifying everyone's status seemed unrealistic from its inception.

NSEERS Procedure

There are three elements to NSEERS: (1) port of entry registration for those entering or (2) leaving the country and (3) domestic registration for some already here. Attorney General Ashcroft announced that the first phase of the NSEERS program would be implemented by the INS[2] at selected ports of entry around the United States starting September 11, 2002. After an initial 20-day period for testing and evaluating the system in these ports, all remaining ports of entry including by land, sea, and air would have the new system in place on October 1, 2002.[3]

The first two elements, consisting of entry and exit controls, were instituted without much fanfare on September 11, 2002. Entry controls include fingerprinting and photographing at the border and exit controls involve the deportation of illegal aliens. These controls apply to both men and women regardless of age or country of origin. The fingerprints of a small percentage of entering foreign visitors would be matched against a database of known criminals and a database of known terrorists. It was stated that the initial list of countries whose visitors required registration was selected according to intelligence criteria based on patterns of terrorist organizations' activities but that, eventually, virtually all visitors to the United States would have to go through a similar entry/exit process (ibid.).

The third element of NSEERS (referred to as 'Special Registration') caused much outcry. It involved the periodic registration of nonimmigrant male aliens above the age of 16 who were nationals or citizens of 25 specially designated countries (see later) who entered the country on or before September 20, 2002 and who would be in the country for more than 30 days. Even if one was a citizen of a nonspecially designated country such as Canada but also the national or a dual citizen of one of the designated countries, registration was mandatory. Such registrants were required to come to a specified INS[4] office to be photographed (no smiling allowed), finger-printed, and interviewed under oath within the scheduled time period. At the interview registrants were also required to provide travel documents, including passport and I-94 card, proof of residence such as a rental agreement, proof of employment, and proof of enrollment at an educational institution. The fingerprints would be matched against a database of known criminals and one of known terrorists. Some registrants were asked for copies of their credit cards while others were questioned about their political or religious beliefs. Registrants were allowed to bring attorneys or interpreters for the initial interview but not for the secondary screening, although not everyone was aware of this facility. Nor were some aware of the risks of deportation, such as student visa holders who did not have the requisite number of credits to demonstrate full-time enrollment, or those who had been arrested and released but whose fingerprints appeared on a criminal database.

If the nonimmigrant registrant planned to remain in the United States for more than 1 additional year, he was required to report back to the specified INS office within 10 days of the anniversary of the date on which he first registered. When leaving the United States, the registrant must appear in person before an INS inspecting officer at one of the designated ports and leave the country from that port on the same day. If a nonimmigrant who is required to register does not do so, he may be considered out-of-status and deportable. He may also be subject to arrest, detention, fines, and/or removal from the United States. Any future application for an immigration benefit such as U.S. citizenship may also be adversely impacted. If the registrant does not properly exit through a designated port, any future attempts to reenter the United States may be affected.[5] These draconian provisions do little to secure our borders, but have done immeasurable damage to our global image as a free and fair nation. They have deterred many people from visiting the United States and frustrated countless others already in the country. Uneven and incompetent application by the government compounds the problem.

Special Call-in Registration was set up with a series of rolling deadlines. The first registrations began on November 15, 2002 for visitors who were nationals or citizens of Group 1 countries Iran, Iraq, Libya, Sudan, and Syria, countries that the State Department had designated as sponsors of terrorism.[6] The second Call-in, Group 2, included visitors from Algeria, Bahrain, Eritrea, Lebanon, Morocco, North Korea, Oman, Qatar, Somalia, Tunisia, United Arab Emirates, and Yemen.[7] The third group originally consisted of men from Armenia, Saudi Arabia, and Pakistan,[8] until it was revised on December 18, 2002 to exclude Armenia. Despite Pakistan's role as a partner in the War on Terror and its strong criticism of the new registration rules, it was unsuccessful in its attempts to be removed from the list of countries whose nationals were required to register. Armenia was the only country successful in removing its name from the call-in Special Registration.[9] The fourth and last group of countries whose male nationals were subject to Special Registration included Bangladesh, Egypt, Indonesia, Jordan, and Kuwait. Men from these countries were required to register between February 24, 2003 and March 28, 2003.[10]

Special Registration and Terrorism

In reality this "simple monitoring" system turned out to be anything but simple. Targeting men from mostly Muslim countries and, no less, using inconsistent procedural application and limited public outreach, Special Registration did not lead to the arrest of a single terrorist. Immigrant rights groups also complained that many of those affected did not learn of the registration requirements until the last minute. The government's outreach was especially misguided in the beginning and resulted in incorrect or insufficient information about the process being sent to the affected communities. While information about the registration process increased as more groups were added—and extended grace periods were granted for those who had not registered during their slotted times—staff shortages and inadequate training led to many improper registrations. Moreover, as mentioned earlier, while the policy originated with the Department of Justice, the INS was charged with implementation. It soon became clear that INS had not been given enough time or resources to carry out its duty effectively. What is more, in the middle of the Group 4 registrations INS was subsumed under the DHS, of which Immigration and Customs Enforcement (ICE) became a part. With the December 16 registration deadline approaching, immigration offices were ill-equipped to handle the flood of registrants or the outrage it generated.[11]

Not surprisingly, after the fourth group of registrations ended, no new groups of countries were selected for call-in registration. All 25 countries whose nationals were required to register were predominantly Muslim or Arab, with the exception of North Korea. Since the United States does not have full diplomatic relations with North Korea, there were not many North Korean registrants. India, a country with one of the world's largest Muslim populations, was not included. Again, only one non-Muslim majority country, Armenia, was able to successfully petition off the list of original registering countries. It is little wonder that Muslims and Arabs saw Special Registration as a policy directly targeted toward their men. Yet Jorge Martinez, a spokesman for the U.S. Justice Department that oversaw the INS until it came under the DHS, is quoted as saying that "the criteria (for registration selection) [are] solely based on intelligence-based matters and national security concerns. It has nothing to do with a person's race, a person's religion or a person's ethnicity."[12]

Despite this strained distinction, by effectively registering *only* Arab or Muslim men, our government seems to equate being Muslim or Arab with being a national security threat. At a time when we need partners in the legitimate fight against terrorism it is counterproductive to alienate this community and to confirm their worst fears that the War on Terror is actually a War on Islam. Special Registration mocks the values of equality and due process that the world used to admire in us.

Effects of Special Registration

On May 20, 2003, the New York Immigration Coalition reported that the Bureau of Citizenship and Immigration Services had registered 82,581 people under the program.[13] Moreover, 13,153 "Notices to Appear" had been issued (this is a "charging document" placing an individual in immigration removal proceedings) and 2,761 men had been detained overall, while 158 were still detained at that time. Only two people had been deported by that date. By the end of the domestic component of Special Registration, which officially concluded later that year, in December 2003, 177,260 men and boys had been registered and 13,799 had been put into deportation proceedings.

When the call-in registrations first began, there was little public awareness or opposition except by some immigrant or Muslim rights activists who requested that the attorney general suspend the program pending a thorough review. Later, in December 2002, Senators Russ Feingold (D-Wisc.), Edward Kennedy (D-Mass.), and Rep. John Conyers (D-Mich.) wrote to Attorney General Ashcroft to protest Special Registration and its implementation. Among other things, they questioned whether "the INS's implementation of NSEERS has struck the proper balance between securing our borders on the one hand and respecting the civil liberties of foreign students, businesspeople, and visitors who have come to our nation legally on the other." The congressmen further pressed the attorney general to "reassure Congress and the American people that the special registration program was not a detention program falling short of widespread internment of Arabs and Muslims."

On December 24, 2002 a coalition including the American-Arab Anti-Discrimination Committee, the Alliance of Iranian Americans, Council on American-Islamic-Relations, and the National Council of Pakistani Americans filed a class-action lawsuit against Attorney General John Ashcroft and the Immigration and Naturalization Service in the United States District Court for the Central District of California, asserting that the INS unlawfully arrested large numbers of people from December 16 through December 18, 2002 in Los Angeles as they came forward to voluntarily comply with the new special registration requirements. The lawsuit sought an immediate injunction to prevent similar detentions in the upcoming registrations.[14] Some in the community felt that Special Registration was less about catching terrorists—as it was highly unlikely that terrorists would show up to register—and more about deporting Muslim and Arab immigrants and intimidating Muslim and Arab citizens. Others saw the suspension of the program as a sign of its ineffectiveness. For example, in October 2003, the American Civil Liberties Union complained in a letter to immigration authorities that they "were not aware of any meaningful efforts undertaken by the Department of Homeland Security to publicize the impending deadlines or any of the other requirements that may be applicable to people who registered."[15]

Regardless of the registration program's intentions, it certainly did create a high level of fear. In one section of Brooklyn, New York—Midwood or "little Pakistan," which had been heavily populated with Pakistani immigrants—20,000 men left the country shortly after NSEERS was instituted.[16] During this time, thousands of Arabs and Muslims went back to their countries of origin or fled to Canada. Again, implementation of NSEERS made a bad situation worse. In some cases, registrants were turned away by one immigration official only to be told by another that they needed to register. Others were improperly registered when they did not even need to register. These types of mistakes had potentially devastating consequences for future immigration relief as the failure to register could lead to harsh penalties. Most devastating was the loss of trust between these communities and immigration and law enforcement. For the first time, the FBI has the authority to detain people solely on the basis of immigration violations.

Since immigration law is considered civil law, not criminal law, many of the legal protections of a criminal defendant do not exist for noncitizens during FBI interrogations. For example, there is no Sixth Amendment right to counsel, no Fifth Amendment protection against self-incrimination (no Miranda right to remain silent), and no Fourth Amendment freedom from unreasonable searches and seizures. At the same time, however, while the vast majority of immigration violations across the board are treated as civil violations, failure to abide by NSEERS is an exception in this regard. It is considered to be a criminal offense, despite its civil nature.

Suspension of Domestic Component to Special Registration/U.S. VISIT

Just as the second round of registrations was to begin, the DHS suspended the domestic component of Special Registration on December 1, 2003. All other requirements are still in effect. NSEERS registration is still required at ports of entry into the United States and the government can require that people subject to NSEERS appear for additional registration interviews on a case-by-case basis. Thousands still face deportation as a consequence of their registration. It was thought that the U.S. Visitor and Immigrant Status Indicator Technology (U.S. VISIT), which was instituted in January 2005 to use photographs and fingerprints to log entries and exits at major U.S. airports and seaports, would meet the national security needs that Special Registration was previously meant to address. We are left to wonder why any portions of Special Registration remain—other than to harass Arabs and Muslims.

Aside from the aforementioned problems with this policy, such as inefficiency, counterproductivity and inconsistency, it also represents a drag on the U.S. economy. Since 9/11 and after the introduction of new stricter immigration standards, foreign students are being solicited to study elsewhere; tourists are vacationing in other destinations; new businesses have chosen to list with the London Stock Exchange rather than deal with U.S. immigration hassles while others have reduced their operations here. The United States is no longer the preferred choice for international conferences or economic migrants. Indeed, data show a marked decline in the number of foreign students, tourists, and members of the international business or scholarship community, among others, traveling to the United States.[17] What is more, these regulations have not only affected those who travel to the United States; they have also damaged our image domestically among the Arab, South Asian, and Muslim American populations as well as internationally in Arab, Muslim, and other affected regions—the very communities we need as allies to protect our national security.

Perhaps in reaction to polling that shows how American treatment of Arab and Muslim immigrants has in some Muslim countries surpassed Iraq and Palestine as reasons for anti-Americanism, one of the first actions of the newly created DHS was to suspend some aspects of the NSEERS program. Despite statements by Asa Hutchinson, undersecretary for Border and Transportation Security, to an Arab-American audience in mid-2004 that "[i]t is our hope to completely end this special registration program because our long term goal is to treat everybody the same way and not based upon where you come from,"[18] the aftermath of the original NSEERS registration remains in effect. Thousands are in various stages of removal proceedings. Expanded security checks have caused year-long delays in the U.S. citizenship process, despite Federal law requiring that U.S. Citizenship and Immigration Service (USCIS) grant or deny citizenship within 120 days of an applicant's citizenship interview and submission of the required documentation and fingerprints. This also impedes the policy goal of the USCIS of processing applications within six months from the time of filing. These background checks for a "National Security Clearance" include "name checks" against FBI records, in addition to the previous standard background check—which can result in backlogs. NSEERS instigated the backlog when DHS submitted 2.7 million names for checks at one time when the program began five years ago.[19] These delays may cause restrictions in travel, work, or in receiving certain benefits. Airport officials frequently stop passengers with "Muslim names" and check them against various watch lists. The national security goal of these checks is ironically circumvented by the delay in identifying potential threats. The Justice Department inspector general's own report concludes that the FBI system for checking the names of immigration applicants suffers from "serious deficiencies" that have produced overwhelming backlogs and questions about the reliability of the information (ibid.).

Recommendations

The most recent White House immigration reform plan in April 2007 did not seek to abolish Special Registration completely, in spite of the fact that the NSEERS program has not adequately met any of its goals. The program has been poorly managed, ineffective, and discriminatory. Although no terrorists were apprehended under the program, it managed nonetheless to erode trust between law enforcement and potential allies, leaving the United States with fewer partners with which to fight terrorism. The government has acknowledged as much by suspending parts of the ill-conceived policy. However, more needs to be done. The DHS should rescind NSEERS in its entirety, terminate removal proceedings against those who complied with the program's registration requirements, and cease proceedings against those whose only violation is their failure to have registered. Adequate mechanisms elsewhere exist within the legal infrastructure to prosecute and/or deport those individuals found to be guilty of terrorism or affiliation with terrorist organizations. Other measures should be dealt with under future comprehensive immigration reform, not via arbitrary profiling based on country of origin.

If the NSEERS program is not abolished, at the very least its staffing should be improved. (This seems improbable, however, since the current immigration system clearly does not have the resources to comply adequately with the program.) More likely, if the program limps along underfunded, then at the least, the FBI database used for checking names for NSEERS and other purposes should be overhauled. When running the name of the applicant against a list of persons with a criminal history, "hits" are often produced because the names have a similar spelling or sound match. Each "hit" must then be pulled up and examined to determine whether the applicant matches the individual with a criminal record. The burden of proof is on the applicant or passenger to establish that he is not the same individual as the one named on the list. There is still no mechanism by which an innocent person can be removed permanently from these lists; so they must provide documentation of their identity each time it is questioned. Again, the best decision would be to abolish the program altogether. Our national security and our international image depend on making the right decisions about immigration. NSEERS neither makes us more secure nor honors our highest ideals.

Notes

1. 67 Federal Register 70526, November 22, 2002.
2. INS was later subsumed within the DHS Bureau of Citizenship and Immigration Services on March 1, 2003.
3. Department of Justice Press Release, August 12, 2002.
4. It was then DHS Bureau of Immigration and Customs Enforcement.
5. Notice For Special Call-In Registration for Certain Immigrants—8 CFR Section 264.
6. Call-In Group 1, Federal Register Notice—November 6, 2002.
7. Call-In Group 2, Federal Register Notice—November 22, 2002.
8. Call-In Group 3, Federal Register Notice—December 17, 2002.
9. Federal Register, December 18, 2002.
10. Call-In Group 4, Federal Register Notice—January 16, 2003.
11. For instance, during the first group registration period it was estimated that 700 men were detained in Los Angeles alone. "Threats and Responses: The Dragnet; U.S. Starts Freeing Foreigners Detained in Anti-Terror Sweep," *New York Times*, December 20, 2002.
12. "Fear and Loathing of U.S. Immigrant Rule," BBC World Service, January 27, 2003.
13. This is data as of May 11, 2003.
14. Complaint for Injunctive Relief SACV021200 AHS Anx.
15. ACLU Immigrant Rights Project letter dated October 30, 2003 by Lucas Guttentag.
16. "Nabe Shrinks in Terror: Scared Pakistanis Leave to Avoid Feds," *New York Daily News*, June 29, 2003.
17. Statement of Bo Cooper, Former General Counsel, Immigration and Naturalization Service on behalf of Global Personnel Alliance, Hearing before the Senate Committee on the Judiciary, Subcommittee on Immigration, Border Security and Citizenship on "U.S. Visa Policy: Competition for International Scholars, Scientists and Skilled Workers," Thursday, August 31, 2006.
18. American-Arab Anti-Discrimination Committee, 21st National Convention, June 11, 2004, Washington, DC.
19. "Audit Faults Delays in Immigrant Name Checks. FBI System Said to Have 'Deficiencies,'" *Washington Post*, June 10, 2008.

8

Civil Litigation against Terrorists and Terrorist States

John C. Blakeman[*]

The aftermath of the September 11, 2001 terrorist attacks have seen a range of policy responses to deterring future attacks and compensating victims of terrorism. The U.S. military is engaged in a multifront war combating terrorists overseas, government agencies are pursuing various domestic policies to forestall another attack, and congress, the president, and federal courts are likewise bound together in an ongoing dialogue about expedient, legal, and constitutional approaches to the War on Terror. One seemingly unlikely policy response has been the use of civil litigation to hold terrorists and states that sponsor terrorism accountable. Relying on tort law principles such as wrongful death, personal injury, and negligence, from both American and international law, victims of terrorism have turned to the American federal court system to establish that those linked with terrorism, from the individuals who carry out terrorist acts, to the foreign states that financially sponsor or otherwise facilitate terrorism, are financially liable for their injurious activities. Indeed, over 95 tort cases have arisen out of the September 11 attacks, and slightly over half have been settled.[1] The vast majority of cases are typical wrongful death lawsuits that target American corporations for not taking steps to protect the 9/11 victims from a terrorist attack. However, a small number of cases name as defendants foreign governments accused of sponsoring

[*]**John C. Blakeman** is Associate Professor of Political Science at the University of Wisconsin–Stevens Point.

terrorist acts, terrorist groups such as al Qaeda, and international banks and other companies that may have helped finance the acts of terrorist groups. For example, in *Burnett et al. v. Al Baraka Investment and Development Corporation et al.* over 2,000 victims of the 9/11 attacks sued foreign governments, corporations, terrorist groups, and individuals, including several high-ranking officials and princes in the Saudi Arabian government, alleging that all of the defendants aided and provided material support to the 9/11 hijackers.[2] Although many of the lawsuits against American corporations have been settled out of court, the cases against foreign government, officials, and others continue to slowly wind their way through the federal judicial process. Many 9/11 cases have been consolidated into one large class-action lawsuit,[3] and at least one 9/11 lawsuit has been decided by default—with a multimillion dollar damage award to the plaintiff, because none of the named defendants, including the states of Afghanistan and Iraq, responded to the lawsuit.[4]

To be sure, civil litigation seems an unlikely way to respond to violent, murderous, terrorist acts, since the primary goal of tort law is to restore injured plaintiffs by making defendants liable for their injuries pay monetary compensation. Whereas federal criminal and military commission prosecutions seek to convict and punish terrorists, civil litigation relies on noncriminal international and federal law to hold states and their officials financially liable for their terrorist activities. Instead of the government bringing all of its prosecutorial resources to bear against captured terrorists, private plaintiffs and trial lawyers initiate tort litigation. Since civil lawsuits are plaintiff driven, government agencies may have little control over how civil litigation in the war against terrorism develops since the plaintiffs amass evidence, structure legal arguments, and try to convince a civil jury or judge that the defendants violated the law. For one scholar, it is fair to ask whether civil litigation is "an appropriate normative tool for combating state-sponsored terrorists," and whether "unleashing lawyers, lawsuits, procedural rules, delay, and other characteristics of American-style tort litigation on foreign state defendants" may unduly interfere with the ability of the United States to wage an aggressive, and successful, global campaign against terrorism.[5] Washington think-tanks have been critical of tort litigation too, noting that that such cases intrude into executive branch policy-making in foreign affairs and may lead to a decrease in direct foreign investment in the United States by foreign corporations and governments.[6] A conservative think-tank, the American Enterprise Institute, similarly argues that "individual litigants in individual cases should not be able to use the combination of civil liability rules and the power of the civil courts to interfere with larger national policy."[7]

Tort law may well interfere with the national security powers of the federal government, but for its supporters using tort law to hold terrorists and states accountable has many benefits. The goal of tort law is to restore the injured plaintiff; thus, at a basic level, tort law is used to financially compensate those injured by others, and in the context of terrorism cases victims can seek compensation for their injuries, or the injuries of other victims such as family members. However, the trial process in civil litigation also serves to establish the relevant facts underlying a dispute, with a resulting public record to preserve those facts for the future. Tort litigation therefore can be used for a "detailed determination of the facts and a permanent record of those facts" relevant to incidents of terrorism.[8] By using the fact-finding processes intrinsic to fair civil trials, tort law can serve as a "form of truth commission" that will show the "interweaving of states and terrorist groups," thus exposing publicly and holding accountable foreign governments that sponsor acts of terrorism.[9] For many victims of terrorism, establishing a factual record about who funded and carried out a terrorist act may be as important as getting compensation for the injuries caused by the same act.

In addition to the fact-finding process, tort litigation also imposes financial penalties on those found liable for committing and aiding terrorist acts. Although the threat of paying a financial penalty probably will not deter many ideologically driven terrorists, "it is conceivable that actors who are on the periphery…may be given pause" by the threat of financial liability arising out of tort law.[10] Indeed, as one federal appellate court put it in a terrorism case unrelated to 9/11, "the only way to imperil the flow of money and discourage the financing of terrorist acts is to impose liability on those who knowingly and intentionally supply the funds to the persons who commit the violent acts."[11] American courts are supportive of holding sponsors of terrorism financially accountable. Since 1996, federal judges and juries have awarded over $18 billion dollars in compensatory and punitive damages to victims of terrorism.[12] Since under law federal foreign governments can now be sued for sponsoring terrorist acts, tort law allows injured plaintiffs to go after the "deep pockets" of those governments to recover monetary damage awards large enough to deter terrorist activity in the future. However, as discussed later, when successful plaintiffs attempt to collect damage awards, they come into conflict with the national security powers of the federal government.

Finally, tort litigation against terrorist states follows a trend recently noticed by scholars of international relations theory. For some scholars the modern national state is disaggregating as "its component institutions—regulators, judges, and even legislators—are all reaching out beyond national borders in various ways, finding that their once 'domestic' jobs have a growing international dimension."[13] Private actors now supplement state policy-making in the international arena in very important ways.[14]

Scholars are not suggesting that the international state system is breaking apart, only that private actors are now more prominent policy-makers in international relations. In terrorism cases plaintiffs act as prosecutors in the international system and thus supplement official state policy-making on terrorism. Litigation is initiated and funded solely by private individuals, not government actors, and it is the plaintiff's responsibility to amass enough evidence and to present valid legal arguments to a federal court to find the foreign government liable. Even though plaintiffs initiate and prepare the entire case, federal courts provide the forum, and are thus implicated in official policy-making that concerns the activities of foreign sovereigns. Plaintiffs thus act as substate actors who mobilize government resources—the national court system—in holding terrorists accountable.

Terrorism tort cases have a sound jurisdictional basis in federal law that predates 9/11, and Congress has frequently changed the law to make it easier for plaintiffs to sue. In 1992, Congress enacted two statutes that established a legal foundation for Americans to sue officials of foreign governments for causing personal injury in violation of domestic and international law. The Torture Victim Protection Act (TVPA) and Antiterrorism Act (ATA) allow American citizens to start civil lawsuits in federal courts for torture, extrajudicial killing, and acts of international terrorism. However, Congress limited the statutes' reach to individuals who torture and kill with the sanction and support of a sovereign state government; the laws do not cover the conduct of sovereign states themselves. Individuals who commit terrorist acts can be accountable, but not the states that fund, support, and sponsor those acts. Even though an individual defendant may be found liable for committing terrorism-related torts, it is still easy for individual defendants to evade lawsuits and ignore civil judgments against them. States, on the other hand, may find it far more difficult to ignore lawsuits against them as states, and given that many foreign governments maintain significant property and other financial resources in the United States, civil judgments against them can, theoretically, be satisfied through property and asset seizures initiated under federal law and enforced by federal courts.

Suing states that sponsor terrorism is preferable to suing individuals, since states have reachable assets that can be seized to satisfy damage awards owed to plaintiffs. Thus, tort damage awards may financially deter states from supporting terrorist acts. Civil litigation may embarrass states in the international community too, with repercussions in terms of economic sanctions and declines in direct investment. However, international law and U.S. federal law recognize an expansive foreign sovereign immunity. Thus, foreign states are immune from litigation in American federal courts *unless* the state is engaged in certain activities defined by federal law. Immunity is codified in the Foreign Sovereign Immunities Act of 1976, and that statute lists the exceptions to immunity; thus, states can be sued when engaged in commercial activities, when seizing property in violation of international law, and with certain personal death and injury claims (not including terrorism). Historically terrorism was not one of the exceptions under which states could be sued. Therefore, to make federal antiterrorism law more comprehensive, and to address the sovereign immunity surrounding terrorist states, Congress modified the legal framework again with the 1996 Antiterrorism and Effective Death Penalty Act (AEDPA) and the Civil Liability for Acts of State Sponsored Terrorism Act (CLASSTA). The AEDPA removed sovereign immunity for states that sponsor or commit certain kinds of terrorist activities in violation of federal and international law. The statute only applies to victims who are U.S. nationals, and more importantly it waives immunity in a very limited fashion: only those foreign states defined as "terrorist states" by the State Department lose their sovereign immunity. As of mid-year 2008, only 5 states were listed as terrorist states: Cuba, Iran, North Korea, Sudan, and Syria. The CLASSTA created a cause of action for litigants to ensure that federal courts would have subject-matter jurisdiction over state-sponsored terrorism.

It is notable that Congress created the comprehensive framework for terrorism-related tort cases in American courts. Since the framework for such lawsuits was in place before the 9/11 attacks, victims of those attacks could choose to use tort law to seek compensation and to establish a factual record regarding the attacks. In part to deter tort litigation, especially against American corporations, Congress created the September 11 Victim Compensation Fund to financially compensate victims (especially surviving family members) of 9/11. Those who accepted government compensation waived their right to sue.[15]

More importantly, the legal framework for terrorism lawsuits was created by the democratic political process, not by federal judges, and thus has an added legitimacy because it springs from the elected political branches. As one federal court noted, "if we failed to impose liability on aiders and abettors who knowingly and intentionally funded acts of terrorism, we would be thwarting Congress' clearly expressed intent to cut off the flow of money to terrorists at every point along the causal chain of violence."[16] Finally, the creation of the legal framework shows a gradual policy-making approach to terrorism litigation, in that Congress over the course of several years created and modified the legal framework to fit the needs of citizens harmed by the terrorist activities of foreign governments. Indeed, debate in Congress continues on other changes to the framework: since the late 1990s Congress has debated, but not passed, measures to remove all state immunity for terrorism in order to facilitate civil cases against any state, not just those labeled as state sponsors of terrorism by the U.S. State Department.[17]

Terrorism tort cases now have a sound footing in federal law, and plaintiffs have had measured success in winning against foreign governments and terrorist groups.[18] However, just because a plaintiff is successful in establishing the liability of a foreign government for a terrorist act, it does not mean that the plaintiff will collect all or even some of the damages awarded by a court. Even though Congress has created the legal framework to facilitate litigation against terrorist states, it has also empowered the president to block federal courts from seizing the assets of terrorist states in civil cases. Thus, a winning plaintiff may find it very difficult to collect any monetary damages arising from litigation. A good case example concerns a civil lawsuit against the Islamic Republic of Iran. In *Flatow v. Islamic Republic of Iran*, Steven Flatow, a U.S. citizen, successfully sued Iran for sponsoring a terrorist bombing in Israel that killed his daughter Alicia Flatow.[19] Flatow was awarded $22.5 million in compensatory damages and $226 million in punitive damages. Yet, he found it very difficult to collect the money. Iran refused to even respond to the lawsuit and thus was not going to pay any damage awards. To compel Iran to pay, Flatow made several requests that federal judges seize Iranian government-owned properties in the United States, such as the former Iranian embassy and military chancellery in Washington, and other consulates and buildings located elsewhere, and offer them for auction, with the proceeds going to satisfy the *Flatow* judgment.[20] Even though the United States and Iran had not maintained diplomatic relations since the late 1970s, and most of the Iranian properties were not occupied, the Clinton administration blocked the seizures as an interference with the executive branch's broad powers over diplomacy and national security. The Clinton administration also relied upon powers in the Omnibus Consolidated and Emergency Supplemental Appropriations Act of 1999, which allowed the president to exercise control over the assets of terrorist states in the United States on grounds of national security. Under §117 of the statute, the U.S. Treasury could block access to those assets, and President Clinton ordered the Treasury to do so in a comprehensive fashion, thereby blocking access to Iranian, Iraqi, and Cuban assets held in the United States.[21] Importantly, in this case the president's power to control the assets of terrorist states stems directly from a congressional grant of power to the executive branch, meaning that the president has a strong constitutional basis upon which to base his power to interfere with civil litigation.

In response to the president's actions, several senators introduced legislation to help Flatow and similarly situated plaintiffs to collect judgments from foreign states, and their bill amended the Foreign Sovereign Immunities Act to explicitly allow federal courts to attach the diplomatic and consular properties of foreign states to satisfy civil judgments against those states. After extensive discussion between the House, Senate, and president, a different bill was adopted by Congress and signed into law by President Clinton in October 2000. Instead of chipping away at sovereign immunity, Congress and the president approved a completely different strategy in the 2000 Victims of Trafficking and Torture Act: plaintiffs with outstanding judgments against terrorist states such as Iran (and Cuba and Iraq) would be able to collect part of their damage awards directly from the federal government, provided they give up all legal claims associated with those damage awards. In turn, the federal government could choose to seek collection from the defendant states, and the statute mandates that resolution of damage awards should factor into attempts to normalize diplomatic relations with terrorist states. Importantly, the act is limited in scope and applies only to those litigants that received final judgments by July 20, 2000. Thus, only a certain group of successful plaintiffs are entitled, by statute, to compensation.

Interestingly, Congress still included a national security wavier provision in the legislation that allows the president to prevent attachment and seizure of foreign-owned property in the interest of national security, provided the state was on the list of terrorist states maintained by the State Department. Although the statute offers no guidelines concerning how the national security waiver is to be used, Congress, in committee hearings, clearly stated its intent that "it is generally in the national security interest of the United States to make foreign state sponsors of terrorism pay court-awarded damages to American victims." Presidents should block assets "only where U.S. national security interests would be implicated in taking action against particular blocked assets or where alternative recourse—such as vesting and paying those assets—may be preferable to court attachment." Finally, presidents should "find the best way to help victims of terrorism collect on their judgments and make terrorist states pay for their crimes."[22]

In 2002 Congress amended the law yet again with the Terrorism Risk Insurance Act (TRIA) that mandated plaintiffs could have foreign terrorist state assets seized even if those assets are blocked by the executive branch. In a series of cases concerning terrorism litigation against Iran and Iraq, plaintiffs have sought to use the TRIA provisions to satisfy their outstanding cases. However, federal courts have interpreted the statute's provisions restrictively, and have refused to seize state assets that the Bush administration has blocked or placed under its control, also per its powers under several federal statutes.[23] For example, courts refused to seize Iranian funds held in American banks, since those funds were being used by the federal government for the upkeep of Iranian properties in Washington, DC, Chicago, and San Francisco. Similarly, courts refused to seize Iraqi assets to satisfy a terrorism tort claim because President Bush, pursuant to authority given to him by Congress in an Iraq war appropriations act, suspended provisions of American law (such as TRIA, and others) that apply to terrorist states.

The terrorism tort structure that Congress has created contains conflicting goals. On the one hand Congress has facilitated tort cases against terrorist states by creating new substantive federal law to allow civil lawsuits for terrorism, and by removing the sovereign immunity of terrorist states. It encourages private plaintiffs to take the initiative against terrorist states by suing and holding them financially accountable for sponsoring terrorist activity. Indeed, plaintiffs have responded to the new legal framework by filing lawsuits, and as a group successful plaintiffs have been awarded several billion dollars in damages against foreign states over the past several years. Federal judges have responded by finding terrorist states liable for the harm and violence they create, and by awarding plaintiffs large damage awards too. Yet, the same framework that facilitates litigation, with the goal of holding terrorist states accountable, also permits the executive branch to block terrorist state assets in the United States, thus making it very difficult for successful plaintiffs to collect damage awards. Holding terrorist states financially accountable, then, hinges upon executive power and the demands of national security and foreign policy. And, when the executive does block terrorist state assets, Congress has spent federal money to satisfy damage awards owed to American citizens by foreign governments. When the federal government assumes the damage award costs, tort law's goal of holding terrorist states financially accountable is greatly diminished and thus dilutes the ability of civil litigation to deter terrorist states by depriving them of the financial resources for sponsoring terrorism. Moreover, by allowing the executive branch to block the collection of civil judgments by prohibiting the seizure of a foreign state's diplomatic properties and assets held in the United States, Congress effectively subordinates the satisfaction of civil judgments to the national security and diplomacy concerns of the executive branch. To be sure allowing the executive to block attachment of assets increases the president's flexibility in foreign affairs, and also means that the threat of seizure of another state's assets can be a diplomatic bargaining chip.

Congress fully recognizes that the executive must have suitable powers to fight the War on Terror, and limiting the president's control over some foreign-owned assets located in the United States will seriously hamper his ability to conduct foreign affairs. By still granting a broad power to the president to block access to terrorist state property and assets, however, Congress ensures that while civil lawsuits against rogue states will proceed, and may well be successful, satisfaction of large judgments will ultimately depend on the executive branch's understanding of, and responses to, larger global events. By making the collection of civil judgments against terrorist states dependent on national security concerns and larger global events, the use of civil litigation to "imperil the flow of money and discourage the financing of terrorist acts" by rogue states is dramatically undermined.

Perhaps most importantly, the model of terrorism tort litigation in which foreign states are sued seems to be successful only when Congress and the president intervene with a financial settlement such as the victims' compensation fund set up for the *Flatow* litigants and others. In support of that model, the United States and Libya signed an agreement (approved by Congress) in August 2008 setting up a Humanitarian Settlement Fund, with no monies from the United States, to bring about "rapid recovery of fair compensation for American nationals with terrorism-related claims against Libya" arising out of Libya's bombing of a Pan Am flight over Lockerbie, Scotland, in 1988.[24] Although several terrorism lawsuits were filed against Libya in the United States (with countersuits filed in Libya against the United States), the resolution of those cases has been achieved through diplomatic means.

For 9/11 terrorism tort cases, the pressures discussed earlier certainly apply. Suing states that sponsor terrorism will be difficult due to sovereign immunity issues, and due to the executive branch's ability to invoke national security and diplomacy concerns to block the seizure of state assets. Past practice shows that when plaintiffs collect damages through terrorism tort cases it is because the federal government either created a compensation fund or negotiated settlement with the offending state, as in the aforementioned Libyan case. Thus, the damage awards arising from federal terrorism tort cases are payable, typically, only when the other branches take action. Whether this interbranch cooperation truly imperils the flow of money from terrorist states to terrorist groups remains to be seen. Testifying before Congress in 2003, State Department legal advisor William H. Taft IV noted that the "piecemeal" legislative approach of the Congress does not work: "the current litigation-based system of compensation is inequitable, unpredictable, occasionally costly to the U.S. taxpayer and damaging to the foreign policy and national security goals of this country."[25] Taft noted that some litigants, in order to collect, had to compete with other plaintiffs for the same terrorist state assets in the United States. Other litigants have not been able to collect at all, and, as of 2003, the U.S. Treasury had paid American plaintiffs $383 million to satisfy some outstanding damage awards. The realistic scenario for terrorism litigation arising out of 9/11 and post–9/11 events, then, is that even if tort plaintiffs are successful in winning against terrorist states, it is likely that they will not collect any damages from those states, and the American taxpayer may foot the bill.

Notes

1. Anemona Hartocollis, "Little-Noticed 9/11 Lawsuits Will Get Their Day in Court," *New York Times*, September 4, 2007.

2. *Burnett et al. v. Al Baraka Inv. and Dev. Corp., et al.* 274 F. Supp. 2d 86 (DDC, 2003).
3. *In re: Terrorist Attacks on September 11, 2001*, 471 F. Supp. 2d 444 (SDNY, 2007).
4. *Smith ex rel. Smith v. Afghanistan*, 262 F. Supp. 2d 217 (SDNY 2003).
5. William P. Hoye, "Fighting Fire with...Mire? Civil Remedies and the New War on State-Sponsored Terrorism," *Duke Journal of Comparative and International Law* 12 (Winter 2002): 126.
6. See generally Gary Clyde Hufbauer and Nicholas K. Mitrokostas, *Awakening Monster: The Alien Tort Statute of 1789* (Washington, DC: Institute for International Economics, 2003).
7. American Enterprise Institute for Public Policy Research, "Should Trial Lawyers Make Terror Policy?" *Liability Outlook* no. 4 (September 2007): 5.
8. John Norton Moore, ed., *Civil Litigation against Terrorism* (Durham, NC: Carolina Academic Press, 2004), 8.
9. Ruth Wedgwood, "Civil Remedies and Terrorism," in *Civil Litigation against Terrorism*, ed. John Norton Moore, 170.
10. Ibid., 168.
11. *Boim v.Quranic Literacy Institute*, 291 F.3d. 1000, 1021 (7th Cir. 2002).
12. See Congressional Research Service, *Suits against Terrorist States by Victims of Terrorism* (Washington, DC: Congressional Research Service, 2008).
13. Anne-Marie Slaugther, *A New World Order* (Princeton, NJ: Princeton University Press, 2004), 31.
14. Robert O. Keohane, *Power and Governance in a Partially Globalized World* (London: Routledge, 2002), 202.
15. Edward L. Lascher and Ellen E. Martin, "Beyond the September 11 Victim Compensation Fund: Support for Any Future American Terror Casualties," *PS: Political Science* (American Political Science Association, January 2008), 147–152.
16. *Boim v.Quranic Literacy Institute*, supra note 11, 1021.
17. See Jack Goldsmith and Ryan Goodman, "U.S. Civil Litigation and International Terrorism," in *Civil Litigation against Terrorism*, ed. John Norton Moore, 152.
18. See generally Congressional Research Service, *Suits against Terrorist States by Victims of Terrorism*.
19. *Flatow v. Islamic Republic of Iran*, 999 F. Supp. 2d 1 (DDC 1998).
20. See generally *Flatow v. Islamic Republic of Iran*, 74 F. Supp. 2d 18 (DDC 1999).
21. Presidential Determination No. 99-1, 63 Fed. Reg. 59, 201 (October 21, 1998).
22. House of Representatives, Conference Report 106-939 (October 5, 2000).
23. "Terrorist-State Litigation in 2002–03,"*American Journal of International Law* 97, no. 4 (October 2003): 966–974.
24. "Libya Claims Settlement," Press Release, U.S. State Department, August 14, 2008.
25. Quoted in "Terrorist-State Litigation in 2002–03," 973.

Part II

Legal Changes to Structures and Systems

9

How 9/11 Changed the Prosecution of Terrorism

Christopher A. Shields, Kelly R. Damphousse, and Brent L. Smith*

September 11 impacted U.S. counterterrorism policy in several key areas, and through the end of 2008 it continues to do so. Policy changes implemented after the attack had a dramatic impact on how the federal government investigates and prosecutes those suspected of engaging in terrorism. Perhaps the most profound policy change occurred when the United States redirected its domestic antiterrorism policy from its earlier focus of infiltrating and beheading terrorist organizations to the more proactive goals of intercepting and disrupting terrorist groups before their members could successfully launch attacks. That change resulted in a dramatic increase in the number of cases the government prosecuted after 9/11. The shift also changed the types of cases the government prosecuted and, ostensibly, its success in gaining convictions.

Not as obvious is the impact that post–9/11 policy changes have had on the strategies that U.S. attorneys use to prosecute terror-related cases. Due in part to the new goals of intervention and prevention, the government pursued cases that were generally less serious and less complicated than the cases it prosecuted before 9/11. In fact, an entirely new category of

* **Christopher A. Shields** is a Visiting Assistant Professor and ATS Project Manager for the Terrorism Research Center at the University of Arkansas.

Kelly R. Damphousse is Presidential Professor of Sociology and Associate Dean in the College of Arts and Sciences at the University of Oklahoma. He is the Associate Director of the American Terrorism Study.

Brent L. Smith is Professor of Criminal Justice at University of Arkansas and author of *Pipe Bombs and Pipe Dreams*.

terrorism cases was pursued. The changes in prosecutorial strategies had several consequences: after 9/11, a higher proportion of terrorism cases were treated like traditional crimes by prosecutors. In addition, terrorist defendants were more likely to behave like traditional offenders and enter guilty pleas than were terrorist defendants who were tried before the attacks. The events of September 11 heightened the amount of scrutiny the public, policy officials, and the media placed on the overall effectiveness of U.S. counterterrorism policy. Moreover, the changes in counterterrorism policy created confusion and that has fostered criticism concerning the government's effectiveness in the War on Terror. In the discussion that follows, we will explore research produced from the American Terrorism Study to provide an overview of each of these topics.

Investigating and Prosecuting Terrorism

Simply put, the federal response to terrorism is a product of political considerations. Terrorism is a political crime motivated by the desire to force social change through the use of violence. Counterterrorism is the effort by the government to repress these violent efforts toward social change.[1] Even though the United States has traditionally avoided the concept of "political crime" in the federal criminal code,[2] it is not possible for federal agencies charged with the responsibility of responding to terrorism to avoid being affected in some way by the manner in which the public and their congressional representatives define and demand enforcement of politically motivated violence.[3]

Defining Terrorism

Although no universal definition of terrorism exists,[4] the definition used by the polity remains a critically important guide in understanding the prosecution of terrorism. Since the FBI is charged with exclusive authority to investigate acts of terrorists both within the U.S. borders, and acts committed against U.S. persons or property overseas, the manner in which it defines terrorism sets the stage for the majority of prosecutorial intervention. Citing the *Code of Federal Regulations*, the FBI defines terrorism as "the unlawful use of force and violence against persons or property to intimidate or coerce a government, the civilian population, or any segment thereof, in furtherance of political or social objectives."[5] The FBI divides these crimes into two categories: domestic and international. Domestic terrorism is limited to "groups or individuals operating entirely within the United States, Puerto Rico or other U.S. territories without foreign direction," while international terrorism includes acts of terrorism that "occur outside the United States, or transcend national boundaries in terms of the means by which they are accomplished, the persons they appear intended to coerce or intimidate, or the locale in which their perpetrators operate or seek asylum."[6]

FBI and the Attorney General Guidelines

In practice, these definitions are filtered through two sets of attorney general's guidelines, depending on whether the investigations are domestic or international. Since the international guidelines are classified, our discussion will generally be limited to the domestic guidelines. The domestic guidelines, most recently entitled *The Attorney General's Guidelines on General Crimes, Racketeering Enterprise and Terrorism Enterprise Investigations*,[7] dictate the rules for opening a terrorism investigation and limit the extent of its scope. Unlike general crimes investigations, FBI terrorism investigations may be opened only under specific situations. For example, "circumstances must reasonably indicate that two or more persons are engaged in an enterprise for the purpose of" using violence to further political or social goals.[8] Furthermore, these investigations are intended to focus upon "the investigation of entire enterprises, rather than just individual participants and specific criminal acts..."[9]

To appreciate the impact of 9/11, it is important to understand how the guidelines have changed over the past 30 years. During that time, federal responses to terrorism and the subsequent number of persons indicted for terrorism-related activities have been affected by three sets of Attorney General Guidelines.[10] Implementation of each set of guidelines was preceded by an "intervention crisis"—a significant event that brought national attention to FBI practices.[11] In the first case, the crisis was brought about by FBI responses to political extremism. The second change occurred in response to armored car robberies perpetrated by left-wing extremists and the third change was ushered in after 9/11.

The *Levi Guidelines* (1976) were a response to abuses under the FBI's Counterintelligence Program (COINTELPRO) identified by the Church Committee.[12] The effect of these guidelines was dramatic: the number of domestic security investigations in the United States dropped from over 20,000 in 1973 to less than 300 in 1977.[13] From 1976 to 1983, the FBI was severely restricted in domestic security/terrorism investigations. As a result, several groups, most notably leftist extremists including members of the United Freedom Front, the Puerto Rican FALN and Macheteros, the Black Liberation Army, and the Weather Underground, operated almost with impunity throughout this period.[14]

In 1981, however, increasing concern by congressional critics about terrorism led FBI director William Webster to pacify efforts to force the FBI into conducting more domestic intelligence investigations.[15] In testimony before a Senate subcommittee on security and terrorism, Webster testified that "there is no known coalescing of an ideological synthesis among (domestic terrorist) groups, nor do we have any sense that they have become effective."[16] This statement was followed almost immediately in October 1981, by the second of the "intervention crises," when members of the Black Liberation Army (BLA), the Weather Underground, and the Black Panther Party reemerged as the May 19 Communist Organization (M19CO). The robbery of a Brinks armored truck in Nyack, New York, made national news and cast serious doubt on Webster's assessment just a few weeks prior.[17]

The response by federal agencies was swift. In March 1983, the *Smith Guidelines* (named after Attorney General William French Smith) replaced the Levi Guidelines, effectively reintroducing the FBI to the work of domestic security and terrorism intelligence investigations. An important counterterrorism mechanism—the FBI Joint Terrorism Task Force concept—emerged as a result of this new crisis. During the next few years, the FBI conducted a national sweep of terrorist groups in America, decimating the remaining leftist groups and successfully interdicting the emerging extreme Right's "War in '84." The roundup included members of the United Freedom Front, one of America's most prolific leftist terror groups; FALN, Weather Underground, and BLA participants in M19CO activities, along with the arrest and indictment of scores of members of the Order, the Covenant, Sword, and Arm of the Lord, Posse Commitatus, Aryan Nations, and other white supremacy organizations.[18]

Then, following the Oklahoma City bombing in 1995, calls for modifications to the Smith Guidelines occurred.[19] However, both the FBI and congressional subcommittees seemed reluctant to implement any changes. The subsequent attacks of September 11, 2001 left little room for nonresponse. While the previous crises that led to changes in the guidelines had come primarily from domestic threats, this third intervention crisis resulted from international terrorism. Partly because of the magnitude of the destruction and partly due to the fact that perceived changes to the guidelines would focus upon non-U.S. citizens, the *Ashcroft Guidelines* (implemented by Attorney General John Ashcroft) ushered in some of the most sweeping changes to the attorney general's terrorism guidelines since 1983.[20]

Despite these changes, "the FBI had not forgotten the stinging public and congressional rebukes for its COINTELPRO indiscretions."[21] Demands that the FBI become once again engaged in "political policing" through domestic intelligence activities were originally met with reluctance by FBI officials.[22] Criticisms by the 9/11 Commission, for example, suggest that the FBI had a "culture entrenched in law enforcement, one not geared to carry out intelligence missions."[23] Despite this reluctance, the number of indictments from terrorism investigations increased dramatically in the three years following the September 11 attacks.[24]

Procedurally, the changes between the Smith Guidelines and the Ashcroft Guidelines were significant. Under the Smith Guidelines, local field offices were required to obtain approval from FBI headquarters ("FBIHQ") before terrorism investigations could be opened. More pointedly, the guidelines required FBI field offices to refer potential terrorism investigations, involving two or more persons, to the director or assistant director of the FBI; they, and only they, could authorize a domestic security/terrorism enterprise investigation. Once the director authorized a terrorism investigation, he had to report that fact to the Office of Intelligence Policy and Review. The Smith Guidelines also required the director (or another top official) to monitor the progress of the investigation at 180-day intervals. Section (B)(4)(a) of the Ashcroft Guidelines loosened those standards by giving agents in the field the authority to open terrorism investigations for a period of up to one year. Unlike the Smith Guidelines, the Ashcroft Guidelines allow the Special Agent in Charge to renew the investigations without approval from FBIHQ.

The Ashcroft Guidelines require field offices, within one year, to report any terrorism investigations they initiate and provide reports to FBIHQ. The guidelines centralized the analysis of fieldwork at FBI headquarters. The changes in guidelines after 9/11 had a significant effect not only on the number of investigations conducted, but also on the manner in which defendants were charged, who was charged, and what was officially recorded as acts of terrorism. Indictments under these investigations formed the basis for counting the number of terrorist incidents that "occurred" and were "prevented" by the FBI in its annual (until recently) reports entitled *Terrorism in the United States*. At the time this piece was written, the Ashcroft Guidelines remained in place. But on December 1, 2008, the FBI will implement a completely new set of guidelines. The implications of that change will be addressed later in this chapter.

Other Significant Policy Changes after 9/11

Other strategies used to combat terrorism in the United States underwent dramatic change after 9/11. In broad terms, American antiterrorism policy focused on terrorist organizations, affiliated networks, and state sponsors in an effort to identify potential terrorist threats and proactively prevent future attacks. In a statement released after 9/11, Attorney General Ashcroft explained that the policy of the U.S. government changed from prosecuting terror-related crimes that had already occurred to thwarting attacks before they happen.[25]

To facilitate these new proactive goals, Congress changed policies to provide legal tools for the Department of Justice to combat terrorism. Some policies expanded legal authority to engage international terrorism that occurs away from American soil.[26] Other policies expanded legal authority to intercept, investigate, and prosecute domestic terrorists. For example, the Anti-Terrorism and Effective Death Penalty Act was revisited and the USA Patriot Act of 2001 was created to extend and strengthen U.S. counterterrorism policy. In addition, the executive branch changed Department of Justice policy on how, and, more importantly, when, the FBI and U.S. attorneys would handle the investigation and prosecution of terror suspects.

Decentralizing the authority for FBI terrorism investigations and implementing proactive policy goals changed the types of cases the FBI labels "terrorist." In particular, Attorney General Ashcroft's directive to the Department of Justice to interrupt, arrest, and prosecute suspected terrorists before an act of terrorism could be committed, fundamentally altered the timing of when cases were formally entered into U.S. District Courts. The proactive policy goals probably forced the FBI to refer cases to U.S. attorneys before the FBI had time to collect enough evidence to convict defendants of complex conspiracies. This helps to explain the post–9/11 change in the type and severity of charges with which terrorist defendants were indicted.

Measuring Terrorism Prosecutions

The FBI conducts numerous investigations regarding suspected terrorist activities each year. Occasionally, the crimes committed indicate a pattern or suspected pattern that involves the continued threat of political violence from an individual or group.[27] As mentioned earlier, the FBI may open a "terrorism enterprise" investigation (in lieu of a "general crimes" investigation). Many of these crimes are investigated through FBI Joint Terrorism Task Forces. During the 1990s, the FBI routinely was investigating between eight and twelve terrorist groups under these guidelines at any one time.[28]

Once an indictment is issued, however, these cases become a matter of public record, retained in the federal criminal case files at the federal district courts where the cases were tried. Information on these cases has been provided through periodic releases by the FBI to American Terrorism Study (ATS) staff personnel.[29] Due to a Supreme Court ruling in 1989 restricting the *compilation* of open source data from FBI files, data released since 1990 has been "sponsored" by either the U.S. House of Representatives Judiciary Subcommittee on Crime or the U.S. Senate Judiciary Committee.[30] Under this arrangement, the FBI submitted the requested information to the Congressional Committee which, in turn, provided the data to ATS personnel for further data collection and analysis. The information provided by the FBI includes the names of those indicted, the federal district court in which the indictments were issued, the federal court case numbers, date of arrest and indictment, and name of terrorist group, if available.

The ATS began monitoring federal prosecutions of terrorists in 1988 (dating back to 1980) and continues to the current time. The study uses the FBI's definition of terrorism. Despite criticism regarding the FBI's application of the definition,[31] FBI data on terrorism provides the greatest continuity over time. Furthermore, the study ensures "adherence to the practical application of the definition by restricting itself to data collection only on cases that occurred as a result of an indictment stemming from a federal 'domestic security/terrorism investigation' (more recently called terrorism enterprise investigations)."[32] These investigations, conducted by the FBI in accordance with the Attorney General Guidelines, "set forth the predication threshold and limits for investigations of crimes…in support of terrorist objectives."[33]

Using the list of indicted persons provided by the FBI, ATS project personnel contacted the U.S. District Court where each case was tried and made arrangements to review the case files and make copies of pertinent records. If archived, arrangements were made with the appropriate Federal Records Center where the records are stored. The ATS comprises approximately 80 variables that measure defendant demographic information (e.g., *race, sex, age, income, education level, marital status,* etc.), general case information (e.g., *number of counts, year of indictment, criminal statute, length of case, case outcome, sentence length,* etc.), terrorism-specific information (e.g., *type of terrorism, group affiliation, length of membership, role in group, how recruited, intended targets, actual targets,* etc.), and some case information unique to terrorism (e.g., *prosecution methods, defense methods, amount of community sympathy*).

The FBI supplemented the first list of names with four additional lists. The ATS includes the names of over 1,000 persons who have been indicted as the result of an FBI terrorism investigation from 1980 through 2004. The ATS database contains information on 706 indictees charged with 9,633 criminal violations in 254 court cases.[34] In addition, there are data on approximately 75 different terrorist groups. The ATS was recently supplemented with data from a National Institute of Justice-sponsored (NIJ) project, the Prosecution and Defense Strategies study ("PADS").[35] Using the same case file source material collected for the ATS, staff members created a database containing approximately 150 new variables measuring trial-specific data.

For example, variables from the PADS project track information about the type of attorney used. The database includes variables that measure whether the defendant received bail; and if not, the reason bail was denied. A set of variables track whether a superseding indictment was filed in each case, and another set of variables track the number of counts added or dropped from the original indictment. These counts are coded by statute number and by U.S. Code chapter. These data also track defense motions and their outcomes, for example: defense challenges to FISA; motions to suppress physical evidence; motions to suppress electronic surveillance; motions to sever counts; motions to suppress statements, and; an entire range of pro se motions. Similarly, PADS data track prosecution motions and outcomes (e.g., whether CIPA protection was sought, motions to exclude defense evidence, challenges to defense strategies, and others).

Prosecution Strategies before and after

Changes in how the FBI was allowed to investigate domestic security/terrorism enterprise cases brought about a change in the methods used by U.S. attorneys to prosecute terrorists. In the 1960s and 1970s, a few prosecutors experimented with politicizing terrorism cases, but the practice was generally avoided.[36] Prosecutors used one of two methods, *explicit politicality* or *exceptional vagueness*, to prosecute "political" defendants.[37] Explicit politicality was characterized by the government's use of a terrorist label in trial documents and the portrayal of the defendant as a terrorist to the public through the news media. This strategy involved an extensive discussion of the defendants' motives and the use of charges that include an element of conspiracy—alleging that the defendant engaged in some type of politically motivated behavior. The most extreme example of this type of charge would be seditious conspiracy or treason.

When the exceptional vagueness strategy was employed, the government avoided describing the defendant as a terrorist. Instead, the defendant was depicted as a traditional offender. Terrorism research referred to this strategy as *conventional criminality*. Subsequent research expanded the typology to include a third prosecutorial strategy—a middle-ground approach.[38] After a string of acquittals in highly politicized terrorism cases, the government began prosecuting terrorist defendants under either a presumed liability statute or with some "traditional" crime where motive was not an issue. But at trial, prosecutors "dropped" a series of subtle hints that the defendant was part of a terrorist group. Later research found evidence that prosecutors sometimes did more than drop subtle hints.[39] On occasion, prosecutors labeled the defendants "terrorist" or directly linked them to terrorist groups, but unlike explicit politicality cases the prosecution did not delve into their political motive directly. Based on these observations, the middle-ground approach was called *political innuendo*.[40] Prosecutors used all three strategies before and after 9/11. The proportional use of those strategies, however, changed considerably between eras.

After September 11: A New Approach

Two separate critiques have challenged the Department of Justice's (DOJ) claims of success in prosecuting defendants linked to terrorism in the post–9/11 era. The "data reliability" critique questioned the data used by them because some of the cases listed in DOJ annual reports contained defendants with no link to a terrorist ideology/group and those defendants were charged with violations of law that did not appear to be related to terrorism.[41] The "soft sentence" critique focused on the defendants' prison-sentence lengths, reporting that the War on Terror was not as successful as the DOJ claimed because "terrorists" were receiving sentences of just a few months.[42] Recent research, focusing on the distinction between case-types, has addressed both critiques.[43]

Focusing on case-type, in the light of post–9/11 changes in counterterrorism policy and policy goals, sheds light on the federal response to terrorism. Shifting away from the goal of infiltrating terror groups, Attorney General Ashcroft directed the FBI and the Executive Office of U.S. Attorneys to intercept and disrupt terrorist planning before an act of terrorism could occur. Toward that end, the FBI and U.S. attorneys targeted immigration and financial fraud after 9/11 with the argument that making it difficult for anyone to engage in these crimes would make it difficult for terrorists—who relied on both forms of criminality—to succeed in gathering the resources and personnel necessary to carry out future attacks.[44] In other words, targeting and pursuing these kinds of crime is designed to diffuse the terrorist threat.

Research has provided the framework for establishing case-type categories.[45] The following case-type categories are used: the *event-linked* category comprises cases where the defendant was linked to a terrorist group or ideology and was indicted on charges related to an act of terrorism (planned or completed); the *pretextual* category contains cases where the defendant was linked to a terrorist group or ideology, but was charged with crimes not directly related to an act of terrorism; and the *diffusion* category contains cases where the defendant was neither linked to a group or ideology, nor a crime related to an act of terrorism.[46]

Case Outcomes before and after 9/11

As mentioned earlier, the counterterrorism policy shift that followed September 11 had a profound impact on the types of cases the federal government pursued. Research conducted earlier this year using the ATS, and the PADS supplemental variables, indicates just how strong the impact affected terrorism prosecutions.[47] The study found that there were no diffusion cases listed by the FBI prior to 9/11, yet this category represents almost half of the cases filed afterward (see table 9.1). That means, prior to September 11, 2001, every defendant referred for prosecution as a result of a domestic security/terrorism investigation was linked by the FBI to a terrorist group or ideology. Yet, only half of the defendants referred after 9/11 were similarly linked.[48] Taking the diffusion cases out of the post–9/11 sample is important because the resulting mix of event-linked and pretextual cases closely resembles the composition of cases filed prior to 9/11.

That study also found that before 9/11, 85 percent of all terrorism cases were event-linked, while only 15 percent were pretextual (see table 9.2).

Table 9.1   Case-type frequencies by indictee pre– and post–9/11.

	Pre–9/11	Post–9/11	Total
Diffusion	0	79	79
Pretextual	81	38	119
Event-linked	431	50	481
Total	512	167	679

Table 9.2   Case type by outcome pre–9/11.

	Trial conviction	Plea guilty	Acquitted at trial	Dismissed	Total
Event-linked	156	149	40	36	381
	40.9%	39.1%	10.5%	9.4%	100.0%
Pretextual	8	52	0	9	69
	11.6%	75.4%	.0%	13.0%	100.0%
Total	164	201	40	45	450
	36.4%	44.7%	8.9%	10.0%	100.0%

In other words 85 percent of the defendants referred by the FBI for prosecution were not only linked to a terrorist group or ideology, they were also linked to a completed or planned terrorist attack. After 9/11, with diffusion cases removed, only 57 percent of the terrorism cases were event-linked, while the percentage of pretextual cases increased to 43 percent (see table 9.3). This finding is not surprising. The policy shift ushered in by Attorney General Ashcroft refocused law enforcement efforts toward intercepting and interrupting terrorist groups before those groups could successfully plan an attack. It makes sense that there would be less evidence available for prosecutors to use to link defendants to terrorist acts when those defendants are charged as soon as criminal violations occurred.

The average number of defendants indicted, per year, in event-linked cases was slightly lower in the post–9/11 era, decreasing from approximately 22 to 17 annually.[49] The average number of defendants indicted in pretextual cases increased from 4 to 13 annually. In this study, the total number of defendants who were indicted in cases that were linked to a terrorist ideology (total of event-linked and pretextual cases) increased slightly from 26 to 30 per year.[50]

Before 9/11, terrorism cases comprised only pretextual and event-linked cases, with most of those cases falling into the latter category. The study showed that prosecutors also relied on the explicit politicality prosecution strategy in the majority of cases. Even if prosecutors had aggressively sought plea bargains among terrorist defendants, the type of cases they filed and the prosecution strategies they used lowered the chances of plea bargaining. In the post–9/11 era, much of that changed. The Ashcroft Guidelines affected that change in two ways.

First, requiring the FBI and U.S. attorneys to intercept and prosecute cases sooner likely served to lower the amount of evidence necessary to

Table 9.3   Case type by outcome post–9/11.

	Trial conviction	Plea guilty	Acquitted at trial	Dismissed	Total
Event-linked	5	28	2	5	40
	12.5%	70.0%	5.0%	12.5%	100.0%
Pretextual	3	22	0	2	27
	11.1%	81.5%	.0%	7.4%	100.0%
Diffusion	5	68	1	3	77
	6.5%	88.3%	1.3%	3.9%	100.0%
Total	13	118	3	10	144
	9.0%	81.9%	2.1%	6.9%	100.0%

pursue event-linked cases. Second, the lower amount of evidence may be responsible for the dramatic reduction in the percentage of cases in which prosecutors used an explicit politicality prosecution strategy. So it is possible that the Ashcroft Guidelines inadvertently made it easier for prosecutors to secure guilty pleas by taking some of the politics (and religion) out of terrorism cases. As the study noted, "the more that terrorism cases resemble traditional criminal cases, the more likely that terrorism defendants will behave like traditional criminal defendants. Couple that with the likelihood that 9/11 left terrorist defendants less willing to take a chance with a jury, and higher plea rates make sense."[51]

The study also found an increased number of dismissed cases in the post–9/11 era, and that may also be related to the Ashcroft Guidelines. Even though the rate of guilty pleas increased and the number of acquittals decreased, the number of cases dismissed went up in the post–9/11 era (when diffusion cases were removed). Moreover, the average number of counts dismissed per case doubled (these figures do not include counts dismissed due to plea bargaining). The study noted at least two reasons for this. First, "the increase in the number of cases dismissed may be the direct result of prosecutors having less evidence. Second, it is possible that net widening resulted in prosecutors charging defendants with extra counts while planning to dismiss some in order to negotiate a guilty plea."[52]

The study also looked for potential consequences of net widening. The basic proposition in net widening is that get tough policies, like the counterterrorism policies enacted after 9/11, will result in the federal government pursuing a higher proportion lower-severity crimes than it did before the policies were enacted. A consequence of this focus is a shift toward prosecuting terrorist defendants for crimes that the government may have largely ignored prior to the policy change. For terrorism cases in the post–9/11 era, the study predicted an increase in the proportion of pretextual cases as compared to event-linked cases, a smaller proportion of highly politicized prosecution strategies among all cases, and an overall decline in the severity of charges filed against post–9/11 terrorist defendants.[53]

As predicted, the findings showed that the proportion of defendants indicted in pretextual cases nearly tripled in the post–9/11 era. Prosecutors not only pursued less serious charges (via diffusion cases) but they also relied on less politicized prosecution strategies (across all case types). The findings suggest that those results were likely due to the impact of Ashcroft Guidelines and federal prosecutors' desire to appear more proactive to the general public. In addition, the results of the study showed "that the average number of defendants indicted in event-linked cases dropped by half, to less than two people per case. Even though the Ashcroft Guidelines continued the trend of the preceding guidelines and defined terrorism as a group activity, the number of individual defendants, even in event-linked cases, grew."[54]

An explanation for this trend can be found elsewhere in the Ashcroft Guidelines. The process to open domestic security/terrorism enterprise investigations prior to 2002 required FBI field agents to obtain permission from the FBI headquarters before a terrorism investigation could be opened. The Ashcroft Guidelines placed complete authority for opening those investigations into the hands of field agents. Remember also that a terrorism investigation could be conducted over a much longer timeframe than a general crimes investigation, and terrorism investigations also provided legal authority via the USA Patriot Act (among others) for field agents to use more invasive techniques (e.g., roving wire taps, secret records checks, etc.). Consistent with net widening, it is probable that the combination of the new guidelines and the attorney general's mandate to prosecute cases sooner led to the FBI referring cases with fewer defendants.

One of the more surprising findings from that research concerned the expected impact of Attorney General Ashcroft's "early prosecution" mandate. It was predicted that early prosecution would impede the government's ability to infiltrate extremist groups with agents, and likewise, it would limit the amount of time government agents had to develop relationships with potential informants who were associated with group members. The findings were consistent with the predictions. Indeed, there were fewer confidential informants and the number of agents who were able to infiltrate extremist groups dropped significantly. But the consequences were not as expected. It was predicted that fewer confidential informants and undercover agents would result in a lower conviction rate. That did not occur. As noted earlier, conviction rates increased in the post–9/11 era across all case-types.

Why, then, did conviction rates increase? The policy shift was likely responsible for limiting the amount of evidence available to prosecutors. Lower amounts of evidence probably caused a shift in the type of cases prosecutors pursued and the type of prosecution strategies they employed. In simple terms, prosecutors were forced to pursue fewer complex and risky cases—even within the event-linked and pretextual categories. Instead, they pursued cases that more closely resembled traditional criminal cases, and terrorism defendants behaved more like traditional defendants by entering guilty pleas.

Diffusion Cases

The study found that 79 defendants were indicted in diffusion cases—all after 9/11. As expected with cases where defendants are not linked to completed or planned acts of terrorism, prosecutors relied almost exclusively on a traditional prosecution strategy (conventional criminality prosecution strategy). The overall conviction rate for diffusion cases was 94.8 percent—the highest of all case-types. The high conviction rate is expected, because diffusion cases are most similar to traditional cases in that the defendants are not linked to terrorism. Of the diffusion cases studied the guilty plea rate was 88.3 percent, and only 6 defendants took their cases to trial. Again, this is no surprise. A majority of the charges filed against defendants indicted in diffusion cases were relatively cut-and-dry instances of immigration fraud and financial fraud.[55]

New FBI Guidelines

On December 1, 2008, the FBI will begin operating under a new set of Attorney General's Guidelines. These guidelines, approved by Attorney General Michael B. Murkasey (the *Murkasey* Guidelines), make it clear that the FBI's role is now one of a "full-fledged intelligence agency—with respect to both intelligence collection and intelligence analysis—and a key participant in the U.S. Intelligence Community gathering service."[56] Murkasey states that the issuance of the guidelines represents the culmination of the evolution of the FBI since the September 11, 2001 terrorist attacks.[57] The guidelines seek to eliminate distinctions between different types of investigations and to create uniform standards "wherever possible."

The distinction between "general crimes investigations" and "intelligence investigations" is eliminated. The new guidelines create three levels of investigation and authorize different methods at each level. Section I.C.2.a. makes it clear that the choice of the least invasive method of investigation is preferred, but leaves the choice up to the judgment of the FBI. Moreover, the guidelines authorize using the most intrusive methods legally available in cases of foreign intelligence and, specifically, terrorism investigations.[58]

Section II defines and authorizes a much broader investigative role for the FBI than under the previous guidelines. This section defines "investigation" in terms of the FBI's ability to "provide critical information needed for broader analytic and intelligence purposes to facilitate the solution and prevention of crime, protect the national security, and further foreign intelligence objectives." Noting that the scope of authorized activities is "not limited to . . . solving particular cases or obtaining evidence for use in particular criminal prosecutions" the guidelines go on to say that the FBI is authorized to retain and disseminate information "incidentally obtained" that is related to matters outside their primary investigative responsibility.[59]

The first level of investigation is the *Assessment.* Assessments are authorized as long as there is "an authorized purpose," but they do not require "any particular factual predication." The guidelines permit the "proactive information gathering functions [of] assessments" anytime the FBI receives a tip concerning crimes or threats to national security. Assessments do not require supervisory approval.[60] The second level of investigations is *Predicated Investigations.* Predicated investigations require supervisory approval and "allegations, reports, facts or circumstances indicative of possible criminal or national security-threatening activity, or the potential for acquiring information responsive to foreign intelligence requirements." Predicated investigations are subdivided into *preliminary investigations* and *full investigations* depending on the predicate facts.[61]

Preliminary investigations are authorized to run for six months and may be renewed by the Special Agent in Charge for an additional six months. Preliminary investigation lasting more than a year can only be authorized by FBIHQ. Importantly full investigations have no preset time limits, and may be authorized for violations of criminal law or national security-threatening activity based upon reasonable suspicion. With regard to terrorism investigations, ostensibly, this is a considerable expansion from the Ashcroft Guidelines—which limited domestic security/terrorism investigations to specific circumstances and to one-year time periods. Moreover, the old requirement of "two or more people"—which focused the FBI's attention on terrorist groups—has been eliminated.

The third level of investigatory tool is the *Enterprise Investigation.* Enterprise investigations are full investigations that focus on groups and organizations and require the same level of predicated facts as the full investigations mentioned earlier. Unlike the previous guidelines, however, racketeering activities and organized terrorism fall under the same umbrella. Moreover, these investigations are expressly authorized for groups that may be involved in activities described in the material support of terrorism statute under 18 U.S.C. §2332b(g)(5)(B).[62] Field offices must report opening a full investigation to FBIHQ within 30 days from when it is first authorized.

The substantive differences between the enterprise investigation and the investigations authorized under the Ashcroft Guidelines are significant. The new guidelines expand the possible time an investigation may be open and require only reasonable suspicion to trigger the full arsenal of investigatory tools at the disposal of the FBI. In terms of terrorism investigations in particular not only are the tools and time limits expanded, but the investigations are no longer separated operationally from other FBI investigations. The expansion of FBI investigatory power under the Murkasey Guidelines may further increase the proportion of pretextual and diffusion cases that the government prosecutes each year. That is a question we may not be able to answer. The guidelines hold a potential, at least, of making future evaluations of the federal government's response to terrorism more difficult to perform as the bright-line between domestic security/terrorism investigations and general crimes investigations has been erased.

Summary

The prosecution of federal terrorism cases changed significantly after the attacks of September 11, 2001. The changes were the result of heightened scrutiny on existing counterterrorism policies and the subsequent changes that federal policy-makers made to correct a perceived intelligence failure. New policy tools were created and policy goals were altered, which refocused the government's counterterrorism response from one of infiltrating and beheading terrorist groups and organizations to one of identifying and interrupting terrorist plots before they could be perpetrated.

Toward that end, Attorney General Ashcroft implemented a new set of FBI Guidelines and issued a mandate to the FBI and U.S. attorneys ordering them to prosecute suspected terrorists as soon as there was sufficient evidence of any wrongdoing, terror-related or not, to win a conviction. The result was a dramatic increase in the number of federal terrorism prosecutions—more in the three years following September 11, 2001, than in the previous 20 years combined. The proactive policy change resulted in a new type of terrorism case: the prosecution of individuals with no identified link to terrorist groups or extremist ideologies, for the purpose of diffusing terrorism.

However, over half of the cases filed after 9/11 involved defendants who were, at a minimum, linked to a terrorist group or ideology. But even among those cases, which outwardly resembled cases filed before 9/11, there was a shift in case-types. Before September 11, 2001, the vast majority of cases involved defendants who were linked to a terrorist group or ideology and who were accused of planning (or committing) an act of terrorism. In the post–9/11 era, by contrast, the number of event-linked cases diminished. The proportion of pretextual cases, those involving defendants who were linked to a terrorist group or ideology but not an attack, increased three times over—providing some evidence that the government was successful in getting proactive.

Not only did the type of cases change after 9/11, but so did the strategies that prosecutors used to prosecute the cases. Before the attacks, prosecutors were much more likely to use highly politicized prosecution strategies than they were afterward. These changes in prosecutorial strategies had several intended and unintended consequences. The government pursued cases that were generally less serious and less complicated, and the defendants in those cases were treated more like traditional criminals by prosecutors. In turn, terrorist defendants were more likely to behave like traditional offenders by pleading guilty. The higher guilty plea rate was matched by a decrease in the number of acquittals. The conviction rate for terrorist defendants tried after 9/11 was significantly higher than it was before. The higher conviction rates in the post–9/11 era are probably the product of several factors. Chief among them was the mandate by Attorney General Ashcroft to prosecute early.

Notes

Portions of this research were funded by the National Institute of Justice (Grant Number 1999-IJCX-0005 and Grant Number 2006-IC-JX-0026) and the Oklahoma City National Memorial Institute for the Prevention of Terrorism (Grant Number MIPT 106-113-2000-064) through the Department of Justice and the Department of Homeland Security. The opinions presented here do not represent the official position of the Department of Justice, the Department of Homeland Security, the MIPT, or the NIJ.

1. Brent Smith, Kelly Damphousse, and Chris Shields, "Two Decades of Terror," unpublished manuscript, 2008, 1.
2. B. L. Ingraham and Kazuhiko Tokoro, "Political Crime in the United States and Japan: A Comparative Study," *Issues in Criminology* 4, no. 2 (1969): 145–170.; Brent Smith and Kelly Damphousse, "Punishing Political Offenders: The Effect of Political Motive on Federal Sentencing Decisions," *Criminology* 34 (1996); Brent Smith and Kelly Damphousse, "Terrorism, Politics, and Punishment: A Test of Structural-Contextual Theory and the 'Liberation Hypothesis,'" *Criminology* 36, no. 1 (1998): 67–92; Brent Smith, Kelly Damphousse, Freedom Jackson, and Amy Sellers, "The Prosecution and Punishment of International Terrorists in Federal Courts: 1980–1998," *Criminology & Public Policy* 1 no. 3 (2002): 311–338.
3. Smith, Damphousse, and Shields, "Two Decades of Terror," 1.
4. See Alex Schmid and Albert Jongman, *Political Terrorism: A New Guide to Actors, Authors, Concepts, Data Bases, Theories, and Literature* (Amsterdam, North Holland: Transaction Books, 1988), for an excellent review of these conceptual efforts.
5. 28 C.F.R. Section 0.85.
6. Federal Bureau of Investigation, *Terrorism in the United States: Counterterrorism Threat Assessment and Warning Unit Counterterrorism Division* (Washington: U.S. Department of Justice, 1999), ii.
7. Office of the Attorney General. *The Attorney General's Guidelines on General Crimes, Racketeering Enterprise and Terrorism Enterprise Investigations* (Washington: U.S. Department of Justice, 2002); similar titles were created in 1975, 1983, and 1989.

8. Office of the Attorney General, *The Attorney General's Guidelines on General Crimes, Racketeering Enterprise and Terrorism Enterprise Investigations* (Washington: U.S. Department of Justice, 2002), 15.

9. Ibid.

10. A. G. Richard Thornburgh made minor changes, mostly semantic, to the guidelines in 1989.

11. Smith, Damphousse, and Shields, "Two Decades of Terror," 2.

12. U.S. Senate, 1976, Books II and III of the *Final Report of the Select Committee to Study Governmental Operations with Respect to Intelligence Activities of the United States Senate*, 94th Congress, 2nd Sess., U.S. Government Printing Office.

13. John T. Elliff, *The Reform of FBI Intelligence Operations* (Princeton: Princeton University Press, 1979).

14. Smith, Damphousse, and Shields, "Two Decades of Terror," 2.

15. Tony Poveda, *Lawlessness and Reform: The FBI in Transition* (Pacific Grove, CA: Brooks/Cole, 1990).

16. Senate Judiciary Committee 1982, 10.

17. Brent L. Smith, *Terrorism in America: Pipe Bombs and Pipe Dreams* (New York: State University of New York Press, 1994).

18. Ibid.

19. United States House Judiciary Subcommittee on Crime, *Hearings on Combating Domestic Terrorism*, 104th Cong., 1st Sess., May. 3, 1995 (Washington, DC: U.S. Government Printing Office).

20. Smith, Damphousse, and Shields, "Two Decades of Terror," 3.

21. Ibid.

22. Phillip Shenon, "9/11 Panel Criticizes Reform Effort at the FBI," *The New York Times*, October 21, 2005, A. 19.

23. Pam Benson and Kevin Bohn, "FBI Slammed for Fighting 9/11 Reforms," *CNN.Com*, October 20, 2005; National Commission 2004.

24. Dan Eggen and Julie Tate, "Few Convictions in Terror Cases; U.S. Often Depends on Lesser Charges," *Washington Post*, June 11, 2005.

25. Office of the Attorney General, *Ashcroft Fact Sheet on New FBI Investigative Guidelines, Politechbot.com*, September 21, 2002.

26. Rapheal Perl, "Terrorism, the Future, and American Foreign Policy," *Issue Brief for Congress*, Order Code IB95112, Foreign Affairs, Trade and Research Division, 2003.

27. Smith, Damphousse, and Shields, "Two Decades of Terror," 6.

28. The exact number of groups being investigated and the names of groups under active investigation are classified. The statement that "8–12 groups are being investigated at any one time" was provided by an FBI JTTF supervisor, December 10, 1998.

29. The procedure for release of the data was evaluated and approved by the Office of General Counsel at both FBI Headquarters and the U. S. House of Representatives.

30. Smith, Damphousse, and Shields, "Two Decades of Terror," 6.

31. See, e.g., Joseph Carlson, "The Future Terrorists in America," *American Journal of Police* 14 (1995): 71–91.

32. Smith, Damphousse, and Shields, "Two Decades of Terror," 7.

33. Federal Bureau of Investigation, *Terrorism in the United States*, 2.

34. Chris Shields, An Analysis of Prosecutorial and Defense Strategies in Federal Terrorism Trials from 1980 to 2004, unpublished manuscript, 2008.

35. NIJ Grant number 2006-IJ-CX-0026.

36. Brent Smith, Kelly Damphousse, Freedom Jackson, and Amy Sellers, "The Prosecution and Punishment of International Terrorists in Federal Courts: 1980–1998," *Criminology & Public Policy* 1, no. 3 (2002: 311–338.

37. Austin Turk, *Political Criminality* (Beverley Hills, CA: Sage, 1982).

38. Smith, Damphousse, Jackson, and Sellers, "The Prosecution and Punishment of International Terrorists in Federal Courts," 311–338.

39. Kelly Damphousse and Chris Shields, "The Morning After: Assessing the Effect of Major Terrorism Events on Prosecution Strategies and Outcomes," *Journal of Contemporary Criminal Justice* 23, no. 2 (2007): 174–194.

40. Shields, *An Analysis of Prosecutorial and Defense Strategies in Federal Terrorism Trials from 1980 to 2004*.

41. Government Accountability Office, *Justice Department, Better Management Oversight and Internal Controls Needed to Ensure Accuracy of Terrorism-Related Statistics*, GAO-03-266, January 2003; Government Accountability Office, "Combating Terrorism: Evaluation of Selected Characteristics in National Strategies Related to Terrorism," U.S. Government Printing Office, Washington, D.C., GAO-04-408T, 2004; Government Accountability Office, *Federal Law Enforcement, Information on the Use of Investigation and Arrest Statistics* GAO-04-411, March 2004; Office of the Inspector General, The Department of Justice's Internal Controls over Terrorism Reporting, OIG-07-04, February 2007.

42. Transactional Record Access Clearinghouse, "Criminal Terrorism Enforcement since the 9/11/01 Attacks," *A TRAC Special Report*, December 8, 2003 found at http://trac.syr.edu/tracreports/terrorism/ report031208. html.

43. Shields, *An Analysis of Prosecutorial and Defense Strategies in Federal Terrorism Trials from 1980 to 2004*; and Robert Chesney,, "Federal Prosecution of Terrorism-Related Cases: Conviction and Sentencing Data in Light of the 'Data Reliability' and 'Soft Sentence' Critiques," available at ttp://ssrn.com/ abstract_id=1005478.

44. Chesney, "Federal Prosecution of Terrorism-Related Cases."

45. Shields, *An Analysis of Prosecutorial and Defense Strategies in Federal Terrorism Trials from 1980 to 2004*, developing the concepts created by Chesney, "Federal Prosecution of Terrorism-Related Cases."

46. Shields, *An Analysis of Prosecutorial and Defense Strategies in Federal Terrorism Trials from 1980 to 2004*.

47. Ibid.

48. Ibid., 76.

49. It should be noted that there are more terrorism cases to be collected from the 2002–2004 FBI list (ATS and PADS). Anecdotally, the proportion of pretextual vis-à-vis event-linked cases should not change dramatically, if at all.

50. The total number of event-linked and pretextual cases in the post–9/11 era will increase as the remaining cases are collected and added to the database, and the total number of defendants indicted in event-linked cases after 9/11 should remain close to the average for the pre–9/11 era. Similarly, I expect the average number of defendants indicted for pretextual cases to climb slightly higher than the figures reported.

51. Shields, *An Analysis of Prosecutorial and Defense Strategies in Federal Terrorism Trials from 1980 to 2004*, 138.

52. Ibid., 139.

53. Ibid., 138–139.

54. Ibid., 139.

55. Ibid., 14.

56. Michael Murkasey, *Memorandum for the Heads of Department Components*, September 29, 2008, 3.

57. Michael Murkasey, *The Attorney General's Guidelines for Domestic FBI Operations*, December 1, 2008, 5.

58. Ibid., 12–13.

59. Ibid., 16.

60. Ibid., 18.

61. Ibid.

62. Ibid.

10

The Commander-in-Chief after 9/11

Aziz Z. Huq*

One of the most contested questions of constitutional law after September 11 has been the meaning of Article II, Section 2's first clause: "The President shall be Commander in Chief of the Army and Navy of the United States."[1] This chapter aims to answer three questions: What disputes over the meaning of the so-called Commander-in-Chief Clause did post–9/11 policies and practices incite? Why did such controversies arise? And, how will such debates about the Commander-in-Chief Clause's meaning likely be settled in the future?

Founding Era Understandings

The Framers did not envisage the Commander-in-Chief Clause as a source of confounding constitutional difficulties or confusion. At the Philadelphia Convention of 1787 delegates debated at length the method of presidential selection, but devoted scant time to determining what authority "the executive Power" of Article II would confer on the president, let alone the specifics of the terse Commander-in-Chief Clause.[2] Writing in the *Federalist Papers* to support ratification, Alexander Hamilton indeed claimed that "little need be said to explain" the Commander-in-Chief Clause.[3] The absence of an executive office under the pre-1787 Articles of Confederation also meant there was no exact post-Revolutionary precedent for the office that George Washington was first to occupy.

---

* **Aziz Z. Huq** teaches at the University of Chicago School of Law.

Undisputed guidance about the original public meaning of the Clause is thus elusive.

But, the Commander-in-Chief Clause has proved to be a source of interbranch friction and has provided grist for scholarly debate in ways that belie Hamilton's epistemic optimism. The Clause has generated different lines of interpretative disagreement, with debate after 9/11 focusing on a cluster of issues that received little attention prior to 2001.

The Puzzles of the Commander-in-Chief Clause

The Commander-in-Chief Clause settles one question and opens two others. It resolves the question whether the military will be independent of civilian, democratic control (it will).[4] It is a sign of the Clause's triumph that concerns about military coups d'état play little role in American history. In stark contrast to other presidential systems in the Americas, the U.S. Constitution has proved resistant to military destabilization and overt autocratic rule.[5]

Two other questions implied by the Clause, however, have not been settled so successfully. One dominated pre–9/11 debates on the Clause. The other has surged to the fore since 9/11.

Before 9/11, a principal axis of debate concerned the distribution of authority between the White House and Congress in determining large-scale strategic deployment of military forces or the initiation of hostilities against another sovereign state. The Commander-in-Chief Clause coexists with a clause in Article I of the Constitution assigning to Congress the power to "declare War." This textual division of strategic war-making powers between the elected branches under these Clauses yielded the dominating fissures in twentieth-century academic- and political debates.[6]

Given America's post–World War II role in the global order—in locales as far flung as Korea, Vietnam, Cambodia, Lebanon, Grenada, Panama, Kuwait, Somalia, Bosnia, and Kosovo—this should be no surprise. Each international conflict involving American forces pressed the question whether Congress or the president would have the first or final say on the use of armed force.

Frictions reached their zenith over the Vietnam War. In 1973, Congress enacted the War Powers Resolution over President Nixon's veto in an effort to settle this question. At its core, the Resolution requires the president to report to Congress within 48 hours of introducing U.S. forces "into hostilities or into situations where imminent involvement in hostilities is clearly indicated by the circumstances," and to withdraw such forces after 60 days absent authorizing legislative action.[7] But presidents have resisted recognition of the Resolution's binding force, even if they have—grudgingly, more or less—complied with it.[8]

Since 9/11, debates about strategic war-making powers have taken a backseat. Unlike cold-war conflicts, post–9/11 military deployments in Afghanistan and Iraq have not been the subject of close conflict between the White House and Capitol Hill (at least at the time of their authorization). In both instances, President George W. Bush easily secured legislative authority long before boots hit the ground.

To be sure, military engagements since 2001 have not been limited to those theaters. But other deployments, such as the discrete military strikes used in Yemen in November 2002 and Somalia in 2007 to kill specific individuals, raised few eyebrows in Congress—however dubious they might have been under international law. As a result, the distribution of strategic war-making powers at the macro level sparked little debate during the Bush presidency.

New Debates for New Conflicts

However, this does not mean that Commander-in-Chief Clause has ceased to be a point of contention. Rather, changes in the nature of America's transnational and international conflicts opened a new front in debates about the Commander-in-Chief Clause's meaning: does the Commander-in-Chief Clause give the president a zone of *tactical* discretion that Congress cannot enter? Specifically, does the Commander-in-Chief Clause allow the president to authorize tactics that are in violation of federal law that Congress has enacted, international treaties to which the United States is party (including those prohibiting cruel, inhuman or degrading treatment and torture), and the uncodified customary rules of international law?

In the decades prior to 9/11, Congress had enacted a series of restrictive statutes and treaties constraining the retail use of coercive force—that is, the use of individualized tactics such as detention and surveillance—in addition to its regulation and direction of large-scale force deployments. The 1949 Geneva Conventions, which American delegates helped negotiate and draft, established a baseline of minimum humanitarian treatment for civilians and soldiers *hors de combat*.[9] The 1978 Foreign Intelligence Surveillance Act, or FISA, provided that its warrant mechanism was the "exclusive means" for national-security-related surveillance in the United States.[10] In addition, a panoply of federal statutes and treaties prohibited and criminalized torture and its sibling, "cruel, inhuman, and degrading" treatment.[11]

Like many international commitments that seemingly constrain American freedom of action, many of these statutes and treaties were conceived from a need to protect *Americans*. Negotiating the Geneva Conventions, for example, American diplomats emphasized the brutal Japanese treatment of American prisoners of war, and specifically sought to preclude their repetition by clear legal prohibition.[12] Laws on surveillance similarly were designed to protect Americans' constitutional rights. Coming in the wake of revelations about the FBI's COINTELPRO program (which targeted leftist domestic dissidents) and Watergate, FISA sought to channel electronic surveillance into a judicially supervised legal framework so it would not be turned against perceived political foes at home.

Anti-torture statutes and treaties were not responses to the real and prevalent abuses in twentieth-century American prisons or among American allies overseas, but rather an elaboration of the leadership role of the United States on human rights questions. For the five decades after World War II, America championed international treaties that put torture out of bounds during war and peacetime. Foreign torturers, at least in theory, found no haven in America. State Department human rights reports condemned tyrannies around the world for using torture. Federal courts issued path-breaking rulings declaring the torturer, "like the pirate and slave trader before him... [to be] *hostis humani generis*, an enemy of all mankind."[13] Even if these treaties did not directly protect Americans, they served a larger strategic goal of asserting America's moral primacy against the iniquities of the Soviet system.

In the wake of 9/11, however, statutes and treaties crafted to protect Americans' constitutional rights or to cement American leadership in world affairs came to be viewed by the executive branch as constraining barriers to effective security. The White House and allies in the Department of Justice thus developed a series of legal opinions articulating the authority to exercise a "prerogative power" to disregard statutory and treaty restrictions on torture, surveillance, and detention. The legal theory used to circumvent or override these laws rested on several components of Article II, including the Vesting Clause,[14] the president's putative foreign affairs authority, and the Commander-in-Chief Clause.

Like the British kings of the sixteenth- and the seventeenth century, President Bush claimed a "prerogative power" to override otherwise applicable federal law on surveillance, torture, and detention in the name of national security.[15] The core of the claim is nicely articulated by a 2002 legal opinion from the Department of Justice concerning the coercive interrogation of suspected terrorists—commonly known as the "Torture Memo": "Any effort by Congress to regulate the interrogation of battlefield combatants would violate the Constitution's sole vesting of the commander-in-chief authority in the President....Congress can no more interfere with the President's conduct of the interrogation of enemy combatants than it can dictate strategic or tactical decisions on the battlefield."[16]

The Justice Department lodged a similar objection to legislative limits on electronic surveillance.[17] Indeed, even after Congress acquiesced to an expansion of surveillance authority in the face of executive-branch fear-mongering, Justice Department lawyers nevertheless insisted that the resulting law was "just advisory. The President can do what he wants to do [because]...the [P]resident's Article II power trumps any ability by Congress to regulate the collection of foreign intelligence."[18]

This theory of prerogative presidential power found initial articulation in a series of legal opinions from the Office of Legal Counsel, or OLC, a division of the Justice Department tasked with authoritative interpretation of federal law that binds the rest of the federal bureaucracy. The previously mentioned torture memos were OLC memos.[19] Initially these opinions were classified and secret. They furnished the basis for executive orders authorizing the National Security Agency to bypass FISA and engage in a sweeping program of electronic surveillance,[20] and they authorized the CIA to engage in a new program of extrajudicial arrest, detention, and "rendition" of terrorism suspects in collaboration with countries such as Jordan, Syria, and Egypt.[21]

In addition to providing a legal basis for presidential actions OLC's legal opinions worked as "cover" for intelligence agencies' employees, who often had grave concerns about their exposure and the financial liability they might face as a consequence of tort suits. Without legal opinions from OLC, it is doubtful career intelligence officials would have agreed to the White House's policy choices. Evidence for this comes from what happened when OLC opinions justifying "enhanced" interrogation tactics were leaked to the public and were cast into doubt by vociferous and uniform criticism of their results-oriented analysis: absent the confidence that they had the law behind them, CIA officials suspended the use of enhanced measures citing a fear of liability.[22] Without the *legal* theory that justified the circumvention of laws barring new forms of intelligence gathering and interrogation methods, the *on-the-ground* government responses to 9/11 would have looked significantly different.

Catalysts of Change

The nature of debate about the Commander-in-Chief Clause shifted after 9/11 in part because of "the peculiar nature of the war on terrorism."[23] Confronting al Qaeda, the United States faces an asymmetric enemy lacking a state or a clear geographic base, a disaggregated, dispersed terrorist network that ebbs and flows to include new individuals and groups over time.[24] Intelligence, not military might, is thought to be at a premium. The decision about how to gather intelligence outside battlefield situations—from a menu of options that includes surveillance, detention, licit coercion, and tortuous interrogation—seems centrally important in counter-terrorism success. Where the cold war generally sparked overt conflict over the political control and direction of states in Southeast Asia, Central America, or the Caribbean, the confrontation with al Qaeda atomized conflict—dispersing and personalizing it beyond the territory previously understood to be the battlefield in a way that put pressure on commitments to seemingly foundational values regarding human dignity and privacy.

It would be a mistake, nevertheless, to ascribe the shift in constitutional debate to the changing nature of transnational conflicts alone. After all, the post–9/11 threat environment was not entirely novel. Soviet adversaries had attempted espionage and sabotage during the cold war. And some of al Qaeda's attacks, such as the October 2000 assault on the *U.S.S. Cole* in Aden, Yemen, had the feel of a traditional military endeavor.[25] Moreover, it is far from clear that the Bush administration even needed to develop a new vision of presidential power in order to accomplish its goals. As Harvard Law Professor (and former OLC Chief) Jack L. Goldsmith has pointed out: "[t]he American public largely shared the government's anxieties on 9/11." It is not unreasonable to think that the White House would have received most, or all, of what it wanted by seeking new legislation from Congress. Indeed, Goldsmith points out, on the occasions that President Bush sought legislative authorization for detention and surveillance policies rejected by the courts, he obtained successfully through the legislative process "a lot of what he thinks he needs for national security."[26] Why then did the White House go it alone?

According to Goldsmith, who served in the Bush administration, "[t]he answer . . . is that the administration's conception of executive power had a kind of theological significance."[27] Indeed, there is ample evidence that well before 9/11, key members of the Bush administration, most importantly Vice President Richard Cheney and his legal counsel, David Addington, had an idiosyncratic "theology" of presidential power that brooked no possibility of compromise with Congress, its laws, or the federal courts that enforce those laws.

In 1987, then-Representative Cheney (R-Wyoming) engineered a response to the Iran-Contra scandal of the late 1980s in a congressional minority report. This report articulated a vision of executive power to override Congress's directives on national security. It even asserted that the executive branch should exercise "monarchical prerogatives" in the event

Congress tried to regulated intelligence operations.[28] The Iran-Contra affair did not directly concern the question whether the president could turn aside laws in the name of national security. Rather, the debate focused on whether officers of the executive branch could deceive Congress in the name of national security.[29] In the Cheney-led minority report, such affirmative deception was artfully redescribed as an exercise of the "constitutionally protected power of withholding information from Congress."[30]

Cheney's argument was a variant of former President Richard Nixon's claim that "when the President does it, that means it's not illegal."[31] But—at the very least—Nixon made his claim *after* he resigned from office. By contrast, Cheney made his claim *before* entering the White House as vice president. In December 2005, Cheney explained, in terms worth quoting at length, to reporters during a trip to Muscat, Oman, that he had not abandoned this view of executive prerogatives:

> [O]ver the years there had been an erosion of presidential power and authority…a lot of the things around Watergate and Vietnam, both, in the '70s served to erode the authority, I think, the President needs to be effective especially in a national security area. If you want reference to an obscure text, go look at the minority views that were filed with the Iran-Contra Committee; the Iran Contra Report in about 1987. [T]hey were actually authored by a guy working for me, for my staff, that I think are very good in laying out *a robust view of the President's prerogatives with respect to the conduct of especially foreign policy and national security matters.* … I do believe that, especially in the day and age we live in, the nature of the threats we face, it was true during the Cold War, as well as I think what is true now, *the President of the United States needs to have his constitutional powers unimpaired, if you will, in terms of the conduct of national security policy.* That's my personal view.[32]

Although 9/11 and the concomitant changes in the security environment presented the opportunity to alter constitutional constructions and understandings, it was thus an idiosyncratic "personal view," presumably shared by others in the Bush administration, that drove the White House's new understanding of the Commander-in-Chief Clause. That understanding was not articulated and defended in the public sphere but instead brought to bear directly to justify new modes of interrogation, detention, and surveillance.

The Future of the Cheney Doctrine

The proposition that the Commander-in-Chief Clause vests the president with wide-ranging authority to set aside or violate federal statutes and duly enacted treaties is flatly contradicted by all traditional sources of constitutional meaning: its text, the Founding understanding, subsequent practice, and Supreme Court precedent.[33] Advocates for sweeping, prerogative presidential powers drew succor from the British monarchical model of executive power.[34] But the Founders "expressly rejected" the British monarchical model of executive power.[35] Having lived most of their lives as subjects to the British king, the Founders were steeped in British constitutional history—a history that furnished them with a powerful warning *against* vesting the executive branch with open-ended power.

The claim of unilateral presidential authority also runs headlong into the extensive range of congressional authorities under Article I of the Constitution on martial matters, including the power to issue rules for "Captures on Land and Water" and the authority to "make Rules for the Government and Regulation of the land and naval Forces."[36] Historical experience endorses the Constitution's textual *sharing* of war powers. Professors David Barron and Martin Lederman, in an impressively compendious article, have demonstrated that the actual practice of presidents and Congress does not reflect a prerogative presidential power. Rather, history "reflects an understanding that Congress could control the Commander in Chief by statute even for such clearly tactical matters as the movement of troops."[37]

And yet this does not mean that the theory of prerogative Commander-in-Chief power will die with its Bush administration progenitors. On the contrary, underlying dynamics of political and institutional change mean that the idea of sweeping prerogative presidential powers may have a significant half-life. For what is correct as a matter of constitutional text and history is not necessarily what works in Washington, DC, or Peoria, IL, for that matter.

The United States has a most peculiar constitutional culture: superficially, constitutional meaning is tightly tethered to the Founding era's understandings. The U.S. government, however, has undergone dramatic transformations in the absence of any formal constitutional change through Article V of the original, organic document.[38] In the twentieth century, the United States had the New Deal, created the postwar administrative state, witnessed a second Reconstruction, and enabled a new birth of civil rights without formal constitutional change. The latter has, by and large, been reserved for matters of minor significance.[39] Constitutional meaning as facts on the ground depends on more pragmatic considerations than text or historical meaning: it has at bottom rested less on legal form and more on underlying political and socioeconomic fact.

So while the prerogative power theory of the Commander-in-Chief Clause can be traced to the confluence of 9/11's exigencies and a small clique's idiosyncratic ideology, that theory would have had little effect without the institutional ecology or instrumental means to give it weight. Even after the end of the Bush presidency, the federal executive branch continues to wield ample power and opportunity to act unilaterally. This is consequence of three trends. Since none of these trends expired with the Bush administration's close, the potential for the prerogative power's renewed application remains.

The first trend is the rapid growth of the executive branch's sheer size, especially in the security sector, to the point where effective congressional or public oversight is all but infeasible. Simple numbers tell the story. In 1930, the federal government had 608,915 employees. In 2004, it had 2,649,319.[40] In 1946, the United States had no permanent intelligence apparatus. In 2005, the federal government spent 44 billion dollars on its 16 permanent intelligence agencies and their staff of 100,000.[41]

Second, the White House's ability to control directly this growing web of agencies has expanded. Whereas in the 1930s, "White House staff could barely be described in the plural,"[42] by the turn of the twentieth century the vice president's office alone had a staff estimated at up to 80; the exact number, remains classified.[43] In 2001, former Harvard Law School and U.S. Solicitor General Dean Elena Kagan described, without contradiction, the ascendance of "presidential administration," whereby presidents had "personal ownership" of the activities of federal agencies, and could use this ownership to impose policy change across the federal policy spectrum from health care and welfare reform to gun control and civil rights.[44] Centralized control has been especially pronounced in the national security field.

Finally, there has been a shift of de facto legislating authority from Capitol Hill to the White House. Today, national security policy is almost always achieved via unilateral directives from the White House known as executive orders. Presidents initially used executive orders to convey instructions inside the executive branch. But as the federal government swelled, their reliance on such orders increased. Between 1920 and 1998 presidents issued more than 10,000 unilateral directives, many concerning national security matters.[45] Unilateral executive directives issued without congressional approval were in the background of the most controversial of the Bush administration's post–9/11 security policies, including military tribunals, "extraordinary rendition," "enhanced" interrogation measures, and warrantless electronic surveillance. Combined with the president's veto power, these make congressional rollback of executive preferences difficult: once the president has set a policy, the Congress needs to muster a two-thirds vote to erase it. Rising use of such orders means it is no longer Congress, but rather the White House, setting ground rules for much federal policy.

These trends mean that the ability of other branches, especially Congress and the courts, to check the president has withered. And those branches show little sign of recognizing their increasing frailty, let alone addressing it. As a result, the space and capacity for executive unilateralism, deploying former Vice President Cheney's vision of prerogative powers, remains open.

Until Congress and the courts recognize and compensate for the tremendous functional and institutional changes that the twenty-first century wrought to the executive branch, the idea of prerogative presidential power under the Commander-in-Chief Clause will remain a loaded weapon, hidden in constitutional folds awaiting its next bearer.

Notes

1. U.S. Constitution, art. II, §2, cl.1.
2. Forrest McDonald, *Novus Ordo Seclorum: The Intellectual Origins of the Constitution* (Lawrence: University of Kansas Press, 1985), 247, 249–253.
3. Alexander Hamilton, James Madison, and John Jay, *The Federalist Papers*, ed. Clinton Rossiter (New York, Mentor, 1961).
4. David Luban, "On the Commander in Chief Power," *Southern California Law Review* 81 (2008): 477.
5. See generally Juan Linz, "The Perils of Presidentialism," *Journal of Democracy* 1 (Winter 1990): 51.
6. Important examples include John Hart Ely, *War and Responsibility: Constitutional Lessons of Vietnam and Its Aftermath* (Princeton: University of Princeton Press, 1993); Louis Fisher, *Presidential War Power* (Lawrence: University Press of Kansas, 2004); Francis D. Wormuth and Edwin B. Firmage, *To Chain the Dog of War* (Urbana: The University of Illinois, 1989). The academic literature in the journals is too large to catalog.
7. War Powers Resolution, Pub. L. No. 93–148, 87 Stat. 555 (codified at 50 U.S.C. §§ 1541–1548).
8. For this history and an argument supporting noncompliance, see John C. Yoo, "The Constitution of Politics by Other Means: The Original Understanding of the War Powers," *California Law Review* 84 (1996): 167, 186–188.
9. The most salient is the Third Convention. The Geneva Convention (III) Relative to the Treatment of Prisoners of War, August 12, 1949 [1955] 6 U.S.T. 3316, 3318, T.I.A.S. No. 3364.
10. 50 U.S.C. §§1801 et seq.
11. For example, 18 U.S.C. §§2340–2340A.
12. Raymond Yingling and Robert W. Ginnane, "The Geneva Conventions of 1949," *American Journal of International Law* 45 (1951): 407.
13. *Filártiga v. Pena Irela*, 630 F. 2d 876, 890 (2d Cir. 1980).
14. "The executive Power shall be vested in a President of the United States," U.S. Constitution, art. II, §1.

15. Carolyn A. Edie, "Tactics and Strategies: Parliament's Attack upon the Royal Dispensing Power 1597-1689," *American Journal of Legal History*, 29 (1985), 197.

16. Memorandum from Jay S. Bybee for Alberto R. Gonzales, Counsel to the President, "Standards of Conduct for Interrogation under 18 U.S.C. §§2340–2340A," August 1, 2002, in Mark Danner, *Torture and Truth: America, Abu Ghraib, and the War on Terror* (New York: New York Review Books, 2004), 149.

17. Faced with a federal statute regulating *all* electronic surveillance of American citizens and residents within the United States, the Justice Department simply asserted "constitutional limits on Congress's ability to interfere with the President's power to conduct foreign intelligence searches." The Justice Department invoked the president's role in foreign affairs and his "authority to direct the Armed Forces in conducting a military campaign." U.S. Department of Justice, "Legal Authorities Supporting the Activities of the National Security Agency Described by the President," January 19, 2006, 30–35.

18. James Risen and Eric Lichtblau, "Concerns Raised on Wider Spying under New Law," *New York Times*, August 19, 2007, A1.

19. Randolph D. Moss, "Executive Branch Legal Interpretation: A Perspective from the Office of Legal Counsel," *Administrative Law Review* 52 (2000): 1303.

20. James Risen and Eric Lichtblau, "Bush Let U.S. Spy on Callers without Courts," *New York Times*, December 16, 2005, A1.

21. Dana Priest, "CIA Holds Terror Suspects in Secret Prisons: Debate Is Growing within Agency about Legality and Morality of Overseas System Set Up after 9/11," *Washington Post*, November 2, 2005.

22. Dana Priest, "CIA Puts Harsh Tactics on Hold," *Washington Post*, June 27, 2004, A1.

23. David J. Barron and Martin S. Lederman, "The Commander in Chief at the Lowest Ebb—A Constitutional History," *Harvard Law Review* 2121 (2008): 941, 945.

24. The former commander of U.S. forces in Iraq has succinctly outlined the challenges involved. David W. Barno, "Challenges in Fighting a Global Insurgency," *Parameters* 36 (2006): 15.

25. Lawrence Wright, *The Looming Tower: Al Qaeda and the Road to 9/11* (New York: Knopf, 2006), 319–320.

26. Jack L. Goldsmith, *The Terror Presidency: Law and Judgment inside the Bush Administration* (New York: W.W. Norton, 2007), 187, 207–208.

27. Ibid., 212.

28. Report of the Congressional Committees Investigating the Iran-Contra Affair, with Supplemental, Minority, and Additional Views, S. Rep. No.100-216, H. Rep. No. 100-433, at 465 (1987) (hereinafter Iran-Contra Report).

29. See Harold Hongju Koh, *The National Security Constitution: Sharing Power after the Iran-Contra Affair* (New Haven: Yale University Press, 1990), 113–116 (summarizing Iran-Contra affair with careful attention to the role of the president).

30. See Iran-Contra Report, supra, 448–452; 457–460.
31. Nixon quoted in Derek Jinks and David Sloss, "Is the President Bound by the Geneva Conventions?" *Cornell Law Review* 90 (2004): 97, 149.
32. Vice President's Remarks to the Traveling Press, December 20, 2005, emphasis added; available at http://www.whitehouse.gov/news/releases/2005/12/20051220-9.html.
33. The argument is rehearsed in nontechnical terms in Frederick A. O. Schwarz and Aziz Z. Huq, *Unchecked and Unbalanced: Presidential Power in a Time of Terror* (New York: New Press, 2007), 151–184.
34. For example, see John Yoo, "Transferring Terrorists," *Notre Dame Law Review* 79 (2004): 1183, 1202–1203.
35. McDonald, *Novus Ordo Seclorum*, 248.
36. U.S. Const., art. 1 §8.
37. Barron and Lederman, "The Commander in Chief at the Lowest Ebb," 946.
38. One of the most interesting treatments of this problem is Bruce Ackerman, *We the People: Foundations* (Cambridge: Belknap Press, 1993).
39. See Bruce Ackerman, "The Living Constitution," *Harvard Law Review* 120 (2007): 1737.
40. Neal Katyal, "Internal Separation of Powers: Checking Today's Most Dangerous Branch from within," *Yale Law Journal* 115 (2006): 2314, 2342, 2316.
41. See Mark Mazzetti, "Spymaster Tells Size of Secret Spy Force," *New York Times*, April 21, 2006, A21; Mark M. Lowenthal, *Intelligence: From Secrets to Policy* (Washington: CQ Press, 2000), 24–39.
42. Andrew Rudalevige, *The New Imperial Presidency: Renewing Presidential Power after Watergate* (Ann Arbor: University of Michigan Press, 2005), 43.
43. Barton Gellman and Jo Becker, "A Different Understanding with the President," *Washington Post*, June 24, 2007, A1.
44. Elena Kagan, "Presidential Administration," *Harvard Law Review* 114 (2001): 2245, 2246–2248.
45. William G. Howell, *Power without Persuasion: The Politics of Direct Presidential Action* (Princeton: Princeton University Press, 2003), 1–7.

II

Intelligent Oversight

Anne Joseph O'Connell[*]

The structure of the American intelligence community has shifted in significant ways in recent years, moving from decentralized and redundant agencies to a more unified system. In 2004, Congress established the Director of National Intelligence (DNI) position and provided that person with some budgetary and personnel authority over the nation's 16 intelligence agencies. Congressional oversight of the intelligence community, however, has largely remained fragmented in the aftermath of September 11, 2001. There is no primary oversight committee in either the House of Representatives or the Senate, with the Appropriations, Armed Services, and Intelligence Committees all exercising significant power.

The stability of congressional oversight structures, even before the 2001 attacks, cuts against the recommendations of many commentators. The National Commission on Terrorist Attacks upon the United States and the Commission on the Intelligence Capabilities of the United States Regarding Weapons of Mass Destruction—more commonly known as the 9/11 and WMD Commissions, respectively—forcefully called on members of Congress to consolidate their overlapping committees tasked with intelligence matters. Congress made some efforts to address these proposals after the Commissions issued their reports and again after the Democrats took control of both chambers in the November 2006 election. But those efforts produced relatively minor changes.

In this chapter, I detail the Commissions' recommendations for reform of congressional oversight and subsequent congressional responses. I then

[*]**Anne Joseph O'Connell** is Assistant Professor of Law at University of California-Berkeley.

discuss whether the suggested reforms are desirable, both in terms of protecting our nation's safety and fostering the rule of law. Finally, I explain why members of Congress have not adopted significant changes and propose several alternative reforms for congressional oversight that likely will improve national security, promote democratic values, and are more politically feasible to implement.[1]

Calls for Reform and Congressional Response

The 9/11 Commission, after reviewing more than 2.5 million pages of documents, conducting more than 1,200 interviews, and holding 19 days of prominent hearings, concluded that both the executive and legislative branches' intelligence efforts should be more centralized.[2] One of the Commission's five major proposals focused on congressional oversight: "unifying and strengthening congressional oversight to improve quality and accountability." Seventeen committees appear to wield power over at least one intelligence agency.[3] The Commission called for a joint intelligence committee for the House of Representatives and the Senate, or, in the alternative, for a single committee to replace the multiple committees in each chamber.[4] This was not the first appeal for a joint committee on intelligence. That came in 1948 from Representative Edward Devitt (R-MN),[5] and it has been repeated throughout the intervening decades.[6]

Ideally, in the Commission's view, this joint committee (or separate committee in each chamber) would have the "power of the purse," controlling authorizations and appropriations.[7] If that were not possible, the 9/11 Public Discourse Project, a nonprofit organization formed by the members of the 9/11 Commission, recommended that each chamber's Appropriations Committee form a new intelligence subcommittee. The Commission also wanted the Intelligence Committees to abolish term limits for membership and to reduce their size.[8]

The WMD Commission endorsed the 9/11 Commission's call for consolidation of congressional oversight. The WMD Commission also offered several "more modest" proposals. Like the 9/11 Public Discourse Project, it recommended that each chamber create an intelligence subcommittee in its Appropriations Committee. It also counseled that the Senate Intelligence Committee be given the same authority over joint military intelligence programs and tactical intelligence programs that the House Intelligence Committee now possesses. Those programs and the national intelligence program make up the entire intelligence community's budget. The WMD Commission also stressed the need for more expertise and cooperation—between the two parties on the Intelligence Committees and between the Committees and the intelligence community. To this end, it recommended, among other items, that each chamber's Intelligence Oversight Subcommittee be restricted to forward-looking "strategic oversight" and that the Intelligence Committees abolish term limits.[9]

The 9/11 Commission report, in particular, garnered significant attention and contributed to the enactment of the Intelligence Reform and Terrorism Prevention Act in December 2004.[10] The Act, in addition to other mandates, established a DNI with cabinet rank and created a National Counterterrorism Center.[11] The major legislation did not, however, change congressional oversight. Congressional reform, to the extent it has occurred, has been far more piecemeal.

Before the shift in party control of Congress from the Republicans to the Democrats in January 2007, the House of Representatives had adopted fewer reforms than the Senate. In 2002, the House created a Homeland Security Committee. Initially established as a select committee, it became a standing committee in January 2005. The Committee does not, however, have exclusive jurisdiction over any issue, including intelligence.[12] The House Intelligence Committee also formed a subcommittee devoted to oversight.[13] Some House members backed more extensive changes. In October 2004, Representative Carolyn Maloney (D-NY) proposed that the House elevate its Intelligence Committee from a select committee to a standing committee and give it exclusive jurisdiction over the intelligence community, including members within the Department of Defense.[14] In July 2006, Representatives Jeff Flake (R-AZ) and Adam Schiff (D-CA) called for the House Intelligence Committee to disclose considerable classified information to at least eight other House committees.[15] Neither proposal was voted out of committee.

Two months before the adoption of the Intelligence Reform and Terrorism Prevention Act, the Senate made several internal changes to its oversight of the intelligence community.[16] For its Intelligence Committee, the Senate reduced the number of members from seventeen to fifteen, gave party leaders the power to choose the chairman and vice chairman, eliminated the eight-year term limits for members, established an oversight subcommittee, and promoted the committee to category "A" status (generally senators can serve on no more than two "A" committees). It voted to create an intelligence subcommittee of its Appropriations Committee, but as of September 2008 that subcommittee did not exist. The Senate also changed the name of its Governmental Affairs Committee to the Committee on Homeland Security and Governmental Affairs. The significance of these reforms is unclear. The Congressional Research Service termed them "the most significant change in Senate [Intelligence] committee operations since 1977,"[17] but the *New York Times* editorial staff labeled them "cosmetic."[18]

In 2005, the 9/11 Public Discourse Project awarded Congress a "D" for intelligence oversight in the organization's final report card for the implementation of the 9/11 Commission's recommendations, finding that the House of Representatives and the Senate "have taken limited positive steps, including the creation of oversight subcommittees" but that congressional oversight "is still undermined by the power of the Defense Appropriations subcommittees and the Armed Services committees."[19]

The 2006 election created a critical opportunity for congressional reform. Many Democrats campaigned on a promise to implement the remaining recommendations of the 9/11 Commission. But after the Democrats won majorities in both chambers, House Speaker Nancy Pelosi (D-CA) felt that she could not ask Representative John Murtha (D-PA), chairman of the Defense Appropriations Subcommittee, to give up control of the intelligence community's budget because Murtha had just lost the contest for majority leader, despite her backing.[20]

The House of Representatives instead established a new Select Intelligence Oversight Panel within the Appropriations Committee in January 2007. The House's political leaders select the panel's thirteen members, three of whom have to be from the Intelligence Committee and two of whom have to be the Chairman and Ranking Minority Member of the Defense Appropriations Subcommittee. The panel oversees spending on intelligence and drafts the classified part of the Defense Appropriations bill, but the Defense Appropriations Subcommittee retains its authority to set funding levels. As part of its oversight authority, the panel can request the Appropriations Committee or Defense Subcommittee to subpoena witnesses.[21] House Intelligence Chairman Silvestre Reyes (D-TX), whom Pelosi had named to his position, appeared pleased with the formation of the new panel: "I believe we've had the kind of better understanding and coordination between authorizers and appropriators that we need." Amy Zegart, a national security scholar, however, noted that "it's not the same as having appropriating powers."[22]

The Senate did not follow the House. In March 2008, all but one of the members of the Senate Intelligence Committee wrote to Senate leaders requesting appropriations power or for the creation of an intelligence subcommittee within the Appropriations Committee. The Appropriations Committee responded, opposing those requests. Both of the Committee's suggestions have been proposed more formally: the former by Senators Richard Burr (R-NC) and Evan Bayh (D-IN),[23] the latter by Senators Christopher Bond (R-MO), John Rockefeller (D-WV) and Sheldon Whitehouse (D-RI).[24] But no action has been taken.

The 9/11 Commission had also recommended that the intelligence community's budget be made public to improve oversight and accountability.[25]

In 2007, Congress agreed to require the DNI to disclose publicly the size of the national intelligence program every fiscal year, unless the president waives the mandate on national security grounds. Although the administration opposed it, President Bush signed the requirement into law.[26]

Desirability of Consolidation of Congressional Oversight

Intelligence commissions typically have pushed for congressional oversight to become more centralized (along with the structure of the intelligence community itself). Even Judge Richard Posner, who favors redundancy in the intelligence community to foster competition and reliability, supports more consolidation in Congress.[27] The American Civil Liberties Union (ACLU), however, opposes consolidation of congressional oversight.[28] Should congressional oversight be unified? To answer that question, the benefits and costs of different institutional arrangements for the protection of national security and democratic values must be compared.[29] Reformers understandably, but mistakenly, focus on the benefits of unification and the costs of fragmentation and redundancy. The proper comparison is between the net benefits of each.

Consider first the appeal of unification for congressional oversight. Most important, the consolidation of congressional jurisdiction, supporters contend, will lead to more meaningful oversight. The 9/11 Commission determined that Congress had failed to perform sufficient oversight. The Commission made much of the fact that congressional committees held only about three dozen hearings on terrorism from January 1998 to September 2001.[30] In light of its policy proposals, the Commission must have thought that more hearings (and thus improved oversight) would have occurred during that same period if there were a joint intelligence committee or only one committee in each chamber with exclusive authority over intelligence matters.

The reasoning behind this conclusion could derive from the perspective of the intelligence agencies or of the committees. According to former staff members of the Intelligence and Appropriations Committees, intelligence agencies "play one committee against the other, often getting the funding [they] nee[d] without the level of oversight and scrutiny that every other federal agency has come to expect."[31] Indeed, Congress has failed to pass annual intelligence authorization legislation, which would bring more oversight, since 2005.[32] Intelligence agencies might face substantially more oversight if they had to answer to one committee.

Alternatively, if there are multiple committees with jurisdiction over intelligence matters, individual committees may focus on other issues in their exclusive jurisdiction and free-ride off the supposed efforts of other overseers. By contrast, the argument goes, members and congressional staff assigned to a committee with complete authority over the intelligence community would develop the necessary expertise and would be more diligent if they knew that no other committee could conduct oversight and consequently that they faced more accountability for their work.[33]

The consolidation of congressional oversight, proponents argue, also would encourage more cooperation by the White House and intelligence agencies. Even after September 11, 2001, congressional committees complained that they were not getting the information they believed they needed from particular agencies.[34] Supporters of a joint intelligence committee contend that the executive branch "would be more open and forthright with a single, small [joint] oversight body than with two with a larger combined membership."[35]

The White House and intelligence agencies may believe that the current structure of congressional oversight allows members of Congress to use their oversight powers more for political gain than for improving national security. The executive branch, in turn, treats Congress with "contempt," according to some key congressional observers.[36] If there were only one committee in each chamber with authority over it, the intelligence community may be less skeptical of that committee and less able to suggest that oversight is politicized. To be certain, the executive branch might find it easier to block oversight if it has to fend off only one committee, though a single committee presumably would wield more power than any one of the current multiple committees.

Finally, if we extend a primary argument made for unification of the intelligence community to Congress, the unification of congressional oversight will permit Congress to "connect the dots" in intelligence efforts. Multiple committees that split up the monitoring of the intelligence agencies may find it difficult to get a complete picture of intelligence operations. In sum, unification of congressional oversight promises more oversight, more cooperation from intelligence agencies, and better substantive outcomes.

Consider now the costs of consolidating congressional oversight. Most critically, because each committee, with its own memberships, adopts a particular perspective on intelligence efforts, a fragmented and overlapping committee structure provides, according to proponents of the status quo, necessary redundancy to avoid a national security failure and to protect core democratic values.[37] For instance, the Senate Homeland Security and Government Affairs Committee may emphasize a potent threat that the Senate Intelligence Committee mistakenly might ignore. Or the House Judiciary Committee, if notified, may raise questions about the legality of warrantless surveillance of international communications with people inside the United States that the House Intelligence Committee would not challenge.[38]

In addition, the consolidation of congressional oversight, opponents fear, will promote uncritical monitoring if intelligence agencies or relevant interest groups are better able to "capture" their overseers, when they are fewer in number.[39] If congressional committees have cozy relationships with the agencies they oversee, they are less likely to press those agencies to improve national security or to foster the rule of law. Because the ALCU fears that the Intelligence Committees will not ask tough questions about the legality of intelligence activities, it wants the House and Senate Judiciary Committees to "retain jurisdiction over intelligence matters affecting legal and constitutional rights."[40] Having multiple committees with power over the intelligence community likely matters more when the same party controls the White House and Congress; agency capture may be less of a problem during periods of divided government.[41]

Finally, the unification of oversight may hinder the development of congressional expertise. Overlapping congressional committees, proponents argue, permit more members of Congress to learn about the intelligence community.[42] To the extent that individual members play particularly important roles in the oversight that gets conducted, redundancy in the committee system may ameliorate any negative consequences if certain members retire, fail to get reelected, or devote attention elsewhere.[43] In addition, because redundancy results in more committees approving an initiative, thereby encouraging consensus among members, legislation is more likely to pass when it comes to a vote.[44] In short, decentralized oversight has the potential to increase reliability, to avoid capture by the intelligence community, and to build expertise and consensus.

Weighing these benefits and costs to congressional consolidation is a complex task, even if we just look to structural choices between unification, on one hand, and redundancy and fragmentation, on the other. To start, the structure of the targets of oversight—here, the intelligence community—affects how Congress should organize itself. One study by scholars interested in both preserving national security and protecting civil liberties concluded that the decentralization of counterterrorism functions prior to the 2004 Intelligence Reform and Terrorism Prevention Act had prevented the emergence of a "single oversight structure, not simply in Congress, but also within the executive branch."[45] To the extent that the DNI now manages all of the intelligence agencies, and this assumption is contested by many experts and news accounts,[46] fewer congressional committees may be needed to oversee the intelligence community. Members of Congress could concentrate their oversight on the DNI's actions. Nevertheless, if we worry that there are now fewer competing voices within the intelligence community, a redundant oversight system where committees take their responsibilities seriously may get better results from a unified intelligence community than a single committee could.

In assessing these structural choices, we want to determine which arrangement will produce better quality oversight, which may not be the same as more oversight. In Loch Johnson's words, we need more "guardians" who will seriously review the activities of the intelligence community and fewer "ostriches" who do not engage, "cheerleaders" who do not question, and "skeptics" who automatically question.[47] It may be possible to obtain the benefits of consolidation *and* redundancy by cutting the number of committees with jurisdiction over the intelligence community but not by as much as the 9/11 Commission desired. Some overlap but more responsibility may foster cooperation with the executive branch, increase accountability of Congress, improve reliability to avoid national security failures, and better protect democratic values. I take up this suggestion in more detail in the next section.

The number of committees, of course, is not the only choice that we should consider in institutional design. I should at least mention two other important variables. First, the composition of oversight committees and committee staff may affect national security and the rule of law more than the number of those committees. Studies on group polarization suggest that congressional oversight would be more effective if committees were evenly balanced in terms of party membership and if committee staff were nonpartisan. Furthermore, commentators have lamented the often fierce party conflict playing out in the Intelligence Committees, which maintain partisan staff, in recent years. As Zegart quips, "members are rewarded more for airing dirty laundry than cleaning it."[48] L. Britt Snider emphasizes the importance of bipartisanship: "Nothing will make a greater difference in terms of enhancing the effectiveness and credibility of the oversight committees than restoring bipartisanship to their operations."[49] Here, unlike in assessing the ideal number of committees, balancing is not necessary, at least for normative concerns of effectiveness and legitimacy: less partisanship would be beneficial. By contrast, committee term limits have competing effects. On one hand, they prevent committee members from developing expertise; on the other, they permit new insights. To foster expertise and alternative perspectives, the terms of committee members could be lengthened and staggered—an idea to which I return later.

Second, the transparency of congressional committee activities also may shape national security and democratic values in significant ways. The 9/11 Commission stressed that "[s]ecrecy stifles oversight, accountability, and information sharing."[50] If committee work on intelligence matters were more transparent, members may be more accountable and thus more diligent in their oversight, no matter how many committees there are with jurisdiction over the intelligence community. On the other hand, intelligence is inherently secretive; too much transparency may harm national security efforts. A compromise might be reached, as discussed later, to increase transparency, at least within the government. The desirability of reform for national security and the rule of law is separate from its feasibility, to which I next turn.

Feasibility of Reform

It is important to consider political realities of institutional design choices, whether of the intelligence bureaucracy or, in the case here, of Congress itself. Much of the congressional response to the oversight recommendations of the 9/11 and WMD Commissions can be explained in political terms. Simply put, committees do not want to relinquish their turf; indeed, committees often try to expand their authority.[51] As the *New York Times* editorial page lamented: "The main recommendation [of the 9/11 Commission], for fewer committees and a more focused panel with hands-on power over intelligence budgeting, clearly lies beyond the present level of selfishness bristling among traditional committee leaders."[52]

Although the 9/11 and WMD Commissions recognized, to varying degrees, the political constraints on reorganizing congressional oversight, neither explicitly explained how change might occur. They seem to have believed that the importance of national security would trump these constraints. But in the decade preceding September 11, 2001, Congress had refused to adopt any of the recommendations concerning oversight of the intelligence community made by seven commissions. As Zegart explains, "Congress was the only government entity that failed to implement a single recommendation during the decade—a record worse than either the CIA's or the FBI's."[53]

To the extent that they contemplated the likelihood of their reforms being adopted, the 9/11 and WMD Commissions must have thought that the tragic events of September 11, 2001 would provide the necessary jolt for Congress to modify well-established structures. The constant hammering for congressional reform by Commissioners and the media did produce some change. The 2006 election presented a second opportunity for changes in congressional oversight because the new Democratic majorities wanted to better monitor the executive branch. The House Democrats did push through some consolidation in intelligence appropriations.

More can be done, however, to improve congressional oversight. Keeping political constraints in mind, I offer five proposals, some of which draw from the Commissions' reports and all of which are targeted at fostering national security and the rule of law. To start, the number of committees with jurisdiction over the intelligence community should be reduced, but not by as much as recommended by the 9/11 Commission. Each chamber's Intelligence, Armed Services, Judiciary, and Appropriations Committees should continue to exercise oversight, but the House and Senate Appropriations Committees should establish a subcommittee for intelligence with actual power, not just advisory input, over intelligence appropriations. By modifying appropriations, intelligence agencies will not be able to play the authorizers off the appropriators to the same extent as they do today.[54] We might again see authorizing legislation, in addition to annual appropriations. By preserving some redundancy and specialization, Congress can better protect national security and democratic values. The Judiciary Committees may be better suited to foster the rule of law, while the Armed Services and Intelligence Committees may be better able to protect national security. The National Security Agency's eavesdropping program, for example, raises intelligence and constitutional concerns. A single committee in each chamber likely cannot adequately address both critical goals.

To complement this reduction in the number of committees overseeing the intelligence community, the Intelligence Committees, at least, should be as evenly balanced by party as possible. In addition, staff should be nonpartisan. If the Intelligence Committees function in a bipartisan manner, the executive branch is more likely to cooperate in oversight efforts. Contrary to the 9/11 Commission's recommendation, Intelligence Committee members should have term limits, though those terms should be long enough to promote the development of helpful expertise and should be staggered so that some members always have important knowledge about the intelligence community while others contribute potentially critical new ideas.

These reforms likely could attract sufficient support to be enacted. Their most politically unpalatable component is the creation of intelligence subcommittees of the Appropriations Committees; unlike advisory panels, these subcommittees would take power away from defense appropriators (and connected authorizers on the Armed Services Committees). Because of the immense size of the nonintelligence budget they control, however, defense appropriators would lose authority over only about 10 percent of funds they currently oversee. Perhaps those members can be enticed to relinquish power by having some of them named to the new subcommittees. At the least, the eight committees that retain some oversight authority under this proposal are likely to support the stripping of jurisdiction from the other committees. Other members may support this consolidation as well because they can take credit for correcting some of the problems identified by the Commissions. Staggered term limits and near-party parity may also generate support, if members believe they have some chance of serving on one of the consolidated committees. A member on a committee that would lose power may agree to that loss for the opportunity to serve a fixed term on a committee that oversees more of the intelligence community. In addition, members of the minority party may support consolidation if it is accompanied by better party parity on the committees that remain.

I offer three other recommendations for reform of congressional oversight. First, more members of Congress should receive notification of critical intelligence activities. Current law requires the president to notify the Intelligence Committees of covert intelligence operations before they take place. In extraordinary circumstances, the president can limit his reporting to the "Gang of Eight," which includes the chairmen and ranking minority members of the two Intelligence Committees, the speaker and minority leader of the House of Representatives, and the majority and minority leaders of the Senate. Under President George W. Bush's administration, prior notification was not provided, even to the Gang of Eight, for covert operations by military special operations forces.[55] The law should be clarified to include those activities. The law should also extend notification in extraordinary circumstances to more key members of Congress and to critical staff—a Gang of Sixteen or Twenty-Four, perhaps. Secrecy can be protected by making the consequences to public disclosure by anyone "read in" to an operation sufficiently severe. As Heidi Kitrosser explains in proposing information funnels for national security information, the scope of disclosure should balance the need for deliberation with the need for secrecy.[56] This reform seems feasible to implement, with Congress motivated to strengthen its hand and with the Obama administration publicly committed to increasing transparency and protecting civil liberties.

Second, the ranking minority members of the Intelligence Committees should be able to subpoena witnesses and call hearings. Presently, no ranking minority member has that authority.[57] In rare circumstances, Congress has permitted deviations from this rule to foster bipartisanship and the legitimacy of oversight. When the House of Representatives established its Select Bipartisan Committee to Investigate the Preparation for and Response to Hurricane Katrina, it gave the ranking minority member powers equivalent to the chairman.[58] By giving ranking minority members such authority, Congress is creating redundancy within the Intelligence Committees, which could offset the potential costs of consolidation for reliability and for the rule of law. It may also reduce the politicization of intelligence. To be certain, this reform calls for a fundamental change in how Congress organizes itself. Minority members should favor this proposal; members who are in the majority may also support such a proposal because they anticipate being in the minority at some point in the future or because they believe intelligence is a unique policy area. To be certain, the recommendation may be extremely difficult to adopt.

Third, Congress should strengthen the Government Accountability Office (GAO)'s ability to investigate the intelligence community and then task the GAO to evaluate and report on intelligence activities at regular intervals. The GAO is Congress's primary auditor of the administrative state; it reviews agency programs on its own initiative, by statutory mandate, and at the request of members of Congress. The GAO, however, has officially complained that the intelligence community rarely cooperates with its investigations: "[U]nless and until we receive such cooperation [from the intelligence community], and given GAO's limited recourse, we will continue our long-standing policy of not doing work that relates directly to intelligence matters unless requested to do so by one of the select intelligence committees."[59] In particular, the GAO cannot obtain necessary materials from the CIA.[60] Congress could pass legislation requiring the CIA and other intelligence agencies to respond to GAO's requests for information, but, despite some recent attempts by Senator Daniel Akaka (D-Alaska), it has not done so.

By tasking the GAO to evaluate the intelligence community's efforts on a recurrent basis, Congress can delegate on the beat "police patrols" to its watchdog agency and then use its own scarce resources to pursue identified concerns. Currently, congressional oversight of the intelligence community depends heavily on "fire alarms" rung by the media or interest groups.[61] GAO reporting would help shift congressional attention from a "flood of second-guessing at the back end, after each flap, that further demoralizes and enfeebles the spies" to "scrutiny on the front end that could improve performance and check abuses."[62] Like increased disclosure requirements, this reform seems feasible in today's political climate, with Congress more willing to stand up for congressional oversight and with a White House at least talking about the need for greater openness. The reform also complements the previous proposal for more authority to be accorded to ranking minority members of the Intelligence Committees. The GAO is one of few tools that minority members have to monitor the bureaucracy as the GAO treats requests from chairmen and ranking minority members similarly.[63]

Conclusion

The intelligence community faces many overseers, within and outside the legislative branch. As the community adapts to changes in the aftermath of September 11, 2001, so will its monitors. Congressional overseers may not change in fundamental ways desired by popular, bipartisan commissions. But legislative monitoring may change in ways that are politically palatable. Those politically attractive changes will hopefully foster national security and the rule of law, nonpolitical values that we hold dear.

Notes

The writing of this chapter was supported by the National Science Foundation, Human and Social Dynamics Division, Grant No. 624296. Ellen Gilmore, Dean Rowan, and especially Tess Hand-Bender provided excellent research assistance. From 2001 to 2003, I was a trial attorney at the Federal Programs Branch of the U.S. Department of Justice. As a team member helping to review designations of entities linked to terrorism before their assets were frozen and defend those designations when legal challenges were brought, I interacted with members of the intelligence community. Nothing in this chapter is based on confidential or classified information, and none of my views should be attributed to the Department of Justice.

1. This chapter draws from my longer article on the structure of the intelligence community and its congressional overseers. See Anne Joseph O'Connell, "The Architecture of Smart Intelligence: Structuring and Overseeing Agencies in the Post–9/11 World," *California Law Review* 94 (2006): 1655–1744. By focusing on congressional oversight, I do not mean to suggest that other forms of oversight are unimportant. Within the federal government, the Privacy and Civil Liberties Oversight Board, the President's Foreign Intelligence Advisory Board, the Office of Management and Budget, Inspectors General, the White House, and the courts, among others, play important roles in intelligence oversight. Outside the government, the media and organizations such as the American Civil Liberties Union oversee, in various ways, the intelligence community. I also concentrate on oversight of the intelligence community and leave aside oversight of the non-intelligence components of the Department of Homeland Security, which has also generated considerable attention from the 9/11 Commission and others.

2. For the executive branch, the Commission recommended that the intelligence community be unified under a national intelligence director who would, among other duties, "manage the national intelligence program and oversee the agencies that contribute to it." National Commission on Terrorist Attacks upon the United States [9/11 Commission], *The 9/11 Commission Report* (New York: W.W. Norton & Co., Inc., 2004), 407.

3. Bert Chapman, *Researching National Security and Intelligence Policy* (Washington, DC: CQ Press, 2004), 234–243. The following committees in the House of Representatives have authority over at least one intelligence agency: Intelligence; Appropriations; Armed Services; Budget; Energy and Commerce; Government Reform; Homeland Security; International Relations; and Judiciary. The following Senate committees have jurisdiction over at least one such agency: Intelligence; Appropriations; Armed Services; Budget; Energy and Natural Resources; Foreign Relations; Homeland Security and Governmental Affairs; and Judiciary. In both chambers the Intelligence Committee is a select committee, not a standing committee. See O'Connell, "The Architecture of Smart Intelligence," 1662.

4. *The 9/11 Commission Report*, 400, 420.

5. Frederick M. Kaiser, *A Joint Committee on Intelligence: Proposals and Options from the 9/11 Commission and Others* (Washington, DC: Congressional Research Service RL32525, 2004), 1.

6. Glen Hastedt, "Foreign Policy by Commission: Reforming the Intelligence Community," *Intelligence and National Security* 22 (2007): 443–472.

7. No congressional committee currently has both authorization and appropriation authority.

8. *The 9/11 Commission Report*, 421.

9. Commission on the Intelligence Capabilities of the United States Regarding Weapons of Mass Destruction, *Final Report* (Washington, DC, 2005), 20, 337–341.

10. *Intelligence Reform and Terrorism Prevention Act of 2004*, Public Law 108–408, *U.S. Statutes at Large* 118 (2004): 3638.

11. It is unclear how much those changes will improve the effectiveness of the intelligence community. See O'Connell, "The Architecture of Smart Intelligence"; Tim Starks, "Intel: Lost in the Reshuffle," *CQ Weekly*, May 5, 2008; Amy B. Zegart, *Spying Blind: The CIA, the FBI, and the Origins of 9/11* (Princeton: Princeton University Press, 2007).

12. 9/11 Public Discourse Project, *Final Report on 9/11 Commission Recommendations* (Washington, DC, 2005), 8–9.

13. Ibid., 8.

14. *Amending the Rules of the House of Representatives to Establish a Standing Committee on Homeland Security and a Standing Committee on Intelligence*, H.R. Res. 837, 108th Congress, 2d sess.

15. *To amend the Rules of the House of Representatives to specify conditions under which the Permanent Select Committee on Intelligence of the House of Representatives shall be required to exercise its authority to make classified information in its possession available to certain standing committees of the House, and for other purposes*, H.R. Res. 5954, 109th Congress, 2d sess.

16. *To eliminate certain restrictions on service of a Senator on the Senate Select Committee on Intelligence*, S. Res. 445, 108th Congress, 2d sess.

17. Paul S. Rundquist and Christopher M. Davis, *S. Res. 445: Senate Committee Reorganization for Homeland Security and Intelligence Matters* (Washington, DC: Congressional Research Service RS21955, 2004), 5.

18. "Unfinished Intelligence Work," *New York Times*, October 11, 2004.

19. 9/11 Public Discourse Project, *Final Report*, 3.

20. Jonathan Weisman, "Democrats Reject Key 9/11 Panel Suggestion," *Washington Post*, November 30, 2006.

21. *To enhance intelligence oversight authority*, H.R. Res. 35, 110th Congress, 1st sess.

22. Starks, "Intel: Lost in the Reshuffle."

23. *Amending Senate Resolution 400, 94th Congress, and Senate Resolution 445, 108th Congress, to improve congressional oversight of the intelligence activities of the United States*, S. Res. 375, 110th Congress, 1st sess.

24. *To improve congressional oversight of the intelligence activities of the United States*, S. Res. 655, 110th Congress, 2d sess.

25. *The 9/11 Commission Report*, 416.

26. *Implementing Recommendations of the 9/11 Commission Act of 2007*, Public Law 110–153, *U.S. Statutes at Large* 121 (2007): 266.

27. Richard A. Posner, *Preventing Surprise Attacks: Intelligence Reform in the Wake of 9/11* (New York: Rowman & Littlefield Publishers, Inc., 2005), 36, 43, 63, 97, 140.

28. Timothy H. Edgar, *ACLU Analysis of the 9-11 Commission's Recommendations for Intelligence Reform* (New York: American Civil Liberties Union, 2004), http://www.aclu.org/natsec/emergpowers/14501leg20040730.html (accessed October 8, 2008).

29. The 9/11 and WMD Commissions, along with Judge Posner, seem more concerned with national security. This emphasis on national security is understandable in the aftermath of September 11, 2001. But congressional oversight of the intelligence community has deep roots in the protection of the rule of law. Congress established the House and Senate Intelligence Committees in the 1970s largely because of unconstitutional actions by intelligence agencies. As a normative matter, it seems that we should want the intelligence community to work effectively within our Constitution.

30. *The 9/11 Commission Report*, 104–107; Zegart, *Flying Blind*, 144–146.

31. Denis McDonough, Mara Rudman, and Peter Rundlet, *No Mere Oversight: Congressional Oversight of Intelligence Is Broken* (Washington DC: Center for American Progress, 2006), 17.

32. Tim Starks, "Intelligence Authorization Bill Collapses amid Conflicting Explanations," *CQ Weekly*, March 23, 2009.

33. More oversight is not necessarily better than less. A similar argument could be made if multiple congressional committees engaged in too much oversight, calling agency officials to testify so frequently that the work of the agencies suffers. Commentators have suggested that such a context exists in homeland security. The Center for Strategic and International Studies and the Business Executives for National Security found that 79 congressional committees and subcommittees have "some amount of jurisdiction over various aspects of homeland security." CSIS-BENS Task Force on Congressional Oversight of the Department of Homeland Security, *Untangling the Web: Congressional Oversight and the Department of Homeland Security* (Washington, DC: Center for Strategic and International Studies, 2004), 2. Consolidating oversight would, in this context, decrease oversight and thus improve agency effectiveness.

34. Philip B. Heymann, *Terrorism, Freedom, and Security: Winning without War* (Cambridge: MIT Press, 2003), 152–156; Zegart, *Flying Blind*, 54.

35. Kaiser, *A Joint Committee on Intelligence*, 9; see also Mathew D. McCubbins and Thomas Schwartz, "Congressional Oversight Overlooked: Police Patrols versus Fire Alarms," *American Journal of Political Science* 28 (1984): 165–179.

36. Norman J. Ornstein and Thomas E. Mann, "When Congress Checks Out," *Foreign Affairs*, November/December 2006, 75.

37. Jonathan B. Bendor, *Parallel Systems: Redundancy in Government* (Berkeley: University of California Press, 1985); Martin Landau, "Redundancy, Rationality, and the Problem of Duplication and Overlap," *Public Administration Review* 29 (1969): 346–358.

38. On the other hand, such redundancy may encourage free-riding. Michael M. Ting, "A Strategic Theory of Bureaucratic Redundancy," *American Journal of Political Science* 47 (2003): 274–292. A committee may forgo the costs of oversight, because it thinks that another committee will engage in necessary oversight or because it believes the costs of failure are not sufficient to induce oversight activity. It is unlikely that congressional committees will shirk their oversight responsibilities completely because the political benefits to some oversight are likely greater than its costs. But the oversight that gets conducted in such circumstances may be more targeted to media coverage than to fostering national security or democratic values.

39. Loch K. Johnson, *America's Secret Power: The CIA in a Democratic Society* (New York: Oxford University Press, 1989), 222; Kaiser, *A Joint Committee on Intelligence*, 10.

40. Edgar, *ACLU Analysis*.

41. To be certain, multiple committees encourage specialization, and such specialization could increase the possibility of capture—especially if the public pays less attention to any one committee.

42. Kaiser, *A Joint Committee on Intelligence*, 14.

43. Members of Congress, however, juggle several committee assignments, making it hard to "giv[e] adequate time and attention to anyone of them." Marvin C. Ott, "Partisanship and the Decline of Intelligence Oversight," *International Journal of Intelligence and Counterintelligence* 16 (2003): 87. Indeed, in the intelligence context, a majority of members on the Intelligence Committees turned up at approximately one-third of public hearings from 1975 to 1990. If there were fewer committees, members would have fewer assignments and could spend more time developing expertise and attending committee meetings—though Senators, with more committee responsibilities, were more likely to turn up at Intelligence hearings than Representatives. See Loch K. Johnson, *Secret Agencies: U.S. Intelligence in a Hostile World* (New Haven: Yale University Press, 1996), 97.

44. Nancy Staudt, "Redundant Tax and Spending Programs," *Northwestern University Law Review* 100 (2006): 1219–1220.

45. Philip B. Heymann and Juliette N. Kayyem, *Preserving Security and Democratic Freedoms in the War on Terror* (Cambridge, MA: Belfer Center for Science and International Affairs, 2004), 258.

46. Starks, "Intel: Lost in the Reshuffle."

47. Loch K. Johnson, "Ostriches, Cheerleaders, Skeptics and Guardians: Role Selection by Congressional Intelligence Overseers," *SAIS Review* 38 (2008): 93–108.

48. Zegart, *Flying Blind*, 58.

49. L. Britt Snider, "Congressional Oversight of Intelligence after 9/11," in *Transforming US Intelligence: Challenges for Democracy*, ed. Jennifer Sims and Burton Gerber (Washington, DC: Georgetown University Press, 2005), 245.

50. *The 9/11 Commission Report*, 24.
51. E. Scott. Adler, *Why Congressional Reforms Fail: Reelection and the House Committee System* (Chicago: University of Chicago Press, 2002); David C. King, *Turf Wars: How Congressional Committees Claim Jurisdiction* (Chicago: University of Chicago Press, 1997); David C. King, "The Nature of Congressional Committee Jurisdictions," *American Political Science Review* 88 (1994): 48–62.
52. "Energizer Bunnies," *New York Times*, December 31, 2004; see also Starks, "Intel: Lost in the Reshuffle."
53. Zegart, *Flying Blind*, 154.
54. As Zegart explains, intelligence agencies try to skirt greater scrutiny by the authorizing committees by seeking refuge with the appropriations committees (and in particular, with the Defense appropriators). Starks, "Intel: Lost in the Reshuffle."
55. Seymour M. Hersh, "The Redirection," *The New Yorker*, March 5, 2007, 65; Snider, "Congressional Oversight of Intelligence after 9/11," 251.
56. Heidi Kitrosser, "Congressional Oversight of National Security Activities: Improving Information Funnels," *Cardozo Law Review* 29 (2008): 1049–1090.
57. Frederick M. Kaiser, Walter J. Oleszek, T.J. Halstead, Morton Rosenberg, and Todd B. Tatelman, *Congressional Oversight Manual* (Washington, DC: Congressional Research Service RL30240, 2007), 56.
58. The minority leader refused to appoint members to this Committee, fearing that the Committee would sugarcoat its assessment. Under 5 U.S.C. § 2954, groups of the general oversight committees in Congress (e.g., Senate Homeland Security and Governmental Affairs Committee) can seek information from agencies without the permission of the chairmen, though there seems to be no way to enforce compliance. Kaiser et al., *Congressional Oversight Manual*, 57–61.
59. Government Accountability Office, *DoD Personnel Clearances: Questions and Answers for the Record Following the Second in a Series of Hearings on Fixing the Security Clearance Process* (Washington, DC: GAO 06-693R, 2006), 1, note 1.
60. Kaiser, *A Joint Committee on Intelligence*, 14, note 20; Frederick M. Kaiser, "GAO versus the CIA: Uphill Battles against an Overpowering Force," *International Journal of Intelligence and Counterintelligence* 15 (2002): 330–389.
61. Ornstein and Mann, "When Congress Checks Out," 68.
62. David Ignatius, "Intelligence Oversight in Free Fall," *Washington Post*, December 13, 2007.
63. Anne Joseph O'Connell, "Who Walks the Watchdog? Bureaucratic Oversight and the Government Accountability Office," working paper, School of Law, University of California, Berkeley, 2008.

12

The Failure of Institutionalized Accountability in Matters of National Security since 9/11

*William G. Weaver and Rene Flores**

There are four main ways to bring the executive branch to heel for abuse of power. Three of these methods are based in constitutionally authorized exercises of power, and the fourth arises from apostasy from within the executive branch. First, the Congress may inquire into executive branch activities through hearings, subpoenas, and studies by support agencies to Congress and other investigatory mechanisms. Congress may also threaten funding or cut off funding altogether in order to force executive acquiescence or strangle programs that have become questionable. Finally, Congress has the power to impeach and remove the president. The powers of Congress are extensive, but are rarely used with any vigor and the maneuverability of the modern presidency almost always works to outflank the lethargic, deliberate, and cumbersome processes of the legislative branch.

Second, the executive branch may be made answerable to judicial authorities for their actions. Numerous statutes transfer congressional oversight power into the hands of the judiciary, where more thorough, systematic, and privately driven actions lead to broader oversight of the executive than is possible by Congress to achieve on its own. For example, one of the greatest transfers of oversight authority occurred under the Federal

*****William G. Weaver** is Associate Professor of Political Science at the University of Texas, El Paso, and author of *Presidential Secrecy and the Law* and *New Perspectives on American Law.*

Rene Flores is a graduate student in political science at the University of Texas, El Paso.

Tort Claims Act, where Congress authorized suits against the United States for tortious injury caused by governmental actions. The creation of a money damages remedies in law against the United States relieved Congress of much of the onerous and divisive problems associated with the rather unillustrious history of so-called private bills.[1] Private citizens, through the power of suit, now undertook oversight of executive branch actions by demanding money damages for wrongs committed by federal agencies and their employees. Many such suits have been filed against the United States since the events of September 11, 2001 that concern abuse of authority in the name of national security; but new and revitalized devices have arisen to thwart accountability.

Third, and perhaps historically the most effective check on executive branch abuse of power, is the free press. There is nothing like embarrassment to cause damage to the executive branch and the presidency for stepping outside the bounds of propriety and law. But this check only works so long as the press and reporters have reasonable freedom to publish, have avenues of access to information, and are not co-opted by federal agencies or the considerations of powerful corporate interests. Since 9/11 the executive branch has engaged in significant efforts to manipulate the mainstream media and to undermine the influence of alternative, presumably less controllable, publication venues.

Finally, fraud, waste, abuse, or violations of law perpetrated by executive agencies may come to light through whistleblowing. Every employee of the federal government is commanded by rule or oath to report wrongdoing to appropriate agencies, but those who take these duties seriously often find themselves punished, fired, demoted, referred for psychiatric evaluation, isolated or threatened with criminal prosecution. While some whistleblowers have become icons of virtue and morality, most are relegated to obscurity and are handled with impunity by the agencies they work for. And in the areas of law enforcement and national security, whistleblowers are afforded no legal protection whatsoever when they report government wrongdoing.[2]

All four of these mechanisms of executive branch oversight have become more problematic since 9/11. Layered onto the already difficult matter of subjecting the executive to scrutiny and checks on abuses of power, the specter of national security now looms in virtually every oversight effort directed at executive actions or programs. Here we undertake an overview of how oversight efforts have become more difficult in the years since 9/11 and how even greater power now resides in the executive branch to withstand scrutiny and avoid answering public inquiries. Due to space constraints this examination will be summary in nature and can only hit on main points with respect to each area considered.

We should be clear that we have no disagreement whatsoever that the executive branch rightly has the power necessary to effect national security; the tools to fight enemies must be updated as our enemies and their tactics change. And Congress has willingly engaged in granting broad power to the executive branch in various areas after 9/11. But concomitant to any transfer or increase of power in the executive branch should be mechanisms to make sure that new powers are subject to oversight and internal controls that provide a reasonable guarantee that agencies will not overstep the law or the Constitution, or encroach on the powers of the coequal branches of government. In our opinion, post 9–11 transfers of authority to the president have not been matched by mechanisms to ensure that those powers are not abused.

The principal obstacle to oversight of the executive branch since 9/11 has been the comprehensive use of secrecy to screen even innocuous information from disclosure to Congress, courts, and the public. Virtually all classified documents, rules concerning classification, and declassification decisions are controlled by the executive branch through authority under executive orders, statutes, and case law. The stance of every recent president is that he has "ultimate and unimpeded authority over the collection, retention and dissemination of intelligence and other national security information.... There is no exception to this principle for those disseminations that would be made to Congress or its Members."[3] We should note that very little classified material is authorized under statute, and that almost all national security information is classified on the basis of executive order and the judgment of civil servants and nothing else. The U.S. Supreme Court has never issued a clear constitutional holding that the president has plenary authority to determine what is national security information and to retain exclusive control over its dissemination, but it is clear that the executive branch is owed great deference in its decisions to classify information.

In the early part of last century military and bureaucratic secrecy merged under uniform classification systems and orders, and blossomed into the "national security state" beginning in the 1940s. Presidents, of course, even from the beginnings of the Republic, have often refused to disclose information on various grounds. These grounds were, for the first 140 years of the United States, generally left undifferentiated; with the incipient beginnings of executive privilege, the state secrets privilege,[4] and classification power collapsed under the general claim of separation of powers in the justifications for refusal of disclosure. There was little urgent need to differentiate the grounds of these claims, since the presidency was modest in size and scope of activity. It is difficult to tease out the exact early provenance of the president's power to control national security information, but a path toward this end can be traced from presidential action in specific events to the modern constitutional and statutory bases for such control.

All administrations engage in secrecy for partisan advantage or to prevent congressional enemies from acquiring useful information, but the trajectory of presidential secrecy power has been on an uninterrupted upward course since the beginning of last century. The early attempts described earlier to shield executive branch information became increasingly awkward as the federal government grew and the national security environment burgeoned with complexity. More formalized mechanisms were needed, and these could only be created with the help of Congress. At the end of the nineteenth century, there existed two broad bases for withholding information; one based in separation of powers and the other in consideration of bad consequences that would flow from release of information. The separation of powers argument is designed to protect the functioning of the presidency and to prevent overreaching by Congress and the courts. The concern under this argument is for a preservation of constitutional divisions of authority.

On the other hand, the protective power argument flows from nothing more than the purely pragmatic and functional necessity to prevent damage to the nation and its citizens from the disclosure of sensitive information that could aid our enemies. While these powers were not insignificant they were exercised on an ad hoc basis. But the press of technology and entanglement in large-scale war in the twentieth century provided the ground that allowed the presidency to lay claim to unlimited control over all national security information. Through statutory intervention just before and during World War I, the separation of powers and the protective power arguments began to coalesce into the single claim that the Constitution commits to the president sole authority over control of national security information.

A question that is seldom explored is how much opacity in governmental activity the Constitution and our democracy will tolerate. On the one hand, we expect executive branch officials to maintain the security of the nation and its citizens, which can often times be accomplished only through secret activity. On the other hand, we expect that the president and executive branch officials will be held legally accountable for their abuses of power, and accountability requires publicity of actions and policies. These two desires are often incompatible and pose difficult issues for courts and politicians. But since the 1950s, and with increasing speed through the 1970s to the present, the balance toward secrecy has shifted decisively in favor of the executive branch. Before the events of 9/11, executive powers of secrecy were a set of non-interlocking privileges, powers, and policies that operated in ad hoc ways—which partially obscured the secrecy power that Congress and the courts ceded to the president over the previous years. The events of 9/11 catalyzed these disparate powers into a set of interlocking mechanisms that have fundamentally transformed the office of president and the powers of the executive branch in a manner that creates challenges to effective accountability and oversight of executive branch activity.

From the perspective of executive branch power to control national security information and to provide for the safety of the nation we briefly look at the four chief means of holding the executive branch accountable and how those mechanisms have changed in light of the events of 9/11.

Congressional Oversight of the Executive Branch since 9/11

Thomas Jefferson had great fear of legislative tyranny, and indeed early in the Republic considered the legislative branch the most dangerous body. In a March 15, 1789 letter to James Madison he noted that "The executive power in our government is not the only, perhaps not even the principal, object of my solicitude.... The tyranny of the executive power will come in its turn, but at more distant period."[5] It is arguable that the "distant period" Jefferson spoke of is now upon us. With the advent of what Theodore Lowi terms the plebiscitary presidency[6] combined with a now highly developed and coherent presidential claim to plenary power to classify and control national security information, the president is now in a position to make direct appeals to the public for support and to cut off Congress from information for reasons of national security. This combination of sophisticated mobilization of public opinion through complex strategies and the claimed ability to refuse information to Congress greatly reduces the accountability of the presidency and agencies of the executive branch. And if we also consider the influence of the controversial "unitary executive" theory, which emphasizes unreviewable presidential power in a time of emergency, the result is that in no time in history has the presidency had to answer for so little of what it does.[7]

In the aftermath of the terrorist attacks of 9/11, the Bush administration made unprecedented claims of executive powers of secrecy and asserted broad powers to withhold information from Congress, the courts, and the public. In response to these claims Congress initially contributed to expansion of executive power by rushing into effect a number of statutes either creating or extending executive authority to engage in surveillance and searches and protect the United States from both internal and external threats. Public expectations changed on 9/11 and Congress suddenly became compliant in the arena of domestic security. Presidential power expanded behind a moving wall of secrecy pre-justified to the people, and accepted by them, as necessary to protect their lives and the wealth of the country. With no means of inspection of how such expanded power is used, the people and Congress, made malleable through fear, largely accepted presidential action without complaint.

The quickest and easiest way to avoid congressional scrutiny of executive action is to simply classify information. It is true that executive orders prohibit the classification of material in order to "conceal violations of law, inefficiency, or administrative error" or to "prevent embarrassment to a person, organization, or agency."[8] But any violation of these prohibitions is at most subject to administrative sanction, and it is so unlikely that a person will be sanctioned for overclassification or fraudulent classification that it never enters a classifier's mind when making decisions. Indeed, diligent search has found no case where a classifier was sanctioned for wrongfully classifying material.

To be blunt, Congress is simply cowed when it comes to claims of national security made by the president or executive branch agencies. In one notable example of congressional fear to cross the executive branch on matters of claimed national security, the Department of Justice, under orders from Attorney General John Ashcroft, retroactively classified documents that had already been in the public realm and on the Internet for two years. These documents had been downloaded some 30,000 times in the years they were on the U.S. Senate website. The goal of this retroactive reclassification appeared to be an attempt to prevent Congress from using the documents in public hearings, and thus to limit executive branch embarrassment.[9] Congress acquiesced to the classification and removed the documents from its website and did not introduce them in the hearing in question, even though the documents were, and still are, readily available on numerous other sites on the web.

Even organizations that exercise minimal oversight of executive branch functions are targeted for retribution if they attempt to perform their legislatively defined duties. For example, the Information Security Oversight Office (ISOO), a small office with less than 30 employees, is responsible for making sure that the 4 million federal and civilian classifiers adhere to executive orders and statutes concerning the proper classification of information. As part of this process, the ISOO requires from each agency or office the number of documents classified and by which category (confidential, secret, or top secret) during the previous year. Vice President Cheney not only refused to provide information for the 2006 annual report for the Office of the Vice President, he attempted to have the ISOO abolished.[10]

Since 9/11, Congress has held a number of hearings on matters ranging from the state secrets privilege to the Foreign Intelligence Surveillance Act to the practice of extraordinary rendition to domestic surveillance by the

National Security Agency, but none of these hearings translated into law or even greater oversight effectiveness of the executive branch.

Judicial Oversight

"National security" is a notoriously dim term, and most definitions do little to make its meaning any clearer. For example, former Presidential Adviser Frank Press testified before Congress that "we have to take a broad view of what constitutes national security" and that "we have to define it in terms of economic growth in the country, of the cultural life in the country, the quality of life for our citizens, and the example we portray to other nations."[11] And Sidney W. Souers, the first director of Central Intelligence, wrote that "'national security' can perhaps best be understood as a point of view rather than a distinct area of governmental responsibility."[12] The problem, especially since the attacks of 9/11, is that the federal judiciary accepts executive branch assertions of this "point of view" almost always without even cursory scrutiny.

There has been a distinct abdication of judicial responsibility for oversight of executive branch actions and the failure to maintain separation of powers where security issues are concerned. Whenever national security concerns are raised, time and again the courts simply capitulate to presidential and executive branch desires. Federal judges are extremely reluctant to second-guess presidential claims that exposure of information, operations, and policies may imperil the United States. The theoretical underpinnings for this deference are sound, but sometimes this deference reaches remarkable levels—as when courts agree with the president that admission of the existence of a single car battery on an Air Force base,[13] or the admission into evidence of already published bank records, jeopardize national security.[14]

And courts are often more than merely passive participants in these efforts, sometimes actively taking part in denuding their own power through the creation of legal doctrines that inure to presidential wishes. For example, the federal judiciary often explicitly or implicitly employs a doctrine known as the "mosaic theory" to prevent exposure and accountability of executive branch activity. The disturbing feature of the mosaic theory is that it is most often used to prevent the disclosure of information that is neither classified nor directly connected with national security concerns, with the justification that individual bits of information, though unclassified, may add up to a classified picture of U.S. activities or capabilities.[15] Not surprisingly, the mosaic theory, among other legal doctrines, leads to abusive efforts by presidents to keep information secret to prevent embarrassment or exposure of evidence of crime.

Recently, facing executive branch assertions of national security, courts have also been willing to strike deposition questions to private citizen deponents such as "When and where were you born?" and "Where did you go to school." Information that could be revealed and discussed over coffee at a Starbucks was found by a federal judge to more than likely cause "grave damage" to the national security of the United States if revealed.[16] In various suits against the United States for violation Courts have also shown a willingness to expand the privileges and immunities of the president based both on Article II powers and on separation of powers doctrine.

The Free Press

The notion that the free press is indeed a check on government abuse is quite possibly the greatest innovation in politics in human history. By insulating a press against government influence and turning them loose to report all the wrongdoing they can find has done a great deal to preserve the Republic. This approach, at least in its degree, is almost uniquely American. Because our government is fixed with terms of office and may not be dissolved like those in parliamentary systems, there is less sense of immediacy of accountability to the people. The American press is supposed to fill this gap; it is supposed to engage in the hue and cry of scandal.

Consider that *The New York Times* had the story concerning warrantless National Security Agency (NSA) surveillance of Americans a full 13 months—before the general election of 2004—before it was finally published in December 2005. We can disagree about the legality of the underlying program, but since the *New York Times* revealed nothing sensitive about the program, what excuse can there possibly be for the nation's leading newspaper to keep the public in the dark for so long? It turns out that the pressure and pleas from the Bush administration were used against the paper, including personal face-to-face appeals by President Bush to *The New York Times* publisher, Arthur Sultzberger. Indeed, the story would not have come out if one of the original authors of the NSA story had not written about *The New York Times'* shameful acts in a book that was due to be released. One wonders what kind of information and access *The New York Times* traded for holding off on the story for 13 months. If *The New York Times* is supposedly the most professional and effective venue of investigation and reporting, vignettes such as that of the NSA case do little to inflate our optimism that the "free" media is a check on government abuse.

In an article *The New York Times* did manage to publish, a federal program authorized by President Bill Clinton and accelerated and expanded after 9/11 by the Bush administration reclassified "thousands of historical documents that were available for years, including some already published by the State Department and others photocopied years ago by private historians." J. William Leonard, then head of the ISOO, found after reviewing a representative sample of the documents that were reclassified that "[t]he stuff they pulled should never have been removed.... Some of it is mundane, and some of it is outright ridiculous."[17]

Since 9/11 the executive branch has also apparently systematically attempted to surreptitiously influence public opinion through manipulation of news sources. Instances of these kinds of actions abound, for example: Armstrong Williams received $400,000 to press for President Bush No Child Left Behind program;[18] the use of "phony" reporters by the Bush administration to engage in media manipulation;[19] the use of paid propaganda overseas;[20] creation and distribution of staged video "news" releases using actors posing as reporters that support positions taken by the Bush administration.[21] With such ranging manipulation of the news media, it is difficult to know what news sources and stories to trust. Recent efforts by the executive branch to control the news concerning the wars in Iraq and Afghanistan and political positions at home cause an uneasy perception that the accountability that a free press is supposed to provide is seriously compromised.

Whistleblowing

In other cultures, the idea of the whistleblower as someone turning against government or business for the good of the people is a strange and unfamiliar concept. Many languages do not have a word for such a person, or simply borrow from English. So perhaps in the United States we are lucky that it receives some attention and some minor protection, but this "concern" and protection also act as lures—coaxing people into believing that if they act to correct a wrong, if they follow the announced policies of their agencies and organizations and turn in wrongdoing, if they try to prevent violations of law by their colleagues, they will be sheltered. The vast majority of federal workers perform their work with honesty and integrity, but in the area of national security, where the stakes are high, there are temptations to violate laws and procedures to achieve results and ensure the safety of Americans.

Where law and procedure is circumvented for expedience and success, employees who follow reporting directives will find themselves targets of retaliation. On the one hand, law and regulation require the reporting of malfeasance, but on the other, to follow those directives is to all but guarantee retaliation. In the federal government, the Office of Special Counsel is tasked with protecting and investigating agency retaliation against whistle-blowers. But, as one of the first Special Counsels (the U.S. official charged with the main duty to protect whistleblowers), K. William O'Connor, explained, "I'd say that unless you're in a position to retire or are independently wealthy, don't do it. Don't put your head up, because it will get blown off." O'Connor complained that "OSC is not a Federal Ann Landers [though] there may be those who wish for one." He referred to whistleblowers as "severed heads," "uninformed, disgruntled or disaffected," "carrying bags and walking up and down Constitution Avenue," "blackmailers, and malcontents." It was his "presumption that management is acting properly," and that whistleblowers are mentally ill malefactors.[22] And the present special counsel seems, if anything, less inclined than Mr. O'Connor to carry out his statutorily mandated duties. Mr. Scott Bloch is under FBI investigation for violation of various federal statutes and is himself accused of punishing whistleblowers and others in his own office for attempting to do their jobs in protecting employees against agency retaliation. In May 2008, a dozen FBI agents seized various items from Bloch's home and office as "part of an investigation into whether the official retaliated against his employees and obstructed justice."[23] Bloch also is accused of arbitrarily dismissing hundreds of whistleblower complaints without investigation. Presently, the chances of a whistleblower seeing justice done are almost nil.

Whistleblowers who work in intelligence and law enforcement agencies labor under greater burdens than their colleagues in unclassified settings. The overused term "Kafkaesque" is accurate for what this category of whistleblower undergoes. National security whistleblowers face a host of impediments and dangers that "normal" whistleblowers do not face. Americans are ambivalent about whistleblowers, and that is how things are likely to remain; loving, admiring, and lionizing many of them in art and culture, while at the same time subjecting others to loathing and ridicule. It is difficult to embrace someone, without reservation, who brings to light facts and acts that cause revulsion, fear, or a loss of faith in the government.

To the whistleblower the choice is often stark: face persecution and not have to worry about moral redemption or retain the comfort of acceptance and anonymity and violate one's moral beliefs. Even in the face of vivid descriptions of what will probably happen to them for reporting wrongs, most people considering reporting wrongdoing feel compelled to ultimately make the complaint. Some believe that this represents a pathology, a mental illness, characterized by narcissism, antisocial tendencies, "black and white" thinking, and a quest for martyrdom. Categorization, of course, works well to dispose of people, to make light of what they have done, and to divert attention from what they have revealed. Categorization also allows whistleblowers as a group to be dismissed out of hand when convenient. Reduction to a stereotype eliminates the need to address reported wrongdoing and allows unique people and their acts to be aggregated into a "personality type."

One journalist, for example, attending a whistleblowers conference held in Washington, DC claimed that "[a]t the beginning of the week, I was skeptical of the proposition that whistle-blowing is a personality type you are born with." But she ended up concluding that "[a]bove all, 'whistle-blower' is a personality type that thinks in absolutes." The author implies that whistle-blowers lack the capacity for subtle thought, and are narcissistic and unreasonable. The author also insinuates that whistleblowers are immature and at least slightly ridiculous, noting that one was shooting spitballs during a presentation. Commenting on Jeffrey Fudin, a pain pharmacologist, she noted that Fudin "started blowing the whistle...when he suspected that the Albany V.A. hospital...was illegally experimenting on cancer patients...[H]e [also] blew it in 2004, when the hospital refused him time off to give a lecture on, natch, whistle-blowing."[24] Juxtaposing Fudin's request for leave to give a conference paper against his disclosure of "suspected" abuse at Stratton VA hospital makes him seem petty. But it would have taken little for the author to add that the unauthorized experimentation was not merely "suspected" but was responsible for the death of at least two men and the premature death of dozens of other VA patients. Destitute and desperate war veterans were browbeaten with threats to withhold treatment and were illegally enrolled in drug studies for pure economic gain. One man engaged in the program was sentenced to seven years in federal prison and Fudin's efforts doubtlessly prevented further loss of life and unnecessary suffering.[25]

No employee with any sense would presently conclude that he or she will be protected from agency retaliation for reporting wrongdoing on the part of the government. Such reporting has never received hospitable treatment, but is even less likely to be encouraged and protected in the post–9/11 environment. As one former employee for the National Security Agency put it, "in these very closed programs and operations, there's no formal system. The IG [Inspector General] is not cleared for these things. In many cases, some levels of supervisory elements...aren't [even] cleared."[26] In intelligence and law enforcement agencies even the mere reporting of wrongdoing becomes problematic. And with the broad and intense move to greater secrecy under the Bush administration post–9/11, it is all the more difficult for employees to report criminal activity of colleagues and supervisors. Employees have been threatened with prosecution for attempting to contact Congress,[27] have been sent for psychiatric evaluation for reporting wrongdoing,[28] had their security clearances terminated, have been reassigned to answer a telephone that never rings,[29] have received poor annual evaluations in an effort to cause termination,[30] and have been subjected to punishment through falsified documents.[31]

Whistleblowing has always been a rather poor check on the executive branch, but since 9/11 its efficacy is further compromised by redoubled efforts of retaliation and secrecy that chill the desire of employees to report wrongdoing in government.

Since 9/11, mechanisms of accountability have been eroded even as greater power is wielded by law enforcement- and intelligence agencies. It is difficult to determine how much abuse of power this increased power and decreased accountability has caused, but history shows clearly and consistently that compromised means of accountability inevitably lead to increased levels of agency abuse of power. Congress, the courts, and the press need to engage in measures to insure that executive branch agencies are subjected to sufficient scrutiny to result in compliance with law and the norms of our democratic society.

Notes

1. For most of the history of the United States, private bills were the chief means of recovery for citizens injured by tortuous actions of federal employees. The Federal Tort Claims Act was not enacted until 1946. See William G. Weaver and Thomas Longoria, "Bureaucracy That Kills: Sovereign Immunity, Federal Governmental Accountability, and the Discretionary Function Exception," *American Political Science Review* 96, no. 2 (June 2002): 335–349.

2. The Whistleblower Protection Act of 1989 does not provide protection to employees of intelligence agencies and some federal law enforcement organizations. Additionally, the Act allows the president to exempt coverage of employees "based on a determination by the President that it is necessary and warranted by conditions of good administration." 5 U.S.C. 2302(a)(2)(B)(ii).

3. *Brief for the Appellees, American Foreign Serv. Ass'n v. Garfinkel*, 488 U.S. 923 (1988) (no. 87-2127), at 42. President Clinton's Department of Justice reaffirmed this view through a memorandum analyzing congressional power to authorize disclosure of classified information to members of Congress by executive branch employees without first seeking executive branch permission. "Access to Classified Information: Memorandum Opinion for the General Counsel, Central Intelligence Agency," Office of Legal Counsel, November 26, 1996, at 4.

4. The state secret privilege is a common law privilege that allows the federal government to cause the withholding of evidence in any trial, whether or not the government is a party to the litigation if the evidence sought would cause harm to national security if made public. The doctrine has its primary origins in the United States in the case of *United States v. Reynolds*, 345 U.S. 1 (1953). See Louis Fisher, *In the Name of National Security* (University Press of Kansas, 2006); William G. Weaver and Robert M. Pallitto, "State Secrets and Executive Power," *Political Science Quarterly* 120(1): 95-112 (Spring 2005).

5. Thanks to Mitchell A. Sollenberger of the Congressional Research Service, who identified this quote in response to an email query on the matter by Professor Robert Spitzer.

6. See Theodore Lowi, *The Personal President: Power Invested Promise Unfulfilled* (Ithaca, NY: Cornell University Press, 1985), 97–133.

7. See, e.g., Steven G. Calbresi and Kevin Rhodes, "The Structural Constitution: Unitary Executive, Plural Judiciary," *Harvard Law Review* 105 (1992): 1153; Steven G. Calabresi and Gary Lawson, "The Unitary Executive, Jurisdiction Stripping, and the Hamdan Opinions: A Textualist Response to Justice Scalia," *Columbia Law Review* 107(2007): 1002; Steven G. Calabresi and Saikrishna Prakash, "The President's Power to Execute the Laws," *Yale Law Journal* 104 (1994): 541, 550; Saikrishna Prakash, "The Essential Meaning of Executive Power," University *of Illinois* Law Review (2003): 703. http://home.law.uiuc.edu/lrev/publications/2000s/2003/2003_3/prakash.pdf.

8. Executive Order 13292, § 1.7.

9. The materials classified were three letters from 2002 written to officials in the Federal Bureau of Investigation and the Department of Justice. Only when it appeared that the letters would be used as evidence in a congressional hearing did Attorney General Ashcroft order their classification in June 2004.

10. Letter from Hon. Henry Waxman, Chair of Committee on Oversight and Government Reform, to Vice President Richard Cheney, June 21, 2007.

11. Quoted in Harold C. Relyea, "National Security and Information," *Government Information Quarterly* 4, no. 1 (1987): 11–28, 13.

12. "Policy Formulation for National Security," *The American Political Science Review*, 43, no. 3 (June 1949): 534–543, 535.

13. *Kasza v. Browner*, 1998. 133 F.3d 1159 (9th Cir.).

14. *Maxwell v. First National Bank of Maryland*, 143 F.R.D. 590 (Dist. of Maryland, 1991).

15. The classic framing of this doctrine occurs in *Halkin v. Helms*, 598 F. 2d 1, 8 (D.C. Cir., 1979).

16. *Al Baraka Inv. & Dev. Corp.*, 323 F. Supp. 2d 82 (D.D.C. 2005).

17. "U.S. Reclassifies Many Documents in Secret Review," *The New York Times*, February 21, 2006, A1.

18. "Department of Education—Contract to Obtain Services of Armstrong Williams," United States Government Accountability Office, September 30, 2005, at http://www.gao.gov/decisions/appro/305368.pdf, (accessed on September 19, 2008).

19. For example, see the reporting of events surrounding the James Dale Guckert matter. The Bush White House credentialed Guckert under the name Jeff Gannon. Guckert would make statements from the reporters' gallery at White House briefings that were biased against Democratic Party positions and he also provided Bush administration officials—including President Bush—with "softball" questions.

20. "Oh What a Lovely War," *The Independent* (London), March 30, 2006, A24.

21. "Video News Releases: Unattributed Prepackaged News Stories Violate Publicity or Propaganda Prohibition," United States Government Accountability Office, May 12, 2005, at http://www.gao.gov/new.items/d05643t.pdf (accessed on September 19, 2008).
22. 131 Cong. Rec. H6407-02, 99th Cong., July 26, 1985.
23. "The Nation; FBI Agents Raid Special Counsel's Office," *The Los Angeles Times*, May 7, 2008, A12.
24. Fairbanks, "Blowing in the Wind," On the Hill in *The New Republic*, June 4, 2007.
25. "Abuses Endangered Veterans in Cancer Drug Experiments," *The New York Times*, February 6, 2005, section 1, page 1.
26. Name of interviewee withheld, Interview of May 14, 2007.
27. See, e.g., the case of Russell Tice, a former employee of the National Security Agency who in 2006 had asked to brief a congressional committee in a secure facility concerning alleged violations of law concerning domestic surveillance. See http://abcnews.go.com/WNT/Investigation/story?id=1491889 (accessed September 22, 2008).
28. This has occurred to numerous employees. The National Security Agency seems to make frequent use of this method of muzzling whistleblowers and cowing employees into silence. While no doubt some employees are legitimately referred for psychiatric evaluation, the author has met with several employee-whistleblowers who were referred and are without any apparent mental defect. In the intelligence world, loss of clearance leads to termination of employment—since holding a security clearance is a requirement to have access to materials to perform the job. So removal of a clearance for psychiatric reasons accomplishes two important goals. First, it removes the employee from the work environment. Second, it diminishes the employee's credibility, since accusations of mental illness against a person still creates substantial bias toward the accused person by third parties.
29. This is what occurred to Mr. Bogdan Dzakocic. As a leader of the FAA Red Team, a team that attempts to breach airport security to discover weaknesses, Mr. Dzakovic explained the security failures behind the events of 9/11 and testified in Congress. He was retaliated against and given the duty of answering the phone that never rings.
30. Of course, this is a common means of retaliating against whistleblowers. It is even sometimes used against high-ranking members of agencies, such as the case of Mr. Sandalio Gonzalez, former Drug Enforcement Agency Agent in Charge for the El Paso Division. Mr. Gonzalez, a senior executive agent with 30 years in service, was forced out of the agency for whistleblowing. He sued the United States and, in a rare event, recovered a sizable judgment.
31. A Drug Enforcement Agency whistleblower was fired through the use of falsified information by supervisors, but was reinstated when the matter came to light. No disciplinary actions were taken against the supervisors. Name withheld.

13

Regulating the Push and Pull of Migration in the Post–9/11 Era on the Southern Border

*Brent G. McCune and Dennis L. Soden**

> …U.S.-Mexican relations have entered their most promising moment in history. Our governments are committed to seizing the opportunities before us in this new atmosphere of mutual trust. The depth, quality and candor of our dialogue is unprecedented. It reflects the democratic values we share and our commitment to move forward boldly as we deepen this authentic partnership of neighbors.[1]

The aforementioned joint statement reflected the atmosphere of U.S.-Mexican relations five days before September 11, 2001. The United States and Mexico were poised for a constructive shared future. President Bush and President Fox recognized that migration-related issues were critical to the neighboring countries' prosperity and well-being. This opportunistic dialogue abruptly ceased, however, with the

---

*__Brent G. McCune__ is Assistant Director at the Institute for Policy and Economic Development and the principal prelaw advisor for the Law School Preparation Institute (LSPI). He teaches in the LSPI and the Master of Public Administration and Intelligence Community Center of Academic Excellence programs.

__Dennis L. Soden__ is Dean of the University College and Executive Director of the Institute for Policy and Economic Development at the University of Texas at El Paso. He is author of over 100 articles and technical reports and author or coauthor of 9 books ranging from *The Environmental Presidency*, *Global Environmental Policy and Administration*, and *Digame: Politics and Policy in the Texas Border*.

terrorist attacks on September 11, 2001. Indeed, the debate changed to one of securing America's borders. Immigration policy is at or very near the center of America's War on Terror, and the nearly 2,000-mile U.S.-Mexico border has received myopic attention after 9/11. As a result, considerable immigration-related legislation has been passed in the name of national security, and significant amounts of money and resources have been spent, and will continue to be spent, on securing the U.S.-Mexico border. The government's active response to 9/11 has resulted in both intended and unintended consequences.

September 11, 2001

September 11, 2001—a day of "unprecedented shock and suffering in the history of the United States"[2]—left America with questions. Congress and the president created the National Commission on Terrorist Attacks upon the United States (9/11 Commission) to prepare a full account of the circumstances surrounding 9/11, to identify lessons learned, and to provide recommendations to guard against future terrorist attacks. The Immigration and Naturalization Service (INS) was identified as the agency that conceivably had the most potential to develop an expanded role in counterterrorism; but, as the 9/11 Commission found, the INS had its hands full with the significant challenges posed by illegal entry over the U.S.-Mexico border, among other things.[3] Ports-of-entry inspectors did not focus on terrorists, perhaps because they lacked needed information to render fact-based determinations of admissibility. Put simply, border security was not viewed as a national security matter.[4] Yet, for many, failed immigration controls were considered a primary cause of the terrorist attacks.[5]

Janice L. Kephart, who served on the 9/11 Commission and coauthored "9/11 and Terrorist Travel: A Staff Report of the National Commission on Terrorist Attacks on the United States," also completed a 2005 report further detailing how terrorists have capitalized on weaknesses within the U.S. immigration system.[6] The report reviewed the immigration histories of 94 terrorists and found that nearly two-thirds (59) committed immigration fraud prior to or in conjunction with terrorism-related activities, and that several of the 59 terrorists violated multiple immigration laws.[7] Notably, temporary visas were a common means of entering the United States.

Ultimately, the 9/11 Commission provided a number of recommendations to protect against and prepare for future terrorist attacks. Those recommendations related to immigration policy include, but are not limited to an integrated U.S. border security system with a larger network of screening points; a biometric entry-exit screening system; and federal standards for the issuance of birth certificates and sources of identification.[8] These recommendations, coupled with the rhetoric that America has "lost control of [its] borders,"[9] the possibility that al Qaeda could turn its attention to America's "porous southern border,"[10] and the strong desire for the government to tighten the border as a visible act in a moment of crisis, fueled an immigration-centered response to the 9/11 terrorist attacks.

Response to September 11, 2001

The most significant change after 9/11 is that immigration is now viewed through a national security lens.[11] National security concerns trump traditional migration motivations when it comes to immigration-related changes. That national security is the preeminent focus of immigration-related policy and legislation following 9/11 is clearly evident in the current immigration debate. The catchphrase "border security is national security" has been used by multiple Washington, DC, politicians. Moreover in his 2008 State of the Union Address, President Bush declared that "America needs to secure [its] borders."[12] Indeed, national security has been the impetus behind much of the post–9/11 immigration-related legislation.

Plenary Power Doctrine

Before reviewing some of the key immigration-related legislation enacted following 9/11, a review of the authority exerted by the Congress and the Executive over immigration is in order. While the U.S. Constitution does not directly address the authority to regulate immigration, it does vest Congress with the power "to establish a uniform rule of naturalization."[13] The plenary power doctrine, which accords Congress and the Executive broad authority to regulate immigration without judicial restraint, was established by the U.S. Supreme Court in the late nineteenth century.[14] Under this doctrine, the government has free reign to treat noncitizens as it sees fit.[15] In essence, the federal government is granted enormous discretion in establishing the laws that govern the admission of noncitizens into the country. While the scope and teeth of the plenary power doctrine has been debated, particularly with the expansion of constitutional protections for resident aliens, the doctrine remains in force today.[16] Presumably, Congress and the Executive have relied on the plenary power doctrine in instituting changes to immigration laws and policies in the post–9/11 national security environment.

USA Patriot Act of 2001

As for immigration-related reform following 9/11, a little more than a month after the 9/11 terrorist attacks, Congress passed the Uniting and Strengthening America by Providing Appropriate Tools Required to Intercept and Obstruct Terrorism (USA Patriot Act) Act of 2001; an Act "to deter and punish terrorist acts in the United States and around the world, to enhance law enforcement investigatory tools, and for other purposes."[17] Title IV of the USA Patriot Act is entitled "Protecting the Border." As it relates to the U.S.-Mexico border, Title IV of the Act expanded the federal government's ability to detain and deport suspected terrorists and significantly increased the immigration enforcement budget.[18] More specifically, section 411, which amends section 212(a)(3) of the Immigration and Nationality Act (INA), expanded the definitions of "terrorist activity" and "terrorist organization" that may be used to deny an immigrant entry into the United States.[19] A spouse or child of an alien who is inadmissible on terrorist-related grounds is himself or herself inadmissible.[20] An alien may also be deemed inadmissible if it is determined that he or she "has been associated with a terrorist organization."[21] Notably, the Act provides for the retroactive application of the changes to section 212(a)(3) of the INA.[22] Finally, the USA Patriot Act articulated Congress's sense that (1) the integrated entry-and-exit data system should be fully implemented at all ports of entry "with all deliberate speed and expeditiously as practicable"; (2) the establishment of the Integrated Entry and Exit Data System Task Force should begin immediately; and (3) the development of the system should particularly focus on the use of biometric technology and tamper-resistant documents that are readable at ports of entry.[23]

Enhanced Border Security and Visa Entry Reform Act of 2002

Approximately eight months after the 9/11 terrorist attacks, President George W. Bush signed the Enhanced Border Security and Visa Entry Reform Act of 2002; an Act "to enhance the border security of the United States, and for other purposes."[24] When it comes to border security, three main provisions of this law come into play.[25] First, section 201 created an interim program whereby federal law enforcement agencies and the intelligence community must share, "to the maximum extent practicable," information relevant to the admissibility and deportability of aliens with the Department of State and the INS.[26] Second, section 202 directed the INS to fully integrate all INS-maintained databases and systems that process or contain information on aliens, and mandated that this integrated system be fully interoperable with the "Chimera system."[27] Third, section 303 required that all U.S. travel and entry documents issued to aliens be machine readable and tamper resistant, and include biometric identifiers.[28]

Homeland Security Act of 2002

On November 25, 2002, President Bush signed the Homeland Security Act of 2002; an Act "to establish the Department of Homeland Security, and for other purposes."[29] The establishment of the Department of Homeland Security (DHS) was the largest transformation of the U.S. government in over a half-century.[30] Part of the DHS's multifaceted mission is to "prevent terrorist attacks within the United States" and to "reduce the vulnerability of the United States to terrorism."[31] Under this Act, the INS was abolished and reorganized into three different agencies: U.S. Customs and Border Protection (CBP), U.S. Citizenship and Immigration Services (USCIS), and U.S. Immigration and Customs Enforcement (ICE).[32] CBP has a "priority mission" of preventing terrorists and their weapons from entering into the United States.[33] USCIS is responsible for administering immigration and naturalization functions and establishing immigration services and priorities.[34] ICE is the largest investigative branch of the DHS and enforces immigration and customs laws by targeting illegal aliens.[35] There have been a number of bills that have appropriated funds to the DHS. Rather than detail each one of the bills individually, it suffices to note that the DHS budget has increased each fiscal year. In fact, the DHS budget request for fiscal year 2009 is $50.5 billion, an amount more than double the fiscal year 2002 budget of $22.1 billion.[36]

Intelligence Reform and Terrorism Prevent Act of 2004

Approximately three years after the 9/11 terrorist attacks, Congress passed the Intelligence Reform and Terrorism Prevention Act of 2004 (IRTPA); an Act "to reform the intelligence community and the intelligence and intelligence-related activities of the United States Government, and for other purposes."[37] Title I of the IRTPA involved another significant restructuring of the government, particularly in the intelligence community, as it amended the National Security Act of 1947 to establish a Director of National Intelligence.[38] Title V—"Border Protection, Immigration, and Visa Matters"—more directly affects migration on the southwest border. Under this Title, the secretary of homeland security is required to increase:

(1) the number of full-time Border Patrol agents by at least 2,000 per fiscal year, from 2006 through 2010; (2) the number of full-time ICE investigators by at least 800 per fiscal year for the same period; and (3) the number of beds available for immigration detention and removal operations of the DHS by at least 8,000 per fiscal year over the same timeframe.[39] Other changes include section 5304, which precludes judicial review of revocations of visas and other travel documents by consular officers or the secretary of state, and section 5402, which renders deportable any alien who has received military-type training from or on behalf of a terrorist organization.[40] Title VII of the IRTPA, also known as the "9/11 Commission Implementation Act of 2004," contains several provisions that impact migration on the U.S.-Mexico border. Section 7208 gives the secretary of homeland security a two-year deadline to fully integrate all databases and data systems that process or contain information on aliens, and to fully implement an interoperable electronic data system.[41] Title VII also establishes minimum standards for birth certificates, and driver's licenses and identification cards.[42] Section 7213 provides for security enhancements to social security cards and numbers, and section 7303 requires the president to coordinate cross-border interoperability issues between the United States, Mexico, and Canada.[43] Finally, Subtitle C of Title VII, also known as the "Homeland Security Civil Rights and Civil Liberties Protection Act of 2004," expands the DHS mission by requiring the DHS "to ensure that the civil rights and civil liberties of persons are not diminished by efforts, activities, and programs aimed at securing the homeland."[44]

Real ID Act of 2005

The Emergency Supplemental Appropriations Act for Defense, the Global War on Terror, and Tsunami Relief, 2005, which included the Real ID Act of 2005, was signed into law on May 11, 2005.[45] Attached as a rider to a military spending bill, the Real ID Act is a highly controversial piece of legislation.[46] Widely known for establishing standards on driver's licenses and identification cards, the Real ID Act also contains important immigration reforms. For example, section 102 amends the Illegal Immigration Reform and Immigrant Responsibility Act (IIRIRA) of 1996 to authorize the secretary of homeland security to waive all legal requirements necessary to ensure expeditious construction of certain U.S. border barriers and roads.[47] The Real ID Act also expands the grounds of inadmissibility and deportability due to terrorist- and terrorist-related activities, as well as the definition of "terrorist organization" to incorporate a broader range of activities.[48] Section 106 bars inadmissible aliens from seeking judicial review of certain removal orders under section 242 of the INA through extraordinary petitions, including habeas corpus and mandamus.[49] Title II of the Real ID Act prohibits federal agencies from accepting, for official purposes, state-issued driver's licenses or identification cards that fail to meet minimum security requirements, including the incorporation of specified information, physical anti-fraud security features, and a common machine-readable technology. It also sets forth minimum issuance standards for such documents, including verification of presented information and evidence that the applicant is lawfully residing in the United States.[50] Section 206 repealed section 7212 of the IRTPA of 2004.[51] Finally, Title III of the Real ID Act calls for the development of a pilot program to utilize ground-surveillance technologies to enhance the border security of the United States, and instructs the secretary of homeland security to develop and implement a plan to improve federal government communication systems and enhance information sharing.[52] Notably, due to heavy resistance from the states in complying with the Real ID Act, the DHS extended the deadline for which states must upgrade the security of their systems from May 11, 2008 to December 31, 2009. Real ID enrollment for all individuals 50 years of age and younger will be completed by December 1, 2014; all others have an extension enrollment up to December 1, 2017.[53]

Secure Fence Act of 2006

A little more than five years after the 9/11 terrorist attacks, Congress passed another controversial law, the Secure Fence Act of 2006; an Act "to establish operational control over the international land and maritime borders of the United States."[54] Section 2 directs the secretary of homeland security to take necessary and appropriate actions to achieve "operational control" over U.S. international land and maritime borders, including systematic border surveillance through more effective use of personnel and technology, and physical infrastructure enhancements to prevent unlawful entry by aliens into the United States.[55] The Secure Fence Act also amends the IIRIRA of 1996 to direct the secretary to provide at least two layers of reinforced fencing and the installation of additional physical barriers, roads, lighting, cameras, and sensors at specified locations along the U.S.-Mexico border.[56] In short, the Secure Fence Act authorizes the construction of a fence along 700 miles of the nearly 2,000-mile southwest border.[57] As of June 27, 2008, 182.2 miles of the pedestrian fence and 151 miles of the vehicle fence have been completed. The DHS plans to complete 670 miles of the southwest border fence (370 miles of pedestrian fence and 300 miles of vehicle fence) by the end of 2008.[58]

Supplemental Appropriations Act, 2008

On June 30, 2008, President Bush signed the Supplemental Appropriations Act, 2008, which includes funding for the Merida Initiative.[59] The latter is a security cooperation initiative with Mexico and the countries of Central America to maximize the effectiveness of existing efforts against drug, weapons, and human trafficking. The Merida Initiative sprang out of the Merida Summit held between President Bush and Mexican President, Felipe Calderon, in March of 2007.[60] The Bush administration pushed Congress to pass the Merida Initiative, which originally planned to provide $1.4 billion of in-kind assistance to the Mexican government and the governments of seven Central American countries over a three-year period.[61] Section 1406 of the Supplemental Appropriations Act, 2008, appropriated $400 million for assistance to Mexico to combat drug trafficking and related violence and organized crime, and for judicial reform, institution building, anticorruption, and rule of law activities.[62] Similarly, section 1407 appropriated $65 million for assistance to the countries of Central America, Haiti, and the Dominican Republic for the same reasons enumerated in section 1406, as well as for maritime security.[63] Both sections stipulate that none of the appropriated funds may be used for budget support or as cash payments. While the Merida Initiative may not appear to be immigration reform, one of its stated objectives focuses on border violence and organized crime. And as will be discussed later, the hardening of the U.S.-Mexico border forces migrants to participate in organized crime.

Clearly, border securing and national security have been the impetus and purpose behind the legislation reviewed earlier. But the question remains—so what? The government has responded to crises before in a similar way, so why is this post–9/11 reaction any different? And how does this national security legislation affect migration on the southwest border?

A Repeat of History?

Much of U.S. immigration and nationality laws should be a source of pride for U.S. citizens. Some U.S. immigration laws, however, indicate a lack of U.S. openness and acceptance.[64] The reviewed legislation clearly shows that the government responded to the 9/11 terrorist attacks with a nativist mentality. The government's nativist reaction to a crisis, however, is not new. Alien and Sedition Acts were passed, which limited immigration and free speech; the Chinese exclusion laws; the First Red Scare during and after World War I, including the Palmer Raids, which involved mass arrests and deportations of radicals; the Second Red Scare following World War II, including McCarthyism's guilt-by-association mindset; and the internment of Japanese Americans during World War II, which was upheld by the U.S. Supreme Court in *Korematsu v. United States*[65] all serve as evidence of previous like responses.

At times, nativism has adversely influenced the treatment of persons of Mexican ancestry in the United States. During the Great Depression, approximately 1 million persons of Mexican ancestry—both noncitizens and citizens—were forcibly removed from the United States. This "forgotten repatriation" campaign sought to save the few available jobs for "true Americans."[66] "Operation Wetback" took place in the 1950s and involved a mass deportation of hundreds of thousands of Mexican immigrants and Mexican-American citizens.[67] U.S. Supreme Court decisions have focused on the "illegal alien" specifically as a Mexican immigrant.[68] In the 1990s, there was the militarization of the U.S.-Mexico border through "Operation Gatekeeper" and "Operation Hold-the-Line."[69] And now, through post–9/11 legislation, there is a hardening of the southwest border. The grounds for inadmissibility and deportability have been expanded, state and local law enforcement have been enlisted to enforce immigration laws, a fully integrated and interoperable entry-exit system has been mandated, the number of Border Patrol agents and ICE investigators has increased on a yearly basis, judicial review of removal orders has been limited, minimum security standards have been mandated for state-issued driver's licenses and identification cards, a 330-mile fence has been erected along the U.S.-Mexico border, with another 370 miles of fence to be built in the future, and over $400 million of in-kind assistance to Mexico has been appropriated to combat, among other things, violence and organized crime along the southwest border. Without question, these changes have directly impacted migration on the U.S.-Mexico border.

Consequences of Post–9/11 Immigration Reform

The government's immigration-related response to 9/11 and nativist response to past crises share both a common purpose and common consequences. In particular, there are stark similarities between "Operation Gatekeeper" and "Operation Hold-the-Line" and post–9/11 immigration reform. The twofold impetus behind "Operation Gatekeeper" was the complaints of residents of San Diego County about illegal aliens crossing the border and the perceived need of the Clinton administration and immigration officials to address the influx of illegal aliens crossing the southwest border.[70] The national strategy of the Border Patrol centered on "prevention through deterrence," whereby the Border Patrol increased the number of agents on the southwest border and made effective use of technology in the hopes of deterring illegal immigration by raising the risk of apprehension.[71] In short, the hope of "Operation Gatekeeper" and "Operation Hold-the-Line" was to "control the borders of the United States between the ports of entry."[72] Similarly, the hope of post–9/11 immigration reform is to secure America's borders. As previously mentioned, Title IV of the USA Patriot Act of 2001 is entitled "Protecting the Border." The purpose of the Enhanced Border Security and Visa Entry Reform Act of 2002 is "to enhance the border security of the United States," and the purpose of the Secure Fence Act of 2006 is "to establish operational control over the international land and maritime borders of the United States." In addition, the Border Patrol's strategic goal is "to establish and maintain operational control of the border of the United States."[73]

The hope of "Operation Gatekeeper" and "Operation Hold-the-Line"—to control the U.S. borders—was never realized. While apprehension levels declined in San Diego and El Paso (the locations of "Operation Gatekeeper" and "Operation Hold-the-Line," respectively), apprehension levels surged in other places along the southwest border especially in nonurban areas. Instead of reducing illegal immigration along the U.S.-Mexico border, "Operation Gatekeeper" and "Operation Hold-the-Line" merely shifted the illegal traffic out of the public eye. The operations also bolstered the smuggling industry and increased the number of deaths among border-crossers[74] at areas of greater risk (e.g., the arid desert). Similar consequences have emerged from post–9/11 immigration reform. Intended and unintended consequences have limited migrants' civil liberties and freedoms. On the U.S.-Mexico border, post–9/11 legislation has affected the number of apprehensions, human smuggling, migrant deaths, and international bridge wait times.

Apprehensions

The relationship between the number of apprehensions to the number of successful illegal entries and the number of attempted illegal entries is unclear.[75] That said, the "prevention through deterrence" strategy assumed that alien apprehensions would decline as the Border Patrol exerted more control of the border.[76] The same assumption underlies the current "operational control" border strategy. There has been a decline in the number of apprehensions after 9/11. Since 1996, the level of apprehensions peaked in 2000 at 1.8 million and reached its lowest level (a little more than 850,000) in 2007.[77] There has not, however, been a steady decline in apprehensions. The number of apprehensions returned to pre–9/11 levels in 2004 and 2005. In 2005, almost all apprehensions (98.5 percent) occurred at the U.S.-Mexico border, and Mexican nationals comprise the majority (86.1 percent) of these apprehensions.[78] The decrease in apprehensions after 2005 is in part due to "Operation Streamline," a CBP-led pilot program where illegal aliens who are not released for humanitarian reasons are prosecuted for illegal entry. Arguably, the possibility of prison time and a criminal record is a powerful deterrent, especially since a conviction jeopardizes any future legal entry into the United States.[79] Assuming there is indeed a relationship between the number of apprehensions and the number of successful illegal entries or the number of attempted illegal entries, then the hardening of the border subsequent to 9/11 has resulted in a decrease in illegal immigration across the southern border. This intended consequence, however, has come at additional costs.

Human Smuggling

As America has tightened southwest border security, undocumented migrants have had to utilize other means of crossing the border. It has become more dangerous and expensive to cross the southern border, which generates business for human smugglers or "coyotes." Because it is more difficult to enter the United States, "coyotes" have increased human smuggling fees to $1,000–$2,000 per person.[80] Human smuggling is big business; at one estimate, there may be 2 million migrants that attempt unauthorized entry into the United States each year, and at $1,000 for each entry, smuggling is a $2 billion-a-year business.[81] Drug gangs are attracted to the money to be made in human smuggling. This "unintended consequence of sealing the border"[82] has resulted in a comingling of drugs and human loads. Indeed, migrants pay for their trips along drug-smuggling routes by serving as "mules," carrying drugs for traffickers.[83] With smuggling there has also been increased border violence. Unauthorized migrants are raped and assaulted along smuggling routes. There are shootings between rival smuggling gangs and hijackings of each others' customers en route to U.S. destinations.[84] Since January 2008, and as of the middle of August 2008, there have been 750 killings in Ciudad Juárez, Mexico, El Paso's sister city across the Rio Grande river.[85] Most of these deaths are linked to a war among drug cartels. All indications are that this turf war developed as a result of a less porous U.S.-Mexico border as drug cartels and smuggling gangs found it harder to transport both drugs and humans across the border.

Migrant Deaths

Another consequence of hardening the southwest border has been an increase in the number of persons who have died crossing the border. A 2006 report by the U.S. Government Accountability Office (GAO) concluded that the number of border-crossing deaths has approximately doubled since the late 1990s.[86] Varying estimates place the number of deaths at 340 (2003), 460 (2004), and 472 (2005).[87] To help place these figures in context, there were more deaths (1,272) in this 3-year period along the southwest border than there were in the 28-year history of the Berlin Wall.[88] As a result of the increasing number of migrant deaths along the southern border the U.S. CBP created the Border Safety Initiative (BSI) campaign, a bilateral effort with Mexico that focuses on disrupting smuggling routes and educating would-be undocumented migrants on the dangers of crossing the border.[89] May to September is known as the "death season" because the death rate along the border soars. Official signs have been posted along the U.S.-Mexico border that read: "¡Cuidado!—No Exponga Su Vida A Los Elementos—¡No Vale La Pena!," which when translated means, "Caution! Do not expose your life to the elements. It's not worth it!"[90] The causes of migrant deaths include dehydration and heat exposure from confined-space smuggling and the extreme heat of the Sonoran desert, in addition to drowning,[91] cold exposure, homicides, and traffic accidents, among others.[92]

International Bridge Wait Times

As it relates to migrants who enter the United States at ports of entry along the southern border, post–9/11 immigration reform has affected international bridge wait times. The U.S.-Mexico border is the busiest land border in the world.[93] In 2006, there were over 88 million personal vehicles, more than 46 million pedestrians, nearly 5 million commercial trucks, and more than 10,000 trains that crossed the southern border at ports of entry.[94] Bridge wait times at the southern border have doubled since the 9/11 terrorist attacks as CBP officials have taken extra care to ensure that terrorists do not enter into the United States.[95] Bridge wait times in the San Diego/Tijuana region illustrate this point. Twenty-six percent of northbound passenger vehicles and 44 percent of northbound trucks at the San Ysidro and Otay Mesa crossings wait two hours or more at the border.[96] Before 9/11, the average wait time during peak hours was less than half an hour.[97] These increased wait times are clearly frustrating for individuals that cross the border daily as a part of everyday life. The increased bridge wait times also choke commerce. For the San Diego/ Tijuana region alone, lengthy bridge wait times result in losses of $1.87 billion in production, 57,000 jobs, roughly $290 million in wages, and $256 million in tax revenue.[98] The southern border backlogs also disappoint investors and hinder the maquiladora industry, in which these experiences clearly produce an adverse economic impact on the southwest border, and to some extent, the entire country.[99] Longer international bridge wait times, increases in the number of apprehensions and migrant deaths, increased border violence and organized crime, and an expanding smuggling industry have all resulted because post–9/11 immigration reform is not aligned with the motivations for migration on the U.S.-Mexico border.

Motivations for Migration on the Southern Border

Hispanics are the largest minority group in the United States, numbering 47 million and representing about 15.5 percent of the total U.S. population.[100] Roughly 64 percent of the Hispanic population is Mexican.[101] Both the legal and illegal Mexican-born population in the United States has grown by about 500,000 people per year from 1995 to 2005.[102] The Pew Hispanic Center estimates that there are currently 11.5–12 million unauthorized migrants living in the United States.[103] Most unauthorized migrants come from Mexico. More specifically, 6.2 million are from Mexico and 2.5 million come from the rest of Latin America, sometimes called "other than Mexican" (OTMs). Together, unauthorized migrants from Mexico and Latin America account for 78 percent of the unauthorized population in 2005.[104] The Mexican government has predicted that mass immigration to the United States will continue at between 3.5 and 5 million people per decade until at least 2030.[105] With Hispanics as the largest minority group in the United States, and Mexicans as the largest ethnic group among Hispanics, and with the sustained mass of both legal and illegal Mexican immigration, in the near future a review of the motivations behind the northward migration on the U.S.-Mexico border is warranted.

Generally, there are various reasons why people migrate. "Push" factors are those living in environment situations that create dissatisfaction with one's present location, and thus relate to the migrant's country of origin.[106] "Push" factors include unemployment, political fear, civil unrest, poor health care, and limited educational opportunities, etc. On the opposite side of the migration coin are "pull" factors. "Pull" factors are those characteristics or attributes of other places that are appealing, and thus relate to the migrant's country of destination.[107] Examples of "pull" factors include job opportunities, political or religious freedoms, prevalent educational opportunities, and family- or friend networks, etc. Both "push" factors and "pull" factors drive Mexican migration to the United States.

Economics is a significant motivation for migration from Mexico to the United States. On the "pull" side of the coin are available "low-paying" jobs in the United States that, by comparison, pay Mexican workers eight to nine times more than jobs in Mexico.[108] On the "push" side of the coin are poor labor conditions in Mexico, including declining real wages and insufficient job creation.[109] In essence, Mexican workers supply much of the labor demanded by American businesses. Mexican workers in the United States also supply the income demanded by family members living in Mexico returned through remittances, a primary source of income in Mexico.[110] Interestingly, the North American Free Trade Agreement (NAFTA), touted as an agreement that would create new jobs and prosperity in Mexico, has driven some of the northward migration as well because it has forced small-business owners, large numbers of famers, and laborers out of work.[111]

Not wholly independent from the economics of migration along the southwest border are the family ties and social networks that both push and pull Mexicans to the United States. Mexicans are indeed pulled to the United States to be with family members living in the United States. But, Mexican workers are also pushed to U.S. jobs to supplement family incomes in Mexico through remittances.[112] Because the United States and Mexico are geographic neighbors, many Mexican migrants have developed "transnational identities" by moving back and forth between the two nations.[113] They move to the United States for seasonal or temporary work and return to Mexico to be with their families. The hardening of the southwest border after 9/11 has slowed down this pendulum-like movement between the countries. Some Mexican migrants have viewed the return to Mexico as too risky, and have opted to remain in the United States. This has resulted in the unintended consequence of an increase in the undocumented population in the United States.[114]

The Future of the Border

One result from the tightening of the southwest border is clear: drugs and unauthorized migrants continue to enter the United States. Despite tough, immigration-related legislation passed after 9/11, as examples, smugglers successfully used an elaborate tunnel to transport drugs and workers from Mexico to the United States, and illegal migrants linked to Mexican cartels ran a sizeable "marijuana garden" in Sequoia National Forest.[115] The "we've lost control of our borders" rhetoric is somewhat misleading because the United States has never had control of its borders. To be sure, it is a tall order, if not an impossible one, to secure the busiest border in the world. The 9/11 Commission Report stated it well: "The challenge for national security in an age of terrorism is to prevent the very few people who may pose overwhelming risks from entering or remaining in the United States undetected."[116] But the national security concern of preventing terrorists from entering the United States only adds to the "needles" of drugs and illegal migrants to be found in the U.S.-Mexico border haystack.

The security of the United States is the most compelling governmental interest.[117] As such, and particularly in a post–9/11 environment, national security will likely continue to influence, if not dominate, immigration laws and policy. This is not necessarily unwarranted because immigration policies are critical to national security. But, immigration reform should not focus solely on securing America's southern border. Studies have indicated that no terrorist has ever entered the United States via the U.S.-Mexico border.[118] And as the 9/11 Commission Report recommended, the border and immigration system of the United States must serve as a critical element of counterterrorism, and at the same time remain a "visible manifestation" of America's belief in freedom, democracy, and the rule of law.[119]

Rather than focusing solely on securing the border, future immigration reforms should seek "prevention through deterrence" via the internal enforcement of current immigration laws. Just as criminal prosecution and the threat of prison time deter some would-be migrants from illegally crossing the U.S.-Mexico border, so too would potential employers be deterred from hiring unauthorized migrants if faced with the same threats. Future immigration legislation and policies should continue to focus on the guidelines and criteria of issuing visas and other travel documents, as well as the training of consulate officials. Lastly, future immigration reforms should be better aligned with the motivations that drive northward migration from Mexico.

Notes

1. President, Joint Statement, "Joint Statement between the United States of America and the United Mexican States," *The Weekly Compilation of Presidential Documents* 37, no. 36 (September 10, 2001): 1277–1278.
2. The National Commission on Terrorist Attacks upon the United States, *The 9/11 Commission Report: Final Report of the National Commission on Terrorist Attacks upon the United States* (Washington, DC: GPO, 2004), xv.

3. Ibid., 80.

4. Ibid., 383–384.

5. Raquel Aldana and Sylvia R. Lazos Vargas, "'Aliens' in Our Midst Post–9/11: Legislating Outsiderness within the Borders," *UC Davis Law Review* 38 (2005): 1683, 1685.

6. Janice L. Kephart, "Immigration and Terrorism: Moving beyond the 9/11 Staff Report on Terrorist Travel," *Center for Immigration Studies*, Center Paper 24 (September 2005), http://www.cis.org/articles/2005/kephart.pdf.

7. Ibid., 5.

8. The National Commission on Terrorist Attacks upon the United States, *The 9/11 Commission Report*, 387–390.

9. This rhetoric has been used by many politicians including President Reagan; see The Public Papers of President Ronald W. Reagan, "The President's News Conference," *The Ronald Reagan Presidential Library*, (June 14, 1984), http://www.reagan.utexas.edu/archives/speeches/publicpapers.html. Echoes of this rhetoric include President Clinton's statement that "our borders leak like a sieve"; see Thomas L. Friedman, "Clinton Seeks More Powers to Stem Illegal Immigration," *New York Times*, July 28, 1993, http://query.nytimes.com/gst/ fullpage.html?res=9F0CE3D7153DF93BA15754C0A965958260; and President George W. Bush's mandate that "America needs to secure our borders," see President, Address to the Nation, "State of the Union," *The Weekly Compilation of Presidential Documents* 44, no. 4 (February 4, 2008): 120.

10. Robert S. Leiken, "Enchilada Lite: A Post–9/11 Mexican Migration Agreement," *Center for Immigration Studies* (March 2002): 9, http://www.cis.org/articles/2002/leiken.pdf.

11. Deborah Waller Myers and Demetrios G. Papademetriou, "The U.S.-Mexico Immigration Relationship: Operating in a New Context by Setting the Stage," *Foreign Affairs en Español* 2, no. 1 (Spring 2002), from http://www.migrationpolicy.org/pubs/foreign_affairs.php.

12. See 109 Cong., 2d sess., *Congressional Record*, 152 (March 30, 2006): S2552 (statement of Senator John Cornyn); Kathy Kiely, "Congress Debates Border Fence, Crackdown on Tunnels," *USA Today*, September 21, 2006, http://www.usatoday.com/news/nation/2006-09-20-border-fence_x.htm (statement of Congressman David Dreier); President, Address to the Nation, "State of the Union," 120.

13. U.S. Const. art. I, § 8, cl. 4.

14. See *Chae Chin Ping v. United States*, 130 U.S. 581 (1889); *Fong Yue Ting v. United States*, 149 U.S. 698 (1893).

15. Kevin R. Johnson, "The Forgotten 'Repatriation' of Persons of Mexican Ancestry and Lessons for the 'War on Terror,'" *Pace Law Review* 26 (2005):1, 3.

16. Kevin R. Johnson, *The "Huddled Masses" Myth: Immigration and Civil Rights* (Philadelphia: Temple University Press, 2004), 14.

17. *Uniting and Strengthening America by Providing Appropriate Tools Required to Intercept and Obstruct Terrorism (USA Patriot Act) Act of 2001*, Public Law 107156, *U.S. Statutes at Large* 115 (2001): 272.

18. Barbara Hines, "An Overview of U.S. Immigration Law and Policy since 9/11," *Texas Hispanic Journal of Law and Policy* 12 (2006): 9, 12.

19. USA Patriot Act, § 411.

20. Ibid.

21. Ibid.

22. Ibid.

23. Ibid., § 414.

24. *Enhanced Border Security and Visa Entry Reform Act of 2002*, Public Law 107–173, *U.S. Statutes at Large* 116 (2002): 543.

25. Rosemary Jenks, "The Enhanced Border Security and Visa Entry Reform Act of 2002," *Center for Immigration Studies*, Backgrounder (June 2002): 1, http://www.cis.org/articles/2002/back502.pdf.

26. *Enhanced Border Security and Visa Entry Reform Act of 2002*, § 201.

27. Ibid., § 202. The Chimera system incorporates "linguistically sensitive algorithms that can account for variations in name formats, spelling and other name elements within a particular language." See Jenks, "The Enhanced Border Security and Visa Entry Reform Act of 2002," 2.

28. *Enhanced Border Security and Visa Entry Reform Act of 2002*, § 303.

29. *Homeland Security Act of 2002*, Public Law 107–296, *U.S. Statutes at Large* 116 (2002): 2135.

30. President, Remarks, "Remarks on Signing the Intelligence Authorization Act for Fiscal Year 2003," *The Weekly Compilation of Presidential Documents* 38, no. 48 (December 2, 2002): 2101.

31. *Homeland Security Act of 2002*, § 101.

32. Ibid., § 471.

33. U.S. Customs and Border Protection, "About CBP," http://www.cbp.gov/xp/cgov/about/.

34. U.S. Citizenship and Immigration Services, "About Us," http://www.uscis.gov/portal/site/uscis/ menuitem.eb1d4c2a3e5b9ac89243c6a7543f6d1a/?vgnextoid=2af29c7755cb9010VgnVCM10000045f3d6a1RCRD&vgnextchannel=2af29c7755cb9010VgnVCM10000045f3d6a1RCRD.

35. U.S. Immigration and Customs Enforcement, "About Us," http://www.ice.gov/about/index.htm.

36. U.S. Department of Homeland Security, "Budget and Finance Documents," http://www.dhs.gov/xabout/ budget/.

37. *Intelligence Reform and Terrorism Prevention Act of 2004*, Public Law 108–458, *U.S. Statutes at Large* 118 (2004): 3638.

38. Ibid., § 1011.

39. Ibid., §§ 5202–5204.

40. Ibid., §§ 5304, 5402.

41. Ibid., § 7208.

42. Ibid., §§ 7211–7212.

43. Ibid., §§ 7213, 7303.

44. Ibid., § 8302.

45. *Emergency Supplemental Appropriations Act for Defense, the Global War on Terror, and Tsunami Relief, 2005*, Public Law 109–113, *U.S. Statutes at Large* 119 (2005): 231.

46. Anita Ramasastry, "Why the 'Real ID' Act Is a Real Mess," *CNN.com*, August 12, 2005, http://www.cnn.com/ 2005/LAW/08/12/ramasastry.ids/index.html.

47. *Real ID Act of 2005*, Public Law 109–113, *U.S. Statutes at Large* 119 (2005): 302, § 102.
48. Ibid., § 103.
49. Ibid., § 106.
50. Ibid., § 202.
51. Ibid., § 206.
52. Ibid., §§ 302–303.
53. U.S. Department of Homeland Security, *Most Jurisdictions Meet Initial Real ID Requirements*, Office of the Press Secretary, April 1, 2008, http://www.dhs.gov/xnews/releases/pr_1207079095443.shtm.
54. *Secure Fence Act of 2006*, Public Law 109–367, *U.S. Statutes at Large* 120 (2006): 2638.
55. Ibid., § 2.
56. Ibid., § 3.
57. David Stout, "Bush Signs Bill Ordering Fence on Mexican Border," *New York Times*, October 26, 2006, http://www.nytimes.com/2006/10/26/washington/27fencecnd.html?_r=1&oref=slogin.
58. U.S. Department of Homeland Security, "Southwest Border Fence," http://www.dhs.gov/xprevprot/ programs/border-fence-southwest.shtm.
59. *Supplemental Appropriations Act, 2008*, Public Law 110–252, *U.S. Statutes at Large* 122 (2008): 2323.
60. U.S. Department of State, *Joint Statement on the Merida Initiative: A New Paradigm for Security Cooperation*, Office of the Spokesman, October 22, 2007, http://www.state.gov/r/pa/prs/ps/2007/oct/93817.htm.
61. Andrew Selee, "Overview of the Merida Initiative," *Woodrow Wilson International Center for Scholars* (May 2008): 2, http://www.wilsoncenter.org/news/docs/Analysis.Merida%20Initiative%20May%208%202008.pdf.
62. *Supplemental Appropriations Act, 2008*, § 1406.
63. Ibid., § 1407. Section 1407 defines "countries of Central America" as Belize, Costa Rica, El Salvador, Guatemala, Honduras, Nicaragua, and Panama.
64. Johnson, *The "Huddled Masses" Myth*, 2.
65. See *Korematsu v. United States*, 323 U.S. 214 (1944). In a stirring dissent in *Korematsu*, Justice Murphy criticized nativism when he expressed: "All residents of this nation are kin in some way by blood or culture to a foreign land. Yet they are primarily and necessarily a part of the new and distinct civilization of the United States. They must accordingly be treated at all times as the heirs of the American experiment and as entitled to all the rights and freedoms guaranteed by the Constitution." *Korematsu*, 323 U.S. at 242 (Murphy, J., dissenting).
66. Johnson, *The Forgotten "Repatriation" of Persons of Mexican Ancestry*, 1–2.
67. Ibid., 10.
68. Johnson, *The "Huddled Masses" Myth*, 159.
69. Johnson, *The Forgotten "Repatriation" of Persons of Mexican Ancestry*, 10.
70. Bill Ong Hing, *The Dark Side of Operation Gatekeeper*, 7 U.C. Davis J. Int'l L. & Pol'y 121, 125 (2001).
71. U.S. Border Patrol, *Border Patrol Strategic Plan: 1994 and Beyond, National Strategy*, (July 1994): 6.

72. Ibid., 2.
73. U.S. Customs and Border Protection, *U.S. Border Patrol, National Border Patrol Strategy*, Office of Border Patrol, September 2004, 2, http://www.cbp.gov/linkhandler/cgov/border_security/border_patrol/border_patrol_ohs/national_bp_strategy.ctt/national_bp_strategy.pdf.
74. Hing, *The Dark Side of Operation Gatekeeper*, 131–135.
75. U.S. Department of Homeland Security, *Fact Sheet: Border Apprehensions: 2005*, Office of Immigration Statistics, November 2006, 1, http://www.dhs.gov/xlibrary/assets/statistics/publications/ois_apprehensions_ fs_2004.pdf.
76. U.S. Border Patrol, *Border Patrol Strategic Plan: 1994*, 4.
77. U.S. Department of Homeland Security, *Fact Sheet: Border Apprehensions: 2005*, 1; Richard Marosi, "Apprehensions of Illegal Border-Crossers Drop 20%," *Los Angeles Times*, November 7, 2007, A-13, http://articles.latimes.com/2007/nov/07/nation/na-immig7.
78. U.S. Department of Homeland Security, *Fact Sheet: Border Apprehensions: 2005*, 2.
79. Spence S. Hsu, "Immigration Prosecutions Hit New High: Critics Say Increased Use of Criminal Charges Strains System," *Washington Post*, June 2, 2008, A1, http://www.washingtonpost.com/wp-dyn/content/ article/2008/06/01/AR2008060102192_pf.html; see also *Immigration and Nationality Act, U.S. Code* 8 (1952), § 1182.
80. Mario Villarreal, Border Patrol spokesman, quoted in Jim Yardley, "Mexicans' Bids to Enter U.S. Rebound to Pre–9/11 Levels," *New York Times*, November 22, 2002, http://query.nytimes.com/gst/fullpage.html?res=9D07E7DA1039F937A15752C1A9649C8B63.
81. Susan Martin and Philip Martin, "International Migration and Terrorism: Prevention, Prosecution and Protection," *Georgetown Immigration Law Journal* 18 (2004): 329, 336.
82. Special Agent Alonzo Peña, chief investigator for ICE in Arizona, quoted in Joel Millman, "Shift Is Afoot on Mexican Border: Security Crackdown Cuts Illegal Crossing but Aids Smugglers," *Wall Street Journal*, October 25, 2007, http://online.wsj.com/public/article_print/SB119327622488470788.html.
83. Ibid.
84. Ibid.
85. Daniel Borunda, "12 Slain in Juárez as Violence Intensifies," *El Paso Times*, August 12, 2008.
86. U.S. Government Accountability Office, *Illegal Immigration: Border-Crossing Deaths Have Doubled since 1995; Border Patrol's Efforts to Prevent Deaths Have not Been Fully Evaluated*, GAO-06-770, August 2006, 3.
87. U.S. Customs and Border Protection, *U.S. Customs and Border Protection Announces Border Safety Initiative Aimed at Preventing Migrant Deaths*, Office of Public Affairs, May 6, 2004, http://www.cbp.gov/xp/ cgov/newsroom/news_releases/archives/2004_press_releases/052004/05062004.xml; Richard Marosi, "Border Crossing Deaths Set a 12-Month Record," *Los Angeles Times*, October 1, 2005, A-1, http://articles.latimes.com/ 2005/oct/01/local/me-deaths1; U.S. Government Accountability Office, *Illegal Immigration*, 1.

88. Associated Press, "Memory of Berlin Wall Casualties Haunts Germany," *CNN.com*, November 6, 1999, http://www.cnn.com/WORLD/europe/9911/06/wall.death.strip/.

89. U.S. Customs and Border Protection, *U.S. Customs and Border Protection Announces Border Safety Initiative*.

90. Catherine Bailey, "Sidebar: Humanity for the Crossing," *Yes! Magazine*, http://www.yesmagazine.org/ article.asp?ID=1688.

91. Drowning occurs in irrigation canals and ditches, as well as a result of flash floods during the summer season in many parts of the southwest.

92. U.S. Government Accountability Office, *Illegal Immigration*, 39.

93. Peter Andreas, "U.S.-Mexico Border Control in a Changing Economic and Security Context," *Woodrow Wilson International Center for Scholars*, U.S.-Mexico Policy Bulletin Issue 1 (January 2005): 6.

94. U.S. Department of Transportation, Bureau of Transportation Statistics, *Border Crossing/Entry Data*, http://www.bts.gov/programs/international/border_crossing_entry_data/.

95. Dean Calbreath, "Border Waits Shown Taking Big Economic Toll on Region," *San Diego Union-Tribune*, February 3, 2008, http://www.signonsandiego.com/news/business/calbreath/20080203-1057-calbreath03.html.

96. Sandra Dibble, "S.D. Border Crossings Called Most Congested," *San Diego Union-Tribune*, July 8, 2008, http://www.signonsandiego.com/news/mexico/tijuana/20080708-9999-1m8border.html.

97. Calbreath, "Border Waits Shown Taking Big Economic Toll on Region."

98. Dibble, "S.D. Border Crossings Called Most Congested."

99. Bureau of Economic Analysis data indicates that for the last five years the southwest region has had the highest regional gross domestic product compared to the other seven regions of the United States. See U.S. Department of Commerce, Bureau of Economic Analysis, *Regional Economic Accounts*, http://www.bea.gov/ regional/index.htm#gsp.

100. "2007 National Survey of Latinos: As Illegal Immigration Issue Heats Up, Hispanics Feel a Chill," *Pew Hispanic Center*, Washington, DC, December 2007: 1, http://pewhispanic.org/files/reports/84.pdf.

101. "Statistical Portrait of Hispanics in the United States, 2006," *Pew Hispanic Center*, Washington, DC, January 2008: Table 5. Detailed Hispanic Origin: 2006, http://pewhispanic.org/files/factsheets/hispanics2006/ Table-5.pdf.

102. Jeffrey S. Passel, "The Size and Characteristics of the Unauthorized Migrant Population in the U.S.: Estimates Based on the March 2005 Current Population Survey," *Pew Hispanic Center*, Washington, DC, March 2006: 9, http://pewhispanic.org/files/reports/61.pdf.

103. Ibid., i.

104. Ibid., 9.

105. David Simcox, "Another 50 Years of Mass Mexican Immigration: Mexican Government Report Projects Continued Flow Regardless of Economics or Birth Rates," *Center for Immigration Studies*, Backgrounder (March 2002): 1, http://www.cis.org/articles/2002/back202.pdf.

106. Guido Dorigo and Waldo Tobler, "Push-Pull Migration Laws," *Annals of the Association of American Geographers* 73, no. 1 (March 1983): 1.

107. Ibid.

108. Hing, *The Dark Side of Operation Gatekeeper*, 146.

109. Elaine Levine, "From Precarious, Low-Paying Jobs in Mexico to Precarious, Low-Paying Jobs in the United States," in *The Politics, Economics, and Culture of Mexican-U.S. Migration: Both Sides of the Border*, ed. Edward Ashbee, Helene Balslev Clausen, and Carl Pedersen (New York: Palgrave Macmillan, 2007), 86–88.

110. Irene Mendoza and Dennis L. Soden, "Economics or Get Tough Policies? A Discussion of the Decline in Illegal Immigration on the U.S.-Mexico Border," paper presented at the Istituto di Sociologia Internazionale di Gorizia, XIV International Summer School: The Mediterranean beyond Borders, University of Trieste, Gorizia, Italy, September 8–19, 2008.

111. Robert Collier, "NAFTA Gives Mexicans New Reasons to Leave Home," *San Francisco Chronicle*, October 15, 1998, A-11, http://www.sfgate.com/cgi-bin/article.cgi?file=/chronicle/archive/1998/10/15/ MN29399.DTL.

112. Levine, "From Precarious, Low-Paying Jobs in Mexico," 65.

113. Johnson, *The "Huddled Masses" Myth*, 164.

114. Ibid.

115. James C. McKinley Jr., "At Mexican Border, Tunnels, Vile River, Rusty Fence," *New York Times*, March 23, 2005, http://www.nytimes.com/2005/03/23/international/americas/23mexico.html; Dan Simon, "Mexican Cartels Running Pot Farms in U.S. National Forest," *CNN.com*, August 8, 2008, http://www.cnn.com/2008/CRIME/ 08/08/pot.eradication/.

116. The National Commission on Terrorist Attacks upon the United States, *The 9/11 Commission Report*, 383.

117. *Haig v. Agee*, 453 U.S. 280, 307 (1981) (citing *Aptheker v. Secretary of State*, 378 U.S. 500, 509 (1964)).

118. Kevin R. Johnson and Bernard Trujillo, "Immigration Reform, National Security after September 11, and the Future of North American Integration," *Minnesota Law Review* 91 (2007): 1369, 1403–1404 (citing Peter Beinart, "The Wrong Place to Stop Terrorists," *Washington Post*, May 4, 2006, A25; and Robert S. Leiken and Steven Brooke, "The Quantitative Analysis of Terrorism and Immigration: An Initial Exploration," *Terrorism and Political Violence* 18, no. 4 (2006): 503–521.

119. The National Commission on Terrorist Attacks upon the United States, *The 9/11 Commission Report*, 387.

Part III

International Law in New Times

14

Fighting Terrorism:
The Role of Military Ethics,
Humanitarian Law, and
Human Rights in Theory
and Practice

Joanne K. Lekea*

After the attacks of 9/11 and the subsequent war against terrorism many questions arose concerning the difficulties of observing international humanitarian law during asymmetrical warfare. On one hand, terrorists do not pay attention to the Geneva Conventions or any other treaties concerning the respect of human rights, the protection of noncombatants, or the permissible means of fighting. In most of the cases, they attack innocent people to accomplish their goals and put pressure on their opponents.

On the other hand, human rights seem to have played an important role on the decision to declare the "war against terror." Initially, the justification of war was based on the self-defense argument. In the course of time, especially after defeating the Taliban regime, the other reason that was used to justify the war was that the Taliban regime was suppressing fundamental human rights, such as the women rights to education and the people's right to religious freedom. In this context, soldiers are obliged to observe the law and protect noncombatants, treat the prisoners of war well, and keep observing the law even if the enemy does not.

* **Joanne K. Lekea** is a visiting lecturer at the Hellenic Air Force Academy and a postdoctoral researcher and a visiting lecturer at the University of Athens.

In theory, thus, the rules and the obligations of the military are well defined—however, in practice things are not quite so simple both on legal and ethical grounds. For example, if we look at the case of Afghanistan, the application of laws of war is notoriously difficult, as the U.S. war against terror changed its legal status after the defeat of the Taliban regime and the establishment of the Karzai administration.[1]

Scope of the Chapter

The main purpose of this chapter is to illustrate the difficult ethical questions raised by the conduct of asymmetrical war. International Humanitarian Law (hereafter referred to as IHL), as well as military ethics, can provide us with the tools necessary not only to evaluate ethical questions on the use of force, but also to prepare us to deal with practical issues about the conduct of hostilities.

The issues I address in this chapter can be summarized in the following questions:

- If the enemy is not acting by the law, could one possibly support the argument that combatants are also justified to do the same, thus vindicating and legitimizing illegal and immoral behavior, which is not in conformity with IHL and the UN Charter? I use the targeted-killing strategy as a case study to answer this question, as it is a much debated issue and a good tool to look at the extent to which the war against terrorism is conducted on fair grounds.[2] The policy of targeted killing is of special interest as it seems to be the most popular antiterror policy and has implications at different levels: IHL, human rights, and the ethical conduct of hostilities. In the following sections I examine both the legality and the morality of this practice.
- When soldiers actually do violate the law, does this mean that the ethical education they and their officers had was in vain? Furthermore, does military ethics teaching prove to be a failure?

Targeted Killing: The Moral and Legal Framework

The strategy of killing certain individuals when they are not posing any direct threat (targeted killing[3]) resembles the policy that Israel applies against Palestinians and seems to be recently adopted by the U.S. forces. The American political and military authorities opposed that policy at the beginning—however, it seems that they started following it lately by preemptively killing terrorist suspects.[4] For the purposes of this study, the definition of targeted killing in the context of the war against terrorism can be given as the decision to kill a suspect for terrorist acts, if he presents a serious threat to public order (according to criminal evidence and intelligence information) with the ultimate aim to cancel, prevent, or at least limit future terrorist attacks.[5] This should be the last resort, where all other methods of incapacitating him have been tested and failed.[6]

In this context, I refer to two characteristic operations of that kind:[7] (1) the attack against six terrorist suspects in Yemen on November 2002;[8] and (2) the attack that took place in June 2006 and lead to the death of Abu Musab al-Zarqawi in Iraq. In the first case, a U.S. missile attack launched from a Predator drone aircraft targeted six suspected al Qaeda terrorists traveling in a vehicle to Yemen. Although civilians were killed, the attack was considered a military action and not an assassination.[9] As a result of this attack Al-Harithi, who was the leader of many al Qaeda attacks, was killed.

The attack against Abu Musab al-Zarqawi was justified on similar grounds. Zarqawi was thought to be the mastermind of numerous acts of violence in Iraq including suicide bombings and hostage executions. He was believed to be responsible for coordinating numerous suicide bombers throughout Iraq. Zarqawi was killed on June 7, 2006 while attending a meeting in an isolated safehouse approximately 8 km north of Baqubah. Two United States Air Force F-16C jets identified the house and bombed the building. Except for Zarqawi, six other individuals were also reported killed. The death of one of his key lieutenants, spiritual adviser Sheik Abd-Al-Rahman, was announced at a later date.

In general terms, three conceptual frameworks can be used to decide on the legitimacy and morality of targeted killing of terrorist suspects at the level of conducting counterinsurgency warfare:

- To treat it as a legal and morally acceptable operation;[10]
- To treat it as an act that violates fundamental human rights and that can be justified only on the grounds of very strict criteria and in special circumstances;[11]
- To treat it as an act that is morally unacceptable, as any kind of violence, and should be condemned even if carried out in the course of a war.[12]

According to the first opinion, terrorists should be dealt with as lawful combatants, who, even if they do not wear uniforms or they do not bear any insignia, retain their status for as long as they are directly involved in military operations. Their classification as lawful combatants is, however, problematic as they do not have distinctive badges all the time that are easily viewable from distance, nor do they show their weapons. International legislation states that protection should be given to them when they have a person in charge who is responsible for the acts of the people under his command, when they have a distinctive badge all the time that can be recognized from far away, when they carry weapons and if they comply to the laws and the customs of war in their operations.[13] In any case, should they try planned and coordinated attacks against military and political targets, it is legal to treat them as military targets.

From an ethical perspective, one can comment on these cases from the just-war tradition (JWT) viewpoint. This tradition has close links with international legislation, especially with reference to the jus in bello part, which was incorporated into IHL.[14] According to the JWT, for the conduct of war to be just, it must be governed by two principles: those of *discrimination* and *proportionality*. The principle of *discrimination* defines who and what can be justly attacked in a war.[15] It is immoral to deliberately kill noncombatants who are "morally and technically innocent, that is, harmless"[16]; this principle is also included in the IHL where it is clearly stated that noncombatants' lives should be protected in the best possible way.[17] This principle creates the obligation for military commanders and other people involved in planning a specific military operation to think carefully about the results of the attack; *civilians and their property should be protected in the best possible way*. In the case of the war against terrorism, the distinction between combatants and civilians is blurred as a result of the terrorists' intentional presence in urban areas. In the cases in consideration, the targets were individuals who were undoubtedly involved in terrorist operations and were high-ranked al Qaeda officers. We could, therefore, conclude that they were legitimate targets and, in this context, the principle of discrimination was observed.

The principle of *proportionality*, on the other hand, is used to resolve issues such as how one should attack and what kind of weapons he might use in order to achieve the military objectives set without causing disproportional collateral damage,[18] for example, civilian casualties or damage to civilian objects. In these non-clear-cut cases, where the enemy is surrounded by civilians, and there is a possibility of harming or killing them as a result of the military operation, the principle of double effect is invoked.[19] A high-level approach to this principle is that if military commanders are planning to perform an act that is likely to harm noncombatants, they can proceed only if the following four conditions are met:[20]

(1) The act must be good in itself; it must be a legitimate act of war;

(2) The direct effect must be morally acceptable (the target must be legitimate);

(3) Any negative effect must not be intended;

(4) The intended outcome must be proportional to the foreseen damage. This means that the good effect(s) resulting from the military operation should outweigh any negative consequences of the attack.

Even when the aforementioned conditions are met, the foreseeable negative consequences must be reduced as far as possible.[21]

In both the examples discussed earlier, there was intelligence about the suspect targets and the attacks were carried out in well-chosen locations with the use of weapons that would minimize any side casualties; in both cases the death of high-rank al Qaeda officers was achieved. The mission was accomplished without casualties for the Americans, and the benefits were important in the case of Yemen (Al-Harithi was killed, the mastermind of many al Qaeda attacks) and the same holds for Abu Musab al-Zarqawi. Thus, the principle of proportionality was also observed.

In general, targeted-killing attacks aim at weakening the terrorist networks, limit their capacities, and prevent their members from planning attacks of a higher magnitude. The tactic of attacking and killing specific targets is superior to other choices for achieving the same results (e.g., the use of troops for engaging in a face-to-face battle with the terrorists or combining these attacks with air force support) as it does not result in wide aggravating consequences to noncombatants and at the same time protects soldiers from battles that can be avoided. This way, the cost of operations is reduced *not only in financial terms but in terms of human lives as well.*[22] This statement could make a strong utilitarian argument, since the benefits of targeted-killing policies extend to noncombatants as well as privates; casualties are reduced in both populations. Beyond that, in the course of war, it is reasonable enough to assume that each opponent organizes his strategy and decides on the tactical moves in a way that will give him the victory having suffered minimal losses.[23]

According to the second opinion, by analyzing the targeted-killing attacks, one can argue that fundamental human rights are violated: suspects are killed without having been tried and found guilty.[24] Besides that, on the basis of the Common Article 3 of the Geneva Conventions of 1949, assassinations that are conducted without a prior court decision are illegal.[25] Apart from that, a number of *targeted-killing* attacks have taken place, where victims were not recognized as terrorists and cases of false intelligence have led to bombing attacks against civilian houses.[26] Beyond the successful operations where it is proved that suspects were indeed involved in terrorist operations, a number of attacks was against civilians and claimed the lives of people whose links to terrorist networks were never proved.

In relation to the Yemen case, it is worth noting that the Amnesty International sent a letter to the president of the United States of America George W. Bush asking him to investigate whether, before the attack, efforts had been made to arrest the terrorist suspects. The letter also asked him to investigate whether the government of Yemen had cooperated in the attack and whether the operation in question was part of a plan for killing suspects rather than attempting to arrest them. The point at which the efforts for arresting suspects of terrorist acts are exhausted is, of course, debatable.[27]

Beyond that, the moral dilemmas that are present in all cases of targeted killing are critical. By authorizing the killing of a suspect, it means that his right to life is violated. If it is proven afterward that the suspect was not involved in the acts that he was accused of, then those who carry out the execution have heavy legal and moral responsibilities. On the other hand, if a suspect is set free and then he carries out missions that will lead to mass killings, do those who set him free have moral responsibilities—if nothing else? How can someone compare the life of a suspect to the life of an innocent civilian? Who is responsible for making such judgments? Is a military commander the suitable judge for these cases? A considerable amount of legal philosophy exists concerning the justification of punishment[28] and who is responsible for deciding these issues, which can be linked to the targeted-killing policies—especially if one considers that the punishment for a suspect terrorist is the death penalty.

These issues are, surely, hard to resolve and anyone can give his own views; however, a minimum level of rights apply, by law, to all suspects and these should be kept. Otherwise, we will have to justify exceptions both at the legal level, as well as the moral level, solely on the grounds of the suspects' degree of danger. But how just is something like that? It would be difficult for someone to support such a view as fundamental rights—such as been innocent until proven guilty and the right to a fair trial—are being violated. In short, fundamental human rights are being violated just for the fear of future actions of the suspects on the basis of strong evidence, at least as current practice demonstrates.[29]

In both our cases, the terrorist suspects were not a direct threat and the "go ahead" for this kind of operations without a court ruling is a violation of both international humanitarian law and human rights law.[30] On the basis of these ideas the second approach was developed—it maintains that regardless of the benefits *targeted-killing* operations may have, the following consequences should be taken seriously into consideration before initiating such an attack:

- the right of suspects to have a fair trial and the legal principle of been innocent until proven guilty are violated;[31] anyone accused of

being a terrorist suspect, even if he participated in terrorist operations, should have the right to a fair trial, where the punishment for
his actions will be decided.

- the ban against arbitrarily taking human lives is violated; the right
  to life is a fundamental human right and should not be violated in
  any case, even in situations of national emergency.
- there is a high chance of creating a vicious circle of violence and a
  chain of terrorist attacks.[32]

The focus can then be diverted to the causes that can justify the killing of certain individuals. I think that the same criteria should hold as for
preemptive attacks, that is, we should have strong and well-founded intelligence information and we should be absolutely certain that the suspect
in question is close to launching a terrorist operation against civilians and
that there is no other way of preventing him from his cause and all other
ways of confronting and arresting him have been exhausted and failed.[33]

Concluding this section, in relation to the three approaches presented
earlier, I believe that the second is the one that sheds light to the tactic of
targeted killing. Neither does it claim that it is the solution to all problems
of the war against terrorism, nor does it reject it in all cases—on the contrary, it takes into account all special parameters that characterize every
operation, making it different from any previous or next one.

In this way, it cannot be claimed (or justified) that terrorist suspects
should become targets and killed in any case, as that would mean that in
order to fight terrorism we should be prepared to accept extended violations of human rights. This would mean that a policy of "kill now and
investigate later" would come in place; in other words, a confirmation that
we are entitled to kill any suspect on the spot, rather than arresting him
and giving him a fair trial—which is a fundamental right of every human
being, guilty or innocent.[34] We should not forget that the war against terrorism is, in essence, a battle for protecting the human rights that are violated by the terrorist operations. Americans and their allies in this war
should be the first to show that they respect human rights.

The War against Terrorism and the Legal and
Moral Framework of War: An Impossible Relationship?

A more general question raised in this context is whether the war
against terrorism needs to be regulated by rules of conduct at all. As
frequently stated, since terrorists do not follow the rules, one can fight
them without respecting any rule of war either. This argument is based

on reciprocity: terrorists disregard human life, so they should be treated accordingly.[35] After all, they started the war, so they are responsible for all the death and destruction that follows.[36] That, practically, means that one can attack suspected terrorists directly or use prohibited methods[37] to keep the pressure on anyone, in order to make the terrorists come out.

This notion is problematic as it makes observing the law optional depending on the enemy one faces; but when a state ratifies a treaty, whether it concerns the rights of civilians and the prisoners of war or the prohibition of certain weapons, it has to adhere to it. If the enemy has not ratified the treaty and probably chooses to use prohibited weapons or methods of war, this is not an excuse for the military to act in the same way. States have to adhere to treaties, as a result of the international law governing them; this is not only an obligation of the United States, but rather an obligation of the international community.[38] This is the reason why the U.S. Armed Forces and their allies have to do everything in their power to defeat the enemy using tactics that are in accordance with IHL.

Another important issue that is raised as a result of the targeted-killing operations is the role the American government and U.S. military forces have to play in the war against terrorism, which is a war against a "stateless terrorist enemy." The nature of these attacks against individuals is purely preemptive, as the primary target of these operations is the death of high-rank al Qaeda officials in order to prevent, avoid, or—at least—reduce the numbers of future terrorist attacks. Furthermore, attacks of this kind primarily aim not only at eliminating terrorists but also target those who are offering them operational, military, or any other kind of support.

More specifically, the United States has relied on covert action in their campaign against terrorism and it appears that future targeted-killing attacks will run in cooperation with other governments, in full secrecy if needed.[39] The attacks will be carried out with or without the consent of those governments whose authorities are involved. This kind of reasoning can become very dangerous as the U.S. government and military forces will be able to act as an "international police force," responding to any new security challenges unilaterally and even preemptively.[40] That scenario gives them full power to interfere and intervene wherever they suspect that there is ongoing terrorist activity.[41]

If one looks at this issue from the viewpoint of international legislation, one will see that military operations for any reason on other nation's territory are problematic, especially if they do not have the consent of the home government. The UN Charter unambiguously states the cases where an operation is permitted: an approval is needed either from the Security Council or a peripheral organization, or the military action should be justified on the basis of exercising the legal right of states to self-defense, either individually or collectively.[42] It becomes even more complex and hard to justify it legally when someone realizes that the operation on foreign territory happens on the suspicion of terrorist act. In this case any principle of sovereignty is overlooked.[43]

The justification is problematic on moral grounds as well. Even if arguments about ending the war sooner with less side casualties are used, they remain in essence unconvincing. The effort to justify this type of operations on the basis that they are being carried out for securing world peace that is in danger from terrorists is not fully acceptable, as fundamental rights—also part of international legislation—are being violated.[44]

With respect to the benefits arising from those interventions and military actions we should scrutinize them carefully, as the results of the American policy will be visible in the years to come. The United States has turned out to be the most powerful country in the New World Order and their contribution so far may indeed be considered as vital, although we have to keep in mind that the great power they hold should not suppress other states' rights or violate human rights. Anytime the U.S. intervention is deemed necessary by the Security Council or is requested by a particular state the situation is different, but the power to use military force against any possible suspected enemy could provoke counteractions and become a major source of international disputes leading to breaches of peace.

Thus, it is clear that the way U.S. military and its allies fight this war—as well as the way it treats terrorists and their organizations—is crucial as it will form a predecessor for future operations. It is very important that the latest technology (especially weapons with a high degree of accuracy) is employed in order to minimize civilian casualties. However, even in this case we should be very careful when targeting terrorist suspects; in the cases under discussion, the attack was indeed launched against terrorists. In the past U.S. forces attacked groups of people whom they mistook for terrorists.[45] Therefore, the operations for locating and targeting suspects should be carried out in such a way that will ensure that the people targeted are the right ones and, even so, eliminate the possibility of other people being in the vicinity and getting hurt.

Beside the practical aspect of this matter, it follows that a major theoretical issue we have to resolve is whether ethical principles, especially those governing the conduct of war, are applicable in the "war" against terrorism. Many people would argue that the principles of discrimination and proportionality cannot be applied because terrorists get intentionally mixed up with civilians.[46] This tactic renders futile the efforts by U.S. forces to avoid civilian casualties; at the same time this will only make the war last longer, leading to more casualties.[47]

It is true that the war against terrorism is a new form and a new kind of war. Although, what is really important, is to take into account the characteristics that are specific to this type of war and make it unique with regards to former wars we have seen and fought so far: such as the fact that it takes place in towns, villages and urban areas; that the terrorists blend in with civilians; and that there is no 'visible' enemy to fight. Moreover, terrorists intentionally use non-combatants either to form a 'human shield' around them or to harm them; both actions serve as means of making their voice heard and their demands met. With these characteristics in mind, many would argue that it is pointless to try not to harm civilians or not to cause disproportional damage. This will make the US Forces and their allies lose their ability to achieve the military objectives set, bringing the war to an end as quickly as possible.[48]

Nevertheless, every new challenge should not become a reason for abandoning or modifying fundamental moral values in order to be in line with any temporal interests. Even before the formulation of IHL regarding the conduct of war, there were moral principles governing what was acceptable and what was not: Plato, Aristotle, and Cicero grant special status to noncombatants. The right to go to war and its just conduct are analyzed in depth by St. Augustine[49] and Hugo Grotius.[50] The Just War concepts morally ground IHL.[51] Therefore, the development of the existing legislation was carried out on moral grounds and principles concerning war. Abolishing the rules and the obligations stemming from the treaties and the conventions that a state has ratified is like giving away its moral values.

On the contrary, one, instead of lowering one's moral standards, should seek alternative ways of achieving one's goals without having to follow an immoral path. As a result, any extension of the capabilities of military technology and, consequently, of military capacity should not make a state give away its moral values. Instead, the most current and accurate weapons should be used in order to fulfil the moral and legal obligations, as these are derived from IHL.

What about the Officers' Ethical Education? Is It in Vain?

The training of officers in issues related to the moral dimension of their profession proves to be really helpful. Especially in situations, like asymmetric war, where the opponent does not follow the moral principles and the rules of international legislation and, as a result, strong dilemmas about the conduct of hostilities come up. In these cases, officers and military personnel of all ranks should have strong positions on issues of morality and justice in order to resist the temptation to act in the same way as their opponent, leaving any thoughts about justice or morality behind. There is a number of ways one can use to teach military ethics; the issue is choosing the best.

War literature[52] and poetry[53] related to warrior ethos, the conduct of hostilities, or other specific aspects of war (such as the treatment of prisoners of war or the protection of civilians) can be an excellent source for identifying and commenting on ethical dilemmas concerning war. One can easily find material that reflects on similar contemporary issues and further analyze the effects these ideas have in today's battlefields. Some ideas expressed in religious and philosophical texts (such as the protection of civilians, the prohibition of using certain types of weapons and so on) are now part of IHL.[54] Analyzing texts may prove a critical tool and precious supplement when thinking about what action one should take in war, but cannot help officers or soldiers to solve practical ethical problems alone. One needs a more systematic approach to deal with them efficiently, especially when urgent answers are needed in the heat of the battle.

Moral theories can further provide officers with a useful framework to resolve ethical dilemmas in a more organized context. Of course there is no moral theory of any kind that can solve every possible problem that could arise. After all, there has never been an ideal theory that could meet all the challenges effectively. Decision-making in a war is not an easy task. Moral theories can help military and political personnel in charge of planning this kind of operations to realize the ethical perspectives and consequences of their choices.

Another way of reflecting on ethical dilemmas and ambiguous cases is by resorting to the rules of conduct as stated in every nation's military legislation and IHL. In fact, a subset of moral rules with the lapse of time formed the moral baseline of international legislation relating to war issues and actually became a part of IHL.

Is this sufficient though? The answer is negative as both ethical theories and international legislation tend to be rather generic by nature and, thus, unable to deal with situations where a large number of interdependent factors are involved. The combination of ethical theories with international legislation can provide officers with valuable directions on which the operation will be based, but can do very little with helping them to design and run it.

Game theory, on the other hand, will allow them to cater to these aspects as it offers the necessary tools for studying practical issues about the costs and benefits of a war, evaluating ethical questions on the use of force in the battlefield or in urban environments where the protection of civilians is crucial.[55] Game theory and rational choice theory prove to be necessary in strategic- and tactical decision-making.[56] The benefits one can enjoy from applying this framework include getting answers in uncertain situations, as well as foreseeing the reactions to each course of action taken; identifying the pros and cons of each alternative and selecting the course of action that minimizes costs while maximizing benefits.

In any case, no matter how military ethics are taught, it is never a futile effort. They help officers of all ranks to realize the moral dimension of their profession and to choose their actions responsibly.[57] This is very important in the war against terrorism since a new way of operations will need to be undertaken and special attention should be paid to the choice of methods used to confront the opponent—which will see that military forces will not end up using practices not supported by international legislation that cannot be morally justified.

Even in the case of unacceptable tactics, such as the bad treatment of prisoners or the use of illegal methods during the interrogation of terrorist suspects, it does not mean that training on moral matters failed. One should take into account the fact that participants in a war face extreme situations and sometimes breaking moral rules and moral principles is more a matter of psychology rather than a deliberate choice. In any case, it is better if one is trained in all aspects of his profession—and morality *is* an important aspect of the officer's profession, as his actions are always related to the value of life.

Concluding Remarks

Summarizing, it is worth questioning whether the strategies that the United States has adopted in practice suppress the ethical parameters and the legislation governing military conflicts so far. There is a popular argument claiming that since terrorists refuse to respect human life and hurt noncombatants, since they are not bound to moral and legal rules, then the behavior of those having to fight them should be similar.[58] As terrorists are responsible for starting the war with their acts (9/11), they are to be held responsible for all damages and deaths caused by it[59] and the troops fighting them can apply all strategies, even prohibited or unorthodox ones, to win the war.

This approach is clearly problematic on both moral and legal grounds. It implies that the war code of conflict as well as the ethical principles governing the conduct of hostilities can be observed or not depending on who the enemy is. All international treaties should be adhered to and that is a responsibility independent of the enemy's behavior. In this case, Americans and their allies should not refer to the tactical choices of the terrorists and use them as an excuse for violating the moral and legal war framework, since they end up doing what they are trying to fight: using methods that violate fundamental human rights.

Another very important issue is the extent to which military can react in an ethical manner to the new threats and methods employed by terrorists. For example, what happens with the protection of civilians and the related difficult choices that officers have to make in the battlefield? One might think that terrorists intentionally mix with civilians, making any attempt to avoid noncombatant casualties futile; this only results in the longer duration of the hostilities thereby causing more casualties.[60]

In relation to the aforementioned issues, the advances in war technologies, which determine to a great extent how battles are fought, should come into play. Every new challenge should not become a reason to quit, discount, or alter fundamental moral values (such as the respect to human life). On the contrary, new ways of achieving the aims set, without using immoral or illegal ways, must be found. The advances in military technology might provide the military with the ability to be effective in carrying out the operations and meeting the objectives set while, at the same time, observing all ethical principles and legal obligations.

One should keep in mind that the way one fights determines—to a great extent—the kind of peace that will follow the war. The just conduct of hostilities and the respect to the opponent's fundamental human rights can be used as a model for the kind of peace we are trying to achieve. As peace should be the prime objective whenever a war is started, U.S. Armed Forces and their allies need to make every possible effort not to undermine it with unacceptable and illegal methods in the battlefield. It is therefore crucial to prove in practice that human life and human rights are respected in the war against terrorism.

Notes

1. Robert Cryer, "The Fine Art of Friendship: Jus in Bello in Afghanistan," *Journal of Conflict and Security Law* 7, no.1 (2002): 37–83. Also, Marco Sassòli, "Terrorism and War," *Journal of International Criminal Justice*.6 (2006): 959–981.

2. There are other examples whose legality and morality has been discussed in length, e.g., the treatment of prisoners held as terrorist suspects. These topics are not covered in this chapter due to limited space. For more information, see Joanne K. Lekea and Nikolaos V. Bochlos, "Arresting, Imprisoning and Interrogating Terrorist Suspects. Is There Room for Intelligence Ethics?" paper presented at the *Second International Conference on the Ethics of National Security Intelligence*, January 26 and 27, 2007, Washington, DC.

3. Eric Patterson and Teresa Casale, "Targeting Terror: The Ethical and Practical Implications of Targeted Killing," *International Journal of Intelligence and CounterIntelligence* 18, no.4 (2005): 638–652.

4. Orna Ben-Naftali and Keren R. Michaeli, "Justice-Ability: A Critique of the Alleged Non-Justifiability of Israel's Policy of Targeted Killings," *Journal of International Criminal Justice* 1, no. 1 (2003): 368–405. Also, Joan Fitzpatrick, "Speaking Law to Power: The War against Terrorism and Human Rights," *European Journal of International Law* 2 (2003): 241–264.

5. Fitzpatrick, "Speaking Law to Power," 247.

6. Robert F. Teplitz, "Taking Assassination Attempts Seriously: Did the United States Violate International Law in Forcefully Responding to the Iraqi Plot to Kill George Bush?" *Cornell International Law Journal* 28, no. 2 (1995): 569, 610–613.

7. Other cases could be used as well, such as the Israeli attack on Sheikh Yassin of Hamas. I chose the two cases (the Yemen and Zarqawi cases) as my study concentrates on the U.S.-led war against terror. One can find interesting information on the Israeli policy on targeted killing and the U.S. attack in Yemen in David Kretzmer, "Targeted Killing of Suspected Terrorists: Extra-Judicial Executions or Legitimate Means of Defence?" *European Journal of International Law* 16, no. 2 (2005): 171–212.

8. Jeffrey Addicott, *The Yemen Attack: Illegal Assassination or Lawful Killing?* available online at http://jurist.law.pitt.edu/forum/forumnew68.php, 2002. Also, Joanne K. Lekea, "Missile Strike Carried Out with Yemeni Cooperation— The War against Terrorism: A Different Kind of War?" *Journal of Military Ethics* 2, no. 3 (2003): 230–239.

9. Walter Pincus, "Missile Strike Carried Out with Yemeni Cooperation: Official Says Operation Authorized under Bush Finding," *Journal of Military Ethics* 2, no. 3 (2003): 227–229.

10. Addicott, *The Yemen Attack*.

11. Patterson and Casale, "Targeting Terror."

12. This is the position of those who follow pacifism and I mention it here only for reasons of completeness of the presentation. As I do not think it is realistic for one to expect that there would be a war without casualties or that in the future war operations would stop existing, I go no further in analyzing this particular opinion.

13. *Convention (II) for the Amelioration of the Condition of Wounded, Sick and Shipwrecked Members of Armed Forces at Sea*, art. 13. Similar arrangements exist in the *Geneva Convention (I) for the Amelioration of the Condition of the Wounded and Sick in Armed Forces in the Field*, art. 13, and in the *Convention (III) Relative to the Treatment of Prisoners of War* of August 12, 1949, art. 4.

14. James Turner Johnson, *Morality and Contemporary Warfare* (New Haven, CT, and London: Yale University Press, 1999), 8–40.

15. Nicholas Fotion, "Who, What, When and How to Attack," paper presented at the Joint Services Conference on Professional Ethics (JSCOPE), held in Washington, DC, January 27–28, 1996; available online at http://atlas.usafa.af.mil/jscope/JSCOPE96/fotion96.html, accessed September 25, 2006.

16. David R. Mapel, "Realism and the Ethics of War and Peace," in *The Ethics of War and Peace: Secular and Religious Perspectives*, ed. Terry Nardin (Princeton, NJ: Princeton University Press, 1998), 67. See also, Robert L. Holmes, *On War and Morality* (Princeton, NJ: Princeton University Press, 1989), 104.

17. *Convention (IV) Relative to the Protection of Civilian Persons in Time of War*, arts. 4, 273/34. *Protocol Additional to the Geneva Conventions I*, art. 2. Also, Common Article 3 of the 1949 Geneva Conventions. *Protocol Additional to the Geneva Conventions I*, art. 48. Finally, *Geneva Convention (I) for the Amelioration of the Condition of the Wounded and Sick in Armed Forces in the Field*, arts. 19, 21, 24, 25; *Convention (II) for the Amelioration of the Condition of Wounded, Sick and Shipwrecked Members of Armed Forces at Sea*, arts. 22–35. *Protocol Additional to the Geneva Conventions I*, arts. 12 and 23.

18. Michael Schmitt, "State-Sponsored Assassination in International and Domestic Law," *Yale Journal of International Law* 17 (1992): 609–685.

19. Fitzpatrick, "Speaking Law to Power," 247.

20. Emanuel Gross, "Self-Defense against Terrorism—What Does It Mean? The Israeli Perspective," *Journal of Military Ethics* 1 no. 2 (2002): 105. Also, Johnson, *Morality and Contemporary Warfare*, 132–133. For further details, see Richard J. Regan, *Just War: Principles and Cases* (Washington, DC: Catholic University of America Press, 1996), 95–96. Finally, Michael Walzer, *Just and Unjust Wars: A Moral Argument with Historical Illustration* (New York: Basic Books, 2006), 153.

21. Walzer, *Morality and Contemporary Warfare*, 155.

22. Gross, "Self-Defense against Terrorism," 96–97. Also, Daniel Statman, "Targeted Killing," in *Philosophy 9/11: Thinking about the War on Terrorism*, ed. Timothy Shanahan (Chicago: Open Court Publishing Company, 2005), 183–202.

23. This could be regarded as a very realistic argument indeed. Amichai Cohen and Yuval Shany, "A Development of Modest Proportions. The Application of the Principle of Proportionality in the Targeted Killings Case," *Journal of International Criminal Justice* 5 (2007): 310–321.

24. Sabine von Schorlemer, "Human Rights: Substantive and Institutional Implications of the War against Terrorism," *European Journal of International Law* 2 (2003): 265–282.

25. There is a major difference between assassination and targeted killing. When we talk about assassination, we have to distinguish between peacetime assassination and wartime assassination. Peacetime assassination requires all of the following three elements to be present: (1) a murder, (2) of a specific individual, (3) for political purposes. Assassination in wartime has the following characteristics: (1) the specific targeting of a particular individual and (2) the use of treacherous or perfidious means. Other forms of extrajudicial execution, targeted killing, or elimination are not synonymous with assassination. Assassination, whether in peacetime or wartime, constitutes an illegal killing, while targeted killing is the intentional slaying of a specific individual or group of individuals undertaken with explicit governmental

approval. For more information, see Major Tyler J. Harder, "Time to Repeal the Assassination Ban of Executive Order 12,333: A Small Step in Clarifying Current Law," *Military Law Review* 172 (2002): 1–39.

26. Tony Pfaff, "Non-Combatant Immunity and the War on Terrorism," (online paper), paper presented at the Joint Services Conference on Professional Ethics (JSCOPE), January 2003, accessed September 25, 2006; available at http://www.usafa.af.mil/jscope/JSCOPE03/ Pfaff03.html; Internet.

27. There have been efforts, of course, to give strict instructions about when the use of lethal force is allowed. In the case of *McCann and Others v. the United Kingdom* (European Court of Human Rights) the judgment gives very specific criteria for the use of lethal force. For more information, see Amichai Cohen and Yuval Shany, "A Development of Modest Proportions. The Application of the Principle of Proportionality in the Targeted Killings Case," *Journal of International Criminal Justice* 5 (2007): 310–321. Also, see Federico Sperotto, "Violations of Human Rights during Military Operations in Chechnya," working paper no. 41, accessed June 15, 2007; available online at http://www.du.edu/gsis/hrhw/working/2007/41-sperotto-2007.pdf.

28. More generally, see David Wood, "Retribution, Crime Reduction and the Justification of Punishment," *Oxford Journal of Legal Studies* 22, no. 2 (2002): 301–321.

29. For more details see, Pfaff, "Non-Combatant Immunity and the War on Terrorism."

30. Amnesty International, "Yemen/USA: Government Must Not Sanction Extra-Judicial Executions," available online at http://web.amnesty.org/library/index/EN-GAMR511682002, 2002.

31. Schorlemer, "Human Rights," 265–282.

32. Statman, "Targeted Killing," 183–202.

33. Gross, "Self-Defense against Terrorism," 96–97 and Kretzmer, "Targeted Killing of Suspected Terrorists," 171–212.

34. Chris Downes, "'Targeted Killings' in an Age of Terror: The Legality of the Yemen Strike," *Journal of Conflict and Security Law* 9, no. 2 (2004): 277–294.

35. Ian Klabbers, "Rebel with a Cause? Terrorists and Humanitarian Law," *European Journal of International Law* 2 (2003): 311.

36. Adam Roberts, "Counter-Terrorism, Armed Force and the Laws of War," *Survival* 44, no. 1 (2002): 10.

37. *Protocol Additional to the Geneva Conventions I*, art. 51.

38. Luigi Condorelli and Laurence Boisson de Chazournes, " Quelques remarques a propos de l'obligation des Etats de 'respecter et faire respecter' le droit international humanitaire en toutes circonstances," in *Etudes et essais sur le droit international humanitaire et sur les principes de la Croix-Rouge en l'honneur de Jean Pictet*, ed. Christophe Swinarski (Geneva: International Committee of the Red Cross, 1984), 17–35.

39. Sean D. Murphy, "International Law, the United States, and the Non-Military 'War' on Terrorism," *European Journal of International Law* 2 (2003): 363.

40. Eyal Benvenisti, "The U.S. and the Use of Force: Double-Edged Hegemony and the Management of Global Emergencies," *European Journal of*

International Law 15, no. 4 (2004): 677–700. The consent of the state concerned can be linked to discussions on the evolving notion of state sovereignty. For more information, see David A. Lake, "The New Sovereignty in International Relations," *International Studies Review* 203, no. 5 (September 2003): 303–323.

41. A number of related interesting issues also arise from the Yemen incident; one of these, which due to limited space we cannot fully analyze here, is that the U.S. military forces took military action outside their borders.

42. UN Charter, Chapter VII, arts. 39, 42, 51–54.

43. Steven Lee, "International Governance and the Fight against Terrorism," *Ethics and International Affairs* 20, no. 2 (2006): 241–246. Also, Jean L. Cohen, "Whose Sovereignty? Empire versus International Law," *Ethics and International Affairs*, 18, no. 3 (2004): 1–24. Finally, Jens Bartelson, "The Concept of Sovereignty Revisited," *European Journal of International Law* 17, no. 2 (2006): 463–474.

44. George R. Lucas Jr., "The Role of 'International Community' in Just War Tradition- Confronting the Challenges of Humanitarian Intervention and Preemptive War," *Journal of Military Ethics* 2, no. 2 (2003): 122–144.

45. We must not forget the accidental bombing of an Afghan wedding party, which was considered to be a Taliban gathering. For more details see, Pfaff, "Non-Combatant Immunity and the War on Terrorism."

46. Daniel S. Zupan, "Just War Theory, Law Enforcement and Terrorism: A Reflective Equilibrium," (online paper), paper presented at the Joint Services Conference on Professional Ethics (JSCOPE), January 2003, accessed September 25, 2006; available at http://www.usafa.af.mil/jscope/JSCOPE03/Zupan03.html.

47. Pfaff, "Non-Combatant Immunity and the War on Terrorism."

48. Ibid.

49. Paul Ramsey, "The Just War According to St. Augustine," in *Just War Theory*, ed. Jean Bethke Elshtain (New York: New York University Press, 1992), 8–22.

50. Paul Christopher, *The Ethics of War and Peace: An Introduction to Legal and Moral Issues* (Upper Saddle River, NJ: Prentice Hall, 1999), 81–103.

51. William V. O' Brien, *The Conduct of Just and Limited War* (New York, 1981), 37–70. Also, Ted Westhusing, "Taking Terrorism and ROE Seriously," *Journal of Military Ethics* 2, no. 3 (2003): 3.

52. Diane P. Thompson. *The Trojan War: Literature and Legends from the Bronze Age to the Present* (Jefferson, NC: McFarland & Company, 2004). Also, Vincent Sherry, ed., *The Cambridge Companion to the Literature of the First World War (Cambridge Companions to Literature)* (Cambridge: Cambridge University Press, 2005). Finally, Philip K. Jason and Mark A. Graves, eds., *Encyclopedia of American War Literature* (Westport, CT: Greenwood Press, 2000).

53. Jon Stallworthy, *The Oxford Book of War Poetry* (New York: Oxford University Press, 2008). Also, Janis P. Stout, *Coming Out of War: Poetry, Grieving, and the Culture of the World Wars*, (Tuscaloosa, AL: University of Alabama Press, 2005).

54. Karma Nabulsi, *Traditions of War: Occupation, Resistance and the Law* (New York, 1999), 66–240. See also, Terry Nardin, *The Ethics of War and Peace* (Princeton, NJ, 1998), 14–213 and Terry Nardin, David R. Mapel, and Steve Smith, eds., *Traditions of International Ethics (Cambridge Studies in International Relations)* (Cambridge, 1993), 62–84, 136–179, 270–296. Finally, Tuck, Richard, *The Rights of War and Peace: Political Thought and the International Order from Grotius to Kant* (Oxford, 1999), 1–234.

55. Rogers B. Myerson, *Game Theory: Analysis of Conflict* (Cambridge, MA: Harvard University Press, 1997), 1–35 and Michael E. Brown, ed., *Rational Choice and Security Studies: Stephen Walt and His Critics* (Cambridge, MA: MIT Press, 2000), 1–44.

56. Philip D. Straffin, *Game Theory and Strategy* (Washington, DC: The Mathematical Association of America, 1996), 27–31 and Martin J. Osborne, *An Introduction to Game Theory* (New York: Oxford University Press, 2003), 1–358. Finally, see Hebert Gintis, *Game Theory Evolving: A Problem-Centered Introduction to Modeling Strategic Interaction* (Princeton, NJ: Princeton University Press, 2009), 357–399.

57. Joanne K. Lekea and George K. Lekeas, "Quantitative Military Ethics: Applying Game Theory to Strategic and Tactical Decision-Making," paper presented at the *Joint Services Conference on Professional Ethics* (JSCOPE), held in Washington, DC, 2006; available online at http://www.usafa.af.mil/jscope/JSCOPE06/Lekea-Lekeas06.html, accessed May 14, 2007.

58. Klabbers, "Rebel with a Cause?" 299–312.

59. Roberts, "Counter-Terrorism, Armed Force and the Laws of War," 7–32.

60. Zupan, "Just War Theory, Law Enforcement and Terrorism."

15

The Torture Memo

*Tara McKelvey**

The people who work in the Eisenhower Executive Office Building on Pennsylvania Avenue, next to the West Wing of the White House, stand out for their seriousness even in a city not known for its *joie de vivre*. Yet the building itself has a rakish charm, with exterior walls made of granite and cast iron, its architectural roots in the French Renaissance. Inside, it has the feel of a slightly seedy, Old World-style Gramercy Park hotel. Attorney Timothy E. Flanigan, a senior administration official, worked on the second floor of the building from 2001 to 2002. He had acted as deputy of the Justice Department's Office of Legal Counsel in the first Bush administration[1] and was an advisor during President George W. Bush's campaign—along with a young legal scholar named John C. Yoo—steering Bush on legal issues that came to include the Florida recount.[2]

As a White House legal advisor, Flanigan, 49, and his boss, Alberto R. Gonzales, serving as White House counsel, were responsible for analyzing issues ranging from domestic security law to international war crimes statutes in the wake of the 9/11 attacks.[3] Indeed, Flanigan had taken up the subject of terrorism as part of a small group of legal experts that included Gonzales; David S. Addington, a counselor to Vice President Dick Cheney; and Yoo, who was at the time a 35-year-old deputy assistant attorney general at the Justice Department's Office of Legal Counsel. Unlike many legal

* **Tara McKelvey** is a senior editor at *The American Prospect*, a frequent contributor to *The New York Times Book Review* and a former research fellow at NYU School of Law's Center on Law and Security. A 2009 Templeton-Cambridge fellow, she is the author of *Monstering: Inside America's Policy on Secret Interrogations and Torture in the Terror War.*

issues that Flanigan had dealt with in the past as a presidential advisor, this one was neither dry nor abstract.

Flanigan was living with his family in Great Falls, Virginia, on September 11, 2001. That day, he huddled with other advisers in the White House situation room and wondered what would happen next. He had personal cause to worry about a future attack—14 reasons, counting all his children. A graduate of Brigham Young University, Flanigan has been included in publicity materials as a participant in Federalist Society activities.[4] He has a broad face, a slightly heavy build, a receding hairline, and a penchant for dark suits, white shirts, and ties. In the hot, sticky summer following 9/11, Flanigan, Gonzales, and Yoo, along with other high-level officials, worked on advising the president on legal dimensions of some of the most important new counterterrorism policies. During that time, Flanigan would find himself soaked in sweat, waiting outside the Eisenhower Office Building, as the manholes on Seventeenth Street let off steam in the afternoon heat.

"The overall response to the war on terror was a very dramatic realignment of thinking in the government as a whole," Flanigan tells me in a telephone interview on December 22, 2004, from his office at Tyco International, where he had taken a position as a senior lawyer. "We moved away from viewing a response to terror as a sort of one-off, criminal-law approach, where you're dealing with a discrete number of defendants, to viewing this as a broader line of attack that would require a higher level of coordination between the FBI and the CIA."[5]

The Office of Legal Counsel's Yoo, a Harvard graduate with dark hair parted on the left side, also found weaknesses in the criminal-justice approach to terrorists. He believed a more vigorous effort, led by the president, was required. Yoo and his Office of Legal Counsel colleagues "went into overdrive," as he wrote in his book *War by Other Means: An Insider's Account of the War on Terror*, attending meetings with officials from the FBI, CIA, the Pentagon, and the State Department in which they discussed the treatment of detainees in U.S. custody.[6] The subject of detainees—and interrogations—was difficult and emotionally trying.

Yoo was working in his office in the Robert F. Kennedy Building in Washington when the first United Airlines jet flew into the World Trade Center on September 11, 2001. His friend, Barbara Olson, the wife of Solicitor General Ted Olson, was killed that same day when the American Airlines jet that she was on crashed into the Pentagon. Most of the participants in the detainee-policy discussions had—like Yoo and Flanigan—experienced the terrorist attacks firsthand. They wanted to stop al Qaeda in its tracks.

"It's not a cops-and-robbers exercise," Flanigan says. "If you arrest bin Laden and bring him back to the U.S. for trial, and he gets a lawyer who tells him to shut up—that's a problem. If we believe a future terrorist attack is possible, or that bin Laden has information that could prevent the event, then we need to find out what he knows. The focus has got to be on getting the information we need to protect American citizens. If you view this as war—and not as a normal, criminal-justice matter—then you are going to have a somewhat different approach. You can be more forward leaning. You're not going to provide everyone with a lawyer."[7]

Defining Torture

On August 1, 2002, Jay S. Bybee, head of the Justice Department's Office of Legal Counsel, signed a memo that provided a narrow definition of torture: interrogators could do what they wanted as long as the intensity of pain inflicted on suspects was less than "that which accompany serious physical injury such as death or organ failure."[8] Yoo is widely acknowledged as the author of the document, which later became known as the "Torture Memo." "Our intent in the Justice Department's original research was to give clear legal guidance on what constituted 'torture' under the law, so that our agents would know exactly what was prohibited, and what was not," Yoo wrote.[9] In fact, the memo created conditions under which almost any type of physical duress could be inflicted on detainees during interrogations.

Specific types of interrogation methods "were discussed by the administration and then blessed," Flanigan tells me. "Nothing was approved that had not been done to U.S. troops during training."[10]

It was a major policy development, and many individuals in the administration found fault with it. "It will reverse over a century of U.S. policy and practice in supporting the Geneva Conventions and undermine the protections of the law of war for our troops, both in this specific conflict and in general," Secretary of State Colin L. Powell wrote in a memorandum to the counsel to the president and the assistant to the president for National Security Affairs one week later.[11]

The views of Secretary of State Powell were not shared by the president. On February 7, 2002, President Bush issued a memo to the vice president, the defense secretary, and intelligence-agency directors about the importance of garnering information from terrorists fighting for the Taliban and al Qaeda.[12] At a press conference on the following day, Defense Secretary Donald Rumsfeld said, "The reality is that the set of facts that exist today with respect to al Qaeda and Taliban were not necessarily the kinds of facts that were considered when the Geneva Convention was fashioned some half a century ago."[13] For this reason, argued Rumsfeld and other administration officials, harsh interrogation techniques may be used on certain types of prisoners.

Less than a year later, in October 2003, Jack Goldsmith, a former University of Chicago professor, took a position in the Office of Legal Counsel. It was, as he writes in his memoir, a scary place. Many of his colleagues had access to a daily "threat matrix," sometimes dozens of pages long, that listed potential terrorist attacks, and often seemed on edge. (It was "like being stuck in a room listening to loud Led Zeppelin music," says Jim Baker, former head of the Office of Intelligence Policy and Review.) It was a tense environment—not only because of the terrorist threats. Officials were also dealing with hostile forces in their backyard—namely, Christopher Hitchens, *The Village Voice*, and "the human rights industry," all of which had gone after Henry Kissinger for war crimes and, according to Goldsmith, posed a threat to current officials.[14]

About a month after he started his job, Goldsmith says, he came across the torture memo but did not "have the time or the resources to devote to the problem."[15] At that point, he did nothing. During this time, Specialist Charles A. Graner Jr. was overseeing detainees in Tier 1A at Abu Ghraib. Yoo has claimed that administration officials have nothing to do with the abusive acts committed at Abu Ghraib. Yet the techniques that were used on the Iraqi prisoners had been approved for al Qaeda suspects by Yoo and the other officials. In fact, Graner was apparently responsible for the implementation of some of these techniques, a list that included, as Yoo wrote, "limiting a captured terrorist to six hours' sleep."[16] Graner and Lynndie England also forced the detainees to exercise—a technique cited by Yoo. Among soldiers, the method is known as "smoking" a detainee, or making him exercise to the point of collapse. Many of these techniques are depicted in photographs taken with Graner's 5.0. megapixel Sony. The pictures range from smudged, dark images of men standing in the prison hallway to vivid portraits of abuse that took place in well-lit corridors.

In one picture, England is shown holding a naked detainee with a strap wrapped around his neck like a leash. Other naked detainees are placed in a human pyramid and, according to court documents, Specialist Megan M. Ambuhl observed "a group of detainees masturbating, or attempting to masturbate, while they were located in a public corridor of the Baghdad Central Correction Facility."[17] A detainee is photographed standing in a cell with his arms draped along the prison bars. His head is covered in a hood. A naked prisoner is reaching his arms across a bed frame in a dark room. A pair of women's underpants is pulled over his head, and light reflects off his arms and back. An interpreter is standing next to naked prisoners shackled together and lying on the floor in a wide hallway bathed in yellowish light.

Eventually Goldsmith did try to correct things, working long hours—"when he had young children at home," wrote journalist Charlie Savage in his book *Takeover*—and trying to come up with a revise of the torture memo.[18] But it was too late. In April 2004, the Abu Ghraib photographs were released. "This is going to kill us," Gonzales "quietly muttered" when he saw the photographs, wrote Goldsmith.[19]

Indeed, the torture memo was presented as evidence at Ambuhl's court-martial for detainee-related misconduct in October 2004. Her lawyer claimed there was a connection between the memo and the abuses that occurred at Abu Ghraib: "It should be noted that, accepting the fact that the actions depicted in the photographs at the prison were wrong, the Attorney General of the United States stated otherwise."[20]

On December 30, 2004, a new version of the torture memo was issued. But the damage had been done. Besides, wrote Savage, the revised memo included a footnote "declaring that everything the CIA and the military had been doing under the old memo was still legal."[21]

The Legal Meaning of Torture

He is a high-level officer who was stationed at Guantanamo in 2003 and visited Abu Ghraib frequently in 2004, and he knows as much as anyone in the army does about the subject of interrogations. In his early forties, not too tall, and a little pale, he is a daredevil (and a bit of a showoff) who likes to speed through Baghdad in a Hummer. Still, he is a thoughtful man. He says that a few weeks after he arrived at Guantanamo, he began to have misgivings about the way detainees were being treated at the military installation. He was not specific about what bothered him, but he said he had gone to speak with the commander, General Geoffrey Miller, about the situation.

> "I asked him, 'Are we doing the right thing here?' I was coming to grips with it myself. And he sat down and talked with me about it and assured me that, 'Yes, we're doing the right thing.' It was early on in the global war on terrorism, and we were trying to come to some understanding of the operation."
>
> "As a soldier, I think that the problems that happened at Abu Ghraib—well, it all boils down to leadership. You're trying to lead a chaotic situation and make sense of things. People are making the best decisions based on the information they have. It's part of the whole human equation. You put people in there trying to do the right thing and what's right for the defense of our nation. Hopefully they're falling back on moral values."

He says he believes that the people in charge of detention facilities set the tone for the interrogations and for the handling of detainees and should be held responsible for what takes place on their watch. Only there is an aspect about the chain of command, and the responsibility for the detention facilities, that he did not discuss. In fact, the people in control may not be the military men and women or even officers such as General Miller, but individuals at a higher level or located within another organizational chart altogether.

Take John Yoo, for example. He was the man in charge of interpreting the legal perimeters for handling detainees in the terror war. He and Flanigan both thought they were doing the right thing. They believed the harsh interrogations provided interrogators with the tools needed to protect the United States from a terrorist attack and that these techniques are necessary for the good of the country. They are not the only ones who defend their position in this manner. In an essay for *Theology Today*, William T. Cavanaugh, a professor at the University of St. Thomas in St. Paul who has studied the Pinochet government, said, "Those who torture tend to think of their work in extremely high moral terms."[22]

> "Would limiting a captured terrorist to six hours' sleep, isolating him, interrogating him for several hours, or requiring him to exercise constitute 'severe physical or mental pain and suffering'?" wrote Yoo. "The legal meaning of 'torture' is not as all-inclusive as some people would like it to be. Legally, we are not required to treat captured terrorists engaged in war against us as if they were suspects held at an American police station. Limiting our intelligence and military officials to polite questioning, and demanding that terrorists receive lawyers, Miranda warnings, and a court trial would only hurt our ability to stop future attacks."[23]

Not everybody agrees that methods such as sleep deprivation and forced exercise should be incorporated into interrogations. "These tactics should be considered for what they are from a moral, legal, and medical perspective: torture," said Allen S. Keller, director of Bellevue Hospital's Program for Survivors of Torture in New York.[24]

Yoo and Flanigan, however, have both argued that these techniques should be used as part of the administration's new counterterrorism strategy. The two lawyers have employed different approaches, and personal styles, to defend their positions. Yoo can sound strident, or at least free of doubt, when he states his case. Flanigan is not like that. When I told him that Iraqi women and children were subjected to the harsh methods, including the use of military dogs and sleep deprivation, his tone softened. He spent a long time with me on the telephone, explaining how these techniques were intended only for high-level members of al Qaeda and the Taliban. He, too, regretted that they were used on Iraqi civilians.

Iraqi civilians were protected by the Geneva Conventions and should not have been subjected to the harsh interrogation techniques that were approved for al Qaeda and Taliban members. Yet these methods were used on Iraqis. "These procedures were designed for use on detainees picked up in the Afghan theater and yet they were applied, as the [Taguba and Fay-Jones] Reports included in this volume demonstrate, to alleged terrorists and to prisoners in Iraq," wrote Karen J. Greenberg in *The Torture Papers*. "The justification for this is hard to find."[25]

Administration officials have blamed rogue soldiers in Abu Ghraib's Tier 1A for using harsh methods on Iraqi detainees and for subjecting them to humiliating treatment. Yet harsh interrogation methods such as stress positions were taught in classrooms at Abu Ghraib. There were guidelines for the implementation of "limited stress—by forcing detainees to assume uncomfortable physical positions, or limiting their sleeping patterns or food," which are the methods Yoo described in his book.[26] These methods were not officially intended for Iraqi prisoners, according to Yoo and other administration officials. Still, they were adopted at Abu Ghraib and in other U.S.-run detention facilities in Iraq during a time when things were going badly in the war. There was intense pressure to obtain information about the insurgency and about the Iraqi forces that opposed the U.S. troops. That may have led in part to the decision to use the harsh methods on Iraqi prisoners.

Army supervisor Steven L. Jordan testified that the interrogation reports from Abu Ghraib were being scrutinized. "I was told a couple of times by Colonel Pappas that some of the reporting was getting read by Rumsfeld," Jordan explained.[27]

One sergeant who was stationed at another facility, Camp Nama, said he recalls watching a PowerPoint presentation on the methods that could be used on detainees. "They were saying things like we didn't have to abide by the Geneva Conventions because these people weren't POWs," he said. "People wanted to go harsh on everybody. They thought that was their job and that's what they needed to do."[28]

"Graner says every time a bomb goes off outside the wire, which is outside the walls of Abu Ghraib, one of the OGA members would come in to say, 'That's another American losing his life,'" one soldier, Ken Davis, told journalist Trish Wood. "'Unless you help us get this information, their blood is on your hands as well.'"[29]

Administration officials claimed, improbably, that the officers or civilian contractors who devised Abu Ghraib interrogation plans (modeled on the Guantanamo Tiger Team approach) were not responsible for the abuse of Iraqi prisoners; nor was Alberto Sanchez, the highest-ranking officer in Iraq, though he had approved of the methods. Nor was Defense Secretary

Rumsfeld, despite the fact he had encouraged the use of the techniques. Yet conditions for the abuse of prisoners were set early in the terror war by Yoo and other individuals at the White House and in the Justice Department.

The implementation was left to people such as Graner and "the muscle," as one soldier calls his friends at the prison. The vast majority of prisoners at Abu Ghraib had no information about the insurgency or about possible future acts of terrorism. Yet American interrogators, guards, and contractors applied harsh techniques and then used some of their own methods that did not appear on the list of approved methods. The explanation for this decision is still in dispute. Some things are certain, though. The detainees were hooded and naked. They did not speak English. They had nicknames such as "Clawman," "Spiderman," and "Gilligan." It became that much easier to treat them inhumanely.

In addition, high-level administration officials expressed ambivalence over the Geneva Conventions that protected the prisoners at Abu Ghraib—even after the scandal broke. On May 4, 2004, one week after the Abu Ghraib photographs appeared on television, Defense Secretary Rumsfeld told a journalist that the Geneva Conventions "did not apply precisely" in Iraq. Instead, they were "basic rules" for handling prisoners. On May 14, Rumsfeld visited soldiers at Abu Ghraib and said, "Geneva doesn't say what you do when you get up in the morning."[30]

Tick, Tock

Many people believe military leaders and government officials should allow, or even encourage, interrogators to torture a suspect under certain circumstances. That's the ticking-bomb theory, a notion familiar to anyone who has watched *24*. The water-boarding of accused al Qaeda suspect Khalid Shaikh Mohammed is used as an example by journalists, members of the military, and scholars who believe torture is—however abhorrent—a method of last resort. If things get out of hand, and an interrogator accidentally kills a suspect, the courts can sort it out.

Human rights lawyers, physicians, and scholars claim that torture does not produce the intended results. "I know from years of listening to torture survivors describing their experiences that individuals so brutalized will often say whatever they think the torturer wants to hear in order to stop the nightmare," wrote physician Keller.[31]

The truth is that torture, as well as beatings, assaults, and random arrests, can be effective. Saddam Hussein was tracked down by unraveling a "social network" of friends, relatives, and acquaintances, says John E. Pike, director of Globalsecurity.org, an Alexandria, Virginia-based defense information organization. Many of them were taken out of their homes and roughed up by soldiers.[32]

The army officer who served at Guantanamo believes that Americans should use every tool available to us in the terror war and that harsh techniques can be justified under certain circumstances. When criminal acts, going beyond the boundaries of permissible interrogation methods, occur, he says, they should be blamed on poor military leadership. Like Yoo and Flanigan, I was in Washington on the day of the terrorist attacks. I left my office building in Rosslyn, Virginia, and ran across Key Bridge to make sure my children were safe, and I looked back and saw the Pentagon in flames. Protecting our country from another attack is important to me, too. But I do not believe abusive interrogation techniques are an effective tool in the War on Terror. The question is not whether or not torture works. Instead, we should ask ourselves whether we want to live in a society that condones it.

Notes

Portions of this essay appeared in *Monstering: Inside America's Policy of Secret Interrogations and Torture in the Terror War* (Basic Books) and in a March 14, 2008, book review, "Power Grab," in *The American Prospect*.

1. "Nomination of Timothy E. Flanigan to Be an Assistant Attorney General," *Public Papers of the Presidents*, Pres. Doc. 623, April 9, 1992.
2. Carl M. Cannon, James A. Barnes, Alexis Simendinger, Bruce Stokes, David Baumann, Marilyn Werber Serafini, and Jason Ellenburg, "The White House Profiles," *The National Journal* (June 23, 2001).
3. Dana Milbank, "White House Counsel Office Now Full of Clinton Legal Foes," *Washington Post*, January 30, 2001.
4. "Federalist Society to Hold Annual Conference in D.C., Nov. 15–17," PR Newswire, November 13, 2001.
5. Timothy Flanigan, telephone interview, December 22, 2004.
6. John Yoo, *War by Other Means: An Insider's Account of the War on Terror* (New York: Atlantic Monthly Press, 2006), 19.
7. Flanigan, telephone interview, December 22, 2004.
8. Karen J. Greenberg and Joshua L. Draytel, eds., *The Torture Papers: The Road to Abu Ghraib* (New York: Cambridge University Press, 2005).
9. Yoo, *War by Other Means*, ix.
10. Flanigan, telephone interview, December 22, 2004.
11. Memo 8, United States Department of State, Memorandum, To: Counsel for the President, Assistant to the President for National Security Affairs, From: Colin L. Powell, Subject: "Draft Decision Memorandum for the President on the Applicability of the Geneva Convention to the Conflict in Afghanistan," *The Torture Papers*, 122.

12. Memo 11, Subject: "Humane Treatment of Al Qaeda and Taliban Detainees" [Signed George Bush], *The Torture Papers*, 135.

13. Donald H. Rumsfeld, "Joint Strike Fighter Signing Ceremony," Defense Department news briefing, M2 Presswire, Washington, DC, February 8, 2002.

14. Jack Goldsmith, *The Terror Presidency: Law and Judgment Inside the Bush Administration* (New York: W.W. Norton, 2007), 59.

15. Goldsmith, *The Terror Presidency*, 157.

16. Yoo, *War by Other Means*, 170–171.

17. Verbatim Record of Trial, Specialist Megan M. Ambuhl, HHC, 16th Bde (ABN), III Corps, U.S. Army, Victory Base, Iraq, by General Court-Martial, Convened by Commanding General, Headquarters III Corps, Victory Base/ Mannheim, August 11, 23, and 25, 2004.

18. Charlie Savage, *Takeover: The Return of the Imperial Presidency and the Subversion of American Democracy* (New York: Little, Brown and Company, 2007), 191.

19. Goldsmith, *The Terror Presidency*, 142.

20. Verbatim Record of Trial, Specialist Megan M. Ambuhl, HHC, 16th Bde (ABN), III Corps, U.S. Army, Victory Base, Iraq, by General Court-Martial, Convened by Commanding General, Headquarters III Corps, Victory Base/ Mannheim, August 11, 23, and 25, 2004.

21. Savage, *Takeover*, 196.

22. William T. Cavanaugh, "Making Enemies: The Imagination of Torture in Chile and the United States," *Theology Today* 63, no. 3 (October 2006): 307–323.

23. Yoo, *War by Other Means*, 171–172.

24. Allen S. Keller, testimony, Hearing of the Eminent Jurists Panel on Terrorism, Counter-Terrorism and Human Rights, an independent body of the Geneva-based International Commission of Jurists, Washington, DC, September 6, 2006, http://www.ejp.icj.org/IMG/DrKellerTestimony.pdf.

25. Karen J. Greenberg, "From Fear to Torture," *The Torture Papers*, xiii.

26. Yoo, *War by Other Means*, 178.

27. Steven L. Jordan, sworn statement, Camp Doha, Kuwait, February 24, 2004 in "Article 15-6 Investigation of the 800th Military Police Brigade," 112.

28. "No Blood, No Foul: Soldiers' Accounts of Detainee Abuse in Iraq," *Human Rights Watch* 18, no. 3(G), New York, July 2006.

29. Trish Wood, *What Was Asked of Us: An Oral History of the Iraq War by the Soldiers Who Fought It* (New York: Little, Brown, 2006), 109.

30. "Leadership Failures: Firsthand Accounts of Torture of Iraqi Detainees by the U.S. Army's 82nd Airborne Division," *Human Rights Watch* 17, no. 3(G) (New York: September 2005): 21.

31. Allen S. Keller, testimony, Eminent Jurists Panel, 6.

32. John Pike, telephone interview, Arlington, VA, January 31, 2005.

16

The "Bush Doctrine" and the Use of Force in International Law

*Leanne Piggott**

International law has traditionally distinguished between rules concerning the recourse to force by states (the *jus ad bellum*) and rules concerning the actual conduct of hostilities, or international humanitarian law (the *jus in bello*). In response to the 2001 al Qaeda attacks against the United States, the so-called Bush Doctrine[1] was developed in part as an attempt to rewrite the rules of the *jus ad bellum*. This chapter examines whether, and if so how, the Bush Doctrine has succeeded in altering the law regulating the resort to force by states. It argues that the Bush Doctrine has failed to change the *jus ad bellum* concerning the preemptive use of force by a state (i.e., to forestall an apprehended future attack). However, it is also argued that the Bush Doctrine has succeeded in changing another aspect of customary international law, namely, the attribution of acts of violence by a terrorist organization to a state supporter of that organization.

General Rules Governing the Resort to Force by a State

The UN Charter

Since 1945, the resort to force by a state, in order to be lawful, must among other things overcome the general prohibition against the threat or use

***Leanne Piggott** is Deputy Director of the Centre for International Security Studies at the University of Sydney.

of force contained in Article 2(4) of the United Nations (UN) Charter.[2] Chapter VII of the UN Charter expressly recognizes two exceptions to the general prohibition against force. First, the Security Council can authorize military action under Article 42 of the Charter "to maintain or restore international peace and security" in circumstances that it has decided constitute "a threat to the peace, breach of the peace or act of aggression."[3] Second, absent a Security Council decision to use force, a state also has an inherent right of individual or collective self-defense under Article 51 of the Charter. It is to this second exception that Part V of the Bush administration's *National Security Strategy* is addressed.

Article 51 opens with the words: "Nothing in the present Charter shall impair the inherent right of individual or collective self-defense if an armed attack occurs against a Member."[4] If Article 51 is the only source of a state's right to defend itself, the qualifying words "if an armed attack occurs" would appear to preclude any right to resort to force to preempt an expected attack. The Charter does not define "armed attack" or the apparently related expressions "threat or use of force" (Article 2(4)) and "acts of aggression" (Article 1(1)). However, it has become accepted that neither of the latter two expressions would necessarily entail a sufficiently high level of force to constitute an "armed attack" giving rise to a right of self-defense.[5] Accordingly, even if the concept of "armed attack" is expanded so that it can be said that the attack begins to "occur" when military preparations for it commence, the scope for stretching the meaning of Article 51 in a way that would permit a state to resort to force preemptively is limited.

Customary Law

Yet Article 51 is not the sole source of a state's right of self-defense. Its own terms suggest that there is a concurrent and preexisting customary law right of self-defense. (Otherwise there would be nothing to "impair," and the right of self-defense would not be "inherent" but derived from Article 51.) This was confirmed by the International Court of Justice in the *Nicaragua* case,[6] where the majority decided that while the customary law right of self-defense has developed in such a way that "its present content has been confirmed and influenced by the Charter," the Charter "does not go on to regulate directly all aspects of its content." Accordingly, "[i]t cannot therefore be held that Article 51 is a provision which 'subsumes and supervenes' customary international law. It rather demonstrates that in the field in question…customary international law continues to exist alongside treaty law. The areas governed by the two sources of law thus do not overlap exactly, and the rules do not have the same content."[7]

There are many difficulties in defining how the customary law right of self-defense differs in scope and content from that which is affirmed expressly in Article 51. These difficulties are in no small way due to the nature of customary international law itself. In international law, customary rules are derived from the way states actually behave (state practice) and their subjective views about the legal status of their acts (*opinio juris*).[8] For a customary rule to emerge, there must be "extensive and virtually uniform" acts that "amount to a settled practice, but they must also be such, or be carried out in such a way, as to be evidence of a belief that this practice is rendered obligatory by the existence of a rule of law requiring it."[9] A change in the "use of force" policy of a state (especially a superpower), as occurred when the United States announced the Bush Doctrine, and in the justification it gives for the change, may either be rejected or accepted by other states and thus seen respectively as either a violation of existing customary international law or a step in the evolution of a new customary rule.

Rules Governing the Preemptive Resort to Force by a State

Prior to the Bush Doctrine

There has never been universal agreement between states as to all the types of situations in which a state may lawfully have recourse to force, and the views of particular states on such matters have often changed over time. States have differed not only about the applicability of particular principles to a given set of facts but also about the content of the principles themselves. These differences are reflected in the writings of eminent jurists. Some have argued for a narrow, restrictive interpretation of the customary law right of self-defense that would allow little or no scope for a preemptive recourse to force.[10] Others advocate a more expansive interpretation that would make such recourse permissible in a range of circumstances.[11]

Yet prior to the Bush Doctrine there was a widely accepted view that it is lawful for a state to resort to force in self-defense to preempt an armed attack that is "imminent." The starting point of most modern analyses of whether this view reflects customary international law is the formulation of U.S. Secretary of State Daniel Webster in his note dated April 24, 1841 to Mr. Fox, the British minister at Washington, concerning the *Caroline* case.[12] The case arose out of the Canadian Rebellion against British rule in 1837. The rebels had been receiving supplies from sympathizers in the United States, despite attempts by the U.S. authorities to prevent such assistance being given. The supplies came from an American ship, the *Caroline*, which was moored in an American port near the border with Canada. A

British force had entered American territory, seized the *Caroline*, set it alight, and sent it over the Niagara Falls, killing two U.S. nationals.

Webster called upon the British government to show a "necessity of self-defense, instant, overwhelming, leaving no choice of means, and no moment for deliberation. It would be for it to show also, that the local authorities of Canada, even supposing the necessity of the moment, authorized them to enter the territories of the United States at all, did nothing unreasonable or excessive; since the act, justified by the necessity of self-defense must be limited by that necessity and kept clearly within it."[13] The terms of the U.S. protest accepted that if it could be demonstrated that Webster's criteria had been satisfied, the British government was entitled to protect itself in anticipation of further raids by the rebel force, and the British response accepted that Webster's formulation was an accurate statement of the applicable law.[14] The dispute was about whether or not the British use of force had met Webster's criteria, the application of which raises many questions.[15]

It is arguable that customary law concerning the use of force, as it existed in 1945 when the UN Charter came into force, had evolved significantly during the inter-War period toward the rules that were ultimately articulated in the Charter, and the principles enunciated by Webster more than a century earlier had therefore been superseded.[16] However, the more widely held view after the Charter entered into force has been that the *Caroline* principles remain compatible with the principles developed in the inter-War period, and enshrined in the Charter, and have continuing relevance to the contemporary world.[17] The survival of the *Caroline* principles was affirmed by the International Military Tribunal in the trial of the major Nazi war criminals at Nuremburg in 1946. In its judgment in *Re Göring*, declaring the German invasion of Denmark and Norway in World War II to be illegal, the Tribunal said, "[i]t must be remembered that preventive action in foreign territory is justified only in case of 'an instant and overwhelming necessity of self-defense leaving no choice of means, and no moment of deliberation.'"[18]

The Tribunal's decision is also notable for its rejection of the defendants' contention that it was for Germany alone to decide whether its invasions of Denmark and Norway were a "necessity" or that Germany's assessment of the situation was conclusive. Instead, the Tribunal held that these matters must be "subject to investigation and adjudication, if international law is ever to be enforced."[19] The Tribunal's decision, therefore, affirmed that the application of such principles in any given circumstances is capable of being determined by a court of law according to objective criteria, and not by a subjective appraisal of the circumstances by the state that has used force.

Thus, prior to the Bush Doctrine, a state seeking to use preemptive force lawfully against an anticipated attack needed to be able to demonstrate the "necessity" of its resort to force by producing evidence that such an attack was imminent and nothing other than forcible action would forestall it. It would also have to be able to demonstrate that its recourse to force was not "unreasonable or excessive" in the sense that it constituted a proportional response to the nature and gravity of the apprehended attack. It could be called upon to satisfy both requirements in a court of law.

As regards the requirement of "necessity," the "imminence" test was reaffirmed most strikingly by the international community, including the United States, in 1981 when the Israeli air force bombed and destroyed a newly built nuclear plant at Osirak in Iraq. Israel sought to justify its action by invoking the right to use force preemptively in self-defense. The Iraqi regime had declared itself to be engaged in a war of annihilation against Israel since 1948 and the development of a nuclear weapons capability would have given Iraq the means to realize its objective.

Yet the Israeli action was unanimously condemned in the United Nations. The U.S. representatives, and most others, accepted that a state's right of self-defense extends to a preemptive use of force against an imminent attack but argued that the Iraqis were a long way from developing the capacity to make nuclear weapons. Accordingly, the threat to Israel of an attack from a nuclear-armed Iraq was not "imminent" and no legal basis existed for Israel's preemptive recourse to force.[20]

In contrast, Israel was not condemned in the United Nations for its use of force against Egypt, Syria, and Jordan in June 1967 after the latter states had massed troops on their borders with Israel. Egypt's President Nasser ordered a blockade of Israel's southern port of Eilat and publicly acknowledged that this act meant war with Israel in which the Arabs' objective would be "Israel's destruction."[21] Israel won the ensuing war and captured large parts of its enemies' territories.

Between June and November 1967 draft UN resolutions in both the Security Council and General Assembly condemning Israel over the 1967 Arab-Israeli war were defeated or withdrawn for lack of support six times. Draft resolutions demanding that Israel withdraw its forces unilaterally from territories it captured in that war were defeated or withdrawn four times.[22] The UN reaction to Israel's resort to force in 1967 remains the clearest example of state practice and *opinio juris* that tacitly accepts a state's right to use force preemptively in self-defense against a threat of imminent attack, even if the evidence that such an attack would have occurred is not conclusive.

The Bush Doctrine

The "imminence" test of when a preemptive use of force will be considered to be a necessary and therefore lawful exercise of a state's right of self-defense was what the Bush Doctrine self-consciously set out to change. Under the Bush Doctrine, a preemptive resort to force by a state can be accepted as a legitimate exercise of its right of self-defense if it is in response to "a grave and gathering danger"[23] rather than an "instant, overwhelming" danger. This was enunciated more fully in Part V of *The National Security Strategy of the United States* published on September 17, 2002:

> For centuries, international law recognized that nations need not suffer an attack before they can lawfully take action to defend themselves against forces that present an imminent danger of attack. Legal scholars and international jurists often conditioned the legitimacy of pre-emption on the existence of an imminent threat—most often a visible mobilization of armies, navies, and air forces preparing to attack.
>
> We must adapt the concept of imminent threat to the capabilities and objectives of today's adversaries. Rogue states and terrorists do not seek to attack us using conventional means. They know such attacks would fail. Instead, they rely on acts of terror and, potentially, the use of weapons of mass destruction—weapons that can be easily concealed, delivered covertly, and used without warning…
>
> The greater the threat, the greater is the risk of inaction—and the more compelling the case for taking anticipatory action to defend ourselves, even if uncertainty remains as to the time and place of the enemy's attack. To forestall or prevent such hostile acts by our adversaries, the United States will, if necessary, act pre-emptively.
>
> The United States will not use force in all cases to pre-empt emerging threats, nor should nations use pre-emption as a pretext for aggression. Yet in an age where the enemies of civilization openly and actively seek the world's most destructive technologies, the United States cannot remain idle while dangers gather.[24]

The difference between this policy and the preexisting law is profound. The "imminence" test of necessity is imperfect but legally workable, requiring a demonstrably high level of probability that an apprehended attack is about to occur, whereas its proposed replacement is inherently vague and fails to draw a clear line. What criteria should determine whether a perceived future threat is "grave" and "gathering"? How far developed must the threat be before one can say that alternatives to the use of force have been exhausted?

Permitting states to use force against threats of attack that may be years away from crystallizing opens the door wide to abuse and mistakes, since it is always a matter of judgment and accurate intelligence whether a state is genuinely threatened to a degree that would justify a preemptive strike.

The Bush Doctrine is silent as to precisely how such a permissive approach can be circumscribed so as to prevent a state from making spurious allegations of "gathering dangers" in order to create "a pretext for aggression" and to ignore its obligation under Article 2(3) of the UN Charter to resolve disputes by peaceful means. This is of special concern if the state making the allegations is a permanent member of the UN Security Council with a right to veto any attempt to constrain its behavior or to place its subjective apprehension of the existence of a "grave and gathering danger" and the urgency it creates under any kind of objective, evidence-based assessment. The Bush Doctrine therefore sought not so much to "adapt" the concept of imminent attack to the changed circumstances of a post–9/11 world as to replace it altogether.[25]

The Bush Doctrine Applied

It was in relation to Iraq in March 2003 that the United States first invoked the Bush Doctrine of preemption as legal justification for its decision to use force.[26] In a series of speeches in late 2002 and early 2003, President Bush held up the Iraqi regime of Saddam Hussein as a paradigm of the kind of developing threat against which preemptive military action would be justified.[27] As an alternative legal basis for using force against Iraq, and in accordance with a pledge made by President Bush in the UN General Assembly,[28] the United States attempted, with the assistance of the United Kingdom and Spain, to secure the passage of an explicit Security Council resolution under Chapter VII of the UN Charter declaring Iraq to be a threat to international peace and security, by reason of its weapons of mass destruction and terrorist connections, and authorizing the use of force against it. The U.S. case against Iraq as a direct threat to the peace was put forward by U.S. Secretary of State Colin Powell in his speech to the Security Council on February 5, 2003,[29] but the authorizing resolution sought by the United States, the United Kingdom, and Spain did not gather the support of a majority of members of the Security Council and was withdrawn.

Thereafter the United States reverted to relying on the justification of self-defense under the expanded criteria of the Bush Doctrine. The United States had been careful to reserve self-defense as its fall-back position in case it failed to enlist Security Council support.[30] Debate has raged ever since about whether the decision of the U.S. government and its allies to intervene militarily in Iraq on March 19, 2003, was a violation of the UN Charter and customary international law, or a step in the evolution of a new customary rule.[31]

The International Response to the Application of the Bush Doctrine

A list published by the White House named 49 countries that supported, militarily or verbally, the 2003 invasion and subsequent military occupation of Iraq.[32] Of those 49, only 4 besides the United States contributed troops to the invasion force (the United Kingdom, Australia, Poland, and Denmark) and 33 provided some number of troops to support the occupation after the invasion was complete and Saddam's regime overthrown.

Most of the rest of the international community was firm in its opposition to the U.S.-led action in Iraq and in its rejection of the various legal arguments that were advanced to justify the war, including the Bush Doctrine rationale that the action was justified by the "grave and gathering" danger posed by the combination of the Iraqi regime's alleged possession of weapons of mass destruction and alleged links with al Qaeda. The position of the 152 states that opposed, or declined to support, the use of force in Iraq was articulated by UN Secretary-General Kofi Annan in an address to the UN General Assembly on September 23, 2003:

> Article 51 of the Charter prescribes that all States, if attacked, retain the inherent right of self-defense. But until now it has been understood that when States go beyond that, and decide to use force to deal with broader threats to international peace and security, they need the unique legitimacy provided by the United Nations.
>
> Now, some say this understanding is no longer tenable, since an "armed attack" with weapons of mass destruction could be launched at any time, without warning, or by a clandestine group. Rather than wait for that to happen, they argue, States have the right and obligation to use force pre-emptively, even on the territory of other States, and even while weapons systems that might be used to attack them are still being developed. According to this argument, States are not obliged to wait until there is agreement in the Security Council. Instead, they reserve the right to act unilaterally, or in ad hoc coalitions.
>
> This logic represents a fundamental challenge to the principles on which, however imperfectly, world peace and stability have rested for the last fifty-eight years. My concern is that, if it were to be adopted, it could set precedents that resulted in a proliferation of the unilateral and lawless use of force, with or without justification.[33]

Although the secretary-general's comments were carefully measured, they amount to an unequivocal repudiation of a central tenet of the Bush Doctrine–that even in the absence of authorization by the Security Council, the use of force to preempt the threat of an attack that is not imminent may nevertheless be legally justified as self-defense. The secretary-general's views continue to reflect state practice and *opinio juris* among the states that did not support the military intervention in Iraq.

Perhaps more significantly, there has also been a conspicuous reluctance to accept the "grave and gathering danger" test as a substitute for the "imminence" test even among America's principal allies who supported the use of force in Iraq. None of the various legal justifications advanced by the United Kingdom, Australia, Poland, and Denmark for sending their troops to Iraq placed any reliance at all on the Bush Doctrine.

Instead, the leaders of each of these states, either directly or through official pronouncements of their respective attorneys general, sought to frame their legal arguments in terms of the UN Charter and other already established principles of international law, contending that the authority to use force against Iraq contained in Security Council resolution 678 (1990) had been revived and that a further such resolution was therefore unnecessary.[34] The argument relied on Iraq's "material breach" (a technical term in the law of treaties) of various provisions of the ceasefire treaty that ended the 1991 Gulf war.

A succinct summary of the legal argument was provided by Australia's Prime Minister John Howard in his speech to the Australian Parliament on the eve of the 2003 invasion of Iraq:

> We supported, and would have preferred, a further Security Council resolution specifying the need for such action. We did so to maximise the diplomatic, moral and political pressure on Iraq, not because we considered a new resolution to be necessary for such action to be legitimate. Our legal advice, provided by the head of the Office of International Law in the Attorney-General's Department and the senior legal adviser to the Department of Foreign Affairs and Trade, is unequivocal. The existing United Nations Security Council resolutions already provide for the use of force to disarm Iraq and restore international peace and security to the area. This legal advice is consistent with that provided to the British government by its Attorney-General.
>
> Security Council resolution 678, adopted in 1990, authorized the use of all necessary means not only to implement resolution 660, which demanded Iraq withdraw from Kuwait, but also to implement all subsequent relevant resolutions and to restore international peace and security in the area. Resolution 687, which provided the cease-fire terms for Iraq in April 1991, affirmed resolution 678. Security Council resolution 1441 confirms that Iraq has been and remains in material breach of its obligations, a point on which there is unanimous agreement, including by even the Leader of the Opposition.
>
> Iraq's past and continuing breaches of the cease-fire obligations negate the basis for the formal cease-fire. Iraq has by its conduct demonstrated that it did not and does not accept the terms of the cease-fire.

Consequently, we have received legal advice that the cease-fire is not effective and the authorisation for the use of force in Security Council resolution 678 is reactivated.[35]

It is outside the scope of this chapter to assess the legal validity of this argument. Its significance, in terms of the Bush Doctrine, is that neither Australia nor any of the other participants in the U.S.-led military intervention in Iraq invoked as their legal justification the principle of preemptive self-defense against a grave and gathering danger. Even though the leaders of each participating state clearly accepted as a matter of fact that the Iraqi regime constituted a growing danger to international peace and security, they each claimed that their resort to force to meet this danger was authorized by a "reactivated" resolution 678. At least tacitly, they thereby rejected the option of invoking an expanded right of self-defense under the Bush Doctrine of preemption as a possible legal justification.

Among the non-U.S. leaders who sent their country's troops to Iraq, Britain's Prime Minister, Tony Blair, came the closest to invoking a second legal justification based on a state's right of individual- or collective self-defense. Some 10 weeks before the commencement of hostilities he told the Foreign Office Conference in London, "[s]o when as with Iraq, the international community through the UN makes a demand on a regime to disarm itself of WMD and that regime refuses, that regime threatens us."[36]

But whenever the British prime minister described the nature of the threat posed by the Saddam regime, he was at pains to characterize it as an immediate, rather than a developing, threat. In a speech to Britain's House of Commons opening the Iraq debate just before the start of the war he said, "[a]nd these two threats have different motives and different origins but they share one basic common view: they detest the freedom, democracy and tolerance that are the hallmarks of our way of life. At the moment, I accept that the association between them is loose. But it is hardening. And the possibility of the two coming together—of terrorist groups in possession of WMD, even of a so-called dirty radiological bomb is now, in my judgment, a real and present danger."[37]

The alleged immediacy of the threat was also central to the intelligence assessment report concerning Iraq, which was prepared by Britain's Joint Intelligence Committee and, somewhat unusually, made publicly available.[38] In his Foreword to the report, Prime Minister Blair emphasized the disclosure that "[Saddam's] military planning allows for some of the WMD to be ready within 45 minutes of the order to use them."[39] The report itself makes that point three times.[40] Thus, to the extent that Prime Minister Blair sought to rely on Britain's right of self-defense as its legal justification for resorting to force in Iraq, he did so on the basis of the classical "imminent danger" test of the *Caroline* case rather than the nebulous "grave and gathering danger" test of the Bush Doctrine.[41]

At times the Bush administration itself appeared to move away from reliance on an expanded concept of self-defense under the Bush Doctrine as its legal justification for the foreshadowed use of force in Iraq. Instead administration spokespersons occasionally emphasized that the Iraqi regime was "pursuing weapons of mass destruction in defiance of a decade of U.N. resolutions"[42] and that the authority to use force against Iraq contained in Security Council resolution 678 (1990) had been revived.[43]

The Failure of the Bush Doctrine to Change International Law Concerning the Preemptive Resort to Force

It follows that the attempt by the Bush Doctrine to expand the scope of a state's right of self-defense beyond what is permitted under Article 51 of the UN Charter and by the customary law *Caroline* principles has failed. State practice and *opinio juris*, even among the states that joined the United States in sending troops to Iraq, has conspicuously avoided anything that might be construed as an endorsement of the Bush Doctrine's attempt to substitute a "grave and gathering danger" test for the "imminent danger" test of when a preemptive resort to force in self-defense is legally justified.

In large part this failure is due to the conceptual vagueness of the Bush Doctrine's "grave and gathering danger" test and the absence of any obvious criteria for its application. But that is not to say that, objectively, there is no need for the scope of a state's right to defend itself under international law to be expanded. The risk of terrorist organizations acquiring weapons of mass destruction (WMD) and using them to attack a state without warning is very real. No state that is threatened with such an attack sometime in the future can afford to wait until the threat becomes "imminent." UN Secretary-General Kofi Annan acknowledged the problem:

> But it is not enough to denounce unilateralism, unless we also face up squarely to the concerns that make some States feel uniquely vulnerable, since it is those concerns that drive them to take unilateral action. We must show that those concerns can, and will, be addressed effectively through collective action. And we must not shy away from questions about the adequacy, and effectiveness, of the rules and instruments at our disposal....
>
> The [Security] Council needs to consider how it will deal with the possibility that individual States may use force "pre-emptively" against perceived threats. Its members may need to begin a discussion on the criteria for an early authorisation of coercive measures to address certain types of threats—for instance, terrorist groups armed with weapons of mass destruction.[44]

Yet Kofi Annan's suggestion that developing threats be dealt with through the machinery of the United Nations remains unworkable. The United Nations is essentially a political forum, where each state acts according to its own perceived interests—which may not necessarily lead it to support a proposal for UN-authorized action to deal with a serious emerging threat to another state or other states. Politics and self-interest, rather than an informed and objective assessment of the gravity of the threat to international peace and security, will determine whether support for such a proposal will be forthcoming, or whether the United Nations will instead be paralyzed. This reality was highlighted by Britain's Prime Minister Tony Blair in his criticism of what he saw as a failure of will by the Security Council to enforce its own legally binding resolutions against Iraq: "Just consider the position we are asked to adopt. Those on the Security Council opposed to us say they want Saddam to disarm but will not countenance any new Resolution that authorizes force in the event of non-compliance. That is their position. No to any ultimatum; no to any Resolution that stipulates that failure to comply will lead to military action. So we must demand he disarm but relinquish any concept of a threat if he doesn't."[45]

The problem has not been confined to Iraq. In the post–cold war world, the threat or use of the veto by one or more permanent members has prevented the UN Security Council from acting in a timely and effective manner to prevent or halt genocides and other large-scale humanitarian crises in the former Yugoslavia, Rwanda, southern Sudan, Darfur, the Congo, Liberia, and Zimbabwe, all of which have disrupted peace and security regionally and threatened to do so internationally.

While the Bush Doctrine has failed to change the international law rules that regulate a state's right to resort to force preemptively to defend itself, it is clear that those rules, including the relevant provisions of Chapter VII of the UN Charter, are inadequate to deal with emerging new threats to international peace and security. These include the threat of terrorist networks acquiring and using weapons of mass destruction. The process of reforming these rules, if there is a process, is likely to be slow. In the interim, the inadequacy of the existing rules does little to promote the international rule of law.

Rules Equating Acts by Terrorists to Attacks by State Supporters

The Bush Doctrine

Another tenet of the Bush Doctrine, in contrast, has been almost wholly successful in transforming preexisting customary international law. In relation to a state's right to use force in self-defense to halt or prevent a terrorist attack, the Bush Doctrine asserts, "[w]e make no distinction between terrorists and those [States] who knowingly harbor or provide aid to them."[46] This is a brief restatement of comments made by President Bush on November 22, 2001 that "America has a message for the nations of the world: If you harbor terrorists you are terrorists....If you train or arm a terrorist, you are a terrorist. If you feed a terrorist or fund a terrorist, you're a terrorist, and you will be held accountable by the United States and our friends."[47]

The significance of this proposition for the jus ad bellum is that a state that "harbors" or "provides aid" to individuals or organizations that carry out a terrorist act against another state will potentially be considered by the United States to have authored an armed attack against that other state, within the meaning of Article 51 of the UN Charter. The attacked state and states with which it has formal security agreements will thus have a right to use force in self-defense against the state that harbored or sponsored the terrorists. "Harboring" seems to entail the active provision by a state of shelter or protection to terrorists on territory under its control, or its passive acquiescence in their use of its territory. "Providing aid," however, is a much broader criterion and does not seem to require that the territory from which the terrorists operate is that of the supporting state.

The UN Charter

This tenet of the Bush Doctrine is not, on its face, at variance with the terms of Article 51. Although Article 51 of the UN Charter conditions a state's right of self-defense on the occurrence of "an armed attack," it does not say expressly that the armed attack must emanate from another state. This is in contrast to the language of Article 2(4), which speaks of a use of force by a "Member" (which must by definition be a state) against another state. Article 51, on the other hand, is silent as to whom or what might commit "an armed attack."

Preexisting Customary International Law

The *Caroline* case itself supports the proposition that self-defense is permissible as a reaction to attacks by nongovernmental entities (in that case, private U.S. nationals aiding a rebellion in Canada against Britain). But prior to the Bush Doctrine, customary international law was reluctant to characterize an act of violence against a state or its citizens by a terrorist organization as an armed attack giving rise to a right of self-defense.

This is because the resort to force in response to an act of terrorism only gives rise to international legal issues if the force is exercised either upon territory lying outside that of the state using force, and therefore belonging to another state, or against the troops, ships, aircraft, facilities, or nationals of another state. If the state resorting to force in those circumstances purports to do so in exercise of its right of self-defense under Article 51 of the Charter, it follows that the "armed attack" giving rise to that right is required in some sense to be an armed attack *by* that other state. And for many years there was no clear doctrinal basis for determining whether and when an act of violence by a terrorist organization could be characterized as an armed attack by a state supporter of that organization, even in circumstances in which the state supporter was legally responsible in other respects for the acts of that organization. Being legally responsible for violent acts committed by a terrorist organization did not necessarily equate to the commission of an armed attack by the responsible state.[48]

In 1978 and again in 1982, Israel invoked a right of self-defense to justify its military intervention into Lebanon for the purposes of eliminating Palestine Liberation Organization (PLO) bases from which the PLO had conducted a series of military attacks on civilian population centers in northern Israel. But on each occasion the UN Security Council demanded an immediate withdrawal of Israeli forces from Lebanon and did not accept Israel's rationale of self-defense as a justification for its intervention.[49] In 1985, when Israeli planes bombed the headquarters of the PLO in Tunisia as a response to armed PLO attacks on its nationals, the Security Council "vigorously" condemned the bombing.[50] The United States did not exercise its veto in favor of Israel on that occasion.

However, a year later when two off-duty American servicemen were killed and several others were wounded during a bomb explosion in a Berlin dance club, the United States alleged that terrorists based in Libya were behind the bombing and, claiming a right of self-defense, sent in the U.S. air force to bomb targets in Libya. The American action was condemned by the General Assembly,[51] but condemnation by the Security Council was thwarted by the triple veto of France, the United Kingdom, and the United States.[52]

In 1998 the United States conducted further air strikes against an alleged chemical weapons facility in Sudan and al Qaeda training camps in Afghanistan after the bombings of U.S. embassies in Nairobi and Dar es Salaam in which nearly 300 people died. The United States again invoked its right of self-defense. Neither the General Assembly nor the Security Council condemned the U.S. attacks. The Arab League condemned the attack against Sudan but was silent regarding the attack on Afghanistan (which is not an Arab country). Overall, the international reaction was both mixed and muted, in marked contrast to the reaction to the earlier incidents.

In each of the foregoing cases the defending state sought to justify its use of force as an exercise of the right of self-defense against another state that was said to be "harboring" terrorist organizations, clearly prefiguring the Bush Doctrine. It was argued that the harboring state thereby in some way promoted or at least tolerated terrorism and was therefore an "accomplice" of the terrorists and thus a legitimate target for defensive action.

Yet prior to the Bush Doctrine, the only attempt to state authoritatively the criteria for determining whether a state sponsor of terrorist acts would be considered as the author of an armed attack was in the majority judgment of the International Court of Justice in the *Nicaragua* case, which read:

> There appears now to be general agreement on the nature of the acts which can be treated as constituting armed attacks. In particular, it may be considered to be agreed that an armed attack must be understood as including not merely action by regular armed forces across an international border, but also "the sending by or on behalf of a state of armed bands, groups, irregulars or mercenaries, which carry out acts of armed force against another state of such gravity as amount to" (inter alia) an actual armed attack conducted by regular forces, "or its substantial involvement therein."[53]

The Court was here quoting from Article 3(g) of the Definition of Aggression annexed to General Assembly Resolution 3314 of 1974, concluding that the quoted extracts "may be taken to reflect customary international law." The judgment continued:

> The Court sees no reason to deny that, in customary law, the prohibition of armed attacks may apply to the sending by a state of armed bands to the territory of another state, if such an operation, because of its scale and effects, would have been classified as an armed attack rather than as a mere frontier incident had it been carried out by regular armed forces. But the Court does not believe that the concept of "armed attack" includes not only acts by armed bands where such acts occur on a significant scale but also assistance to rebels in the form of the provision of weapons or logistical or other support.[54]

To paraphrase the Court, an actual "sending" of "armed bands, groups, irregulars or mercenaries" to another state or "substantial involvement therein" and the carrying out of an operation by them that, "because of its scale and effects, would have been classified as an armed attack" if carried out by a state, are all necessary in order to meet the armed attack requirement. The mere "provision of weapons or logistical or other support" is insufficient to meet this requirement.

A corollary of this view is that outside the narrow bounds of the *Nicaragua* principles, assaults against the citizens or territory of a state by externally based militias and terrorist organizations are matters for law enforcement agencies, not defensive military action. Because self-defense measures may only legitimately be employed against an armed attack by a state, so the reasoning goes, a state that goes after terrorists based in the territory of another state would be violating that other state's sovereignty.[55]

But that view and the narrowness of the *Nicaragua* criteria for determining whether a state sponsor of terrorist acts would be considered as the author of an armed attack were already under sustained criticism long before substitute criteria were put forward by the Bush Doctrine. In a powerful dissenting judgment in the *Nicaragua* case itself, Judge Jennings (United Kingdom) criticized the majority conclusion that the provision of arms, coupled with logistical and other support, is not an armed attack—observing that in that event:

> [I]t becomes difficult to understand what it is, short of direct attack by a state's own forces, that may not be done apparently without a lawful response....This looks to me neither realistic nor just in the world where power struggles are in every continent carried on by destabilization, interference in civil strife, comfort, aid and encouragement to rebels and the like. The original scheme of the United Nations Charter, whereby force would be deployed by the United Nations itself [under Article 43] has never come into effect. Therefore an essential element of the Charter design is missing. In this situation it seems dangerous to define unnecessarily strictly the conditions for lawful self-defense, so as to leave a large area where both a forcible response to force is forbidden, and yet the United Nations employment of force, which was intended to fill that gap, is absent.[56]

Jennings's dissenting views were echoed and enlarged upon by academic writers.[57] Measured against the 9/11 attacks and the Bush Doctrine that followed, these critiques seemed, if anything, to be understated. Under the Bush Doctrine, it is not just the provision of arms to terrorists, coupled with logistical and other support, that would constitute an armed attack. A state manifesting *any* degree of "knowing" support for, or acquiescence in, the hostile acts of a non-state actor is to be considered to be not only in breach of its general legal obligations to other states[58] but also as a state against which self-defense rights may legitimately be asserted.

Thus, on October 7, 2001, less than a month after the al Qaeda attacks against New York and Washington, DC, the United States notified the UN Security Council that it had incontrovertible evidence that the attacks were carried out by al Qaeda and that further attacks were planned. The United States asserted its right of self-defense against Afghanistan under Article 51 of the UN Charter because of "the decision of the Taliban regime to allow the parts of Afghanistan that it controls to be used by this organization as a base of operation."[59] That day, U.S. and British forces commenced military operations against the Taliban and al Qaeda strongholds in Afghanistan (Operation Enduring Freedom).

While it can hardly be doubted that the al Qaeda attacks on the United States were grave enough to satisfy the "scale and effects" requirement for an armed attack posited in the majority judgment in the *Nicaragua* case, it was never asserted by the United States (or others) that the al Qaeda terrorists had been "sent" to the United States by the Taliban government in any sense that would satisfy the other *Nicaragua* requirement. (On the contrary, al Qaeda appears to have its own independent command structure.) Nor did the United States allege that the Taliban had provided al Qaeda with arms or logistical or other support beyond allowing it the use of its territory.

The sole U.S. allegation against Afghanistan was that the Taliban regime had knowingly "allowed" al Qaeda to use Afghani territory as a base of operation, thus satisfying the "harboring" requirement of the Bush Doctrine. The mere presence on the territory of a state of a terrorist base from which an attack is carried out will apparently satisfy this requirement unless the state is unable, despite *bona fide* attempts at law enforcement, to prevent or put a halt to that presence.

The International Response to the Application of the Bush Doctrine

Despite its obvious departure from the *Nicaragua* criteria, the implementation of this aspect of the Bush Doctrine by the United States in relation to Afghanistan seems largely to have been accepted by the international community. Only the governments of Iraq, Sudan, and North Korea and, in more muted terms, Cuba, Malaysia, and Iran, condemned the attacks as a punishment of the Afghani people for the crimes of the terrorists, or questioned whether al Qaeda had carried out the attacks on the United States.[60] From all other quarters there was express or tacit acceptance of the principle that a state can legitimately be the target for self-defense military measures merely by harboring terrorists who have attacked another state.

The UN Security Council's first response to the al Qaeda attacks was to pass Resolutions 1368 and 1373 (2001) in which the Council defined those attacks as a "threat to the peace" and also expressly recognized "the inherent right of individual or collective self-defense in accordance with the Charter." The latter resolution, passed under Chapter VII of the UN Charter, also binds all states to cooperate in combating terrorism through a broad range of law enforcement measures and reserves to the UN Security Council the right to take collective action against state sponsors of terrorism.

The references in these resolutions to the right of self-defense has been criticized, as the resolutions are said to "assimilate a terrorist attack by a terrorist organization to an armed attack by a state"[61] and thus blur what had previously been distinct, well-defined, and workable concepts in international law. Despite the criticism, almost all states, and the major regional organizations of states, have similarly embraced the "assimilation" of terrorist attacks of the kind carried out against the United States by al Qaeda to an armed attack by a state.

In the immediate aftermath of the al Qaeda attacks, the secretary-general of NATO publicly announced that the evidence linking al Qaeda to the attacks justified invoking Article 5 of the Washington Treaty, making an attack on one ally an attack on all, and affirmed NATO members' "commitment to collective self-defense."[62] A resolution in similar terms was passed by the Organization of American States, which also stated that "those responsible for aiding, supporting or harboring the perpetrators...are equally complicit" in the attacks.[63] The U.S. air strikes and military intervention against Afghanistan, and the overthrow of the Taliban government, elicited direct assistance from the United Kingdom and indirect assistance from the NATO allies, as well as from Georgia, Oman, Pakistan, Qatar, Saudi Arabia, Turkey, and Uzbekistan.[64]

Even among states that have traditionally been less well disposed to the United States, there was near unanimity in supporting or abstaining from criticism of the U.S.-led military campaign in Afghanistan. The "Final Communiqué" adopted by the Foreign Ministers of the Organization for the Islamic Conference at Doha on October 10, 2001 made no criticism of the military action then underway, and tacitly accepted much of what U.S. government statements were saying about terrorism and the future of Afghanistan.[65] The Secretary-General of the Arab League Amr Moussa merely called upon the United States not to extend its military response beyond Afghanistan to any Arab country,[66] and verbal support for the United States and its allies was given by Egypt.[67]

China and Russia responded to "Operation Enduring Freedom" by cooperating with U.S. requests for intelligence sharing.[68] The Organization of African Unity refrained from criticism and welcomed the adoption of UN Security Council Resolution 1373 and previous resolutions on terrorism, urging its member states "to ensure their effective follow-up and implementation."[69] The Association of Southeast Asian Nations called on its Members to "strengthen cooperation at bilateral, regional and international levels in combating terrorism in a comprehensive manner" and affirmed that "at the international level the United Nations should play a major role in this regard" but made no mention or criticism of "Operation Enduring Freedom."[70]

The Success of the Bush Doctrine in Changing International Law

As one writer has observed, "reactions of governments to a major episode in contemporary history suggest something about their views regarding the underlying legal norms that govern the relevant state of affairs."[71] The reactions of states and organizations of states to the al Qaeda attacks on the U.S. constitute for the most part a significant body of state practice and *opinio juris* affirming that the U.S. invocation of its right of self-defense against Afghanistan under Article 51 of the UN Charter was legitimate. But this could only be the case if the al Qaeda attacks on New York and Washington, DC, constituted an armed attack on the United States *by Afghanistan*, as the United States contended.

In supporting that contention expressly or tacitly, the rest of the international community appears to have quietly jettisoned the *Nicaragua* criteria for determining whether the violent acts of a terrorist organization constitute an armed attack by a state. In their place, the "harboring" criterion of the Bush Doctrine seems largely to have been accepted. The broader "providing aid" criterion has yet to be tested.

Conclusion

In the international legal landscape that has emerged since 9/11, future U.S. administrations and other governments seeking legal justification for using force against another state whose government they perceive to be preparing to launch an armed attack against their country at some time in the future (albeit not imminently) are unlikely to rely on the Bush Doctrine and to use force ostensibly in self-defense against a "grave and gathering danger," or to receive substantial international support if they do. They will either have to wait until they acquire credible evidence that the apprehended attack is imminent or seek authorization from the UN Security Council to use force against the perceived source of the threat.

A third option may become available if the perceived source of the threat is a state that has supported or harbored a terrorist organization that has carried out violent attacks against another state with the threat of carrying out further attacks. In that event, under the expanded Bush Doctrine criteria for characterizing terrorist acts as an armed attack by a state, if both the attacked state and other states with which it has formal security agreements use force against the sponsoring state, they will have a strong argument that they are exercising their inherent right of individual or collective self-defense under Article 51 of the UN Charter. The potential vulnerability of a state sponsor of terrorism to legitimate self-defense measures by state victims of terrorist attacks is arguably one of the more effective disincentives to such sponsorship presently afforded by international law.

Notes

1. The Bush administration's national security policy response to the 9/11 attacks, which has become known as the "Bush Doctrine," was articulated by President Bush in a series of speeches that in September 2002 became the core of the *National Security Strategy of the United States*, http://www.whitehouse.gov/nsc/nss.html (accessed May 31, 2008).
2. Article 2(4) of the UN Charter reads: "All Members shall refrain in their international relations from the threat or use of force against the territorial integrity or political independence of any state, or in any other manner inconsistent with the Purposes of the United Nations." *Charter of the United Nations*, http://www.un.org/aboutun/charter/ (accessed May 31, 2008). See this link for all subsequent references to the UN Charter.
3. See Article 39. A decision of the Security Council under Article 42 is *eo ipso* legally binding on all states unlike most resolutions of the United Nations, which are not of themselves legally binding but may be indicative of state practice and *opinio juris*.
4. The full text of Article 51 reads:
     Nothing in the present Charter shall impair the inherent right of individual or collective self-defence if an armed attack occurs against a Member of the United Nations, until the Security Council has taken measures necessary to maintain international peace and security. Measures taken by Members in the exercise of this right of self-defence shall be immediately reported to the Security Council and shall not in any way affect the authority and responsibility of the Security Council under the present Charter to take at any time such action as it deems necessary to restore international peace and security.
   The right of "collective self-defence" arises where a state, although not itself attacked, has an obligation under a security treaty to come to the defense of another state that has sustained an armed attack.
5. See majority judgment in *Case Concerning Military and Paramilitary Activities in and against Nicaragua (Nicaragua v United States) (Merits)* [1986] International Court of Justice Reports 14, 103–104 (para. 195) and 126–127 (para. 247).

6. *Case Concerning Military and Paramilitary Activities in and against Nicaragua (Nicaragua v United States) (Merits)* [1986] International Court of Justice Reports, 14.

7. Ibid., 94 (para. 176).

8. Majority judgment in *North Sea Continental Shelf cases (Federal Republic of Germany v Denmark; Federal Republic of Germany v The Netherlands)* [1969] International Court of Justice Reports, 3.

9. Ibid., 44 (para. 77).

10. See Ian Brownlie, *International Law and the Use of Force by States* (Oxford: Clarendon Press, 1963), 112–113 and 264; and Hans Kelsen, *The Law of the United Nations* (London: London Institute of World Affairs, 1950), 914.

11. See Derek W. Bowett, *Self Defence in International Law* (Manchester: Manchester University Press, 1958), 185–186; Humphrey Waldock, "General Course on Public International Law," *Receuils des Cours* 106 (1962): 231–237; and James L. Brierly, *The Law of Nations*, 6th ed. (Oxford: Clarendon Press, 1963), 417–418.

12. Letter dated April 24, 1841 from Mr. Webster to Mr. Fox, *British & Foreign State Papers*, vol. 29, 1137–1138.

13. Ibid.

14. Letter dated July 28, 1842 from Lord Ashburton to Mr. Webster, *British & Foreign State Papers*, vol. 30, 195–196.

15. It would be a strange law that would legitimize a resort to force by a state that acted without prior "deliberation," particularly if the state is also required to ensure that its action is limited to, and "kept clearly within," the necessity that gave rise to it. Webster may well have formulated his criteria in the expectation that "he was demanding the impossible." Robert Y. Jennings, "The Caroline and McLeod Cases," *American Journal of International Law* 32 (1938): 89. In their correspondence, both the American and British representatives conflated the concepts of "self-defense," which presupposes an attack, and "self-preservation," which does not. It is therefore unlikely that Webster intended to confine the application of his formulation specifically to a state claiming to act in self-defense, 91–92.

16. Ian Brownlie, "International Law and the Use of Force by States Revisited," *Chinese Journal of International Law* 1 (2002): 5–6. One can also question the post-Charter relevance of Webster's words in the light of the provisions of Chapter VII of the Charter, which empower the Security Council to decide whether "a necessity for self-defense" exists in any given situation, rather than leaving it to a "defending" state to act as its own arbiter of such matters.

17. "To cut down the customary right of self-defence beyond even the Caroline doctrine does not make sense in times when the speed and power of weapons of attack has enormously increased"; Sir Humphrey Waldock, "The Regulation of the Use of Force by Individual States in International Law," *Receuils des Cours* 81 (1952): 498. See also Oscar Schachter, "The Right of States to Use Armed Force," *Michigan Law Review* 82 (1984): 1633–1635.

18. In "Re Göring and Others," *International Law Reports* 13 (1946): 203, 210. See also *Judgment of the International Military Tribunal for the Far East* 2

(1948), 994–995, where the Tribunal accepted that the Dutch declaration of war on Japan in 1941 was a legitimate act of preemptive self-defense.

19. Ibid.

20. See UN Security Council Resolution 487 (1981) and General Assembly Resolutions 36/27 of November 13, 1981 and 37/18 of November 16, 1982, and accompanying debates.

21. Speech by Egyptian President Gamel Abdul Nasser to Arab Trade Union Congress, Cairo, May 26, 1967 in Robert Stephens, *Nasser: A Political Biography* (London: Penguin, 1971), 479. The threats were accompanied by other acts of belligerency against Israel and by Nasser's demand (which was acceded to) for the removal of the UN peacekeeping force in the Sinai separating Egyptian and Israeli troops.

22. Abba Eban, *Personal Witness: Israel through My Eyes* (New York: Putnam, 1992), 439–440. The resolution that was finally passed in November, which was Security Council Resolution 242, endorsed the interdependent principles of "land for peace" requiring both an Israeli withdrawal from territory and a termination by the Arab states of their "belligerency" against Israel and "respect for and acknowledgement of" its sovereignty. Also, the precise extent of the required Israeli withdrawal was purposely not specified.

23. "Radio Address by the President to the Nation," September 14, 2002, http://www.whitehouse.gov/news/releases/2002/09/20020914.html (accessed June 13, 2008).

24. *The National Security Strategy of the United States of America*, "Part V" (2002), http://www.whitehouse.gov/nsc/nss.html (accessed May 30, 2008).

25. The Bush Doctrine does not expressly or by implication purport to revise the other *Caroline* principle—the proportionality rule that "self defence would warrant only those measures that are proportional to the [actual or apprehended] armed attack and necessary to respond to it." This is the way the rule was articulated in the majority judgment in *Case Concerning Military and Paramilitary Activities in and against Nicaragua (Nicaragua v United States) (Merits)* [1986] International Court of Justice Reports 14, para. 176. Accordingly, that rule is not addressed in this chapter even though it has been argued that the U.S.-led military intervention in Iraq violated the rule. See Christian Henderson, "The Bush Doctrine: From Theory to Practice," *Journal of Conflict and Security Law* 9, no 1 (2004): 17–18.

26. See sources at supra notes 23 and 24 and President Bush's speech on Iraq, "Saddam Hussein and his sons must leave," *New York Times*, March 18, 2003, A14, where he states: "We are acting now because the risks of inaction would be far greater. In one year or five years the power of Iraq to inflict harm on all free nations would be multiplied many times over."

27. Ibid.

28. "My nation will work with the U.N. Security Council to meet our common challenge. If Iraq's regime defies us again, the world must move deliberately, decisively to hold Iraq to account. We will work with the U.N. Security Council for the necessary resolutions. But the purposes of the United States should not be doubted. The Security Council resolutions will be enforced—the

just demands of peace and security will be met—or action will be unavoidable." Remarks by President Bush in Address to the United Nations General Assembly New York, New York, September 12, 2002 http://www.whitehouse.gov/news/releases/2002/09/20020912-1.html (accessed June 27, 2008).

29. UN Security Council, Meeting Recordings, February 5, 2003, S/PV.4701, 2–17.

30. See final sentence quoted in supra note 28.

31. For the view that the Bush Doctrine and its invocation to justify the war in Iraq represent new customary law see Benjamin Langille, "It's 'Instant Custom': How the Bush Doctrine Became Law after the Terrorist Attacks of September 11, 2001," *Boston College International and Comparative Law Review* 26 (2003): 145–156; and John A. Kohan, "The Bush Doctrine and the Emerging Norm of Anticipatory Self-Defense in Customary International Law," *Pace University School of Law International Law Review* 15, no. 2 (2003): 283–357. For the contrary view see Joel R. Paul, "The Bush Doctrine: Making or Breaking Customary International Law?" *Hastings International and Comparative Law Review* 27 (2003–2004): 457–479; and Robert M. Lawrence, "The Preventive/Pre-Emptive War Doctrine Cannot Justify the Iraq War," *Denver Journal of Internal Law and Policy* 33, no. 1 (2004): 16–30.

32. The White House, "Coalition Members," http://www.whitehouse.gov/news/releases/2003/03/20030327-10.html (accessed June 27, 2008).

33. Secretary-General's address to the General Assembly, New York, September 23, 2003, http://www.un.org/apps/sg/printsgstats.asp?nid=517 (accessed July 4, 2008).

34. For the United Kingdom, see British Attorney General Lord Goldsmith's Statement dated March 17, 2003, available at http://news.bbc.co.uk/1/hi/uk_politics/2857347.stm (accessed July 4, 2008). For Australia, see Attorney General's Department and Department of Foreign Affairs and Trade, *Memorandum of Advice on the Use of Force against Iraq*, March 18, 2003, http://pandora.nla.gov.au/pan/10052/20030521-0000/www.pm.gov.au/iraq/displayNewsContent4acc.html?refx=96 (accessed July 4, 2008). For Poland, see announcement of President Aleksander Kwasniewski, March 17, 2003. Full English text available at http://www.president.pl/x.node?id=2011993&eventId=1508071 (accessed July 4, 2008). For Denmark, see Danish Ministry of Foreign Affairs statements on February 14, March 16, and March 17, 2003 as quoted and translated into English by Tonny Brems Knudsen, "Denmark and the War against Iraq: Losing Sight of Internationalism?" in *Danish Foreign Policy Yearbook* 2004, ed. Per Carlsen and Hans Mouritzen (Copenhagen: Danish Institute for International Studies, 2004), 57.

35. Commonwealth of Australia, Parliamentary Debates, House of Representatives, Official Hansard No. 4, 2003, Tuesday, March 18, 2003. Fortieth Parliament First Session—Fourth Period, page 12510.

36. Prime Minister Tony Blair's Speech to the Foreign Office Conference, London, January 7, 2003, http://www.number-10.gov.uk/output/Page1765.asp (accessed July 4, 2008).

37. Prime Minister Tony Blair's statement to the House of Commons opening the Iraq debate, London, March 18, 2003, http://www.number-10.gov.uk/output/Page3294.asp (accessed July 4, 2008).

38. *Iraq's Weapons of Mass Destruction: The Assessment of the British Government* (United Kingdom: The Stationery Office Limited, September 2002), ID 114567 9/2002 776073, http://www.official-documents.co.uk (accessed July 4, 2008).

39. Ibid., 4.

40. Ibid., 5, 17, 19.

41. Other reasons for going to war that were put forward by the United States and its allies included the unbridled brutality of Saddam Hussein's regime. This was more of a political rather than a legal justification for resorting to force. Even though the governments of the United States and its allies each made statements highlighting grave ongoing human rights abuses by the Iraqi regime against its own people, no government sought to construct a serious legal argument justifying the war under a doctrine of humanitarian intervention.

42. For example, Radio Address to the Nation by President Bush, September 14, 2002, supra note 23.

43. White House Press Secretary Ari Fleischer cited previous Security Council resolutions as justification in a Press Conference on March 13, 2003, http://www.whitehouse.gov/news/releases/2003/03/20030313-13.html#19 (accessed June 27, 2008).

44. Secretary-General's address to the General Assembly, New York, September 23, 2003, http://www.un.org/apps/sg/printsgstats.asp?nid=517 (accessed June 27, 2008).

45. Prime Minister Tony Blair's statement to the House of Commons opening the Iraq debate, London, March 18, 2003, http://www.number-10.gov.uk/output/Page3294.asp (accessed July 4, 2008).

46. *The National Security Strategy of the United States of America*, "Part III" (2002), http://www.whitehouse.gov/nsc/nss.html (accessed May 30, 2008).

47. Mike Allen, "From Both Sides, Promises to Fight On: Bush Says Hardest Part Is Ahead," *Washington Post*, November 22, 2001, A1.

48. It has been argued that such an equation should be made. See Sean D. Murphy, "Terrorism and the Concept of 'Armed Attack' in Article 51 of the UN Charter," *Harvard International Law Journal* 43, no. 1 (2002): 50–51.

49. UN Security Council Resolutions 425 (1978) and 509 (1982). The latter resolution demanded that the withdrawal of Israeli forces occur "forthwith and unconditionally."

50. UN Security Council Resolution 573 (1985).

51. UN General Assembly Resolution 41/38 of November 20, 1986. The vote to condemn the United States was 79 for, 28 against and 33 abstentions.

52. *United Nations Year Book* (1986), 247–257.

53. *Case Concerning Military and Paramilitary Activities in and against Nicaragua (Nicaragua v United States) (Merits)* [1986] International Court of Justice Reports 14.

54. Ibid., 103–104 (para. 195). The majority elsewhere (at 62, para. 109) said that it had to determine whether the relationship between the terrorist organization and its state supporter is "so much one of dependence on the one side and control on the other" that it would be right to equate the terrorist organization with "an organ" of the state. However, this statement was made in the context of the court's consideration of jus in bello issues, and not in relation to the question of what constitutes an "armed attack" giving rise to the right of a state to resort to force in self-defense.

55. See Antonio Cassese, "Terrorism Is Also Disrupting Some Crucial Legal Categories in International Law," *European Journal of International Law* 12 (2001): 997 and the principle in *S.S. "Lotus" (France v. Turkey)*, Permanent Court of International Justice Series A, No. 10, at 18 (1927), prohibiting a state from exercising its power in any form in the territory of another state without consent. In a nonbinding Advisory Opinion in 2004, the International Court of Justice again attempted to confine the right of self-defense to responses to armed attacks by state actors. See the majority opinion in *Legal Consequences of the Construction of a Wall in the Occupied Palestinian Territory* [2004] International Court of Justice Reports 136 at 194 (para. 139). But this view was pointedly criticized even by some of the judges who comprised the majority. See Separate Opinion of Judge Rosalyn Higgins (United Kingdom) at 215 (para. 33) and Separate Opinion of Judge Pieter H. Kooijmans (Netherlands) at 229–230 (para. 35). See also Dissenting Opinion of Judge Thomas Buergenthal (United States) at 242–243 (para. 6). The majority in any event also found Article 51 of the UN Charter inapplicable for an entirely different reason, which makes the case distinguishable, namely that there was no allegation that the attacks on Israeli civilians by Palestinian terrorist organizations were imputable to a foreign state. See majority judgment at 194 (para. 139).

56. *Case Concerning Military and Paramilitary Activities in and against Nicaragua (Nicaragua v United States) (Merits)* [1986] International Court of Justice Reports 14, 533–534.

57. See Oscar Schachter, "The Lawful Use of Force by a State against Terrorists in Another Country," *Israel Yearbook on Human Rights* (1988): 217–218. It has also been argued that the Court's "scale and effect" requirement is really an issue of proportionality, rather than a question of what constitutes an armed attack. See Rosalyn Higgins, *Problems and Process—International Law and How We Use It* (Oxford: Clarendon Press, 1994), 251.

58. As set out in the *Declaration on Principles of International Law Concerning Friendly Relations and Co-Operation among States in Accordance with the Charter of the UN*, General Assembly Resolution 2625 (XXV), October 24, 1970, 10th para.

59. Letter dated October 7, 2001 from the Permanent Representative of the United States of America to the President of the UN Security Council reprinted in *International Legal Materials* 40 (2001): 1281.

60. See references cited in Steven R. Ratner, "*Jus ad Bellum* and *Jus in Bello* after September 11," *American Journal of International Law* 96, no. 4 (2002): 910,

notes 24 and 25. For Muslim state reactions, see also "Muslim World Ignores Bin Laden's Call for Jihad, Shrugs at U.S. Attacks in Afghanistan," *Al-Bawaba News*, October 9, 2001.

61. Cassese, "Terrorism Is Also Disrupting Some Crucial Legal Categories in International Law," 997.

62. Statement by NATO Secretary-General Lord Robertson on October 2, 2001 reprinted in *International Legal Materials* 40 (2001): 1268.

63. OAS Res. RC.23/RES.1/01, September 21, 2001 reprinted in *International Legal Materials* 40 (2001): 1270.

64. David J. Gerleman, Jennifer E. Stevens, and Steven A. Hildreth, *Operation Enduring Freedom: Pledges of Foreign Military and Intelligence Support*, October 17, 2001, Congressional Research Service, Library of Congress Order Code RL 31152.

65. OIC Foreign Ministers, "Final Comminique," http://www.oic-un.org/home/FQ.htm (accessed July 11, 2008).

66. Dina Ezzat, "Dynamics of Disarray—Arab and Muslim States Have not Formulated a Collective Stance on U.S.-Led Airstrikes against Afghanistan," *Al-Ahram Online Weekly*, Issue No. 555, October 11–17, 2001, http://weekly.ahram.org.eg/2001/555/war101.htm (accessed July 11, 2008).

67. Ibid.

68. Gerleman, Stevens, and Hildreth, *Operation Enduring Freedom*, Library of Congress Order Code RL 31152.

69. OAU Central Organ Communique on Terrorism, New York, November 11, 2001, Central Organ/MEC/MIN/Ex-Ord. (V) Comm.

70. ASEAN Declaration on Joint Action to Counter Terrorism, Brunei Darussalam, November 5, 2001, http://aseansec.org/529.htm (accessed July 11, 2008).

71. Ratner, "*Jus ad Bellum* and *Jus in Bello* after September 11," 910.

17

The 9/11 Attacks and the Future of Collective Security Law: Insight from Islamic Law

Mashood A. Baderin＊

An African philosophical adage says: "When children fall they look forwards, but when adults fall they look backwards."[1] The message therein is that a sensible adult will look carefully backward to identify the cause of a fall so as to avoid it and prevent falling again when he/she passes through that route in future. But a child would inattentively proceed forward without caring to look backward to identify the cause of its fall and will therefore fall again when it passes through that route in future. Borrowing from that philosophy, the starting point of this chapter is that the devastating aftermath of the 2003 United States (U.S.)-led invasion of Iraq places a responsibility on scholars and practitioners of international law to look carefully backward and identify relevant lessons that can be learnt from the Iraqi crisis for the future development of international law generally and Collective Security law particularly. Looking back, the 2003 U.S.-led war on Iraq does raise many legal and moral questions in relation to international law, some of which has been extensively debated by scholars and practitioners of international law.[2] With specific regard to Collective Security, Krisch has observed that since 9/11, Collective Security has both "been strengthened in several ways" but "has also been significantly weakened."[3] He argued that this has caused "a rise of Collective Security, as well as its fall, and both simultaneously,"[4] which, in essence, has left Collective Security in a sort of quagmire.

＊ **Mashood A. Baderin** is Professor of Law at the School of Oriental and African Studies, University of London.

This chapter is a short reflection on that quagmire. Despite the pessimism expressed by some commentators about the effectiveness of Collective Security owing to the Iraqi crisis,[5] this essay argues that the devastating aftermath of the 2003 U.S.-led war on Iraq has actually demonstrated that Collective Security still remains the best option for pursuing international peace and security subject to the necessary adherence to its elements of multilateralism, rule of law, good faith, and exhaustion of all avenues of peaceful settlement before resorting to war. Also, as the U.S.-led war on Iraq gave rise to some anxiety between the "West" and the "Muslim world," the chapter also draws some insight from Islamic law on the subject, being one of the main legal systems with which international law interacts in today's world,[6] to provide evidence to strengthen the argument on Collective Security as the best means for the realization of international peace and security within the context of the UN Charter in a post–9/11 world, particularly in relation to Muslim states. Since this volume is about the effect of 9/11 on international law generally, it is essential to begin with a short analysis of how 9/11 became associated to the 2003 U.S.-led war on Iraq.

The "9/11" Attacks as Pretext for the 2003 U.S.-Led War on Iraq

While it is now apparent that Iraq had nothing to do with the terrorist acts that occurred in the United States on September 11, 2001, the incident was exploited by the United States as a necessary pretext for the 2003 war on Iraq and to sideline the United Nations (UN) in that regard. Although Iraq had been on the UN agenda since the First Gulf War, as a result of its invasion of Kuwait in 1990, and was consequently under a UN weapons inspection regime, it would have been very difficult for the United States to legitimately commence war on Iraq unilaterally without a valid excuse. After the liberation of Kuwait under the U.S.-led UN mandate and the end of the First Gulf War in 1991, there was a debate on whether the U.S. armed forces should have moved on into Iraq and removed Saddam Hussein from power then. The U.S. president at the time, George Bush, Sr., opposed the move by arguing that it would be going beyond the UN mandate to do so at that time. However, from 1998 it was clear that the United States had adopted a formal policy for regime change in Iraq through its enactment of the Iraq Liberation Act of 1998 (hereinafter ILA)[7] after the withdrawal of the UN weapon inspectors from Iraq on allegations of noncompliance of Iraq with the UN inspection regime. Section 3 of the ILA clearly stated that "[i]t should be the policy of the United States to support efforts to remove the regime headed by Saddam Hussein from power in Iraq and to promote the emergence of a democratic government to replace the regime."[8] While the ILA referred to the fact that President

Clinton had earlier in August 1998 "signed Public Law 105-235, which declared that "the Government of Iraq [was] in material and unacceptable breach of its international obligations" and urged the president "to take appropriate action, in accordance with the Constitution and relevant laws of the United States, to bring Iraq into compliance with its international obligations," the ILA did not grant the U.S. president authority to directly use U.S. military force to achieve its aim of regime change in Iraq. Section 8 of the ILA provided that "[n]othing in this Act shall be construed to authorize or otherwise speak of the use of the United States Armed Forces (except as provided in section 4(a)(2)) in carrying out this Act." Section 4(a)(2) of the ILA only allowed U.S. military assistance in form of military education and training to Iraqi democratic opposition organizations to remove Saddam Hussein from power in Iraq, which had, up to the 9/11 terrorist acts in the United States, not succeeded in achieving the stated objective of the ILA.

Thus the 9/11 terrorist acts appeared to have provided the needed excuse to justify the use of direct U.S. military force to effect the U.S. policy of regime change in Iraq. President George Bush, Jr., laid the ground for linking 9/11 to the need for war on Iraq in his speech before the UN General Assembly on September 12, 2002, in which he stated, inter alia that "Iraq's government openly praised the attacks of September the 11th [and that] al Qaeda terrorists escaped from Afghanistan and [were] known to be in Iraq."[9] In his article titled "Justifying the Use of Force in a Post–9/11 World: Striving for Hierarchy in International Society," Kerton-Johnson indicated that between September 2002 and May 2003 the U.S. president cited terrorism as justification for the war on Iraq on 114 occasions.[10] For example, in a televised address aboard the U.S. aircraft carrier *USS Abraham Lincoln* on May 1, 2003 the U.S. president linked the war on Iraq to 9/11 by stating that

> The battle of Iraq is one victory in a war on terror that began on September the 11, 2001–and still goes on. That terrible morning, 19 evil men–the shock troops of a hateful ideology–gave America and the civilized world a glimpse of their ambitions. They imagined, in the words of one terrorist, that September the 11th would be the "beginning of the end of America." By seeking to turn our cities into killing fields, terrorists and their allies believed that they could destroy this nation's resolve, and force our retreat from the world. They have failed.[11]

In his book *From 9/11 to the Iraq War,* McGoldrick has also noted that "[t]he link back [of the 2003 war on Iraq] to 11 September was clearly expressed by U.S. President Bush in a televised White House Press Conference on 6 March 2003"[12] wherein the president stated that: "The attacks of September the 11th, 2001 showed what the enemies of the

United States did with four airplanes. We will not wait to see what terrorists or terrorist states could do with weapons of mass destruction."[13]

In supporting the U.S. position, the then British Prime Minister, Tony Blair, is noted to have also stated in an interview on February 6, 2003 that "there was a serious risk that rogue states, like Iraq, were developing and proliferating weapons of mass destruction, and would supply them to terrorist organisations to which it had links, like Al-Qaeda."[14] Also, in trying to secure a UN Security Council (SC) mandate for the war on Iraq, the then U.S. Secretary of State, Colin Powell, stated before the SC in February 2003 that "[l]eaving Saddam Hussein in possession of weapons of mass destruction for a few months or years is not an option—not in a post–11 September world."[15] Earlier, the eleventh preambular paragraph of the *Authorization for the Use of Force against Iraq Resolution* adopted by the U.S. Congress on October 16, 2002 had also stated as follows: "Whereas members of al Qaida, an organization bearing responsibility for attacks on the United States, its citizens, and interests, including the attacks that occurred on September 11, 2001, are known to be in Iraq."[16]

Thus, despite the lack of a direct nexus between Iraq and the 9/11 terrorist attacks, the latter was eventually linked to it by the United States and some of its close allies as pretext to justify the unilateral U.S.-led war on Iraq commenced on March 20, 2003, which subsequently led to serious divisions within the SC and the UN membership generally on the issue of legitimacy and/or legality of the war on Iraq within the context of Collective Security law and the mandate of the SC to maintain international peace and security.

Effect on Collective Security and International Peace

It is a fact that humanity enjoys social, economic, and political progress better in a climate of peace and security rather than in a climate of war, fear, and insecurity. The idea of Collective Security is thus aimed at ensuring a climate of peace and security in interstate relations. It is based on "… the proposition that aggressive and unlawful use of force by one nation against another will be met by the combined strength of all other nations. All will co-operate in controlling a disturber of the peace."[17] Considered comprehensively, the concept is built on three main principles as follows:

> First, states "must renounce the use of military force to alter the status quo and agree instead to settle all of their disputes peacefully. Changes will be possible in international relations, but ought to be achieved by negotiation rather than force."

Second, states "must broaden their conception of national interest to take in the interests of the international community as a whole. This means that when a troublemaker appears in the system, all of the responsible states will collectively confront the aggressor with overwhelming military force."

Third, and most importantly, states "must overcome the fear which dominates world politics and learn to trust each other. Such a system of security, as Inis Claude has argued, depends on states entrusting "their destinies to Collective Security."[18]

One the one hand, there has been the argument that the U.S.-led 2003 war on Iraq demonstrated that the concept of Collective Security is a myth that does not work.[19] On the other hand, there is also the general view that a SC Collective Security mandate, pursued multilaterally, would have provided international legality and a better chance of success in Iraq than the unilateral U.S.-led war. As the terminology depicts, *Collective Security* is a means for ensuring the collective maintenance of peace and security within the international community of states. Krisch has however noted the U.S. position prior to the war on Iraq as indicated by the U.S. president's spokesman then that "there [were] many ways to form international coalitions [and that] [t]he United Nations Security Council [was] but one of them,"[20] which begs the question of whether there are better alternatives to Collective Security for the maintenance of international peace and security. In responding to that question, it is satisfying to note that in its report submitted in December 2004, the UN Secretary-General's High-Level Panel on Threats, Challenges, and Change observed that the task is not to find alternatives for Collective Security but to make the system work better.[21] Thus, despite any aberration that the 2003 war on Iraq may have cast on the practical processes of Collective Security under the UN system, the devastating aftermath of the war has, in my view, actually proved that Collective Security remains a better alternative for maintaining international peace and security. Alternative forms of global security systems include a balance of power system, a loose bipolar system, a tight bipolar system, a superpower hegemonic system, and a strict regional defense system.[22] In this era of internationalism, it is submitted that Collective Security still appears to be a better option to those other alternative security systems for maintaining peace and security in interstate relations, provided that its fundamental element of multilateralism based on rule of law and good faith is respected. In a global system that practically consists of "big" and "small" states, "strong" and "weak" states, "super-power" and "powerless" states existing side by side within realist assumptions of relentless hegemonic competition between them, the best means to promote the maintenance of peace and security is a collective system that assures all the member states, big and small, of some level of certainty and consistency. Collective Security facilitates such assurance through adherence to multilateralism and rule of law, because under it "states agree to abide by certain norms and rules to maintain stability, and when necessary band together to stop aggression."[23] Thus, rather than abandoning Collective Security, many commentators on the Iraqi crisis have proposed the need for promoting better adherence to the necessary principles that would ensure the effectiveness of the system, especially the principles of multilateralism, rule of law, good faith, and exhaustion of all avenues of peaceful settlement in its application as originally conceived by the drafters of the UN Charter.[24]

Theoretically, the UN Charter provides a most comprehensive Collective Security system in the history of international organizations. Its coverage by three chapters consisting of 22 articles[25] evidences the comprehensiveness of the process under the Charter. The process consists of peaceful settlement of international disputes under Chapter VI, enforcement measures including use of force under Chapter VII, and regional action under Chapter VIII of the UN Charter. This is against the background that the main objective of the United Nations, as stated in Article 1(1) of the UN Charter, is the "maintenance of international peace and security, and to that end: to take *effective collective measures* for the prevention and removal of threats to the peace, and for the suppression of acts of aggression or other breaches of the peace, and to bring about by peaceful means, and in conformity with the principles of justice and international law, adjustment or settlement of international disputes or situations which might lead to a breach of the peace."[26] In discharging this responsibility, the role of the SC is very well reflected in Chapters VI, VII, and VIII of the Charter.[27] Regretfully however, emphasis has usually been placed on the use of force under Chapter VII, which has relatively dwarfed Chapters VI and VIII as important elements of the Charter's Collective Security regime. White thus reminds us of the obvious fact that under the UN Charter "Collective Security can both promote the peaceful settlement of situations that endanger peace (Chapter VI processes) and take action with respect to threats to the peace, breaches of the peace or acts of aggression (Chapter VII action)."[28] The importance of Chapter VIII (regional action) as part of the processes for the maintenance of international peace and security has equally been acknowledged by experts.[29]

Peaceful Settlement of International Disputes

The SC is mentioned in every Article of Chapter VI of the UN Charter (art. 33–38). This is seen as establishing the prominent role of the SC in ensuring peaceful settlement of international disputes as part of its primary responsibility of maintaining international peace and security.[30] Article 33(2) and Article 34 are significant in that regard. While Article

33(2) confers powers on the SC to call upon parties, when it deems necessary, to settle their disputes by peaceful means, Article 34 confers it with powers to "investigate any dispute, or situation that might lead to international friction." Although Bowwett notes that SC resolutions under Chapter VI "are in the nature of recommendations" and "not decisions to which Article 25 applies, and therefore the parties are in principle free to reject them,"[31] he however acknowledged the potential deterrent nature of Chapter VII in ensuring compliance with Chapter VI recommendations. While the deterrent potentials of Chapter VII against members' noncompliance with Chapter VI recommendations may have diminished during the Cold War period due to the use of the veto, it regained some clout after the Cold War, especially through the SC's swift reaction and decisions in response to Iraq's invasion of Kuwait in 1990 and thus strengthened the chances of securing compliance with Chapter VI recommendations especially in relation to disputes or situations identified as a threat to international peace and security. In that regard, it is hereby submitted that before the commencement of the 2003 U.S.-led war on Iraq, there were at least two further possible prospects for peaceful settlement of the crisis with the probability of compliance by Saddam Hussein in the face of the imminent Article 42 action by the SC.

The first prospect related to Chapter VI and it was that, confronted with the imminent threat of an Article 42 collective use of force under the authority of the SC, Saddam Hussein was relatively cowered and had started cooperating again with the UN weapons inspectors acting under Article 34 of the UN Charter, as was reported to the SC by the UN Chief Weapons Inspector Hans Blix and Mohamed ElBaradei of the International Atomic Energy on March 7, 2003 before the war on Iraq was commenced.[32] In retrospect, it could thus be argued that the door to peaceful settlement should not have been closed at that stage of the crisis. In view of the differences in political judgment amongst the five permanent members of the SC and amongst the member states of the United Nations generally at that stage, respect for multilateralism and rule of law would most probably have vindicated recourse to peaceful settlement rather than the rush to war on Iraq by the United States. The second prospect related to regional action under Chapter VIII is analyzed in the following section.

Recourse to Regional Action

In response to criticisms against the war on Iraq and large collateral damages ensuing thereby, both President Bush and Prime Minister Tony Blair argued that despite the large collateral damages suffered, the war on Iraq had succeeded in removing Saddam Hussein from power and thus made the world safer. The second prospect for peaceful settlement of the crisis was in relation to this question of regime change in Iraq and the role that regional organizations within the region could have played in achieving the regime change without the use of military force. While arguing that regime change in form of forcible replacement of the ruling authority of a state by external actors is almost always a bad idea, Reisman has noted that there are times when the need for a regime change could be morally, ethically, legally strong and feasible. He suggested however that even in such circumstances, a military action is not, for diverse moral and political reasons, the wise and right means of achieving such a change.[33] Considering that there was a move by the United Arab Emirates, before the commencement of the war on Iraq in March 2003, to offer asylum to Saddam Hussein, it is valid therefore to raise the question of whether or not the SC could have pursued that prospect to realize a regime change by peaceful means through regional action. This is in view of the fact that, similar to Chapter VI, the SC is also mentioned in every Article of Chapter VIII (arts. 52–54). In my view, the SC could have used its mandate under Chapter VIII to pursue that possibility as happened, in somewhat similar circumstances, in the case of Charles Taylor to save the situation in Liberia later in August 2003. Regional organizations such as the Arab League and the Organisation of Islamic Conference (OIC), acting under Chapter VIII of the UN Charter, could have also intervened at that stage to pursue the peaceful abdication of Saddam Hussein as was done in the case of Charles Taylor in Liberia through the intervention of the African Union and the offer of asylum by Nigeria.[34] Looking back, it is submitted that the two prospects identified earlier were "missed opportunities" for possible peaceful settlement of the crisis under Chapters VI and VIII of the UN Charter, which could, perhaps, have been vigorously exploited to prevent the destruction and unnecessary loss of lives caused by the 2003 U.S.-led war on Iraq, from which lessons need be taken for the future of Collective Security.

Origins of Collective Security and an Insight from Islamic Law

Bennett has identified that the idea of Collective Security "is not unique to the twentieth century" and neither is it an unprecedented creation of modern international organizations.[35] The idea is often traced back to informal collective protective notions of "all for one and one for all" in primitive human communities. He further noted that "political philosophers, in every period of recorded history and in eastern as well as western civilizations, have advocated theories and practices…that might reasonably be labeled Collective Security measures."[36] He then gave examples of the views of Greek philosophers such as Plato, Christian theologians such as St. Augustine, ancient Chinese philosophers such as Confucius and Roman Stoics such as Cicero to substantiate the antiquity of the idea of Collective Security.[37] He, however, makes no specific reference to any antecedent in Islamic thought on the concept. It is observed in that regard that reference is generally rare in this subject area as to whether or not the concept of Collective Security is known to Islamic legal and political thought at all.

However, the war on Iraq did demonstrate the need to examine the possible influence of Islamic law on the application of international law generally and on Collective Security law specifically in the Muslim world in at least two ways. First was the earlier controversy as to whether or not the war on Iraq, after Afghanistan, was a war by "Western" super powers against Islam and the Muslim world. Second was the latter controversy as to whether or not Islamic law should serve as "a source" or "the source" of legislation in the constitution of Iraq.[38] In the first case, both the U.S. President George Bush and the U.K. Prime Minister Tony Blair had to explain many times that the war on Iraq was not a war between the "West" and Islam. After an initial stalemate in the second case, the compromise was to include Islam as "a source" of legislation in the Iraqi interim constitution adopted in March 2004[39] and subsequently as "a fundamental source of legislation" in the main constitution adopted in October 2005.[40] Such controversy raises the question of whether Islamic law and the ideals of international law generally and, in this case, international Collective Security are mutually connected and thus necessitates an insight into Islamic law on the concept to draw upon for the future of Collective Security especially in relation to engagement with the Muslim world in that regard.

It is interesting to observe in that regard that the Qur'an, which is the principal source of Islamic law,[41] specifically established a relative rule of collective measures as early as the seventh century for dealing with apparent "threats to peace and security" within the Islamic community by providing that

> If two parties among the Believers fall into a dispute, then *you all* should make peaceful settlement *(fa aslihū)* between them; but if one of them transgresses beyond bounds against the other, then *you all* should fight *(fa qātilū)* against the transgressing party until it complies with the command of God. If it complies, then *you all* should make peaceful settlement *(fa aslihū)* between the two of them with justice and *you all* should act equitably *(fa aqsitū)*. Indeed God loves those who are equitable. The Believers are but a single Brotherhood, so *you all* should make peaceful settlement *(fa aslihū)* between your two (contending) brothers and be God-fearing so that you may receive mercy."[42] (Emphasis added)

The aforementioned rule, established in the seventh century, reflects the recognition of collective measures as a system for maintaining peace and security under Islamic law. A careful analysis of the verses quoted earlier will indicate six important elements for the application of the collective measures under Islamic law as follows:

1. A golden cord that runs through the provisions from the beginning of the verses to its end is the collective pronoun "*you all*" signifying the importance of multilateralism within the system.
2. The provisions emphasize peaceful settlement and only authorize military action (fighting) in case of defiance and continued transgression by a disputing member of the community.
3. The emphasis on peaceful settlement before resort to military action raises the important question of when and how to decide that all peaceful means have been exhausted and to label a disputing party as a transgressor to be fought collectively. This is answered at the end of the verses by reference to "God-fearing," which implies the concept of good faith in arriving at that decision and in Collective Security generally.
4. Furthermore, the general rule in every conflict under Islamic law is based on the principle "*al-sulh khayr*" meaning "peaceful settlement is always better."[43] Therefore, the door of finding a peaceful settlement is never permanently shut in the process and is thus repeated a third time toward the end of the verses.
5. The provisions reflect the relevance of the rule of law in Collective Security measures by its reference to justice and equity in finding a peaceful settlement.
6. The provisions reflect the relevance of universality and equality of membership within the Collective Security system by its reference to a single brotherhood of the community.

It is evident from the aforementioned analysis that Collective Security is not an unknown concept to Islamic law or alien to the Muslim world. Rather, the concept is recognized as a viable method for collective maintenance of peace and security under Islamic political and legal thought, subject to the elements of multilateralism, exhaustion of all avenues of peaceful settlement before resort to warfare, good faith, rule of law, and the universality and equality of membership within the system.

In contemporary literature on the subject, these elements of collective measures identified under Islamic law earlier are equally considered as part of the indispensable elements of an ideal Collective Security system today.[44] This demonstrates one of the many common grounds that do exist between Islamic law and international law in the maintenance of international peace and security, which needs to be positively explored to achieve a less controversial application of international law generally, and Collective Security law especially, within the Muslim World. Looking back at the war on Iraq, the important lesson from this insight is that the introduction and accommodation of this Islamic perspective of collective measures into the discourse on the enforcement of international Collective Security law could have enriched the debates on the subject and also enhanced a better understanding and accommodation of international Collective Security law in the Muslim World. Perhaps such an informed dialogue could have promoted a more in-depth reflection on the necessary elements of multilateralism, rule of law, good faith, and exhaustion of all possible means of peaceful settlement as envisaged by the modern provisions on Collective Security under the UN Charter and also eliminated charges of an imposition of a Western concept upon Muslim states during the earlier days of the Iraqi crisis.

Conclusion

As it stands now, there is strong support for the position that the 2003 U.S.-led war on Iraq was strongly motivated by the 9/11 terrorist attacks, but that the war defied the "collectiveness" and multilateralism of Collective Security for the maintenance of international peace and security. Neorealist theorists of international relations argue that such defiance demonstrates that the concept of Collective Security is merely idealistic and that powerful states will always have their way and find reason to unilaterally decide when to go to war because it ultimately benefits them by establishing their authority. However, I submit in the conclusion of this chapter that the Iraqi experience must not be ingrained as precedent for destroying Collective Security. Rather the devastation caused to life and property in Iraq by the 2003 U.S.-led war places a duty on practitioners and scholars of international law to exploit every possible legal space within the UN Charter to encourage the commitment of states to Collective Security through the promotion of an adherence to multilateralism, rule of law, good faith, and exhaustion of all avenues of peaceful settlement of international disputes before resort to the use of armed forces in interstate relations in future.

Notes

1. This is a Yoruba proverb. The Yorubas are a tribe in West Africa predominantly from Southern Nigeria.

2. See, e.g., Vaughan Lowe, "The Iraq Crisis: What Now?" *International and Comparative Law Quarterly* 52, no.4 (2003):.859; Nigel D. White, "The Will and Authority of the Security Council after Iraq," *Leiden Journal of International Law* 17 (2004): 645; R. Dobie Langenkamp and Rex J. Zedalis, "What Happens to the Iraqi Oil: Thoughts on Some Significant, Unexamined International Legal Questions Regarding Occupation of Oil Fields," *European Journal of International Law* 14 (2003): 417; Michael Byers, "Agreeing to Disagree: Security Council Resolution 1441 and International Ambiguity," *Global Governance* 10 (2004): 165; James Dobbins, "Iraq: Winning the Unwinnable War," *Foreign Affairs* 84, no. 1 (2005): 16.

3. Nico Krisch, "The Rise and Fall of Collective Security: Terrorism, U.S. Hegemony, and the Plight of the Security Council," in *Terrorism as a Challenge for National and International Law: Security versus Liberty?*, ed. Christian Walter, Silja Vöneky, Volker Röben, and Frank Schorkopf (Heidelberg: Springer Law, 2004), 879–908, 880.

4. Ibid.

5. See, e.g., David Miller, "Collective Security: Is There Such a Thing," http://www.scoop.co.nz/mason/stories/HL0302/S00062.htm (last accessed October 24, 2008) where the author argued that "Collective Security does not work."

6. See generally "Introduction," in *International Law and Islamic Law*, ed. Mashood A. Baderin (Aldershot: Ashgate Publishing Ltd., 2008), xiii–xxxvi.

7. Iraq Liberation Act of 1998 (Public Law 105-338, October 31, 1998), available online on Library of Congress Website at http://thomas.loc.gov/cgi-bin/query/z?c105:H.R.4655.ENR: (last accessed October 24, 2008).

8. Sec. 3, ibid.

9. Text of Speech titled: "President's Remarks at the United Nations General Assembly" is available on the White House website at http://www.whitehouse.gov/news/releases/2002/09/20020912-1.html (last accessed October 10, 2008).

10. See Nicholas Kerton-Johnson, "Justifying the Use of Force in a Post–9/11 World: Striving for Hierarchy in International Society," *International Affairs* 84, no. 5 (2008): 991–1007, 997–1003.

11. http://www.guardian.co.uk/world/2003/may/01/usa.iraq (last accessed October 18, 2008).

12. Dominic McGoldrick, *From "9/11" to the Iraq War 2003: International Law in an Age of Complexity* (Oxford: Hart, 2004), 18.

13. Ibid.

14. Ibid.

15. UN Doc. S/PV/4701 (February 5, 2003), 17.

16. *Authorization for the Use of Military Force against Iraq Resolution* of 2002 (Public Law 107-243, October 16, 2002), available online at http://www.c-span.org/resources/pdf/hjres114.pdf (last accessed October 24, 2008).

17. K.P. Sakensa, *The United Nations and Collective Security* (London: DK Publishing House, 1974), 4–5.

18. John Baylis, "International and Global Security in the Post–Cold War Era," in *The Globalization of World Politics*, ed. J. Baylis, 4th ed. (Oxford: Oxford

University Press, 2007), 253–276, 264, citing Charles A. Kupchan and Clifford A. Kupchan, "The Promise of Collective Security," *International Security* 20, no. 1 (1995): 52–61.

19. See, e.g., Miller, "Collective Security."

20. Krisch, "The Rise and Fall of Collective Security," 898.

21. United Nations, "A More Secure World: Our Shared Responsibility," *Report of the Secretary General's High-Level Panel on Threats, Challenges and Change,* UN Doc. A/59/565 of December 2, 2004, page 13.

22. See, e.g., Morton A. Kaplan, *System and Process in International Politics* (New York: John Wiley, 1957), 21–53. See also A. LeRoy Bennett, *International Organisations, Principles and Issues,* 6th ed. (New Jersey: Prentice Hall, 1995), 18.

23. Baylis, "International and Global Security in the Post–Cold War Era," 264.

24. See, e.g., UN Doc. A/59/565 of December 2, 2004, page 13. Kaplan, *System and Process in International Politics*; Bennett, *International Organisations, Principles and Issues.*

25. Arts. 33–54.

26. Art. 1 (1) UN Charter (emphasis added).

27. See art. 24(2) UN Charter.

28. Nigel D. White, "On the Brink of Lawlessness: The State of Collective Security Law," article delivered at the Hilaire McCoubrey Memorial Lecture, University of Hull, May 15, 2002, page 1

29. Ibid., 5. See also Bruno Simma, ed., *The Charter of the United Nations, a Commentary,* Vol. 1, 2nd ed. (Oxford: Oxford University Press, 2002), 812ff.

30. Simma, ed., *The Charter of the United Nations, a Commentary,* 584, para. 1.

31. D. W. Bowett, "The United Nations and Peaceful Settlement," in Report of a Study Group of the David Davies Memorial Institute of International Studies, *International Disputes: The Legal Aspects* (London: Europa Publications, 1972), 183 See also B. Simma, *The Charter of the United Nations, a Commentary,* 584, para. 2. It is important to note however that the ICJ observed in the *Namibia Case* (1971) ICJ Reports, page16, that in accordance with Articles 24 and 25 of the UN Charter, the Security Council is generally empowered to adopt binding resolutions for the maintenance of international peace and security.

32. See Hans Blix's report to the Security Council on March 7, 2003 at http://www.un.org/Depts/unmovic/SC7asdelivered.htm (last accessed November 1, 2008). The report stated, inter alia, that "… at this juncture we are able to perform professional no-notice inspections all over Iraq and to increase aerial surveillance.'

33. W. Michael Reisman, "Why Regime Change Is (Almost Always) a Bad Idea," *American Journal of International Law* 98 (2004): 516, 522–525.

34. Charles Taylor is now standing trial before the Special Sierra Leone Tribunal in the Hague. For the trial updates, see, e.g., http://charlestaylortrial.org (last accessed April 27, 2009).

35. Bennett, *International Organisations, Principles and Issues,* 144.

36. Ibid., 9, 144.

37. Bennett, *International Organisations, Principles and Issues*, 9, 144.

38. See, e.g., International Crisis Group Report, *Iraq's Constitutional Challenge*, November 13, 2003, pages17–18, para. D. at http://www.icg.org//library/documents/middle_east___north_africa/19_iraq_s_constitutional_challenge.pdf (accessed January 2005).

39. Article 7 of the Iraqi Interim Constitution provided that:

    (A) Islam is the official religion of the State and is to be considered a source of legislation. No law that contradicts the universally agreed tenets of Islam, the principles of democracy, or the rights cited in Chapter Two of this Law may be enacted during the transitional period. This Law respects the Islamic identity of the majority of the Iraqi people and guarantees the full religious rights of all individuals to freedom of religious belief and practice. (B) Iraq is a country of many nationalities, and the Arab people in Iraq are an inseparable part of the Arab nation.

    For a commentary *see* N.J. Brown, "Transitional Administrative Law: Commentary and Analysis," http://www.geocities.com/nathanbrown1/interimiraqiconstitution.html (January 29, 2005).

40. Article 2 of the Constitution of Iraq (2005) provides that:

    First: Islam is the official religion of the State and it is a fundamental source of legislation; A: No law that contradicts the established provisions of Islam may be established. B:No law that contradicts the principles of democracy may be established; C:No law that contradicts the rights and basic freedoms stipulated in this constitution may be established. Second: This Constitution guarantees the Islamic identity of the majority of the Iraqi people and guarantees the full religious rights of all individuals to freedom of religious belief and practice such as Christians, Yazedis, and Mandi Sabeans.

41. See, e.g., Mashood A. Baderin, *International Human Rights and Islamic Law* (Oxford: Oxford University Press, 2003), 32–44.

42. Qur'an 49: 9–10. See Muhammad Hamidullah, *The Muslim Conduct of State*, 7th revised and enlarged ed. (Lahore: Sh. Muhammad Ashraf, 1977), 178, para. 338ff, where the author analyzes this Qur'anic provision as a rule of "Muslim International Law" or "Islamic Law of Nations."

43. See Qur'an 4: 128.

44. See, e.g., Lynn H. Miller, "The Idea and the Reality of Collective Security," *Global Governance* 5, no. 3 (July–September 1999): 303–332; Bennett, *International Organisations, Principles and Issues*, 144.

Index